EVERY NOW AND THEN

EVERY NOW AND THEN

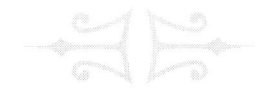

The Amazing Stories of Douglas County, Georgia Volume I

LISA LAND COOPER
History Is Elementary, LLC

Copyright © 2016 Lisa Land Cooper
All rights reserved.

ISBN: 1519234732
ISBN 13: 9781519234735

DEDICATION

To the people of Douglas County – past, present, and future.

TABLE OF CONTENTS

Acknowledgements xiii
Introduction xv
List of Illustrations xvii

Section One   **First Residents** 1
Chapter 1   A Little Digging Regarding Benjamin Hawkins 3
Chapter 2   The Buzz on Buzzard Roost Island 6
Chapter 3   Douglas County's First Residents 9
Chapter 4   On the Fault Line 14

Section Two   **There Once Was a Campbell County** 17
Chapter 5   The Forgotten Town of Campbellton 19
Chapter 6   The Doctor Who Wanted to Fight 24
Chapter 7   The Mother of Confederate Reunions 29
Chapter 8   A Letter for Mrs. Glover 33
Chapter 9   Civil War Sites in Douglas County 35
Chapter 10   Ms. Synthia's Recollections 40
Chapter 11   The Brothers Garrett 46
Chapter 12   The Route to the High 48
Chapter 13   Drinking In the Dog River .51

Section Three	**Early Citizens and Communities**	55
Chapter 14	Blips on a Map - Wilsonville, Hannah and McWhorter	57
Chapter 15	Richard M. Wilson – A Life of Service	62
Chapter 16	Robert Jehu Massey – A Monumental Find	66
Chapter 17	Ephraim Pray – An Amazing Man	72
Chapter 18	Ephraim Pray – Still an Amazing Man	78
Chapter 19	A Succession of Polks	83
Chapter 20	The Green-Rice Mill on Anneewakee Creek	88
Chapter 21	Judge Bowden's Plantation	94
Chapter 22	Arnold Mill	98
Section Four	**The New South**	101
Chapter 23	His Honor and the Sacred Harp	103
Chapter 24	The Poole House – A Historic Gem	106
Chapter 25	How Douglas County Lost Its Extra "S"	109
Chapter 26	Journey to a Town Center	112
Chapter 27	Joseph S. James – Douglasville's First Cheerleader	117
Chapter 28	The Business of the Railroad	122
Chapter 29	A Few Thoughts on the Railroad	125
Chapter 30	The Railroad – Making Connections	129
Chapter 31	Early City Ordinances and Fines	133
Chapter 32	Douglasville's First Schoolhouse	138
Chapter 33	The Anatomy of a Picture – The McElreath and McLarty House	141
Chapter 34	Taking a Minute for the Masons	145
Chapter 35	CSI – Douglasville, 1875	149
Chapter 36	Welcome to the Family Feud or the Sad Tale of William Nottingham	152
Chapter 37	Wilson Steverson – Game-Changer	156
Chapter 38	A Few Snippets from the 1880s	161
Chapter 39	Fed Hudson and the Midway School	167
Chapter 40	When Eagles Won't Fly	170

Chapter 41	Puzzle Pieces from the News Archives 173
Chapter 42	The Social Network along Sweetwater Creek 177
Chapter 43	Contentious Politics 183
Chapter 44	Maroney's Mill 187
Chapter 45	Grover Cleveland and the Election of 1884 190
Chapter 46	The Glorious Fourth 194
Chapter 47	Shortening on the Plaza 198
Chapter 48	Douglasville's Canning and Preservation Company . . . 201
Chapter 49	Promoting Douglasville 206

Section Five **Salt Springs – The Resort Town** 209
Chapter 50	In the Beginning – The Sweetwater Park Hotel 211
Chapter 51	Inman and Marsh – The Men behind the Sweetwater Park Hotel 214
Chapter 52	Let's Go to the Chautauqua Grounds 216
Chapter 53	Senator McKinley's Visit to Salt Springs 218
Chapter 54	Garrett's Views of the Chautauqua 222
Chapter 55	Viewing the Sweetwater Park Hotel through a Writer's Eye 226

Section Six **The Cotton Mill** 233
Chapter 56	The Cotton Mill – An Important New South Ingredient 235
Chapter 57	Mr. Geer and the Granite 241
Chapter 58	Demolition by Neglect or How Douglasville Lost Its Most Important Historic Asset 244
Chapter 59	A Primer Regarding Brownfields 251
Chapter 60	Mother's Day, the Mill, and Memories 255
Chapter 61	The Cotton Mill – One Year after the Fire 259

Section Seven **A Progressive Time** 263
| Chapter 62 | In the Poor House . . . . 265 |
| Chapter 63 | The Italian Peddler . . . . 269 |

Chapter 64	The Brockman Boys of Douglas County	274
Chapter 65	Baptists versus Methodist – Douglasville's Debating Pastors	277
Chapter 66	A Little Background Regarding Mr. and Mrs. Post	282
Chapter 67	When Mr. and Mrs. Post Came to Town	288
Chapter 68	Mr. Post and Third Party Politics	293
Chapter 69	The Posts – The Final Chapter	300
Chapter 70	Douglasville Was in the Hands of the Northerners	307
Chapter 71	The Upshaw Family	310
Chapter 72	Who the Heck is Bill Arp?	316
Chapter 73	A.J. Bryan – The Man Who Built Courthouses	318
Chapter 74	Moonshine in Douglas County	322
Chapter 75	Douglas County's Spanish American War Story	325
Chapter 76	Revisiting Camp Hobson	329
Chapter 77	Shared Space	332
Chapter 78	Dynamite in Douglasville	336
Chapter 79	A Marathon Commencement	339
Chapter 80	Douglas County's Connection to the Silk Industry	344
Chapter 81	How the Election of 1902 became the Lawsuit of 1904	347
Chapter 82	The Roberts-Mozley House	351
Chapter 83	Storage Wars – Then and Now	355
Chapter 84	Farmers and Merchants Bank	358
Chapter 85	Mr. Smith – The Inventor	363
Chapter 86	Tales of Falling Stars	366
Chapter 87	A Post in Three Parts – A Reverse S-Curve, a Wayward Caboose, and Antiquated Blue Laws	370
Section Eight	**Boom and Bust**	377
Chapter 88	The Civic League	379
Chapter 89	A Kozy Theater for Douglasville	381
Chapter 90	Changing Perspective	384
Chapter 91	Five Little Boys – Five Grown Men	387
Chapter 92	Joseph C. McCarley – Make Your Mark!	391

Chapter 93	Living Along the Dog River in the Early 1900s	395
Chapter 94	The Log Cabin Library at Lithia Springs	400
Chapter 95	From Military Road to Bankhead Highway	404
Chapter 96	Douglasville during World War I	409
Chapter 97	The James Boys and World War I	414
Chapter 98	Radio Days	418
Chapter 99	Hugh Watson – Soaring Through Life	421
Chapter 100	Revisiting Hugh Watson	426
Chapter 101	Verifying the Railway Bridge	431
Chapter 102	A Little Light for Douglas County	434
Chapter 103	Mac Abercrombie – Douglasville's Own Mule Whisperer	437
Chapter 104	Take a Bridge to the Past	440
Chapter 105	Douglasville's Presidential Candidate – William D. Upshaw	444
Section Nine	**The War Years**	449
Chapter 106	The Select Few	451
Chapter 107	Birthin' Babies – A Little History Behind Douglas General Hospital	454
Chapter 108	Douglasville, 1948 – A Glimpse	458
Chapter 109	A Submarine for Douglas	461
Chapter 110	Lithia Springs, First Baptist – A Dream Come True	464
Section Ten	**The Fabulous Fifties**	469
Chapter 111	Louise Suggs – Lessons from the Father	471
Chapter 112	Citizen O'Neal – The Man behind the Plaza	474
Chapter 113	Turkeys Away!	478
Chapter 114	The Villa Rica Explosion	481
Chapter 115	January, 1955 – Douglasville Grammar School Burns	487
Chapter 116	My Love Affair with O'Neal Plaza	489
Chapter 117	So Long, Tex	492

| Chapter 118 | Groover's Lake . . . . 495 |
| Chapter 119 | Ruth Blair's Historic Find . . . . 498 |

**Section Eleven Suburbia, Shopping Centers,
               and the Superhighway.** 501

| Chapter 120 | Living Your Dream . . . . 503 |
| Chapter 121 | The Good, the Bad, and the Ugly
               Regarding Cracker. . . . . 507 |
| Chapter 122 | My Interview with Harris Dalton . . . . 510 |
| Chapter 123 | Deputy Tommy and the Bear. . . . . 513 |
| Chapter 124 | The Rigors and Rewards of Growing
               Up in Bill Arp . . . . 516 |
Chapter 125	Parkway Regional Hospital – A History. 519
Chapter 126	Dragracing – The Traffic Tipping Point 524
Chapter 127	A Quilt for Douglas County 527
Chapter 128	Local History IS a Big Deal 529
Chapter 129	The Mule Train 532
Chapter 130	Remembering Those Who Serve 535
Chapter 131	A Little Regarding Sheriff Earl D. Lee 539
Chapter 132	Memories of the Storm of 1973. 544
Chapter 133	Sweetwater Creek State Park – Thirteen Things . . . 548
Chapter 134	A Tragedy at New Hope 554
Chapter 135	The Douglas County Courthouse –
Crash Course in Local History 559
Chapter 136	Douglas County's Little Courthouses 562
Chapter 137	Streets, Roads, and Place Names. 566
Chapter 138	Visit Eight Historic Sites without Leaving
the County 569
Chapter 139	Family History – Real Facts or Wild Exaggerations . . . 573
Chapter 140	History is Alive and Well in Douglas County 577

Bibliography 581
Index 591

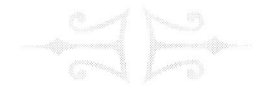

ACKNOWLEDGEMENTS

How do I begin to acknowledge and thank the hundreds of people who have helped me with my research for the past five years?

Many thanks go to the friends and the many acquaintances willing to share their stories, memories, impressions, and opinions with me regarding old Campbell County, Douglas County, and Douglasville history including close to five thousand people who like and participate in the discussion on my Facebook page, *Every Now and Then*.

In particular, I'd like to extend a special thank you to the members of the Douglas County Historical Society, the Douglas County Museum of History and Art, the Douglas County Public Library on Selman Drive, the Douglasville City Council, the Douglas County Board of Commissioners, the Douglas County Chamber of Commerce, and the *Douglas County Sentinel* for their support.

Bob Smith, Gary Tilt, Ron Daniel, Brian Stout, and John and Elaine Bailey also need a special thank you for their help with the details, encouragement, and friendship.

My Mister – David – receives a huge amount of gratitude as he patiently listens as I chatter on and on about whatever I'm working on each week, serves as a sounding board, and doesn't complain as I get involved in my work and forget to plan dinner.

For my children – Matthew and Rachel – your encouragement means the world to me.

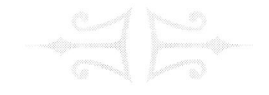

INTRODUCTION

This book is not intended to be a complete history of old Campbell County, Douglas County, or Douglasville, but does represent the bulk of my published research. Some of the contents of this book have appeared online at *Douglasville Patch* (2010-2011) and within my weekly column with the *Douglas County Sentinel* since 2012 – a total of 140 columns.

At this point it was becoming a bit overwhelming for me to remember what I had published and what still "lived" within my notes, so I decided to publish the early columns with a detailed index, so I could have all of the early columns in one easy place to search.

My work to find more pieces of the puzzle is ongoing.

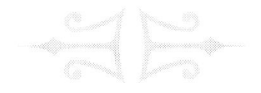

LIST OF ILLUSTRATIONS

Chapter 3   **Skint Chestnut Tree** – The legendary chestnut tree that was used as a directional marker and served as a significant meeting place for Native Americans and early settlers. It stood at the highest point on the ridge close to where the old courthouse sits today. (Courtesy of Douglas County government.)

Chapter 5   **Campbell County Courthouse** – This building served as the seat of Campbell County government in the town of Campbellton until 1870 when the county seat was relocated to Fairburn. This building was left abandoned and eventually torn down. (Courtesy of Jeff Champion.)

Chapter 9   **Irwin-Bomar-Rice-Austin-Bullard-Henley-Sprayberry Home** – This home, still standing in Douglas County, dates to 1835 and was built by Francis Irwin. It originally stood in old Campbell County. (Courtesy of the Douglas County Museum of History and Art.)

Chapter 17   **Ephraim Pray** – One of Douglas County's earliest settlers and served on the first board of commissioners. Pray Street, running between Church and Broad Streets, in

	downtown Douglasville is named for him. (Courtesy of the Douglas County Museum of History and Art.)
Chapter 24	**Poole House** – This Federal style mansion is known as the Poole-Huffine-Bulloch-Rollins-Hudson/Farmer-Rollins home and was built by Dr. William Haynes (W.H.) Poole, the very first physician and surgeon in the area before Douglasville or Douglas County existed by name. After spending a few years as a wedding/event facility the home is once again a private residence. (Courtesy of the City of Douglasville.)
Chapter 26	**Young and Nancy Vansant** – Young Vansant is remembered for providing 40 acres to lay off the county seat for Douglas County and erect a courthouse and jail at Skint Chestnut. (Courtesy of Douglas County Museum of History and Art.)
Chapter 27	**Joseph S. James** – James was elected as Douglasville's first mayor in 1875, and until his death in 1931 he was an ardent Democrat and adhered to the New South philosophy. James was instrumental with getting the cotton mill built in Douglasville, speculated in land and had a thriving law practice. (Courtesy of the Douglas County Public Library.)
Chapter 33	**McElreath-McLarty House** – This house sat on Campbellton Street between Broad and Church Streets. It dated to the 1880s, and at different times it served as a boarding house. Today, the Plaza East parking lot is located there. (Courtesy of the City of Douglasville.)
Chapter 38	**Dr. T.R. Whitley** – Dr. Whitley practiced medicine in Douglas County from the 1880s through the 1930s, was the founder of Douglasville College, and during his time of service in the state legislature he was instrumental in getting Bankhead Highway routed through Douglas County. (Courtesy of Douglas County government.)
Chapter 47	**Snowdrift Shortening Ad at O'Neal Plaza** – The D.H. Gurley grocery ad featuring Snowdrift Shortening at O'Neal

Plaza provides an iconic view of Douglasville. The vintage ad is part of the plaza's charm taking us back to the turn of the century and our earliest roots when Douglasville's commercial district had several grocery stores. (Courtesy of Lisa Land Cooper.)

Chapter 50 **Sweetwater Park Hotel** – Lithia Spring's famous resort opened in the summer of 1887 boasting 250 rooms besides parlors, offices, and billiard rooms. Piazzas stretching for 700 feet with widths of 14 to 28 feet surrounded the hotel with wide halls dividing the rooms. (Courtesy of Douglas County Museum of History and Art.)

Chapter 53 **Piedmont Chautauqua** –The brainchild of Atlanta's Henry W. Grady, the Chautauqua opened in July 4, 1888 and returned for a couple of months every summer for a few years with speakers, seminars, and various entertainments. (Courtesy of the Douglas County Museum of History and Art.)

Chapter 56 **Lois Beaver Cotton Mill** – Douglasville's cotton mill opened in 1908 and through the years had several different names including New Century Cotton Mill, Glendale Mills, Desoto Mills and the Douglasville Spinners. (Courtesy of the City of Douglasville.)

Chapter 66 **Helen Wilmans Post** – Mrs. Post moved to Douglas County in 1887 with her husband, Charles C. Post. She was involved in the mental science movement, and he was intent on making the Progressive Party instrumental in Georgia politics. Instead, they turned the city of Douglasville upside down. (Courtesy of a private source.)

Chapter 73 **Douglas County Courthouse (1896)** – The 1896 Courthouse designed by Andrew J. Bryan & Company had pine floors and ceilings from the forests along the Dog River while a company along the Chattahoochee River furnished the bricks. Tragically, the courthouse was lost in a fire in 1956. (Courtesy of Jeff Champion.)

Chapter 75   **Camp Hobson Dining Tent** - Camp Hobson was a military camp in Lithia Springs that was used during the Spanish-American War. Camp Hobson was set up to provide a place for patients to basically escape after Typhoid broke out at Fort McPherson early in August, 1898. Camp Hobson was short-lived, but because it existed it may have saved the lives of the men who were sent there. The camp was opened in July, 1898 and by September, 1898 the soldiers had been transferred. (Courtesy of a private source.)

Chapter 78   **Douglasville Banking Company** – In 1891, Douglasville Banking Company, Douglasville's first bank began doing business with the public. The bank opened at the northwest corner of Price and Church Street in 1906. (Courtesy of the City of Douglasville.)

Chapter 79   **Douglasville College** – The school was located on Church Street where the National Guard Armory stands today. All grades were covered, and courses from needlepoint to Greek were offered. The school opened in 1889 and closed in 1914. (Courtesy of the City of Douglasville.)

Chapter 82   **W.T. Roberts Family** – The family is sitting on the front porch of their home on Campbellton Street around 1911. Mr. Roberts, an attorney, was also a former mayor of Douglasville and served as state representative. The Cultural Arts Council of Douglasville/Douglas County is now located in the home. (Courtesy of the City of Douglasville.)

Chapter 84   **Farmers and Merchants Bank** – Located at the east corner of Campbellton and Broad Streets the Farmers and Merchants Bank opened in 1907 as part of the Witham bank chain. By 1927, the bank was out of business. (Courtesy of the City of Douglasville.)

Chapter 90   **Hutcheson Building** – This building on Broad Street has the name of its owner designed into the brickwork.

EVERY NOW AND THEN

Judge Robert H. Hutcheson built this building in 1915. He placed his law firm and other offices on the second floor while the U.S. Post Office took over the entire main floor as a testament to how fast Douglasville was growing. (Courtesy of the City of Douglasville.)

Chapter 92 **Joseph C. McCarley** – In 1915, Joseph C. McCarley built the brick building on Broad Street that bears his name. He did what it took to make his novelty store profitable including selling peanuts on the street. (Courtesy of the City of Douglasville.)

Chapter 99 **Hugh Watson** – Already flying before World War I, Watson made a name for himself in the aviation field completing early cross-country flights and eventually running his own airfield in Ohio where he taught aviation. He also taught at Atlanta's Candler Field. (Courtesy of a private source.)

Chapter 101 **Railway Bridge** – The bridge that allowed pedestrians to cross over the railroad tracks from Broad Street to Strickland Street was constructed of cross ties. The bridge was located at the Bowden and Broad Streets intersection. (Courtesy of Mike Garrett.)

Chapter 105 **William D. Upshaw** – William D. Upshaw was the brother of Douglasville businessmen H.M. and L.C. Upshaw. He was a prolific writer, United States Congressman, and ran for president on the Prohibition ticket against Franklin D. Roosevelt in 1932. (Courtesy of a private source.)

Chapter 110 **First Baptist Church, Lithia Springs** – Groundbreaking for their first church building occurred in 1946. From left to right: Mary Gore, Ethel Hodges, Vassie Williams, John and Estelle Rice, Pat Chandler, Jewell Patterson, Amy Copeland, G.W. Southard, Rev. Arnold Patterson, John Cauble, Rev. Pat Johnson, and John Brown. (Courtesy First Baptist Church, Lithia Springs.)

Chapter 111   **Louise Suggs** – Ms. Suggs learned the game of golf from her father, professional baseball player Johnny Suggs, at the Lithia Springs Golf Course. Ms. Suggs went on to win several tournaments and awards and was instrumental in beginning the LPGA. (Courtesy of the Douglas County Museum of History and Art.)

Chapter 118   **Groover's Lake** – This was THE place to be beginning in the 1930s for speed boat races, swimming, dancing and other fun. (Courtesy of Douglas County Museum of History and Art.)

Chapter 125   **Parkway Regional Hospital** – Built in 1973 by Glenmore and Sarah Carter, the eleven-story cylindrical nursing tower with an attached rectangular medical building was an iconic landmark west of Atlanta. (Courtesy of Douglas County Public Library.)

Chapter 131   **Sheriff Earl D. Lee** – Douglas County's well known sheriff who began his career in law enforcement in the mid-1960s. He was elected sheriff in 1973 where he served a few four year terms. (Courtesy of Douglas County Museum of History and Art.)

Section One

FIRST RESIDENTS

Chapter 1

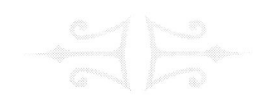

A LITTLE DIGGING REGARDING BENJAMIN HAWKINS

Early on when I started researching and writing about Douglas County history a passage in Fannie Mae Davis' book, *Douglas County, Georgia: From Indian Trail to Interstate 20,* caught my eye. She wrote, "The first known white visitor was Indian agent, Benjamin Hawkins, who had visited the site of Hurricane Creek in 1796 and 1798 and described the destruction of a powerful hurricane or tornado."

I've seen this same passage used again and again in various written histories of Douglas County, and I thought it was intriguing because apparently we could pinpoint the first known white visitor to our area when it was still inhabited by Native Americans.

I decided to do a little more digging.

There is most certainly a Hurricane Creek located in Douglas County. It crosses Post Road, Bill Arp Road (Highway 5), and Old Five Notch Road before spilling into the Chattahoochee River.

It makes sense then that Benjamin Hawkins crossed the creek on his journey across Douglas County lands, right?

Hawkins, born in 1754, got his start by volunteering with the Continental Army during the American Revolution. He served on George Washington's staff as his main French interpreter.

Hawkins served as a delegate to the Continental Congress during the time the U.S. Constitution was ratified, served in the Senate representing North Carolina, and sat in on some negotiations with the Creek Indians brokering several key treaties.

President George Washington appointed Benjamin Hawkins as General Superintendent of Indian Affairs in 1796. Hawkins had authorization to deal with all tribes south of the Ohio River. He took his job very seriously and immediately set out on a journey through Indian held territory to learn as much as he could about the tribes.

During his journey, Hawkins recorded his observations noting topography, details concerning Indian agriculture, wildlife and Indian customs. He also mentioned various white men who were living in the territory at the time among the Indians.

He set out with a few supplies and his horse picking up interpreters and guides along the way. He had no idea how he would be received from place to place, and he was totally dependent upon the people of the Upper Creeks, Lower Creeks and the Cherokee Nation for "shelter, refreshment, information, and guidance."

At the time Hawkins was appointed Indian Agent, the deerskin trade was failing. Southern tribes were also being pressured to hand their lands over to cotton planters. One of the solutions the federal government promoted, and Benjamin Hawkins supported, was to train Indian men and women regarding ranching, farming, and cottage industries such as cloth making. The training would in turn assimilate the people as American citizens, and the hope was Native Americans would willingly dissolve their national sovereignty and simply hand over their territories to the U.S. government.

Unfortunately, an important fact was largely ignored, yet it was staring government leaders and settlers in the face. The Native Americans who inhabited the southern states at the end of the 18th century had been farmers for centuries. Several Indian families had already begun to ranch on their own.

Another factor that seemed to be overlooked was assimilation had been taking place since so many Cherokees and Creeks lived as many of their white neighbors. Apparently the assimilation wasn't going as fast as the U.S. government wanted hence the hopes for an education program.

Unfortunately, after reading through Benjamin Hawkins' journals I haven't been able to find any evidence he crossed the lands that would one day be Douglas County.

It doesn't mean he wasn't here, but he was very meticulous regarding documenting his travels. When you compare Hawkins' words to the maps and examine them closely, it is very apparent Hawkins' travels were to the north and extreme south of where Douglas County is today.

Hawkins' journal is extremely important historically because it records one of the first known journeys through the Chattahoochee River Valley including present-day Harris and Troup Counties. In fact, it is near where the Harris-Troup line exists today that Hawkins actually records a location where the land had experienced some sort of hurricane. It was evident some type of weather event had destroyed trees in not one place along his route but five different places, and it appeared they had occurred at different times due to new growth or the absence thereof.

More than likely our Hurricane Creek in Douglas County was named by Indians or settlers in the area due to some sort of significant storm damage, but the name was not given by Benjamin Hawkins, and his own records do not indicate he ever crossed our county.

The one thing his journals do prove to me, however, is since there were white men living in Native American territory to the north and to the south of us, more than likely there were white men living here among the Indians as early as the 1790s.

I just don't know who they were – yet.

Chapter 2

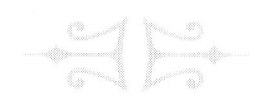

THE BUZZ ON BUZZARD ROOST ISLAND

Hundreds, if not thousands of Douglas County residents travel across the Chattahoochee River every week day to reach school or work.

I've crossed the river numerous times myself – most of the time with hardly a thought to the water flowing underneath me.

I would guess that most of us never get any closer to the river that makes up a portion of Douglas County's borders than our car windows.

What about you?

The closest I've gotten to the river has been to stroll along the stretch near Vinings that passes by Ray's on the River after Sunday brunch or from the patio at Canoe at lunchtime, and then there was the impromptu instance a summer or two ago when I made the Mister walk to the middle of the Highway 92 bridge with me to snap a few pictures.

You should have seen me attempting to dodge dead animals on the side of the bridge and try NOT to fall over the side into the water. Those cement bridge railings look much higher from the safety of your moving car. I also didn't realize the cars zooming by would be so dang close, but we finally did manage to get a picture or two of the river from the middle of the bridge.

The Chattahoochee River doesn't just serve as a geographic border for Douglas County. It figures prominently in our history – especially our earliest history involving Native Americans before there was a Douglas County – before there was a Campbell County.

In fact, per *The River Keeper's Guide to the Chattahoochee River* by Fred Brown "evidence of both Woodland (1000 B.C. to 900 A.D.) and Mississippian (900-1600 A.D.) villages as well as Paleo-Indian (10,000 to 8,000 B.C.) mounds have been found throughout the area." The book also mentions Buzzard Roost Island and describes it as one of the most important archaeological sites in northwest Georgia.

If you take a look at the maps online you see the island in the Chattahoochee River right where the borders of Fulton, Cobb, and Douglas meet along the river.

It just seems natural that the Creeks would have settled near the island as it became a crossing point in the river – part of the Sand Town Trail – said to be one of the oldest "roads" in the southeast. The Indian trail went all the way out towards present day Alabama and was used by natives and then later pioneer settlers. In fact, today's Cascade Road follows the old Sand Town Trail.

East-West trails such as the Sand Town Trail typically crossed waterways at the Fall Line because the streams were shallow making a better place to cross. Travelers sometimes were able to just wade across.

The island is also mentioned prominently in various treaties the Creek and Cherokee Nations made with the government regarding boundaries.

The Treaty at Indian Springs dated January 8, 1821 mentions Buzzard Roost Island as a geographic feature. The treaty states,"…from thence the nearest and direct line to the Chattahoochee River, up the eastern bank of said river along the water's edge to the Shallow ford where the present boundary line between the State of Georgia and the Creek Nation touches the said river, provided, however, that if the said line should strike the Chattahoochee River below the Creek Village Buzzard Roost, there shall be a set-off made so as to leave the said village within the Creek Nation."

I located another description offered by Wilson Lumpkin in April, 1821. Lumpkin would go on to be a governor of Georgia, but in 1821 he was responsible for addressing treaty line disputes with the Creek Indians. He was sent out to the Buzzard Roost area to gather information and report back to then Governor John Clark. Lumpkin sent Clark what was likely one of the few, if not only, visual accounts of a river trip from Buzzard Roost up to Standing Peachtree which is the site of present day Atlanta.

Lumpkin's report says, "From the Buzzard Roost village to the Standing Peachtree I estimate the distance of fifteen miles – this is computed more by the Indians…For several miles on the river, these improvements, is the most striking appearance of a town, the buildings being more compact in this, than any other part of the settlement. But there is no appearance of Capital, Town-house, or public-square about the place…."

I know.

Lumpkin's report doesn't give the kind of description I want either, but he does confirm there were buildings and dwellings of some sort.

Other sources describe the Sand Town/Buzzard Roost settlement with cornfields planted along the river and scattered dwelling structures here and there stretched for one mile north and south from the island on both sides of the river.

It's just as hard to find documented trips to the island today. Occasionally, I run across someone's blog post or Flickr pictures regarding the island.

I would love to hear from any readers who have done any exploring on Buzzard Roost Island or might have a story or two about it!

Chapter 3

DOUGLAS COUNTY'S FIRST RESIDENTS

If I asked you what comes to mind the minute I say the word Douglasville I really doubt you would mention anything having to do with Native Americans, but if you want to be serious about our history we cannot leave them out.

They were here first, right?

You can still see their footprints, IF you know where to look.

If you search back into the recesses of your memory from middle school you might recall this area was home to both the Cherokee and Creek Nations. You might also remember they didn't always get along so well. In fact, in 1821, the United States grew weary of the constant fighting between the two nations here in Georgia, so they established a buffer zone 10-miles across that would separate the two groups.

Fannie Mae Davis' history of Douglas County advises both nations had liberty to hunt and fish in the neutral zone. The border line and the old trail touched the north side of today's United Methodist Midway Church property and crossed the future Southern Railway track approximately one mile east of mid-town Douglasville. She further advises the site where Douglasville would eventually be located close to the skint chestnut tree was in the neutral zone. The skint chestnut was used as a direction marker and was a significant meeting place for both tribes. It stood at the highest point on the ridge close to where the old courthouse sits today.

Many history-types in and around Douglas County will tell you a legendary Cherokee Chief, AmaKanasta, is associated with the eastern part of Douglas County and Lithia Springs where lithium laded waters of a spring were used as a cure for aches and pains and lifted the spirits of partakers. It was recorded the chief's wigwam was located at Salt Springs, the earliest name for today's Lithia Springs. Those same history-types will also advise you can find hollowed out rocks near the springs that were used as soaking tubs.

When Interstate 20 was under construction there are several stories regarding various Native American artifacts being unearthed. Some were taken home by construction workers while others were covered with tons of concrete and asphalt. The realization really makes one wonder what might be under the superhighway cutting through the county lost for all time.

Both the Creeks and Cherokees used the land along the Chattahoochee River to grow corn. Even today stones with handmade depressions in them used for grinding corn can be found along the river if you know what you are looking for.

Native Americans also left behind "bent" trees they used as pointers to identify important places or simply as directional markers. Fannie Mae Davis advises a young tree was trained to grow parallel to the ground, the new upward growth forming a right angle which 'pointed in the direction to a village or spring'. Native carvers favored Beech trees for markers since the wood was easier to sink into. Trees bearing pictograms can be found along many local creeks and the Chattahoochee River. Again, you have to know what you are looking for.

Once the Indians were removed and the city of Douglasville and Douglas County were established, the prime source of income for the area was agriculture. For over one hundred years after the Native Americans were gone, area farmers would find arrowheads, pottery and other artifacts as they plowed their fields. Often these items were simply plowed under and over because they just didn't understand how important or significant the items might be to future generations.

Stories are told regarding one Chapel Hill farmer who found a large stone weapon of some sort on his property, but at the time it was found it could not be removed without tremendous effort. Later on in the 1950s technology existed to finally remove the object the family had been plowing around.

There are also stories of an old Indian burial ground that was unearthed by a farmer in the 1930s along the Dog River.

Then there is the Princess Anneewakee Mound located on the west bank of the Chattahoochee River near what used to be Campbellton.

Yes, the mound existed. You can see it via certain aerial photos of the area taken in the 1950s and available online.

Is it really the burial mound for an Indian princess?

It might be the resting place of the daughter of a Creek chief, but a princess?

No.

The Cherokees and Creeks did hold certain women in high regard, and would have respected the daughter of the chief, but a daughter would not have carried the title princess as we think of a princess today.

One thing we can be certain of is the mound did exist.

George White, a preacher as well as an amateur historian and archaeologist travelled the state in the early 1800s and wrote *Historical Collections of Georgia: Containing the Most Interesting Facts, Traditions, Biographical Sketches, Etc., Relating to Its History and Antiquities, from Its First Settlement to the Present Time.* The publication was what we would think of today as a travel guide.

White advised, "[The tomb was] opposite the village of Campbellton, on the western bank of the Chattahoochee, in a tuft of trees, on one of those mounds so common in Georgia; rests the remains of Anawaqua, and Indian Princess, the former proprietor of the soil. It is situated in a meadow, in a bend of the Chattahoochee, and near the foot of a considerable hill. Ancient fortification are [White's exact words] traced all around the plain, extending from the river to the hill."

Legend tells us the Chief chose that section of the river for his daughter's resting place because he thought it was the most beautiful, and he loved his daughter so much he named Anneewakee Creek after her.

The road would come much later.

Fannie Mae Davis advises in her history that anthropologist had known of the mound from the county's early days, but it wasn't until after World War II when Dr. Robert Wauchope, an authority regarding Georgia's platform mounds, gave the Princess Anneewakee mound an examination. He concluded the mound had been built over an earth lodge or log tomb due to the charred wood and pottery fragments found on the site.

Later on after the land exchanged hands, the new owner needed some fill dirt and began chipping away at the mound. He had no idea what the mound was or might be. Once he was told about the significance regarding the mound he stopped, but by then there was only about a foot to eighteen inches left. Students from the University of Georgia visited the site and found several artifacts. Among the mound periphery there were tapering lenses, deposits from periods of surface erosions and outwash, fragments of pottery or shards from several ancient periods to early 1800 European ceramics. Shards were radio-carbon dated from A.D. 605 to A.D. 725.

According to Ray Henderson's *Self-Guided Driving Tour of Douglas County*, a 400 pound carved stela [or stele] was found on Jacks Hill and was purported to be the headstone of Princess Anneewakee. It was possibly exposed when the timber for railroad ties was cut for the new line to Birmingham. This stele is currently on display at the Interpretive Center at Sweetwater Creek State Park.

A stele is usually stone or a wooden slab with some sort of inscription carved on it. They were used to mark territory but were generally used to mark graves.

Our Native American history is every bit just as important as our history regarding the founding families of Douglasville, the impact of the Civil War, or how Bankhead Highway came to be.

Legends along with documented stories and locations of events and found artifacts need to be gathered and documented.

Chapter 4

ON THE FAULT LINE

Every day thousands of people, many of them residents of Douglas County, travel Interstate 20 east into Atlanta. When you pass Thornton Road and reach the top of Douglas Hill you are met with a wonderful view of the Atlanta skyline, but what most people don't realize is that they on the western edge of the Brevard Fault with the Chattahoochee River positioned at the lowest point of the fault. The eastern edge of the fault is located at Interstate 285 where you see rock cliffs.

Fred Brown and Sherri M.L. Smith, authors of *The Riverkeeper's Guide to the Chattahoochee River* state, "Seen from a globe-circling, picture-snapping satellite high above the Earth's surface, the Brevard Fault looks like a monstrous incision across the torso of Georgia made by the Great Physician operating under battlefield conditions." It's a fairly long incision travelling across the state of Georgia from South Carolina and into Alabama for a total of 160 miles. It is the unofficial dividing line between the Appalachian Mountains and the Piedmont Plateau, and forms a channel for the Chattahoochee River for approximately 100 miles of is 540-mile course…The Brevard Fault zone…runs directly through the Sweetwater basin which gives the area a more mountainous environment than surrounding communities."

Have you ever noticed as you travel around in and near Sweetwater Creek State Park the area has a mountainous feel? The Brevard Fault is the reason why the park has rugged trails, rocky bluffs and rapids to navigate. It is why we see such steep grades, rolling hills, and why the water flows so fast in certain sections like a mountain stream. In fact, the Brown and Smith state, "…Sweetwater Creek, for example drops 120 feet from Austell to the Chattahoochee River; it drops 80 feet within the boundaries of Sweetwater Creek State Park alone. North-facing coves on [the creek] harbor trees, shrubs [like Mountain Laurel], herbs and wildflowers usually associated with the Appalachian Mountains to the north. The Fault also made it possible for the historic mills—New Manchester, Ferguson and Alexander's Mill—to be located along the creek since they needed the water power."

It's amazing to me that minutes from downtown Atlanta, close to Interstate 20, and seconds from most of our homes Sweetwater Creek State Park provides more than approximately 2,500 acres of peaceful wilderness including a 215-acre lake, ambling streams, forests full of all types of flora and fauna, and historic ruins. The park has been described as an extensive wilderness setting within 15 minutes of downtown Atlanta, and the park's extensive size allows it to support a diversity of native fauna.

So, now that you know the eastern edge of Douglas County follows a geological fault should you be worried? Should you rush out and purchase earthquake insurance?

While it's true that the Brevard Fault formed millions of years ago due to pieces of the Earth's crust moving against each other, I don't think we need to be too worried. The Brevard Fault is an ancient one, and geologists tell us it hasn't experienced any movement for 185 million years.

All we need to do is enjoy the beauty the Fault provides!

Section Two

THERE ONCE WAS A CAMPBELL COUNTY

Chapter 5

THE FORGOTTEN TOWN OF CAMPBELLTON

Yesterday was one of those nice lazy days spent with family and friends that you want to bookmark and remember for a very long time. We sat at my sister's house on her lovely porch and watched a steady stream of traffic coming and going from the Cotton Pickin' Fair at Gay, Georgia Like many along the route Dear Sister had filled her front yard with several odds and ends hoping a few of the fair goers would stop and load up on some new found treasures.

We never actually made it down to the fair.

Who really needed to go all the way down to Gay when both sides of the road in Dear Sister's little crossroads of a community was filled to capacity with crafts, odds and ends, signs that exclaimed boiled peanuts and funnel cakes, as well as any other item that could be sold.

Seriously, anything and everything imaginable could be found on the side of Georgia 85 meandering south from Fayetteville towards Gay, Georgia.

Of course, the draw for me wasn't yard sale after yard sale. It had something to do with my niece being in town and something to do with getting to see the newest addition to the family – a sweet little baby boy. Then there were the promises of a grilled feast my brother-in-law can produce, sitting around with friends, and enjoying the community of Alvaton where my sister and her husband now make their home.

And what a home it is! I have to admit I'm drawn to Dear Sister's home – a turn of the century house with lots of character and hints of history that we have yet to discover.

No, it's not hard for me to cross the Chattahoochee River and head south at all when the invite is extended.

Our route home was lit by the Supermoon. I swear we could have turned off the headlights and still could have made our way home.

We headed back into Douglas County along State Route 92, and as we approached the four way crossing at Charlie's Market I couldn't help but notice how bright the remaining features of the town of Campbellton were – the Methodist Church on my left with its old graves, the old Baptist Church cemetery up the hill on my right along with the Campbellton Lodge building which dates to 1848.

I made a silent wish wanting to look up on that hill and see the old Campbell County Courthouse with the moonlight bouncing off the window panes, but no matter how hard we wish sometimes our dreams just can't come true.

The old courthouse was torn down many years ago after it was abandoned.

As we zoomed across the river I turned back towards Campbellton and noticed how the moonbeams lit up the river making a path right through the middle of the water. I was overcome with sadness at that moment – mourning the town that had been along the banks of the Chattahoochee River, and I recalled a description Atlanta's esteemed historian Franklin Garrett had penned in his book *Atlanta and Its Environs.*

Garrett said, "Old Campbellton, upon its eminence overlooking the Chattahoochee with its brick courthouse, Masonic Hall, academy, and ante-bellum homes gleaming through the avenues of magnolia, myrtle, or cedar, were doomed. Most of its old families drifted off to other places, including the newer railroad towns of Fairburn and Palmetto. Weeds rioted and choked neglected flower gardens. Rows of comfortable homes, once housing a population of some 1200, fell into decay. The Masonic Lodge Hall was deserted. For two decades the red brick courthouse stood dark and silent the habitation of owls, bats, and ghostly memories of better days, until it was mercifully dismantled. The names upon mossy tombstones in the Methodist churchyard and the old Baptist cemetery are the only remainder of the once flourishing and beautiful town, the site of which, since 1932, has been in Fulton County."

So, how did Campbellton basically become a ghost town of sorts?

Here's a little regarding how it all played out…

Campbell County was named for Duncan G. Campbell. Part of Campbell's claim to fame is he helped to negotiate the Treaty of Indian Springs – the treaty where the Creek Nation ceded a portion of their land including the land that would become Campbell County.

If an initial settler in the area – Judge Walter T. Colquitt – had gotten his way the county seat for Campbell County would have been established on his property at Pumpkintown eight miles south down the river, but an online publication by the Chattahoochee Hills Historical Society states "another judge – Francis Irwin – offered his eight acres of undeveloped land [along the river]…with an added incentive for free lots for prospective builders and inhabitants…By 1829, establishment of the county government began in earnest with the creation of a judicial system and the appointment of James Black, Jesse Harris, Robert O. Beavers, Thomas Moore, and Littleberry Watts as electoral commissioners and county organizers…and by 1835, streets and lots in Campbellton were surveyed and [ready for construction]".

Eventually, the town would have a courthouse, doctor's office and pharmacy, academy, hotel, blacksmith, stores, lodge hall, post office and many homes.

In his book, *The Courthouse and the Depot: The Architecture of Hope in an Age of Despair*, Wilbur W. Caldwell discusses a Coweta County account that relates in 1830, Samuel Keller, a saddle shop owner and one of the first commissioners for the county, moved from Newnan to Campbellton 'lured by expectations' of steamboats on the Chattahoochee River.

Yes! Steamboats!

Can you imagine?

The Chattahoochee Hills Historical Society website mentions "there were high hopes for the rich loamy soil [which did make the area successful agriculturally, but] there were also high hopes for the Chattahoochee to become a major transportation and shipping channel in the region… but the river proved to be shallow and difficult to navigate."

As far as I can tell there is only one recorded trip made upriver by a steam vessel from West Point to Campbellton. A Troup County source states "in 1831 Reuben Thompson brought a load of goods upriver."

The hope to develop steamship travel on the Chattahoochee all the way to Atlanta persisted until at least the second half of the twentieth century, but the dream finally died as folks had to accept the river just wasn't navigable for steamboats.

The death sentence for the town of Campbellton came about per most sources when the Atlanta & West Point Railroad failed to be built through Campbellton. The line went through Fairburn, Georgia instead. Many local sources state the citizens of Campbellton refused the railroad, but I agree with most historians who realize that thoughts of the railroad being routed through Campbellton were just a dream. The terrain along the current line through Fairburn, which I lived along growing up, is along a natural flat ridge, a much more suitable site.

Even so, the loss of the railroad meant a slow death for Campbellton over the next several years beginning in 1870 when as Caldwell reports "the citizens of Campbellton moved to Fairburn in droves". One local account relates Campbellton residents were "dismantling their homes and moving them as well. The town had close to 1200 citizens at its peak, but by 1860, only 239 white citizens still remained."

The original courthouse in Campbellton was wooden, but was eventually replaced with a brick structure.

A local man – Robert Cook – bought the building and dismantled it. He used the materials to build a barn on his property along Cedar Grove Road.

All that remains of old Campbellton today is Campbellton United Methodist Church and even though the Baptist church building is not original to the town the cemetery is. The Baptist church faces what once was the town square where the courthouse stood. Both Union and Confederate soldiers rest in the cemeteries. Close to the Baptist church stands the Beaver home – a Greek Style farmhouse which was taken over by Union soldiers when they crossed the river at Campbellton during the Civil War. The house sits across from where the original Campbell County Courthouse stood.

You might be asking yourself why I'm discussing a dead town that lies on the Fulton County side of the river today, but back in 1828 Campbell County extended beyond the river into what is today Douglas County. In fact, Douglas County was created from Campbell County in 1870. Many of our county's forefathers were citizens of Campbell County long before they were citizens of Douglas County.

The long forgotten town of Campbellton IS important to Douglas County history.

It is the beginning of the Douglas County story.

Chapter 6

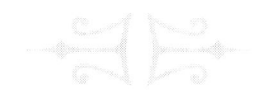

THE DOCTOR WHO WANTED TO FIGHT

One of the things I try to avoid as I share my research regarding Douglas County history is a dry recitation of someone's birth and death dates, where they are buried, who their parents were, their spouse's information and their children's names.

I want to do more than just record a litany of facts.

I wouldn't want to write it, and you certainly wouldn't want to read it.

Even when I was still in the classroom I thought of myself as a storyteller because that's what history is – a collection of true stories.

Thousands of people throughout history have gone to great lengths to record history through newspapers, diaries, journals, saved letters, family Bibles, and oral traditions. I want to gather up as many of the bits and pieces of the story that I can, from as many resources as I can and tell the story.

Sometimes it's a real challenge, but in the case of Dr. Thomas Coke Glover the story is just too compelling not to relate it.

Though Glover was born in Augusta, Georgia he chose to make Campbell County his home.

The genealogy research of Joe Baggett indicates Glover was in Campbellton as early as 1850. He was a medical doctor and evidence suggests he was highly respected and known across the state.

Now you may be asking yourself why I'm discussing a man from Campbell County when my focus is Douglas County history. Please remember Douglas County was birthed out of Campbell and many of our citizens hold ties to the original settlers of Campbell County including Dr. Glover.

Dr. Thomas Coke Glover interests me due to the choices he made during the days leading to the Civil War. He was a respected physician who married Elizabeth (Lizzie) Susan Camp Glover in 1852. Glover was one of the town commissioners of Campbellton in 1854 per the research of Joe Baggett.

Glover also served the people of Campbell County as one of two delegates they sent to represent them at the Secession Convention held in Milledgeville from January 16 to March 23, 1861.

Not only did Glover vote for secession, he also assisted with writing the new Constitution of the Republic of Georgia.

Of course it was assumed Glover would serve in the Confederate Army, and it was naturally assumed he would serve as a medical doctor, but this is where Glover deviates from the expected. By serving as an Army doctor he would have been spared from actual combat, but Glover chose to fight and set about at once organizing a company of men.

Richard B. Stansberry writes in *So Sings the Chattahoochee*...."[Upon returning from the Secession Convention] Dr. Glover organized the Campbellton Blues which became Company A of the Twenty-First Georgia Infantry Regiment. The men drilled on the streets and about the courthouse square [in Campbellton]. They received so much training they were dubbed the 'West Pointers' of the Georgia Twenty-First, and given the roster distinction of Company A."

This might have been the end of my discussion regarding Dr. Glover, but then I happened upon an interesting book titled *History of the Doles-Cook*

Brigade by Henry Walter Thomas. The book was published in 1903 and represents the history of four different regiments of the brigade – the Fourth, the Twelfth, the Twenty-first (Glover's regiment), and the Forty-fourth. Thomas, the author of the book, served in Company G of the Twelfth Georgia, and the book is an extensive history provided mostly by the men who served.

So often we have the information someone fought in the Civil War but Thomas' book provides the details regarding where the men in Company A fought and contains eyewitness accounts of Dr. Glover's actions.

Thomas relates how Glover and Company A didn't reach Virginia until Second Bull Run, and soon after their arrival a feud began between some of the officers that grew and spread and lasted until death claimed the principal, Colonel John T. Mercer.

When the order came to go to Manassas a large number of the regiment was down in their tents with measles. When the order to strike tents was received the rain was pouring down in torrents, and Captain Glover went to Colonel Mercer and asked if the tents could remain over the men sick with measles stating it would endanger their health further if they got wet.

Colonel Mercer refused to listen.

Captain Glover refused to obey the order regarding the sick men under his command and was placed under arrest. The tents were struck leaving about twenty men with measles in the rain.

Almost all the other company officers of the regiment took sides with Captain Glover, and the breach between Mercer and Glover was never healed as long as they lived.

On arriving at Manassas, the regiment went into camp and a few days later the arrested officers were returned to duty without any thing further having been done.

Glover and his men were soon caught up in assisting the Twenty-first North Carolina in capturing the Union supply depot at Manassas Junction. Glover's commanding officer, Brigadier General Isaac Trimble gleefully said, "Give me my two Twenty-ones and I'll charge and capture hell itself!"

Glover and the Twenty-First Georgia took part in the Battle of Sharpsburg or Antietam in September, 1862.

One of the battle reports relates how the Twenty-first Georgia was ordered to wheel to the left, and, taking shelter under a low stone fence running at right angles to their former line, direct their fire upon the wavering Yankee regiment, with the view of breaking the enemy's line at this point. They did so promptly, and a few rounds from them had the desired effect, and the enemy's line was entirely broken.

Discussing the same action Thomas' book states:

"We were given orders to reach the fence. In obedience to this command there was exhibited the most daring bravery that came under our observation during the war – a bravery not surpassed in the charge of the Famous Light Brigade at Balaklava. Volley after volley was poured into the Twenty-first Georgia, mowing down the men by scores, yet they never faltered or waivered, but onward went, closing up the gaps in the lines as if on dress parade, with their gallant commander Colonel [Thomas Coke] Glover, in front with his sword in his uplifted hand calling for his men to follow. And they did. Oh God! What a sight; what carnage. What a feast of death was that!

…The fence was reached the work of death commenced at short range. From this fence we poured volley after volley into them for some thirty to forty minutes…The regiment went over the fence with one of its most blood-curdling rebel yells.

…Then they fled and the day was ours; but at what a cost! … Company A went into the battle with forty-five men, nineteen were killed and twenty-one wounded, some of them fatally and others crippled for life."

One of the wounded happened to be Glover himself who at some point during the battle realized ammunition was getting low and his men were wasting it on an enemy who was too far out of range. The book *Antietam: The Soldier's Story* by John M. Priest relates how Glover sought out Colonel James Walker (C.O. Trimble's Brigade) to ask to move the men under his command. Walker gave the order for the Twenty-first Georgia to move out. As his aide delivered the command to the regiment a ball struck Major Glover through the body and sent him to the ground – severely wounded, but he did live to fight another day.

In fact, he lived to fight many fights before his death leading his men through 107 various engagements with the enemy.

When Colonel John T. Mercer of the Twenty-First Georgia was killed at Plymouth, North Carolina Glover rose to Lieutenant Colonel on April 18, 1864.

Five months later on September 19, 1864 he was shot and killed instantly at Winchester, Virginia and was buried there.

Strangely, it is reported a few hours before his death Lieutenant Colonel Glover heard about the fall of Atlanta and said, "Atlanta has fallen, and I fear all is lost, but I shall not live to see it."

Amazingly prophetic, right?

Thomas relates in *The History of the Doles-Cook Brigade*, "No braver or truer man that he ever drew the breath of life. He was always at his post of duty ready to lead his men to battle. His own safety was of no consideration to him when or where duty called. Not a single battle was ever fought by the regiment, but that this noble officer was with it, encouraging and leading his men to victory and glory…Colonel Glover was to the Twenty-first Georgia what Stonewall Jackson was to the army of the valley."

One final note regarding the Twenty-First Georgia including Company A from Campbell County – of all the regiments engaged in the War Between the States, North and South, the Twenty-first Georgia was the third in number of men killed in battle. The regiment that lost the greatest number was the Eighth New York, and they were killed by the Twenty-First Georgia.

Chapter 7

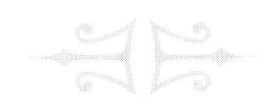

THE MOTHER OF CONFEDERATE REUNIONS

When I was in the classroom I used to show videos and pictures regarding Civil War veterans to students, and invariably one or two of my little sweethearts would wonder how in the world those old men could fight a war.

Of course, they weren't old men during those years the war was fought – far from it, but for many years after the war they continued to get together for reunions.

The website for The Center for Civil War Research explains, "Almost immediately after the end of the Civil War, veterans sought out occasions to gather together, to relive their shared experiences, find solace in their battle-forged bonds, to celebrate heroic deeds, and commemorate their sacrifices of their fallen comrades. These reunions…came eventually to serve as a symbol of a wider national reunification, despite the vast majority of reunions remaining purely separate former Union or Confederate affairs…Attended by hundreds and thousands, reunions of all kinds evoked powerful sentiments and became fertile ground for the construction of Civil War Memory."

But where did the idea for the first reunion come from?

How did they start?

I've written previously about Dr. Thomas Coke Glover from Campbellton and his experience during the Civil War. He organized and fought with Company A of the Twenty-first Georgia Infantry unit, and after leading his men in 107 various engagements with the enemy he was killed in Winchester, Virginia.

Now I want to continue his story by discussing his wife – Elizabeth (Lizzie) Susan Camp.

A marker at her grave in Corsicana, Texas states, "In 1867, after the War Between the States with *for God and county* as her motto she rode the countryside of Campbellton, Georgia to assemble the comrades of her fallen husband to a basket dinner and to *talk over the w*ar…"

Thus began the Confederate reunions.

To be even more accurate Mrs. Glover is often referred to as the "mother of Confederate reunions" organizing the first one in June, 1867.

In 1928, an issue of *Confederate Veteran* advises Company A was comprised of 200 men as the war began. By April, 1865 when the war ended there were only 30 left – including the drummer and the fifer.

Only 12 made it to the reunion.

The magazine article states, "…the orator was Colonel Thomas Latham of Atlanta. They arranged to hold an annual reunion as long as any two of them lived to meet together and talk over the days that tried men's souls… At the next annual meeting a big basket dinner was given and all the veterans in Campbell County were invited to meet with them…They vowed by the help of God to teach their children and charge them to teach their children for all time to come that the cause for which they fought was just and right, to teach them to be proud of the part we took in the conflict, that we were overcome by numbers – not whipped, but overcome."

That language, "we were overcome by numbers – not whipped, but overcome", is familiar because it comes directly from a letter Mrs. Glover wrote many years later to the Atlanta chapter of the Daughters of the Confederacy regarding her vision of the Confederate reunions. I found the contents of the letter in the book *History of the Doles-Cook Brigade* by

Henry Walter Thomas. It is a great read if you are interested in Civil War history.

The letter gives some insight into her thoughts regarding Reconstruction and her purpose behind her attempt to get the men to gather.

Mrs. Glover's letter says:

"After the fateful day of Appomattox the men of the South wended their way to their desolate homes, many broken in health and in fortune.

The first problem to solve was how to support their families; the struggles, trials and hardships undergone to accomplish this is underwritten in history. God alone knows the suffering endured, but the men who had fought under Lee and Jackson were equal to the task of supplying food, shelter and raiment for their loved ones. Soon this was a matter of minor consideration.

The South was in the throes of Reconstruction, bleeding at every pore, under military and carpetbag rule; the Northern press branding the men who fought for the Confederacy as rebels and traitors, urging that our leaders be hanged and imprisoned; here the Union Leaguers trying to get all the landholders to join them to prevent confiscation. If a man refused, or dared hold secession, he was considered a traitor.

Ben Hill was the only man who had courage to denounce the infamous rule of the papers of the day; Dunlap Scott the only man in the Bulloch legislature who dared protest against their wasteful expenditure of the people's money.

My husband was killed at Winchester, Virginia, in 1864, and is buried there in the beautiful Stonewall Cemetery. I had to toil to support and school my children and keep the wolf from the door. Must my children and the children of other brave men who fought and died for the love of home be branded as children of rebels and traitors?

Must the men who were spared with their children, be branded as rebels and traitors for all time?

> *Must the finger of scorn be pointed at these men and their children for having fought for our cause and homes? Must they be disgraced as were the Tories who fought for King George in the Revolution? No, no, a thousand times no!*
>
> *The cause was just and right and by the help of God I vowed to so teach this to my children and to call the men of our company (A, 21st Georgia regiment) together, talk over the war and its incidents and charge them to teach their children for all time to come that the cause for which they fought was just and right: teach them to be proud of the part they took in the conflict; teach their children that we were overcome by numbers, three and five to one – not whipped, but overcome…"*

Joe Baggett's *Who's Who of Douglas County* advised [Mrs. Glover] was one of twelve children born to Benjamin Camp (1801-1884) who was a colonel in the Indian Wars. Her mom was Winifred Arnold (1802-1888) and both parents are buried at Campbellton Methodist Church. `

Mr. Baggett further advises Mrs. Glover's grandfather was Joseph Camp who fought in the War of 1812 and his father, Benjamin Camp had fought in the American Revolution.

Her brothers were members of the Campbellton Guards organized by her husband.

Somehow it makes sense to me that Mrs. Glover would form a reunion group considering every man in her family had been in service at one time or another.

Mrs. Glover briefly lived in Douglas County in the 1880s before moving to Indian Territory then to Corsicana, Texas where she was active in veteran's affairs.

She died on April 14, 1915 and is buried in Texas.

The local Sons of Confederate Veterans, Lt. Col. Thomas Coke Glover, Camp 943 participated in the plaque dedication at Mrs. Glover's grave site in Corsicana, Texas.

Chapter 8

A LETTER FOR MRS. GLOVER

Our story begins in the 1850s. Moses Loeb was a Jewish peddler fresh from the shores of Europe. Back then peddlers traveling through towns and villages were a common sight all over the United States.

In 1852, Loeb reached the then thriving town of Campbellton to peddle his wares, but he fell ill with Typhoid Fever. Fortunately for him a young married couple – Dr. Thomas and Lizzie Glover – took him in and nursed him back to health before sending him on his way.

The Glovers gradually forgot all about the peddler as they began raising a family. Dr. Glover had his medical practice, and he was involved in Campbell County politics.

There were also other issues such as slavery, states' rights and the war that happened to be on the horizon. Dr. Glover was one of two delegates selected from Campbell County to attend Georgia's Secession Convention in 1861. Dr. Glover also organized the Campbellton Blues, a group of Confederate soldiers who served with the 21st Georgia Regiment.

Glover could have entered the Confederate Army as a doctor and escape the horrors of the war by staying well behind the lines, but he chose a different kind of service. Many accounts of the exploits of the Campbellton Blues paint Dr. Glover as brave and always at his post ready to lead his men into battle. In fact, he led his men though 107 various engagements with the Union Army until finally, he was shot and killed instantly in 1864 at Winchester, Virginia.

Lizzie Glover realized when she sent her husband off to war the worst might happen, and it did. She never remarried, but picked up the mantle of service from her husband and carried on raising her children, but she also worried about the children of the other men who had served with her husband.

She was adamant folks should never forget why they went off to war and should teach their children as well. The marker at Lizzie Glover's grave advises that in 1867 she began organizing a reunion of the men who had gone off to war with Dr. Glover in order to talk over the war. For this very reason Mrs. Glover is often referred to as the "mother of Confederate reunions".

Around the middle of December in 1892, Lizzie Glover was living in Douglasville, and as many war widows she had experienced great sacrifice and poverty. One day she received a strange letter. It had a strange postmark and the handwriting and notations looked foreign.

Mrs. Glover read the letter, but it took her a few minutes to understand the details and make a connection to the past when she was just a new bride some years before.

The letter said – *Forty-eight years ago, I lived a stranger in Georgia. I was at the point of death in your house for six weeks, and it was only your tender care that gave me back life.*

I have lived ever since in Weisbaden, Germany…

I send you a slight reminder that, though half a century has almost rolled around since I saw you, I have never forgotten your kindness…

The slight reminder that Moses Loeb sent to Lizzie Glover was a certified draft for $500.

It was just a few years later that Lizzie Glover moved out west with her daughter's family. I have no way of knowing, but I'd like to think that the $500 Moses Loeb sent to Lizzie helped in some way to get her to her new home.

Chapter 9

CIVIL WAR SITES IN DOUGLAS COUNTY

Kennesaw Mountain, Pickett's Mill, Ezra Church, and Jonesboro are all significant locations regarding Civil War history in the Atlanta area.

Douglas County has a few sites as well even if they aren't very high on the name recognition scale and are not marked. Most of the events were nothing more than troop movements from both sides, but Douglas County citizens were heavily affected by the war since both Confederate and Union soldiers lived off the land and took private property when necessary for their own use. It is also important to remember that Douglas County did not exist during the Civil War. The locations that are detailed here were all within Campbell County during the war.

Dark Corner is one area of the county that saw some troop movement. The Confederate Army of the Tennessee camped there, and General Hood deemed the location his headquarters in the fall of 1864. Various orders archived today are addressed to Dark Corner and are dated September 30 and October 1, 1864. If troop numbers are accurate close to 40,000 Confederates moved through Dark Corner, an area between Winston and Douglasville, on their way to Allatoona and then on to Tennessee.

Other areas of the county touched by the Civil War include Flint Hill Methodist Church located at 7156 Highway 5. Two unknown Confederate soldiers were buried there after dying in the arbor close to the church on October 2 and 3, 1864.

At the intersection of Rockhouse Road and Riverside Parkway a two-story rock house stood constructed of flagstone and mortar. The property included a hill which during the skirmishes of July 3rd and 4th, 1864 the state militia and the 3rd Texas Calvary held along a trench line against oncoming Union forces. Douglas Hill is above the intersection. At the time the house was owned by a lawyer named Edge. The Union troops eventually took the property including his home, stock and crops.

Early in July, 1864, General Sherman ordered Generals Stoneman and McCook to flank the Confederates to the right of Kennesaw Mountain and eventually move south and secure Sandtown Road down to the Chattahoochee River. The troops crossed Sweetwater Creek at Powder Springs and entered Salt Springs/Lithia Springs. On July 3, 1864 the Union troops met considerable opposition from General Ross' men in what avid historians remember as The Battle of Sweetwater Bridge, but once Stoneman linked with the 55th Illinois Infantry General Ross and his Confederates were pushed back to the river. Accounts of the battle pinpoint the location as "Riverside Parkway at the bridge over Sweetwater Creek – adjacent to the site of Aderholds Ferry."

General Stoneman's men reached the New Manchester site on July 9th. Most Douglas County residents know about the New Manchester Manufacturing Company ruins at Sweetwater Creek State Park, but many don't realize there was a town of approximately 500 people who supported the factory, a flour mill, a grist mill, and water powered saw nearby. The town boasted a company store, inn, and post office. There had even been talk of building a rail line into the town, but the Civil War delayed the effort.

The manufacturing company was five stories tall making it one of the tallest buildings in the area, and it was powered by a 50,000 pound waterwheel. There was no actual fighting between troops when the mill was taken, but there was a skirmish nearby at Alexander's Mill also located within the grounds of Sweetwater Creek State Park today.

General Stoneman captured the mill and ordered it destroyed since it had been a vital supplier of cloth for tents and sheets to the Confederacy. Mystery surrounds the New Manchester site as many of the people working at the mill were rounded up by the Union soldiers and sent north where they were forced to remain until the end of the war. Since the mill was never rebuilt, many of the workers never returned to the area. The book, *The Women Will Howl: The Union Army Capture of Roswell and New Manchester, Ga. and the Forced Relocation of Mill Workers* by Mary Deborah Petite is an excellent resource to learn more about the incident.

After camping along Sweetwater Creek, Stoneman and his men headed southwest. He and General McCook had received orders to disrupt the West Point Railroad south and west of Atlanta. McCook's men camped along the road towards Campbellton and there was a very short battle with a Confederate unit on the Irwin-Bomar-Rice-Austin-Bullard-Henley property. The home still stands today along Highway 92 before you reach the Chattahoochee River. A Union soldier was killed and the mistress of the house, Susan Miller Bullard was told to provide him a proper burial or risk having her home burned. The solder rests today in the garden near the house.

Before heading on to Newnan, McCook decided the Bullard home would make a fine location for him to "make camp." He enjoyed a fine dinner prepared by Mrs. Bullard while his men camped all around the house and adjacent grounds. Following dinner Mrs. Bullard's daughter, Tallulah Florence Bullard provided the evening's entertainment since she was a very accomplished piano player.

McCook's men made various requests and soon found that "Little Reb" as they called Tallulah could play any song they requested. When they asked her to play *Yankee Doodle*, however, the little girl would launch into *Dixie* instead. They kept requesting *Yankee Doodle*, but she kept pounding out *Dixie* on the piano keys. After hearing *Dixie* over and over General McCook finally walked into the parlor to see what was going on.

Once McCook surveyed the living room scene of conflicting wills, he correctly devised an accommodation for both sides. He is reported to have said, "Men, if you expect Little Reb to play *Yankee Doodle* for you tonight I suspect that you'll have to sing *Dixie* first.

So, it was on a night in 1864 in Douglas County when a group of Yankee cavalry sang *Dixie* while Little Reb accompanied them on the piano!"

Once McCook and his 3,500 cavalry troops reached the Chattahoochee they crossed at Smith's Ferry.

Over the next several days there were a few skirmishes on both sides of the river at Campbellton leaving the town in shambles. Many sources discuss how citizens kept the Campbellton Ferry (where Highway 92 crosses the river today) busy as it was set upon by people trying to flee the small town. I would imagine the Gorman/Austell Ferry up the river at today's Highway 166 Bridge was also busy with refugees.

Other plantations and properties in the area were also commandeered by Union troops as they made their way across the river. The Glennwood plantation located on the west banks of the Chattahoochee near Campbellton and owned by Reverend Henry D. Wood was also disturbed. Reverend Wood passed away in April, 1861, and is buried in the cemetery at the Methodist Church in Campbellton. His widow and daughter, Rosa Emory Wood, tried to keep things going and were on the property to greet the Union soldiers.

Bravely Rosa rode out to greet Sherman's men telling the commanding officer, "My business is urgent." She proceeded to advise the Union soldiers her mother was an invalid, and she wanted an escort to get her and her mother to Atlanta safely. The story goes that she did get her escort, and they even waited patiently for Rosa to pack various belongings for the journey and to give instructions to her slaves. The two women rode off with their Union escort leaving their property entrusted to the Union soldiers and slaves. They eventually made their way to relatives in Virginia where Rosa's mother passed away.

Rosa Emory Wood married Willis Allen Brockman in August, 1866, and in 1870 she returned to Glennwood. Her husband took over the property and – well, that's a story for another time.

Chapter 10

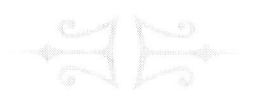

MS. SYNTHIA'S RECOLLECTIONS

One year ago when I mentioned to friends I would be writing a local history column, I had a few people who immediately said, "Oh, you are going to write about the mill at Sweetwater, aren't you?"

It is a foregone conclusion, isn't it?

The New Manchester Mill is one of our most historic sites, and there is a bit of mystery concerning the millworkers who were carried off by Union troops, but I quickly answered that since it was such an expected topic, I would wait and choose other bits of history that aren't so well known.

So far, I have stuck to that plan, but today I'm going to mention the mill because I've stumbled over an interesting story regarding one of the families who lived at New Manchester and what happened to them after the war.

The mill at New Manchester was built along the banks of Sweetwater Creek in 1846. It was the tallest structure around Atlanta at the time with five stories. Ninety looms and six thousand spindles were busy making yarn and fabric. The mill's closest competitor as far as output was a mill located in Roswell, Georgia.

As I wrote in April, 2011 many don't realize there was a town of approximately 500 people who supported the factory, a flour mill, a grist mill and a water-powered saw nearby. The town boasted a company store, inn and post office. There had even been talk of building a rail line into the town, but the Civil War delayed the effort.

In her book, *The Women Will Howl*, Mary Deborah Petite advises William Washington Stewart was the mill boss and lived at New Manchester with his wife, Elizabeth (Lizzie) Russell and their children including their daughter Synthia Catherine Stewart.

Once the Civil War was underway the mill at New Manchester set about making cloth for Confederate uniforms which would make the mill, the mill workers, as well as their children huge targets for the Union as the war drug on.

A narrative by Synthia Stewart is found at a Stewart family genealogy website where she states, "All the men, all the old men, you know, went to the army first." This included her father who joined the Confederate Army by enlisting at Campbell County on March 4, 1862 with the Salt Springs Guards, Company K, 41st Regiment, Georgia Infantry. He was captured at Vicksburg, Mississippi in 1863 but was released after signing a paper that he would not fight with the Confederate forces again. Basically, he lied and returned to the fighting almost immediately.

By July, 1864 Sherman and his forces had reached the west banks of the Chattahoochee River in their quest to reach Atlanta, but first they had orders from Sherman to burn the mill at New Manchester. When the Union commanders balked at burning the mills in Roswell and New Manchester, they sent word to Sherman wanting him to re-verify his original orders. Sherman issued a second order which gave his men permission *to arrest all people, male and female, connected with those factories, no matter what the clamor, and let them foot it, under guard, to Marietta, whence I will send them by cars [railroad] to the North...The poor women will make a howl.*

General Sherman had unleashed "total war" on the people of the South in an effort to destroy Southern morale.

It worked.

Word had already reached those living at New Manchester that the Union soldiers would take or destroy everything of any value.

Synthia recalls how they hid things:

"We took a big pitcher and filled it full of silverware, it was a big old water pitcher, and set it down in a hollow stump. We couldn't put any dishes in it, so we just put the dishes around the edge, and covered them up with trash and went on and left them. Well, they stayed there until after the War was all over with, and when the people got back home, why, then they went and gathered up the things that they had left that way, you know. But they never did get anything that was left in the house. That was all gone.

The next day there came a crowd of northern soldiers. Before they came through, Grandma said, "Well, Lizzie, let's cook the children one more meal of victuals." We had lots of chickens, but we had nothing else much though to go with them, so they cooked the chickens and fixed dinner. Before we could get through, why, the yard was full of men, looked like. They just come on down, and we children walked to the door, and they said, "Well, we're just in time." They didn't ask if they could or not, they just walked in and sat down at the table and ate up all the dinner we had cooked, so we didn't have anything more left to cook another day.

And then they set the factory afire and burned that up."

Union soldiers blasted the dam at New Manchester. The flood destroyed the mill town while they set fire to the mill itself.

Synthia recollects, *"The northern men told the women… to get themselves home and get them a little tad of clothes, some for the children and themselves… Not to try to take anything else out of the house, only just what they could carry…"*

The book *General Sherman and the Georgia Belles: Tales from the Women Left Behind* by Cathy Kaemmerlen includes the story, and Stewart family lore indicates the one possession Synthia took from her family's home was the family Bible.

The assembly point for the mill workers from New Manchester and Roswell were the grounds of the Georgia Military Institute. From there the workers would be shipped north by train. Today, the spot where the Georgia Military Institute was located is the home to the Marietta Conference Center and Resort on Powder Springs Street in Marietta, Georgia.

At some point along the journey to Marietta, the Stewart Family Bible was taken from Synthia by a Union soldier. Once in Marietta she noticed the soldier and pointed him out. Kaemmerlen writes in her book that Synthia caused such a ruckus General Sherman himself came to her to see what was going on. After quizzing the soldier, he immediately had the family Bible returned to the young girl.

The mill prisoners were taken to Louisville, Kentucky and Synthia continues her story – "[We were] *turned ... loose in a big old hospital house...They called* [us] *prisoners ..."*

Yes, they were prisoners, and Sherman's orders dictated the mill workers would stay there until they signed an Oath of Allegiance to the Union. Once the oath was signed people were allowed to cross the Ohio River and find work in the local area.

Day after day stuck in a building with dozens of folks with restless energy – I can only imagine how nerves were frayed and people were at the end of their endurance. However, the story for the Stewart family imprisoned far from home in an old hospital building took a miraculous turn.

Synthia recalls the joyous moment:

"We just fooled around, you know, and wanted to get outside and they wouldn't let us. And we heard a band coming and we wanted to get out then, sure enough! Well, after a while we begged and cut up so that [the adults] *got ashamed of us and let us go out...It was just a*

whole lot of southern prisoners that they were going to keep until the next morning and send them across the Ohio River. Well, we got out there and the band passed and just as it passed, why, the first man behind the band was PA. We thought he was dead, you know, didn't know we ever would see him anymore."

What a coincidence!

Synthia's father, Walter Washington Stewart had been captured again near Atlanta on August 3, 1864. He was being shipped to Camp Chase near Columbus, Ohio, and it was just a strange twist of events that the family members met up under such conditions.

It was at this point that Synthia's mother, Lizzie, signed the Oath of Allegiance and found work in Louisville doing accounting work.

Synthia's story continues:

"We stayed there in Louisville, got us a place, and we children went to school and did the best we could and Ma worked for the government to make her some money. And finally they turned [my father] *loose..."*

Once the family had enough money saved for the trip they returned to Atlanta, and of course, they made the short trip to New Manchester to see what had become of their home, but they found nothing but ruins. It had become a ghost town.

Synthia advises:

"And when we went back home, why, everything was torn up, there wasn't anything growing, only just wild, you know, and believe it or not, but the whole fields... in STRAWBERRIES. We had thousands and thousands of strawberries, and we gathered those strawberries and carried them to Atlanta and sold them and made money to live on, with what Pa was making... A lady who didn't have to refugee,

why she had a little handful of peas and she gave Ma the handful of peas. She planted them and we had several messes off of those peas ... we never did have any strawberries any more. That was God's work, you know, He gave us Holy Manna to eat while we didn't have anything else."

The Stewart family remained in the Atlanta area during those hard years immediately after the war before moving to Gaylesville, Alabama. It was in Gaylesville where Synthia married David Boyd, a young man from Smyrna, Georgia. Family lore advises one hundred guests were present at the wedding and it was recorded in their old Bible.

The romantic in me hopes it was the same family Bible Synthia saved from destruction, and the same Bible General Sherman personally returned to her.

Synthia and her husband eventually settled in Sidney, Texas with their nine children. Her family knew her as Granny Boyd and she shared her Civil War experiences with her grandson when she was 92. Her recollection is on a gramophone recording that is on file with the Friends of Sweetwater Creek State Park and the Atlanta History Center. It is that recording that documents the story regarding the Bible Kaemmerlen writes about in her book.

The family genealogy site advises, "Synthia outlived her husband David by many years and died in October, 1951 a few days before her 97th birthday. Her obituary in *The Comanche Chief* stated, "Through her long and interesting life she was the heart of her home and her family centered closely about her. One of the last gentlewomen of the Old South and its traditions has fallen asleep. The vividness of her life will keep a glow burning in the hearts of her loved ones."

Chapter 11

THE BROTHERS GARRETT

The date was August 12, 1861 when Lemuel Garrett traveled from his farm in Palmetto to Campbellton. Even though he was the husband of one and the father to six – one daughter and five sons – he was intent to fight for the Confederate Cause.

He joined Captain Evan Riley Whitley's Campbell Volunteers, Company E of the 35th Georgia Regiment. The men of Company E were ordered to Evansport, Virginia and by 1862, they were camped at Yorktown, Virginia.

In his book, *Red Clay to Richmond*, John J Fox, III explains how many of the men in the 35th signed up for what they felt would be a short war, but soon found themselves tramping all over Virginia fighting at Manassas, Seven Pines as well as Gettysburg.

Lemuel Garrett was captured at Smith's Ford along the Rapidan River in Virginia on May 6, 1864 during the Battle of the Wilderness. Once a Union prisoner, he was sent to Point Lookout in Maryland. When that camp began to experience overcrowding Lemuel was in a group of prisoners sent further north to Elmira, New York.

The Federal prison at Elmira was referred to as "Hellmira" by the men who were imprisoned there. At one point 2,000 of the 8,000 prisoners were sick and dying. The prisoners suffered due to little or no housing, poor sanitary conditions, and food was almost non-existent. Prisoners took to eating rats in an effort to survive.

Lemuel lived in those conditions for five months until he was paroled and exchanged in Savannah, but by then typhoid was taking his life. Sadly, he died in a Confederate sanitarium in Savannah on November 29, 1864, and is buried in the Laurel Grove Cemetery along with many other Confederate soldiers.

Lemuel's youngest son, Alexander Stephens Garrett who had been named for the vice president of the Confederacy, never knew what life was life before the war since he was born in 1861. More than likely he had no memories of his father.

After the war, farm implements were gone, there was no money, and buildings were in disrepair. Most families had no time for sending their children to school and the Garrett family was no exception.

Lemuel's wife, Martha Cash Garrett, was left alone with a farm to manage as well as raising her young children. However, she overcame the hardship life dealt her, and managed to raise five professional men.

Yes, Lemuel's boys all became professional and well respected men. Two of the boys became lawyers and three became well respected doctors.

Christopher Columbus Garrett or Dr. C.C. Garrett is the brother who is remembered best by the citizens of Douglas County. After obtaining his medical degree from the Atlanta Medical College he began his practice in Lithia Springs. Not only did he have a private practice, he was also associated with the Sweetwater Park Hotel as a staff doctor. Dr. Garrett was the father and grandfather of Dr. Luke Garrett, Sr. and Jr., who both practiced in Austell.

Dr. C.C. Garrett not only served his community as a doctor, he is also remembered as a former mayor of Lithia Springs and served a total of 24 years with the Douglas County Board of Education – 16 of those years as chairman.

Dr. Garrett's home still stands today on South Sweetwater Road while his office was moved at some point to the grounds of the Lithia Springs Water Company where it stands today serving as a museum.

Chapter 12

THE ROUTE TO THE HIGH

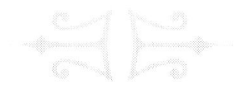

The route to the High Museum of Art in Atlanta seems rather simple, right?

Just head into Atlanta on Interstate 20, follow Interstates 75/85 northbound to the 10th/14th exit. Take a right on 14th, left on W. Peachtree, and a right on 15th. One more left on Arts Center Way puts you inside the parking garage, and then you are free to roam through all of the wonderful pieces of art in a building that is a work of art itself.

But the historical route behind a building or an organization is never quite as simple as it seems.

The museum dates back to 1905 when the Atlanta Art Association was founded. The permanent collection that is now 13,000 pieces strong got its start with furniture store magnate, J.J. Haverty.

Trace the route back far enough regarding the museum and you discover a link to Douglas/Campbell County.

Stay with me now as we follow the historical route.

Following the passage of the Indian Removal Act in 1830 and thirty years before Douglas County came to be, William Ely Green moved his family to the banks of Anneewakee Creek by way of his native New Jersey and Georgia's Morgan County. Sources indicate Green established two important mills along the creek creating cotton cloth in one and rope in the other by 1840.

Green's transport wagons were known to carry cotton cloth and rope out to customers, but would return with such things as a fancy cook stove for his wife's kitchen and a piano for his daughters to play from such places as Charleston. Even in the wilds of then Campbell County, the Greens wanted the finer things and sent their daughter Mary to a fancy female seminary in New Jersey. She supposedly spoke two languages other than English.

Mary became the third wife of a much older James Harwell Wilson. He was a well-known and respected owner of Sandtown Place, a plantation that once existed on Sandtown Road, an extension of Cascade Road. The Wilsons married in 1861 in the midst of the Civil War, and their daughter, Hattie, was born the next year.

During the summer of 1864, Union soldiers commandeered Sandtown Place and used it as a hospital. Sources indicate the Wilson family went south as the Union soldiers came through, but before leaving, J.H. Wilson filled the columns of his home with grain, so there might be something for his family when they were able to return.

Following the war and the death of J.H. Wilson, Mary and Hattie were no longer welcome at Sandtown Place since children from previous marriages inherited the property. Mother and daughter went to Atlanta where Mary sewed and took in borders to get by. Hattie was able to eventually attend the Atlanta Female Institute for a cultured education.

Hattie married James Madison High in September, 1882. Mr. High was a very well-known and successful Atlanta merchant. He owned J.M. High Department Store on Whitehall Street, and Hattie became very well known in Atlanta society. The Highs lived in a few homes over the years along Peachtree Street at a time when fine mansions lined the street instead of skyscrapers.

In 1911, J.M. and Hattie High built a Tudor-style home complete with servants' quarters. The home sat on a hill close to the intersection of 15th and Peachtree.

In 1926, Hattie High donated her home to the Atlanta Art Association. The home would house the associations growing art collection – the same collection that would grow into the High Museum of Art we have today. The High home housed the collection until 1955 when it moved to a brick building adjacent to the house.

So, in a nutshell a granddaughter of one of Campbell/Douglas County's first citizens helped to birth Atlanta's High Museum of Art.

Chapter 13

DRINKING IN THE DOG RIVER

I never know where I'm going with these columns until my deadline looms, I get a little frantic, and I finally sit down to write. As soon as I publish one column I begin to think about the next, but I don't give it real serious thought until I actually begin to let the words flow from my fingertips. This week I've been thinking about historical myths – those bits and pieces of historical lore that get mixed in with actual facts – and how the myths and true facts become muddled in the first place.

The muddling is easy for historians and educators to do. We seem to perpetuate the myths. Don't get me wrong, I don't think we intentionally do this. One reason has to do with new primary sources and how they are constantly being located and examined. The new information counters what we previously thought was fact. Another reason is the structure and content of classroom resources over the last two hundred years does not always set things straight for various reasons.

I don't want this column to perpetuate myths. Therefore I've agonized over each word, sentence and fact wanting to make sure everything I share here regarding the history of Douglasville and the surrounding area is factual, however we don't have many scholarly published resources. Mostly, what we have is a plethora of stories that must be waded through and measured very carefully against what we know regarding facts.

This week I want to discuss the Dog River – the source for our drinking water. For some people it's hard to describe the Dog River as a river because it's more of a creek in places. It begins south of Villa Rica in Carroll County and flows into the western side of Douglas County. Then it travels south and eastward till it spills into the Dog River Reservoir in the southern end of the county. Finally, the water flows into the Chattahoochee River.

However, don't let the fact the Dog River is used for drinking, and a quick glance at the quiet lake fool you. RiverFacts.com advises, "[The seven mile stretch of the Dog River from Highway Five down to the reservoir] is according to American Whitewater a Class III+ section of whitewater."

Many a Douglasville teen has gone to shoot the rapids along the Dog River on transfer truck sized tire tube in past summers. However, it is important to remember they are classified dangerous by the experts. Many other Douglas County residents enjoy the 300-acre Dog Reservoir Lake for fishing and boating.

I became interested in the Dog River as I began reading about the various mills in Douglas County during the 1800s. I found it interesting to discover the original name for the river was not Dog River but Trout Creek, the name Native Americans in the area prior to the 1870s, had given it.

Then I had to wonder how does a creek, a river, a river-creek change from Trout to Dog?

There are a few stories and here is where the historical myth connection comes into play. Fannie Mae Davis' history of Douglas County relates a few interpretations regarding the naming of the body of water. Apparently, she asked around and was told different things. She advises an early settler in the county by the name of M.L. Dorsett claimed mad dogs roamed the banks of the river while having seizures. The dogs fell into the river and drowned. Later it became the spot to shoot mad dogs and dispose of them in the river.

Did they have that many problems with wild dogs back then?

Another gentlemen quoted in Mrs. Davis' book by the name of Tom Sneed advises the Creek Indians actually gave the river its name in memory of a beloved chief named Haujo. His name translates to "dog", and he was the appointed warrior over Chattahoochee Town in 1799. Other sources indicate the word "haujo" translates to mean "mad" or "crazy". It must have been a popular title among Creek Indians because six different men from the Creek Nation signed the Treaty of Fort Jackson in 1814 with the name Haujo.

Is this story possible? Yes, but I have yet to discover any hard evidence.

Ephraim Pray, one of Douglas County's earliest settlers, bought up land along Trout Creek paying fifty cents an acre and using gold coins (per a family story) to make his purchase from the State of Georgia. Pray Street in Douglasville's historic district is named for him, and Pray's Mill Baptist Church was named for his mill. Ephraim Pray is credited with saying the Dog River name had to do with dogs that were drowned after a tussle with a deer. While I don't doubt occasionally dogs would have a major throw-down with deer, I can't believe it happened often enough to change the name of a body of water. Again, I have found no verified story regarding this event.

Then, of course, this being the South we have the Civil War angle to the story. The story goes that during the Battle of New Hope Church near Dallas, Georgia a courier dog used by the Confederates was attempting to swim across the river. The Confederates were waiting on the other side of the river for the vital messages the dog carried within its collar when the dog was shot mid-river by a Yankee spy.

It makes for a good story, doesn't it?

Mrs. Davis' history advises more than likely it's a myth by saying, "Stories of those dark days are part of the lore of every Southern child."

Could it be true? Maybe, but I have found nothing to verify the details and every account I've seen regarding troop movement through the Douglasville area indicates Sherman's men were further southeast from the Dog River.

There is documented evidence the Federals crossed the Chattahoochee close to where the Highway 92 bridge stands today. There were several skirmishes there between Sherman's men and Confederates after the burning of the New Manchester Mill and the Campbell County Raiders who defended Campbellton just across the river.

Could a Yankee spy have been sent up that way for intelligence reasons? Sure, but again, there is no documented evidence.

So, it looks like for now we have no bona fide reason why Trout Creek became the Dog River, but questions like this spurs the historian on.

We may never find the answer, but the journey is just too enjoyable to pass up.

So, which story sounds plausible to you?

Section Three

EARLY CITIZENS AND COMMUNITIES

Chapter 14

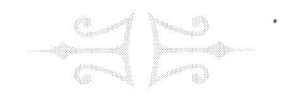

BLIPS ON A MAP - WILSONVILLE, HANNAH AND MCWHORTER

Early maps of Douglas County show places most don't recognize today. For instance on the Douglas County map for 1883 you see a town noted by the name Wilsonsonville.

Wilsonville?

Where the heck is Wilsonville? Why is it on the 1883 map, but isn't so widely known today?

Places just don't disappear, right?

One of the first settlers in the southern part of what would one day be Douglas County was a man by the name of Moses Wilson. Like so many others he packed up his wagon and along with his wife and young boys he made the trek from North Carolina to Georgia in 1829. When Moses first reached Georgia the land he settled on was actually along the Chattahoochee River in Carroll County, but once Douglas County was created he found himself to be a citizen of Douglas.

Over the next few years Moses Wilson added to his land holdings until he acquired several hundred acres of land. In fact, I located one such property transaction between Cheadle Cochran and Moses Wilson recorded in Deed Book C, pages 228-229 for Campbell County dated October 9, 1839.

Moses oldest son, Peter, stayed on the property, but another son named Joseph traveled a few miles over towards Villa Rica which at that time was a rough and tumble gold mining town where he opened up a general store. Years later, his two sons – Ulla and Wallace – became leading Villa Rica merchants.

Moses' youngest child – John A. Wilson, had been born in North Carolina in 1828, and was no more than a year old when the family traveled to Georgia. John traveled again – but this time a shorter distance – when around 1850 he left his father's home and moved to Hurricane Creek just a little further north from his father's holdings. There along the creek John had a wool carder as well as grist and saw mill.

Community names seemed to spring up around mail stops, and in this case since the post office was located on Moses Wilson's land the area became known as Wilsonville. George W. Burnett was listed as postmaster as well as a physician in the area.

One of the Douglas County little courthouses was placed at Wilsonville – the little courthouse for the Fairplay District – where the Justice of the Peace heard cases and citizens could vote during elections.

Douglas County established its first Board of Education on March 25, 1871, and John A. Wilson was installed as the first president. Flint Hill Academy was one of the first schools organized. It was a one room cabin and was located on the back of the lot where Flint Hill Methodist Church stands today.

By 1879, the *Georgia Gazeteer* indicates 75 people were living at Wilsonville. Mail arrived weekly by horseback. The little village had a shoemaker named J.J. Kimbrell.

In 1880, a terrible fire destroyed the mills belonging to John A. Wilson. By this time he and his wife, Lucinda, were elderly, and they decided not to rebuild. The post office moved a few miles south and for a time mail in the area was addressed "Hannah" instead of Wilsonville since John's daughter-in-law, Hannah Wilson (married to Noah) took the duties of postmistress. A school by the name of Mt. Zion was close by and took on the name Hannah as well. Hannah was very close to the area where Tyree Road intersects with Post Road today.

A Gazetteer of Georgia for 1881 indicates the area received mail four times a week. Isham N. Brown was also listed as physician, V.P. Burnett was Justice of the Peace, W.L. Davenport was a Methodist preacher and saw mill owner. E.H. McWhorter was also a Methodist preacher and blacksmith, Allen Manning was a mechanic along with J.S. Moss and Samuel Pate. J.J. Shadix was a Baptist preacher, S.A. Steed was the constable, and Moses' youngest son, John A. Wilson was the grist mill owner.

At some point after he lost the mills, John A. Wilson and his wife moved to Douglasville. Fannie Mae Davis surmises they probably left with a heavy heart since "they [were leaving] the village they had built and loved." The Wilsons moved into one of the first houses along Bowden Street, and John was appointed postmaster of Douglasville in July, 1890. Later, his wife took the position in 1893.

When you look at the Douglas County map for 1899, you no longer see the name Wilsonville, however, you do see the community of Hannah, and there's something new in the vicinity – the community of McWhorter.

By 1883, three years after the Wilson mills were destroyed by fire – the Wilsonville area had become known as McWhorter.

When the Hannah post office closed in 1885, the mail was sent to a popular store in the area operated by Dave Tolar. The name was then registered as McWhorter because the land where the store sat was owned by Matthew McWhorter and his recently deceased brother, Elijah H. McWhorter who had been a pastor in the area.

The little courthouse was moved to McWhorter. Fannie Mae Davis relates, "As people were saying, "it takes a post office and a courthouse to start a town."

The area had been known as Skinner, but the young people had a different name referring to it as Tight Squeeze or Fitsquese. I have yet to discover the reason why, but even the local Douglasville paper referred to the area as Fitsquese.

An issue of the *The Weekly Star*, dated 1886 mentions, "Fitsquese is on the boom."

In fact, the 1886 issue of *A Gazetteer of Georgia* provides the names of some thirty-six farmers working the surrounding countryside. By 1887, the population had increased to 160, and by 1880, there were 200 souls calling McWhorter home.

McWhorter wasn't just a community or a mail stop – it was a town!

McWhorter news regularly appeared in *The New South* – a paper published in Douglasville. In June, 1883, the paper published a story concerning McWhorter. The article stated, "Our town is on the boom. Town plots are selling at $150 each, which is considered a fair price for suburban lots. The Methodist have just completed the best house of worship in the county (Flint Hill). It has a Masonic and Alliance Hall overhead... We have a splendid school...We have two doctors in our town, G.W. and W.K. Burnett, who do a driving business. They both keep fast horses. They run a drug store and have an extensive farming business. M.R. McWhorter is the blacksmith and politician of the town. Dan Gaston of the firm McWhorter-Gaston is the woodwork man. G.T. Giles and S.A. Griffin are real estate agents for this section."

The paper also published social news as well – "J.T. Bartlett while engaged in rolling a log into his saw mill carriage had his head and nose badly mashed. His wife hardly recognized it as the lovely nose of yore. James Gaston and Joe Barron have each lost a mule recently."

By the turn of the century, there were new businesses – a barber shop, ginnery, and shingle mill, two additional doctors, W.L. Friddel, a native of Douglas County and Delvous Houseworth of nearby Clem, Georgia which was between Carrollton and Whitesburg along State Route 27. Mrs. Lizzie Griffith operated a millinery store at McWhorter as well.

Flint Hill Academy had become Flint Hill High School serving grades 1-9 in a larger building and two churches had been added to the area – Basket Creek and Fair Field Methodist.

By 1914, a telephone exchange was installed in a store owned by O.H. and Joseph Hines, but by 1923 it was discontinued as Southern Bell had entered the scene and modern phone service became the norm. Eventually roads were paved and unfortunately that meant the growth of McWhorter would stall since people were able to move around the county a bit easier and reach the larger stores of Douglasville and even Atlanta. Stores in McWhorter began to close, and finally, the intersection of Highway 5 and 166 began to take on the appearance we see today.

When you examine the maps from 1999, you see that places like Wilsonville, Hannah and even McWhorter are just historical footnotes.

As Fannie Mae Davis states, "Two great highways cross paths where years and years ago, a dozen or more businesses were in operation."

People zoom by each and every day without a thought to the thriving town that once existed there.

Chapter 15

RICHARD M. WILSON – A LIFE OF SERVICE

This week's column began with a critical look at my beloved laptop. I took time out long enough from tapping on the keys to really look at the keyboard. I have to admit – it looks terrible.

I've actually typed the letters right off the keys. Luckily I've been typing for years and "know" the keyboard intimately. In other words, I don't have to look at the keyboard.

Every week I begin the process of writing this column by looking through my many pages of notes to see if something speaks to me. This week is no different. I read through my notes, and then I saw it – the phrase "brought the first typewriter into Douglas County."

Seriously, it had to be more than just a mere coincidence I see those words moments after I had been examining my own keyboard, but on second thought, I didn't think I had enough material for a column.

I didn't think there was enough there to hold your attention.

All I had was I knew who brought the very first typewriter into the county, and I had worn out my own keyboard.

I returned to searching through my notes.

A little later I saw the words "Civil War soldier...." along with the phrase "related to an American Revolution printer".

"Hmm…"

I read further. I zeroed in on the Civil War soldier's name.

Richard M. Wilson.

Another "Hmmm…"

Something seemed familiar.

Then

it

clicked.

Typewriter guy and the Civil War soldier was the same person!

Bingo!!!

People, we have a column.

Many months ago I had run across an old *Neighbor News* article by Joe Baggett that concerned Richard M. Wilson. Baggett identified Mr. Wilson as the great-grandson of an English printer who helped spark the American Revolution and as the grandfather of one of Georgia's most influential politicians, Joe Mack Wilson.

Richard M. Wilson was born August 20, 1837 in Pendleton County, South Carolina to Richard T. Wilson and Martha (Miller) Wilson. Unfortunately, he was left without a father at the age of 12. An obituary published in the *Pendleton Messenger*, a paper actually owned by Wilson's maternal grandfather, dated February 23, 1849 states the elder Wilson "died in his 45th year of age, a resident of our village for near 20 years, leaving a wife and six small children."

Baggett's article goes on to state Richard M. Wilson's maternal grandfather, John Miller was born in London and was a well-known printer. There were also claims he was the anonymous author of *The Junius Letters* which were attacks on the government of King George III which helped to spark the American Revolution. Miller eventually made his way to South Carolina at the end of the Revolution.

As a young man Richard M. Wilson clerked in various retail stores in Pendleton, Anderson and Charleston, South Carolina as well as Memphis,

Tennessee where he sold everything from clothing to groceries. Wilson moved to Atlanta where I've read he clerked in a store and a hotel just prior to the beginning of the Civil War.

An article from the *Douglas County Sentinel* dated April 22, 1909 claims Mr. Wilson was the only soldier holding the rank of Captain during the Civil War who was not called by his official military title. Wilson enlisted as a private at the beginning of the war with the First Georgia Infantry, Company D also known as Lee's Volunteers under Captain G.W. Lee for 12 months. Baggett's article further advised this was the first company from Georgia mustered into Confederate service and the mustering in ceremony took place at Montgomery, Alabama in the presence of Confederate President Jefferson Davis, but I have been unable to verify this to date.

Once the year was up the men returned to Atlanta where the company was reorganized and Jazeb Rhodes was the Captain. The company was stationed at Fort Gaines on Dauphin Island near Mobile, Alabama. Later the company was sent to Tennessee where Wilson was captured at Fort Donelson at some point during the third week of February, 1862. He was taken to the POW installation at Johnson Island near Sandusky, Ohio. The prison camp website advises Wilson along with other prisoners taken in 1862 would have been exchanged after only five months, so by September, 1862 Wilson would have been making his way back to his company.

Wilson was also at the Battle of Chickamauga. His company entered the battle with 42 enlisted men. Following the battle twenty-one were wounded and two had been killed. They regrouped during winter quarters at Dalton, Georgia. Wilson was then elected to fill the vacancy of Captain Jazeb R. Rhodes who had been found guilty during a court marshal and ordered shot at Chattanooga. Wilson took on the job of a captain, but technically the paperwork had not been done.

After leaving Dalton, the fighting began to move south towards Atlanta and Wilson ended up participating in most every engagement.

So, Wilson ended the war with a promotion and did his duty as a captain but technically the paper work didn't come through until much later. It has been discovered that Wilson's Confederate Pension papers on file with the Georgia Archives does indeed show Wilson's rank at the end of the war as captain.

Following the war Wilson returned to Atlanta but remembered a girl he had met who lived along the Dog River. He moved to the area and married Mary Frances Dorsett in 1866. Wilson settled in teaching school and operating a small farm in the Harris Community (the area where the Dog River empties into the Chattahoochee River). He also served as a justice of the peace.

In 1889, Richard M. Wilson was elected as Douglas County's first clerk of court, and held the position for some time. Fannie Mae Davis recounts in her history of the county that during the election of 1902, Mr. Wilson received 843 votes out of 1700 registered voters in the county.

Mrs. Davis also writes about an exchange she had with a then 93 year old Frank Wilson concerning his father. He remembered how he had a job in the 1880s assisting his father with keeping the fire going in his office at the courthouse, the second version built in 1880, but abandoned for new construction by 1886. Frank Wilson also remembered his father's offices were on the ground floor of the building along with other offices while the jury, witness and large courtroom took up the second floor. Unfortunately, there are no photographs that have been located to date of this particular courthouse.

An article in *The New South* dated January, 1902 relates how Wilson brought the very first typewriter into Douglas County. Up until then all of the records he created involving the court had to be handwritten. The typewriter would help him be more efficient. The newspaper advises, "The machine was bulky and heavy, weighing 50 pounds or more. The purchase price was $175."

The New South article continued, "A typing instruction booklet came with the purchase from which Mr. Wilson taught himself to use the machine".

Fannie Mae Davis advises in her book, "The typewriter, an heirloom greatly appreciated by the Wilson family, was stored in the home of his grandson, Charlie Wilson, on Bowden Street, until it became missing a few years ago."

Gee, has anyone seen it?

Chapter 16

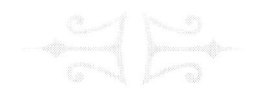

ROBERT JEHU MASSEY – A MONUMENTAL FIND

As you might already be aware historical research interests me. No surprise there, right?

I realize it might not be your thing, but it's mine. I conduct the research in order to find the quirky things that draw people in, the hidden information that never makes it to the textbook or your eleventh grade history teacher's lesson plan.

I use it to remind folks about things they know, but have filed them away somewhere in the dark recesses of their minds.

I use the research to write curriculum so other educators can share it with their students.

I use the research to feed my need to write, and learn.

I do the research to find little pieces of larger history puzzles I'm trying to put together, and that's where the irony comes in. Most of the time I find little puzzle pieces here and there when I least expect them, most certainly when I'm NOT looking for them.

Sometimes those little puzzle pieces are monumental because they hold the key to solving a historical mystery.

I've never been that fortunate to locate something like that, but Hugh Harrington has experienced the joy of a monumental find while looking for something else.

Hugh was on the hunt for information regarding a mass escape from a woman's prison, so he was pouring over microfilmed issues of the *Southern Recorder*, a Milledgeville paper that was published during the Civil War. He happened upon a list of soldiers who had died at Brown Hospital during the last months of the Civil War.

The hospital, named for Governor Joseph Brown had been in Atlanta, but then moved under the direction of Dr. R.J. Massey to Milledgeville when General Sherman began marching south.

The list of soldiers had nothing to do with what Herrington was searching for, but he had hunch that the list might be important.

He knew there was a Confederate Memorial at Memory Hill Cemetery in Milledgeville to unknown dead. He knew this because he had been involved in indexing many of the graves at the cemetery. He knew at least two of the soldiers were named in the Confederate section, and their names were on the same list he had just found in the newspaper archives.

It was more than a hunch. Herrington had stumbled upon the identities of the unknown soldiers - all of them.

Hugh Herrington did just what I would have done.

He went to the cemetery, walked to the memorial and announced to the men at rest there, "I know who you are…"

What a personal moment of joy for Mr. Herrington!

Then he met with members of the United Daughters of the Confederacy and shared his discovery. They immediately agreed with him that he had found a resource to identify the graves.

He went through the list to determine which men were shipped home, and narrowed the list to 24 names. He determined they all died in August or September, 1864 while patients of the hospital. They all died of disease of one sort or another, and they were all citizens of Georgia and part of the militia.

However, between September 6, 1864 when the newspaper article provided the names of the men who died and 1868 when the monument was erected folks didn't remember a list existed, and the names had been lost all that time until Hugh Herrington happened to be looking for something else.

Astounding!

I have to wonder though if Mr. Herrington ever found anything on those wild women who broke out of prison.

I've written about Dr. R.J. Massey, the head surgeon at Brown Hospital. He was instrumental in saving the State House in Millledgeville from Sherman's torch and happened to live in Douglasville for a bit.

Through my months of research I've come to the conclusion that Douglas County history is packed with interesting people who contributed to our area and to our state in very important ways.

Some of those people were born in Campbell/Douglas County, lived here and died here like Joseph S. James. There are others who lived here for a time and then left to make their mark on the world like Hugh Watson, and still others who arrived in Douglasville for a brief time and then moved on like Dr. Robert Jehu Massey.

Dr. Massey was born near Madison, Georgia in October, 1828 and grew up near Penfield, Georgia. He received his degree from the Medical College of Georgia in Augusta and began a medical practice in Penfield before moving to Atlanta, Georgia. He married Sarah Elizabeth Copeland on June 16, 1850.

During the Civil War Dr. R. J. Massey assisted the Confederacy by serving as a surgeon. He often worked right in the field. In fact, an article from *The Atlanta Constitution* from 1908 concerning Dr. Massey's 80th birthday has him recalling his efforts to save the life of General John Bell Hood when he was severely injured at Chickamauga. The article states, "When General Hood was operated on at the old Alexander Bridge Hospital, Dr. Massey administered the anesthetic." In fact, several sources indicate Dr. Massey performed approximately 2,000 surgeries using anesthesia. Hood had been wounded so severely his right leg had to be amputated four inches below his hip. General Hood's leg was sent along with him in the ambulance because it was thought Hood wouldn't live much longer and at least his leg could be buried with him.

Of course, Hood did live to fight another day.

As the focus of the war shifted towards Atlanta Dr. Massey ended up at the Brown Hospital and helped it relocate further south to Milledgeville as Sherman's men advanced on the city. Dr. Massey's position was surgeon in charge.

Governor Brown and other state officials fled Milledgeville ahead of General Sherman's army. The Union soldiers occupied the city of Milledgeville on November 23, 1864.

Lee B. Kennett in *Marching through Georgia: The Story of Soldiers and Civilians during Sherman's Campaign* confirms Brown Hospital and Midway Hospital were the only public institutions still functioning when Sherman's men entered the city.

Basically, you could say that Dr. Brown and the doctor in charge of the Midway Hospital were the only officials, of sorts, available to Sherman during his brief stay in Milledgeville.

Kennett recounts how Massey asked for Union guards at the hospital to keep soldiers from ransacking it. He had to do this more than once because the guards kept disappearing. Apparently Dr. Massey kept his eye on what the Union soldiers were doing in other parts of the city and in particular at the state house even though he had no power to stop them.

It would seem that Dr. Massey's visibility during the brief Union occupation of Milledgeville and his interaction with General Sherman helped save the state house from the torch. Though the building was in great disarray when citizens returned to the city, important documents and records belonging to the state of Georgia were saved.

Years later the Georgia General Assembly acknowledged Dr. Massey's actions.

Kennett also advises how General Sherman left twenty-eight of his injured men with Dr. Massey. Sherman told the doctor to give them a decent burial if the soldiers died, or if they lived to remand them over to the care of the prison at Andersonville. In return for taking care of the soldiers Dr. Massey received ten gallons of rye whiskey that had been discovered. Apparently the whiskey had been hidden by the owner of the Milledgeville Hotel in hopes the soldiers wouldn't get it. Instead, Dr. Massey was able to use the whiskey at the hospital.

Another book, *Civil War Milledgeville: Tales from the Confederate Capital of Georgia* by Hugh T. Harrington discusses Dr. Massey's efforts during the Milledgeville occupation and states Dr. Massey wrote his own articles in *The Sunny South* and *The Atlanta Constitution* regarding his war experiences that were published in the early 1900s.

Dr. Massey's obituary from *The Atlanta Constitution* (March 19, 1915) states, "He possessed a wonderful memory, stored with vast knowledge of the pioneer history of the state, and his writings, which are written in a pleasing style dealt largely with this period."

He was a great friend to Georgia's Governor William J. Northern (1890-1894) and contributed over one hundred biographies to Northern's book, *Men of Mark in Georgia*. *The Library of Southern Literature* also advises Dr. Massey wrote for *Uncle Remus Magazine* at frequent intervals.

After the war Dr. Massey practiced in Gainesville, and St. Simons, followed by a move to Douglasville. Dr. Massey's son, Robert A. (Alexander) Massey, was an attorney, judge and Douglasville postmaster in the late 1800s.

In the book *From Indian Trail to I-20* Fannie Mae Davis relates how Dr. Massey had a kitchen lab in his home which he used to concoct cures from herbs and roots he collected across the county. One such extract he marketed was Compound Georgia Sasparilla which was billed as "The best, cheapest and most complete blood remedy in the world." The extract could be bought directly from Dr. Massey at his office and at area stores for the sum of one dollar. Apparently, Dr. Massey also operated a drugstore in Austell before selling it to Dr. C.C. Garrett around the turn of the century.

While he lived in Douglasville Dr. Massey cultivated his love of history and exercised his writing skills. He was an early editor of *The Weekly*

Star per Mrs. Davis. She states, "He…added great interest in the early paper which gave away to *The New South* a few years later and of several legends, giving the original source of the Skint Chestnut name. Dr. Massey's story has been the most acceptable by lovers of local history."

Thought he spent his last years writing Dr. Massey still practiced medicine. He returned to Atlanta in 1893 and served as the lead physician for the Confederate Soldier's Home.

Dr. R.J. Massey's grave can be found in Douglasville's City Cemetery.

Chapter 17

EPHRAIM PRAY – AN AMAZING MAN

Currently, I have the number twenty on the brain – as in twenty years. When I was twenty I was working as a paralegal for law firm in Marietta. Looking back on it now I had it made. I had my own money, but I lived with my parents. Mother was available as my cook and laundress while Daddy served as my advisor and back up banker. My main activity when not working or sleeping was hanging out with my friends.

Even though I worked, it wasn't back-breaking labor. I was in a very nice air-conditioned office with machines such as a word processor and a copy machine to help me with my job which basically consisted of drafting complaints and researching case law. The attorney I worked with never came in before twelve each day, so twice a week I'd venture over to the courthouse and answer a calendar call on his behalf. I ate lunch out every day in places that had real waiters and cloth napkins.

Even though I was great at my job, and took it very seriously, the words cushy, charmed and spoiled come to mind, but it wasn't lost on this student of history that I was experiencing a much different lifestyle at twenty than many of my female counterparts who had gone before me.

I had more opportunities than my aunts had experienced, much more than either of my grandmothers, and my great-grandmothers would have been shocked I didn't already have three or four kids trailing after me and one on my hip while I took care of the house, the garden full of produce, and a chicken yard outside my back door.

Go back to the 1820s and 1830s and life was just plain hard – not just for women, but things were difficult for men as well when compared to today. Folks didn't have the ease of today's modern fabric regarding clothing choices, education was lacking unless you had money and the right connections, and modern conveniences such as the phone, electricity, and modern travel just didn't exist.

To reach a certain age such as twenty years old and venture off to make your way in the word was a hard thing to do. There was no constant contact with loved ones and friends like there is today. Striking out on your own meant being on your own – TOTALLY! Once you left your family's side a letter could take several weeks to reach its destination. Overnight postal service didn't exist.

In fact, if you left your family and moved to another state or even more than fifty miles away it was very probably you might never see your family again. Yet, people did leave their families and did make their own way in the world including a very important man in Douglasville history.

Ephraim Pray.

One of the area's earliest citizens even before Douglas County or Douglasville existed actually hailed from the North.

Yes!

A Yankee in our midst!

Yet, Ephraim Pray became a model for hard work and responsible citizenship.

Ephraim Pray was born in Augusta, Maine in 1809, and he remained there until he left his father's home and set out to make his mark on the world at the age of twenty. He was armed with an engineering license and a small endowment of gold pieces from his father.

Pray didn't just move to the neighboring county or even adjacent state. He decided the South held his promise and began a journey most of us would find very unappealing in today's modern world, and he did so alone. He first travelled to Boston where he hopped aboard a steamship bound for Savannah, Georgia. From Savannah he reached Augusta, Georgia by riverboat, and finally he took a stagecoach to Greene County, Georgia where Pray remained for two years. While residing in Greene County he used his engineering knowledge and built two mills.

It's hard to know for sure from the historical record I've been able to examine, but I would imagine that Pray had heard about all of the land in North Georgia that had been freed up for settlement based on the McIntosh Treaty of 1825 also known as the Treaty of Indian Springs. The Treaty ceded remaining Creek lands to the government and got the ball rolling for the forced removal of all Native Americans from North Georgia.

Almost immediately the land was set up for purchase by white settlers and land speculators. Pray purchased nine lots with 202 ½ acres in each lot for fifty cents an acre using some of the gold his father had given him. At that time the land actually sat in Carroll County since Douglas County was not officially created until 1870. Pray bought the land with the full knowledge he could possibly be the only white man for miles, but he also knew as did everyone else that the Native Americans would be gone soon – one way or another.

The nine land lots Ephraim Pray purchased were located on Trout Creek now known as the Dog River. The property lay along both sides of today's Highway Five at the Dog River Bridge. In fact, Pray is credited with one of the theories regarding how Trout Creek became the Dog River advising a pack of dogs drowned in the river.

In 1828, Ephraim Pray arrived via stagecoach in the Campbellton-Fairburn area. Before setting out to view his property he bought a slave woman to serve as a cook. They set out down the old Indian Trail that ran from Fairburn west into what is today Douglas and Carroll Counties.

Along the way he stopped at a tavern on Bear Creek. The tavern was owned by Elijah and Ezekiel Owl, Cherokee brothers who also had a gristmill and post office. Today the location is known as Fout's Mill.

The next day Pray left the slave woman with the Owl brothers and travelled back towards Campbellton to purchase two male slaves and either a horse or a mule. Once Pray reached his land he met up with the brother of the two Owl brothers – Abraham Owl.

Abraham lived in a cabin along Trout Creek/Dog River he had built in the 1790s. Fannie Mae Davis advises in her history of Douglas County Pray "had compassion for the old Indian and told Abraham he would have a home with him until the day he died". Pray was true to his word. Abraham Owl remained with Ephraim Pray until 1834 when the old man finally passed away. Four years later the Cherokee were forcibly removed from Georgia.

Ephraim Pray dammed the Trout Creek/Dog River and using the water power he operated a flour and grist mill as well as a saw mill. He also farmed. The second floor of his mill was used by the two male slaves as well as by Pray himself to make furniture.

Up until 1838 Pray lived in Abraham Owl's cabin, but he finally built a proper house which still stands today. He moved into the house in April, 1843. Once he had a proper house his attention turned to finding a wife, and in November, 1843 he married Mary Ann Little, a Villa Rica blacksmith's daughter. The Prays never had children of their own, but adopted Mrs. Pray's sister's children. Many came to admire and love Mr. and Mrs. Pray and referred to them as Uncle and Aunt Pray.

During the 1840s and 50s more and more families moved into the area and the new settlers came to see Ephraim Pray as a leader.

At Pray's invitation Humphrey Posey, a Baptist minister and missionary to Cherokee Indians from as far back as 1819 rode his horse from Villa Rica to Pray's home to preach from his porch to all who would listen.

Soon after Pray donated twelve acres for the purpose of building a church that would become Pray's Mill Baptist Church. Pray's only stipulation was the church had to remain Baptist or the land would revert back to the Pray family. The new congregation wanted to name the new church for Pray, but he refused. Of course, they ended up naming the church for his mill instead.

Pray wanted to join the new church. He had been a Baptist since he was sixteen, after all. The Baptist church Pray belonged to in Maine did not look favorably on him owning slaves, and when he wanted his letter moved to the new church, they refused. Basically, it was the Baptist form of excommunication. He therefore became a constituent member of Pray's Mill and attended church there until he passed away.

During the Civil War, Pray took a job with the Confederate government as superintendent of a salt mine in Montgomery, Alabama. Towards the end of the war when the Union soldiers were advancing on the area we know as Douglas County today a neighbor wanting to gain favor with the approaching enemy burned down Pray's mill. The neighbor was later lynched in Montgomery, Alabama, and the mill was never rebuilt.

After the Civil War when folks began to tire of living in Campbell County and having to travel all the way across the Chattahoochee River to Campbellton to conduct business Ephraim Pray was one of several men who traveled to Atlanta to listen to the state legislature approve a new Georgia county – Douglas, in 1870. In fact, the state legislature named Pray and four other men as commissioners to do the necessary work to set up the new Douglas County government. For his troubles Pray was honored with a street named for him even though today we know the street to be West Courthouse Square. He has the distinction of being a charter citizen of Douglas County, too. In fact, Ephraim Pray has the distinction of being a man who lived in three different counties – Carroll, Campbell, and Douglas – without having to move even one stick of furniture!

Yes, I'd say Ephraim Pray was an amazing man!

Chapter 18

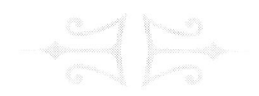

EPHRAIM PRAY – STILL AN AMAZING MAN

Back in January I wrote about Ephraim Pray, one of our earliest settlers. After having a few e-mail conversations with Pray's descendant, Joe Phillips, I feel it's time, actually it's a little past time for me to revisit my column and make a few clarifications.

At the heart of this is history that might contain embellishments. Sometimes stories handed down from family member to family member contain details that can't be verified through legal documents such as birth certificates, land deeds or court cases, and newspapers or even old family photographs are nonexistent.

Sometimes the stories become muddled over time. Details get taken away, and other things are added. The stories are interesting, but we don't know where the facts end and where the fiction begins.

Some family stories can be eliminated as embellishments because they just don't add up to the puzzle pieces we have, and then other stories, most of them in my opinion, fall into the range of "We just don't know".

We might hunt for the verification, but can't find it.

I think family history is a valid resource, but when I use it to write about Douglas County history I should make very clear what is family history and if it has been validated or not.

The website for Prays Mill Baptist Church gives a rather detailed history of Ephraim Pray. Fannie Mae Davis provides similar details in her book regarding Ephraim Pray.

The main source of information for these publications were Pray family members, of course, including Joe Phillips' father and uncle who heard the stories from their father, but a few years ago Joe began a search to verify the stories, to see what could be proven beyond a shadow of a doubt regarding the details of Ephraim Pray's life.

In some instances verification was found, and in some instances Joe came up short. That's why I want to revisit Ephraim Pray, to set the story straight as we know it this very minute.

Of course, a missing puzzle piece could be found tomorrow and then we would need to readjust all over again.

History's a little funny like that, but it's one of the reasons I enjoy it so much.

As I stated in my original column regarding Ephraim Pray, while many of our earliest settlers came from the Carolinas is it said Pray came from up North. Family history tells us he migrated south from Augusta, Maine; however there is no verification of this to date and to further muddle the mix there happens to be an Ephraim Pray who owned a plantation in Liberty County, Georgia.

Of course, the Douglas County Pray and the Liberty County Pray are NOT one and the same.

No matter where Pray came from, at some point he did arrive in Georgia.

In my original column I mention how he might have travelled to Georgia by steamship to Savannah and then overland, however again, this is pure conjecture since we don't have tickets stubs, a journal entry, or even a newspaper clipping.

Our first real proof of Ephraim Pray living in Georgia involves Greene County. Joe Phillips is in possession of an account book Pray used to record where he worked and how much his pay happened to be.

We know that Pray built a mill and possibly a bridge for Dr. Thomas Poullian at Scull Shoals.

The account book also verifies Pray worked for Mr. Shivers at Rock Mill Plantation.

Mr. Phillips advises me the account books also indicate while at Scull Shoals and Rock Mill Plantation Pray built churns, bedsteads and a house to make extra money. Relevant pages of the day books have been sent to the "Friends of Scull Shoals" and the current owner of the Rock Mill Plantation for their records.

In my prior column I advised that in 1828, Ephraim Pray arrived via stagecoach in the Campbellton-Fairburn area, and before setting out for his property he bought a slave woman to serve as his cook.

The year is an educated guess more or less as Mr.Phillips has not been able to verify the purchase of a slave woman, but it is more feasible that Pray would have been in Campbellton as it was a far more established town than Fairburn around that particular time period.

I advised in the next part of the story that Pray met up with the Owl brothers at Bear Creek. Supposedly Elijah and Ezekiel Owl were two Cherokee brothers who had a grist mill and ran the post office at Fout's Mill, but to date I have found no factual evidence to back up the Owl Brother's existence.

I'd love to. It's a great story, but so far we have no real proof.

Joe Phillips advises he has not found anything to document the existence of the Owl Brothers owning Empire Mill. He also advises Fout's Mill was at one time Crumbie's Mill providing the name of "Crumbie's District".

The next part of the story is where I introduced the mythical Abraham Owl.

Supposedly Abraham Owl is Elijah and Ezekiel's brother, and he lived on the land Ephraim Pray had purchased.

In her book, Fannie Mae Davis advises Pray "had compassion for the old Indian and told Abraham he would have a home with him until the day he died." This is what prior members of the Pray family had told her.

Phillips has been unable to find any verification that Abraham Owl and a wife ever lived on the land with Pray, and freely admits that the stories consistently told to him by family members was most likely embellished by his grandfather.

We just don't know, and at this point I would have to say that all three of the Owl Brothers could be a myth.

Part of my original column dealt with a Baptist minister by the name of Humprey Posey and the founding of Pray's Mill Baptist Church.

Mr. Phillip's advises years ago a page from one of Pray's "day books" which was more or less like a journal was copied by Mr. Frank Winn when he was the Ordinary of Douglas County. Today the book cannot be found, but the page Mr. Winn copied referred to the founding of Pray's Mill Church, which was shown in early maps as "Pray's Chapel."

The narrative tells of Pastor Posey arriving with his horse ill, and of the weather that day. He also stated that there was the Jared Smith family, which was buried near the spring, not having the benefit of a Christian burial.

Mr. Philips remains on the hunt for the missing daybook

During the Civil War, I had advised that Pray worked as a superintendent of a salt peter mine in Montgomery, Alabama, but there is no record of this to date. The only salt peter mine found so far in Alabama was near Hunstville, and the archives do not have a listing of Pray in the Confederate civil servant index.

I also discussed that towards the end of the Civil War someone burned down Pray's mill hoping to gain favor with the Union soldiers who were advancing on the community. The sources I had available at the time advised the man was lynched in Montgomery, but Phillips has found other information.

Phillips advises the man who burned Pray's mill was a local "Clinton" man, and he was hanged beside the Dog River in a place where he could see the remains of the mill. His grave is unmarked but I'm told the current owners of the property know the location.

We do know that Ephraim Pray served as postmaster of Campbell County during the war. Phillips has located a copy of a petition for pardon to President Johnson in which Pray states he served as post master and pledges to support the Constitution of the United States on September 21, 1865. The oath was taken before Rueben Crawford Beavers, Ordinary of Campbell County.

I still propose that Ephraim Pray was an amazing man as I stated in the original post. He has the distinction of being a man who lived in three different counties – Carroll, Campbell, and Douglas – without having to move even one stick of furniture.

Chapter 19

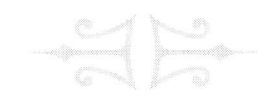

A SUCCESSION OF POLKS

I'm sure everyone thinks they have an interesting family tree, but some, of course, are a little more interesting than others.

One of the perks regarding writing about history is I get to dig around the roots of various family trees, and I have determined everyone's tree has extreme high points to brag about as well as that skeleton folks like to talk about in hushed tones.

Everyone has a branch of the tree that ends in a strange little cul-de-sac that leaves you scratching your head, and sometimes you find situations that at first create visions of three-eyed children with horns coming out of their heads – even the family trees of very important people including presidential family trees.

The particular tree I'm speaking of belongs to our 11th U.S. President – James Knox Polk – a tree that has a branch that reaches all the way to Douglasville, Georgia.

The stories are fascinating regarding the Polk family, but some of the connections are a bit suspect at first and just like many families they like to use the same names for their children from generation to generation. At one point this afternoon I had to create a little family tree on paper just to keep the story straight, so I knew I was talking about the right person.

First of all it would appear that the first Polk arrived on the eastern shore of Maryland sometime in the mid-1600s and had a son named William who was born about 1700. He ended up in Pennsylvania and married Margaret (Taylor) Polk. They had eight children – William, Deborah, Thomas, Charles, Susan, Margaret, John, and Ezekiel. About the time Ezekiel was seven years old the family decided to move south close to where Charlotte, North Carolina is today in Mecklenburg County.

The Polk family is considered to be among the first pioneer settlers of the area and all of the Polk boys were a success. Thomas accumulated vast land holdings through speculation including lands in Tennessee and set himself apart by serving in the Continental Army during the American Revolution. There are documented stories he was in charge of the group of soldiers who helped to move everything of value out of Philadelphia, Pennsylvania including the Liberty Bell as the British approached the town.

Ezekiel is remembered for taking part in the Snow Campaign from November to December, 1775 when North Carolina Patriots flushed Tories out of the area. The men marched in terrible conditions including two feet of snow. Ezekiel also caused a stir when it became apparent the British were going to be in control of Charlotte. He went to the British and asked for protection. This action seems strange today, but it should be in no way construed that Ezekiel had Tory views. He wasn't alone in asking the British to spare his property. Ezekiel also was the subject of neighborhood gossip because he didn't share the Presbyterian views his other family members did. Ezekiel followed the philosophy of Deism, a religious belief that reason and observation of the natural world, without the need for organized religion, can determine that the universe is the product of an all-powerful creator.

Many men during the time period followed Deism including Thomas Jefferson. Ezekiel and his family eventually moved on to Tennessee. Ezekiel's great-grandson would become our 11th President, James K. Polk

Thomas and Ezekiel's brother, Charles Polk is also remembered for his service during the American Revolution by serving in various regiments including the Company of Lighthorse where he served as the Captain.

Charles Polk had a son named Charles and then Charles, Jr. had a son named Ezekiel, and it's through this particular Ezekiel the family reaches Georgia.

Are you beginning to see why my research got a little confusing regarding the Polk family names?

In 1834, Ezekiel formed a caravan with several family members to travel to land just opened up for settlement in northwest Georgia due to the Indian Removal Act. Traveling with Ezekiel was his wife, Melissa Jane "Jenny" (Weddington) Polk, his wife's brother, Alexander Green Weddington and Weddington's wife, Hannah (Polk) Weddington.

Did you notice? Ezekiel's wife's maiden name was Weddington and Alexander's wife's maiden name was Polk.

Hmmm…

Yes, brother and sister married brother and sister. That's a vine of kudzu climbing up that family tree if I ever saw one.

Also traveling to Georgia was Ezekiel's mother, Eleanor, and his mother-in-law, Mary "Polly" (McLarty) Weddington as well as Ezekiel's brother Charles Shelby Polk and his wife Catherine (McLarty) Polk.

The group ended up in the Dark Corner area of what would one day become Douglas County. If you wanted to locate the Dark Corner area today you would find it along Cedar Mountain Road between Douglasville and Winston. Fannie Mae Davis advises in her history of Douglas County, "The Indians judged the red soil as more valuable because the larger trees grew there than on the white land. In certain sections the soil division goes directly from dark to light as if a line was drawn."

A.E. Schole's *Georgia State Gazetteer* confirms the name was due to the color of the soil, but there are also other theories. In one of my earlier columns I advised other historical sources discuss a Cherokee leader known simply as The Dark. His claim to fame included developing the first toll road into Cherokee lands. In another column I wrote about Dark Corner during the Civil War when close to 40,000 Confederates moved through Dark Corner between September 30 and October 1, 1864 on their way to Allatoona and on to Tennessee.

Prior to the Civil War Ezekiel Polk was one of the richest landowners in the area, and with nine children he ensured his name would live on. Many of the families his children married into are recognizable today – Carnes, Winn, and McKelvey, among others.

Ezekiel Polk ended up accumulating 3,000 acres, a sizeable fortune and a number of slaves. Fannie Mae Davis recounted the son of one of his former slaves, Jack Polk, recalls that much of the west side of [Douglas County], spilling over into Carroll County by the Civil War, was owned by Ezekiel Polk. On Emancipation Day Ezekiel called his slaves together and informed them they were free to go or stay. If they stayed they would be paid for their work."

Ezekiel Polk donated the land where Ephesus Baptist Church now stands. Fannie Mae Davis advises in her history of Douglas County, "The original intent of the donation was to set aside a place for people to worship, a separate school area for education, and lastly a place for burial."

That being said Ezekiel's resting place was not at Ephesus but at Douglasville's City Cemetery.

The Weekly Star for January 12, 1884 stated, *"On Tuesday, January 5th Uncle Ezekiel Polk, one of the oldest and most respected citizens of Douglas County, was killed by falling or being thrown from his horse. He had been in Douglasville all that day attending to business, and left town in time to get home, seven miles out of Douglasville, by sundown.*

…He was found about one hundred yards from the house lying on his face with his arm broken. All of his ribs on his right side [were] broken loose from his backbone and three panels of fence torn down where his horse had drug him against the fence…

He died at 2 o'clock that night…In his death Douglas County lost one of her most prosperous, wealthiest and most useful citizens…He was one of the oldest citizens of the county…and died loved by all who knew him. His life was without spot and without blemish, and he left a heritage to his children in that he far excels his worldly possessions although he was called wealthy. Of his old associates there were few left and when they are all gone, the county has lost the best men who ever lived on our soil…

The Polk family piqued my interest initially because in her book Fannie Mae Davis mentioned a place a couple of times called Weddington Grove. Naturally, as I researched through the details of the Weddington family I hit upon the Polk family line. I'm still wondering if Weddington Grove was a family home, and if it still stands today.

Regarding my own family and the quirky details surrounding my mother's relations, how many people can claim their grandfather's wife was also his aunt or that their mother's father was also her grand-uncle? What if your grandmother's father-in-law was also her brother-in-law or your great-grandfather was also your great grand uncle?

My messy and rather scary family tree occurred because a father and son, my great-grandfather and grandfather married sisters, and they were half-sisters, at that.

Chapter 20

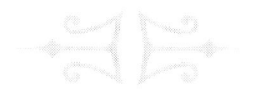

THE GREEN-RICE MILL ON ANNEEWAKEE CREEK

Anneewakee Creek rises to the south of Douglasville and runs southeastward to join the Chattahoochee River at a point a little downstream and opposite the site of the old town of Campbellton.

The name is from the Cherokee language – possibly from a Cherokee family name. Some researchers think members of this family might have lived along the creek. However, I need to point out Anneewakee Creek actually flows through land that was part of the Creek Nation – not the Cherokee.

A Cherokee name in Creek territory is not so strange because around 1815 Cherokees were under the impression they would be able to settle on Creek lands as far south as today's Heard County. In fact, there was a section of land designated as no-man's land that ran from the river up to and across the ridge where Broad Street is in downtown Douglasville where both tribes hunted. It makes sense there would be some overlapping and mixture. The boundaries kept changing as white settlers began moving in and began their plans to seize Native American lands no matter which tribe claimed the lands.

In 1821, both tribes agreed to yet another boundary line that began at Buzzard Roost Island on the Chattahoochee River where Douglas and Cobb Counties meet and ran westward to the Coosa River in Alabama.

The line passed far above the head of Anneewakee Creek.

When looking to early industry in Douglas County you have to zero in on the area along Anneewakee Creek. By the 1830s two important mills were situated on the creek and shared a property line.

One of those mills was the Alston Arnold mill, and the other was the mill first owned by William Ely Green.

Mr. Green came to Georgia from his home state of New Jersey in 1831. Green brought along his wife, Mary Stiles Green and their children. His first stop was the area of Georgia where Morgan, Oconee, and Walton Counties converge.

An article by Arden Williams at the *New Georgia Encyclopedia* advises, "…after the war of 1812 some southern leaders, in an attempt to duplicate the prosperity of cotton mills in New England, built textile factories in the South. Many of the earliest factories were in Morgan and Wilkes County. The idea faltered a little, but due to an economic depression in 1837 alternative sources of revenue for southern businessmen was needed, and the mills began to prosper."

William Green and his family were welcomed to Georgia by a relative – Ephraim Stiles Hopping – Mary Stiles Green's cousin. Hopping had been living in Georgia since 1825 when after graduating from Princeton; he headed south to accept a teaching job at the University of Georgia. Then he decided he would build a mill.

The 1840 census shows William Ely Green living in Morgan County, and by 1846 Hopping's High Shoals Factory was in full operation and remained so for years, however, at some point Green and Hopping parted ways. Perhaps they had a disagreement, perhaps they had an amicable parting, or perhaps Green wanted to stake a claim of his own where new unclaimed lands waited near Campbellton, Georgia following the Indian Removal.

At any rate, Green did purchase a strip of land along Anneewakee Creek that Fannie Mae Davis describes as "laying off Anneewakee Road." It was there William Ely Green began a couple of mills – one for making cotton cloth and thread and a second mill for creating rope. My research indicates the rope mill was the only one at the time in North Georgia. Both mills were fully operational by 1840, but the process could not have been easy.

The area at that time was a wilderness with few folks in the area. It was a full thirty years before Douglas County would exist and at that time the city of Douglasville wasn't even a thought. The area where our old courthouse stands today was merely an intersection of Indian trails close to an old skint chestnut tree.

Green had to physically clear the land with no modern equipment other than an ax. Once trees were cleared those same trunks had to be fashioned to use for building structures. It was back breaking and time consuming work. There were no corner groceries, so the family had to set to planting crops immediately to sustain them.

Fannie Mae Davis' information regarding Mr. Green and his mill explains census records for 1850 and into the Civil War years clearly shows both mills employed men and women on an equal basis. For the most part women didn't work outside the home during antebellum years, but a few women were forced to work out of need. Mrs. Davis names one such woman – a 65-year old widow named Mary Frails. She worked in the mill alongside her two daughters.

Besides providing jobs for those in need, Mr. Green's mills also provided an important market closer to the folks who were raising cotton along the Chattahoochee River and on the Chapel Hill plantations.

Green then shipped his finished products out to various towns that existed near and far. He used ox drawn wagons as his method of transport. Davis states, "A round trip to Atlanta took the wagons four days – a trip to Villa Rica would take two days."

One of Green's first team drivers was Wylie Preston Tackett. He began driving a wagon for the Green mills in 1848 when he was only ten years old!

Driving the wagons was dangerous and lonely work. The roads weren't the roads that we know today. They might have followed some of the same routes, but they were more or less Indian trails that were barely wide enough for wagons let alone people. Wild animals such as wolves and mountain lions were prevalent.

Some of the towns could be a little scary, too. In 1848, Villa Rica was a rough and rowdy gold mining town.

Fannie Mae Davis advises her sources for the information regarding Tackett comes from a written account his daughter left behind following her death in the 1960s. The daughter advised Tackett held the job driving the wagons until he was 23. At that point he volunteered to serve in the Confederate Army.

The area surrounding Green's mills became a little community since he and the neighboring mill Alston Arnold owned provided housing for many of the workers. A thriving community store was set up to help those who lived in the community. Arnold's property adjoined Green's tract of land along the banks of Anneewakee Creek.

In fact, that area was populated to the point that Campbell County leaders placed a district courthouse in the area much like our own mini-courthouses from the past. The district courthouse was basically a rough log cabin and when it was not in use for government purposes it served as a school as well as a religious meeting house. I know that seems strange today with the constant cry for the separation of church and state, but this was a frontier of sorts. Necessity was more important than matters involving how a government building was being used. Since public education didn't exist at the time the school would have been a private concern and folks could make a choice regarding sending their children. There was also a post office. The Anneewakee Factory Post Office was a log structure on Green's property. Fannie Mae Davis indicates the building stood until well into the 20th Century.

Of course, the mill provided Green and his growing family with a nice living. It is reported he had one of the first buggies in the area. His transport wagons were known to carry cotton cloth and rope out to customers, but would return with such things as a fancy cook stove for his wife's kitchen and a piano for his daughter to play from such places as Charleston.

The Green mills survived the Civil War even though Union soldiers were aware they existed. Perhaps Green's Yankee heritage helped keep his property intact.

Even so, the Civil War impacted William Ely Green and his family. His son Henry Martyn Green was killed in action at the Battle of Fort Stevens near Silver Spring, Maryland. Green's first-born, Robert Edgar Green also served in the Confederate Army. He came home from the war and attended medical school while overseeing some of the operations at the mill, but he soon tired of it. Mill work wasn't for him. Dr. Green soon departed for Gainesville where he would end up making his home. He actually began the city's first street car line and served as Gainesville's mayor in 1879.

William Ely Green eventually sold his business to his son-in-law, Major Zechariah A. Rice. Major Rice served in Cobb's Legion during the early days of the Civil War, and during the last months of the war he was an officer with the Fulton County Home Guard. Fannie Mae Davis quotes the deed of sale as, "Deed Book U, page 504, for 870 acres of land lots 100, 101, 102, 103, 112, 113, 1st District, 5th Section, Douglas County – Factory house and all machinery appertaining to it."

Major Rice and his wife Louise lived on the property, but he maintained his interests in Atlanta as well. Rice was actually returning to a "home place", of sorts. You see, Rice's mother was a member of the Bomar family, and his grandfather, Armistead or A.R. Bomar, built the Sprayberry-Henley home that still stands today along Highway 92 near the Chattahoochee River.

Wylie Preston Tackett returned from the war as a captain and became Rice's foreman. Fannie Mae Davis states Tackett, "...operated the factory and rope business almost single-handedly." He and his family – wife Melissa J. Underwood Tackett and his daughter Ella Virginia (1870-1956) lived in the area. Tackett was also a Mason. He died in 1907 and is buried at New Hope Baptist in the Chapel Hill area of Douglas County.

While the business did continue after the Civil War, it never operated on the same level as it did before the war. William Ely Green died on April 14, 1867 and is buried in Atlanta's historic Oakland Cemetery in Block 95, Lot 1.

Chapter 21

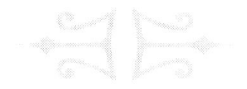

JUDGE BOWDEN'S PLANTATION

We drive by places every day in Douglas County never realizing the significance the place holds in our historical record. The place I have in mind to examine this week was once the hub of a thriving plantation that covered most of the land in and around the intersection of Bankhead Highway and Thornton Road.

The planter's home was always the center of all activities for a plantation, and in this case, the home still exists. I'm certain that you have driven by it more than once. I'm referring to the yellow two-story home with green shutters on the south side of Bankhead Highway as you head towards the Thornton Road intersection. The house is a little deceptive. It doesn't appear to date back to 1849 until you examine it a little closer. The chimneys on each side of the house are important markers.

Long-time residents of Douglas County refer to the yellow house as the Bowden home. It belonged to Judge John C. Bowden, and he controlled several hundred acres surrounding the house. Judge Bowden's holdings were located in Cobb and Campbell (now Douglas) Counties.

Born in 1826, Judge Bowden moved his business concerns from Cave Springs to Salt (Lithia) Springs in 1850. The next year he married Mary Rosa Summerlin, the daughter of a Salt (Lithia) Springs landowner named

Joseph Summerlin who per the 1855 tax digest owned several hundred acres and nearly three dozen slaves.

There are some discrepancies in the historical sources regarding who built the house. Some state Judge Bowden built the house in 1849 while others state Joseph Summerlin gave the house to the newlyweds. The more important point is that Judge Bowden owned the house for many years, and he and his wife raised eight children there. The Salt (Lithia) Springs post office was located for a time at the Bowden home since the Judge was appointed post master in 1859.

Joseph Summerlin died in 1863 and is thought to be buried across the road from the Bowden house in what some records refer to as the Summerlin-Bowden cemetery. I had never noticed the private family cemetery until just the other day after I had begun my research. It's easy to breeze by the spot as you try to keep your eyes on the road. My husband and I visited the small family plot and noted the county refers to the place as the Bowden-Mozley Cemetery. Today the graveyard is wedged between a carwash and a church across the street from the Bowden home. There are several graves, but only two have markers you can actually read.

Judge Bowden's home survived General Sherman's troops when they invaded the area on July 2, 1864, however the troops did vandalize the family cemetery searching for valuables.

It is said that Mary Rosa's step-mother, Susan, was among the women in the area who were sent north when the mill at New Manchester was destroyed. I have no direct confirmation of this but after Joseph Summerlin's death she remarried and was in the Chestnut Log area per records dated 1870, so apparently she is one of the few women who made her way back to Douglas County.

Judge Bowden presided over the Inferior Court in 1864. This was a court that had limited jurisdiction. The staff was generally part time and judges weren't necessarily schooled in the practice of law. The court usually handled minor financial civil cases. Judge Bowden was an original Douglas County commissioner and served as a school commissioner in

1872. Most of the biographies I've located also list him as a merchant, planter, and Mason.

Part of Judge Bowden's land holdings included the springs. Folks in the surrounding area had been aware for years regarding the health benefits the water held. Judge Bowden bottled the water and sold it on a somewhat limited basis.

In the summer of 1881 James A. Watson, an Atlanta businessman, was on the way to visit his mother in Douglasville. The route from Atlanta cut through Salt (Lithia) Springs with the Bowden house serving as a stagecoach stop. Somewhere between Atlanta and Salt (Lithia) Springs Watson fell ill causing him to spend a couple of days at the Bowden home. During his stay he was given some of the water from the springs and credited it with his speedy recovery. He left the Bowden home with a jug of the water and once he was home in Atlanta he had the water tested. It was discovered the water was rich in Lithium bicarbonate. Though Judge Bowden was already selling the water Watson saw a business opportunity and shared his idea with a couple of his friends from Atlanta.

Three years later Judge Bowden sold the springs along with 700 acres to Atlanta businessmen E.W. Marsh and Hugh Inman who along with Watson eventually developed the Sweetwater Park Hotel.

The men began an extensive advertising campaign which must have worked because *The Weekly Star* dated February 17, 1885 advised large quantities of water were being shipped and the company had offices in Atlanta, New York and New Orleans. Willie Bowden, Judge Bowden's son was in charge of the shipping department.

Over time Judge Bowden's plantation was divided among his children and eventually sold off bit by bit. New owners came to live in the yellow house. In 1948, Edwin Arthur Hetzner moved into the historic home. Hetzner was known to locals as Coach Hetzner since he was the basketball coach for Austell High School. Later he transferred to Douglas County High School, and he was the principal of Beulah Elementary as well.

After retiring in 1967, Coach Hetzner devoted his time to his hobbies including a miniature village he constructed called Piddleville he put on display for friends and neighbors to tour. Coach Hetzner and his wife also devoted many hours to restoring and renovating their historic home.

When Coach Hetzner passed away in 1967 his wife, Lois, ran a flower shop as well as a mobile home park on her property before moving to Pennsylvania in 1988.

Today, a plumbing company operates from the Bowden home.

Who would have ever thought that the land radiating from the nondescript yellow house was part of a large plantation or held such significance historically?

Chapter 22

ARNOLD MILL

I love to visit the Irish Bred Pub & Restaurant in downtown Douglasville. I like the exposed old brick inside the dining room, the tall windows at the front, and the old photographs of Douglasville as it used to be hanging along the walls.

The food and fellowship are great ingredients, too!

Earlier this month I had lunch at the pub with a friend to discuss local history. It was the perfect location since the pub building itself has a long history as does the entire commercial district along Broad Street.

The day was cold and rainy. I hurried through O'Neal Plaza and into the pub without much notice of my surroundings. Had my visit to the pub been during the early 1970s or much earlier during the 40s or even back to the 20s I would have seen a round item encased in the cement resembling a wheel of some sort in front of the storefront.

I would have seen a millstone, items long associated with harvest and hospitality. This particular millstone has quite a history and according to a past county historian it symbolizes the gratitude of a people for their time of great need.

The stone is actually from a mill that was located along the banks of Anneewake Creek.

Arnold Mill was built by pioneer Alston Arnold after he came to Georgia via South Carolina in the 1830s. He situated the mill at the mouth of Anneewakee Creek, and it later proved to be a most advantageous spot for him and for the people of Douglas County.

The mill was quite an enterprise for its day. Local historians advise the mill was three stories high and also had the capability of sawing wood as well. A small community even sprang up around the water-powered business.

During the 1880s a terrible drought lasting six months hit north Georgia including Douglas County. Many of the mills could no longer grind grain and corn because the water powering the millstones had dried up.

However, due to its position at the mouth of the creek Arnold Mill was able to put precious corn meal into the hands of hungry settlers.

As time went on, of course, the mill was no longer needed. As we moved from a more agricultural area to a business-oriented community the mills along the Chattahoochee River and creeks such as Anneewakee fell silent. Often times all that is left of these old mills is a foundation and a broken millstone or two.

However, the Arnold descendants realized the importance of their millstone. They realized it did symbolize a long forgotten time in Douglas County when people were very grateful for Arnold Mill. The millstone came to be memorialized in the sidewalk along Broad Street for nearly sixty years.

I wonder in all that time how many people walked over it and had no idea what it was.

Dr. F.M Stewart placed the millstone in the sidewalk in front of his business which was located where the Irish Bred Pub & Restaurant is located today. A family member has advised me Mr. Stewart owned the location after Mr. Selman did, and he was quite the entrepreneur here in Douglasville along with his brother, Rader Stewart.

Dr. F.M. Stewart is remembered as a dentist, Master Mason, and served on the school board. His brother, Rader Stewart, was a banker with interest in the Farmers and Merchants Bank. Together the brothers owned a general store situated on Broad Street, and they also owned Stewart's Mill.

This is the point of my research where a huge question loomed. So, if the Stewart brothers had their own mill how did Dr. F.M. Stewart come to possess the Arnold Mill millstone and place it in front of his business establishment?

One of the historical sources I consulted was Fannie Mae Davis' written historical account regarding Douglas County. She advised the stone was taken up in the late 70s and family members including Charlie and Rebecca Camp considered it a family relic and had possession of it.

Finally – a name I recognized.

Luckily I'm friends with the Camp's daughter- in- law, Julie, so I asked her about it. It hit both of us at the same time. Why were the Camps in possession of a millstone belonging to the Arnold family? Stranger still the Camps daughter-in-law had been born an Arnold. Red flags went up for both Julie and I. Was there some connection between Julie's family and her husband's? Some connection she might not want?

You know the old adage regarding be careful what you look for – you might just find it? Thankfully, this wasn't the case. We didn't discover some genealogical faux pas. There IS a logical explanation regarding why Dr. Stewart came to be in possession of the Arnold Mill stone and why the Camp family keeps it safe today.

You see, the millstone wound its way through his daughter's line of succession. Dr. F.M. Stewart was married to Willie Edna Selman, granddaughter of Alton Arnold, the original mill and millstone owner.

From Dr. Stewart the stone passed to his daughter, Francis "Toot's" Thompson and then to her daughter, Rebecca Camp.

Mrs. Camp and her husband, Charlie, have given the millstone another resting spot in the sidewalk of their Douglasville home where I'm sure it will remain for the next few years.

Section Four

THE NEW SOUTH

Chapter 23

HIS HONOR AND THE SACRED HARP

Summer is almost here and that can only mean one thing – family reunions!

I'm off today to make great memories and remember some old ones with the 21st century version of dinner on the ground – gathering around the air conditioner in the church's activities center.

Yes, it's time for the Land reunion at Sharp Mountain Baptist Church in Ball Ground, Georgia.

In the old days we met under a shelter outside the church. Once there the ladies would spread cotton tablecloths up and down the longest table constructed of slabs of marble and concrete blocks I have ever seen. The various designs on the tablecloths formed a wild checkerboard – a rather strange and beautiful quilt.

The table literally groaned underneath all of the food – every sort of vegetable you could imagine from stewed squash and green beans to fried okra and sweet potatoes. There would be fried chicken, country fried steak and salmon patties, roast with carrots and potatoes, sliced ham, and pork roast, too. Biscuits, corn bread, and every type of dessert you could imagine. I always grabbed one of the largest Chinet plates in the stack and promptly filled it to capacity.

After dinner the kids would go running off up the hill to the cemetery to play tag among the headstones of family members long gone or play school in one of the Sunday school rooms. The adults of every age would talk and contemplate their full bellies in lounge chairs scattered around the table.

And then the singing would begin.

My Great Uncle Homer loved his singing. He'd head into the sanctuary by himself and fuss at any of us who might be running through the church building.

Uncle Homer would begin to holler for the adults to come in and sing or at least listen, and bit by bit most everyone would struggle in to watch and hear him. You couldn't help it. The comforting sound would draw you in.

I loved it and miss it very much. Uncle Homer has been gone for several years and reunions really aren't the same without sitting on that wooden pew with my cardboard fan printed with Jesus at The Last Supper on one side and ads from local businesses on the other trying to keep the hot air moving around me. Everyone from 5 to 85 was flapping those fans, so it's a wonder we all didn't just lift up off the ground and rise to Glory.

Like my Uncle Homer, Douglasville's own Joseph S. James, our first mayor, was a huge champion for singing – shape note singing, that is.

The Fasola.org website advises "Sacred Harp is a uniquely American tradition that brings communities together to sing four-part hymns and anthems…Technically, [the] style of singing is "shape note singing" because the musical notation uses heads in four distinct shapes to aid in sight-reading, but it is often called "Sacred Harp" singing because the books that most singers use today are called "The Sacred Harp".

Judge James had a love of music in his bones. He was born in 1849 to a singing teacher named Stephen James (1821-1872) and his wife, Martha Shipley. James became what is described to be a tireless promoter of Sacred Harp singing in the Atlanta area.

James revised the music book *The Sacred Harp* and compiled many other books regarding shape note singing through the 1920s. Though he was a prominent lawyer in Douglasville as well as Atlanta, he often found himself defending his actions in court regarding matters of business and even regarding his love of shape note music. He was sued at one point for plagiarism, but somehow never let things like that deter him.

He just kept on singing.

So should we.

Chapter 24

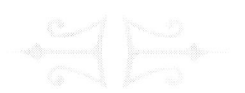

THE POOLE HOUSE – A HISTORIC GEM

When you discuss Douglasville and the topic of historic properties, the Poole-Huffine-Bulloch-Rollins-Hudson/Farmer-Rollins home located at 7125 West Strickland Street instantly comes to mind. At 145 years old the home is one of the oldest properties in the city as well as Douglas County.

The home was built by William Haynes Poole, the very first physician and surgeon in the area before Douglasville or Douglas County existed by name.

Dr. Poole began studying medicine with Dr. M.F. La Dell in Cedartown, and earned his degree from Savannah Medical College where he served one year as an intern at the Marine Hospital.

He graduated in 1860 with first honors in his class and his graduating thesis, *Modue Operandi of Medicines* was published in what would amount to the *American Medical Journal* today for other physicians to review.

After graduation, Dr. Poole returned to Carroll County where his parents lived intending to open his medical practice there, but he served the next four years in the Medical Unit of the Confederate Army. His skill in surgery was reported to have been equal to the best in the entire unit.

Family stories relate how after the war Dr. Poole was traveling through Skint Chestnut – the name Douglasville was known by prior to 1875 – with thoughts of heading west to begin a medical practice. Dr. Poole met up with Rueben Vansant who along with his brother, Young Vansant, owned most of the land surrounding Skint Chestnut. Mr. Vansant advised Dr. Poole there was a great need for a doctor in the area, and that the area would be growing in the future. Dr. Poole decided to stay and rented a room from Vansant.

It wasn't long before Dr. Poole had an extensive and profitable practice as well as a wife. He had fallen in love with Reuben Vansant's daughter, Marcella. They married in 1861, and by 1868, he had built his home on land that Reuben Vansant gave the couple. Over the next few years their growing family of 8 children filled the home.

The slate roof is original to the house and was hauled to Douglasville by two horse wagons from the quarry at Rockmart. Directly behind the house is the smokehouse and what is described as the caretaker's cottage also dating to 1868.

Dr. Poole was very well known in town and took part in many aspects of the development of Douglasville. He owned land throughout the county and served on a committee that made recommendations regarding the construction of the 1896 courthouse. He was also a Mason and member of the Lutheran Church. After the 1896 Courthouse burned, a box that had been placed behind the cornerstone was opened. One of the items inside the box was a $500 Confederate note signed by W.H. Poole and two of his sons, Reuben H. and Thomas J. Poole who were also doctors in the community.

Adjacent to the property is the historic Vansant Cemetery where the Vansant brothers are buried with their wives. Young Vansant gave 40 acres of his own land for the city of Douglasville.

The Huffine family bought the property from Dr. Poole. Mr. Huffine owned a cotton warehouse and had other business concerns in Douglasville.

The next owners were the Bulloch family followed by Keith and Sandra Rollins who were the last owners to actually live in the home. They made many restorative improvements to the home and gardens before passing the property to Susanne Hudson and Jeri Farmer who opened le Jardin Blanc, an events facility.

For the last few years hundreds of people have enjoyed Dr. Poole's home as well as the beautiful landscaped gardens around the house with white climbing roses, hydrangeas, and bricked walks while attending various events such as weddings, teas, and private parties.

Today, the property is once again a private home.

While the home is certainly beautiful inside and out, its tie to Douglasville's history cannot be ignored. It is most certainly a gem among our historic properties!

Chapter 25

HOW DOUGLAS COUNTY LOST ITS EXTRA "S"

I strongly believe the story regarding how Douglas County was named is right up at the top of the list of interesting stories.

The Carl Vinson Institute of Government at UGA as well as the historical marker in front of the old Douglas County Courthouse on Broad Street advises the county was named for U.S. Senator Stephen Douglas who ran against President Abraham Lincoln in 1860.

Celebrate Douglas, the web portal for the government of Douglas County goes a little further stating: "Douglas County…was first named for Frederick Douglass…due to the Republican/military control of the Georgia General Assembly, and later changed to honor Stephen A. Douglas…when local control of the General Assembly was re-established when Reconstruction ended."

Hmmm, so there has to be a story, right?

Did Georgia have an enclave of strong Unionists west of Atlanta who chose to make a stance by naming a Reconstruction-era county after Frederick Douglass?

Prior to 1870 Douglas County was part of Campbell County. Folks on the north side of the Chattahoochee River disliked traveling 20 miles or more on horseback or by wagon to conduct any town business, so a delegation was formed to petition the General Assembly for a new county.

The delegation included Ephraim Pray, John C. Bowden, John A. Wilson and several others. They managed to get Dr. W.S. Zellers, the representative from Campbell County, to prepare a bill regarding its organization.

For most of 1870 the General Assembly had a Republican majority consisting of a large number of carefully placed Northern carpetbaggers and former slaves. The pro-Douglas County delegation wanted to honor Stephen A. Douglas, but knew it would be easier for the bill to pass if they let the General Assembly think the new county would be named for Frederick Douglass.

So far, the only documentation used to back up the claim that they created a ruse is a letter written by Moses McKoy Smith in 1930 which Fannie Mae Davis refers to in her book *Douglas County: From Indian Trail to Interstate 20*. Smith later served as mayor of Douglasville in 1882, state representative from 1884-1885, and had practiced law in the community for over 30 years. His letter testified to the events regarding the scheme that convinced the General Assembly to approve Douglas County as Smith's father was one of the men in the delegation.

I've not seen the letter myself, but everything I have seen through my research during the last four years makes the ruse totally plausible.

The county was approved, but what the General Assembly did not realize was once the lawmaking body of Georgia returned to Democratic hands, the county would quietly remove the extra "S" and state publically the honoree was Stephen A. Douglas.

In all of my research over the last four years I've never seen anything in the newspapers that corroborates any reason why our county is named Douglas until recently.

The other day I happened upon a very short article published in the January, 1873 editions of the *Atlanta Weekly Sun* and *Atlanta Daily Sun* which said, "When this new county was organized in 1870, it was intended to be named in honor of Stephen A. Douglas; but when it came before the Legislature it was recorded in the journals of both Houses as Douglass after Frederick Douglass, the Negro orator and politician, instead of Douglas. It is hoped that this new county shall be known by its proper name. It...should be explicitly known that the county was named for Stephen A. Douglas and not Fred. Douglass."

So, perhaps it was a ruse, but publically in 1873 the disappearance of the double "S" was blamed on clerical error.

Chapter 26

JOURNEY TO A TOWN CENTER

Gather two or more people together in one community, and it won't be long before the disagreements begin.

It's inevitable.

We are human.

Our great city of Douglasville began under a cloud of disagreement including a major lawsuit that went all the way to the Georgia Supreme Court. Head on over to the Douglas County Courthouse and find the very first court docket book dating back to the 1870s. One of the first entries will advise the first Defendants in the county happened to be the Douglas County Commissioners, and the lawsuit concerned the location of the county seat.

The Georgia General Assembly issued an act on October 17, 1870 creating Douglas County. Within the language of the act was a stipulation calling for an election to be held the first Monday of November, 1870 to elect an ordinary, sheriff, clerk of superior court and to choose a location for a county seat where all county business would be conducted.

Many thought it was a foregone conclusion that the Chapel Hill community would be considered. In 1870, Chapel Hill contained a general store and a few other businesses. There was both a Baptist and Methodist church and three different schools including a high school. The area was a very prosperous plantation community with several influential citizens.

Many others preferred the area up on the ridge known as Skint Chestnut where a trading post had been located some years before. It wasn't just the draw of the ancient Chestnut tree or the trading post that enticed folks. It had a lot to do with the proposed rail site the Georgia Western Railroad (today's Norfolk Southern) wanted to create.

The 1870s was a time when attitudes in Georgia were changing. Many of our town father's understood the new 'farm to factory movement' which would result in business opportunities, more industrialization and an established rail line.

The railroad had actually proposed building a rail line through the county prior to the Civil War, but the war had delayed it. The right-of-way would cross the county for nineteen miles, and at one point would parallel the old Indian trail where the road passed the ancient Chestnut tree. By 1870, the land had been cleared for the rail line from Atlanta to Skint Chestnut and beyond to Reuben Vansant's crossroads.

By the time the election rolled around thoughts of Chapel Hill as the county seat had been replaced by a group of folks wanting the center of the county chosen as the location. The geographic center is approximately located off of Highway 5 near Pray's Mill Baptist Church. The folks who supported this area were known as "center" people and included

Moses M. Smith. He argued the railroads could be persuaded to run a line through the area and mentioned the area's water sources–, Bear Creek and Sweetwater Creek –as the fuel to run a million dollars worth of machinery. He did have a few valid points, but many felt it would be too difficult to persuade the railroad to change their plans since much of the land had been cleared.

The ballot listed the "center" location as well as Skint Chestnut as voting choices. White men who were 21 and older showed up on the specified date to vote at designated precincts.

The election resulted in William W. Hindmon taking the office of Ordinary, T.H. Selman as Sheriff, and A.S. Gorman was the first clerk of Superior Court. The Board of Commissioners consisted of John C. Bowden, W.N. McGouirk, J. H. Winn and Ephraim Pray along with Mr. Hindmon since the act passed by the General Assembly provided the Ordinary would also be a member of the board. The act required the newly elected Board of Commissioners to purchase a tract of land at the elected county seat site, lay off lots, sell them at outcry, and use the funds to construct a courthouse and jail.

It sounds simple, right?

The center of the county received 300 votes, and there were many votes for Skint Chestnut.

Events took a murky turn when voters ignored the two choices and wrote in other locations referring to Skint Chestnut, but according to the various histories I've read there was more than just one exact location along the rail line known as Skint Chestnut. So, it was unclear once all of the votes had been cast how many votes the Skint Chestnut location intended by the city fathers had received. In her history of Douglas County, Fannie Mae Davis states, "The commissioners arbitrarily ruled that voting for other sites other than the center were actually votes for Skint Chestnut."

In other words, they decided all ballots not in favor of the center of the county were in fact votes for the proposed Skint Chestnut location.

Of course, the center folks were upset, and so were many other voters who felt it was wrong for the Board of Commissioners to wield that much power, and what about the folks who had not voted for the center of the county or the intended Skint Chestnut area?

Yes, the election ended up being a debacle.

Moses M. Smith, Ephraim Pray and many others who were "center" people hired Thomas W. Latham as their attorney and filed a petition of protest against Commissioners Hindmon, Bowden, Winn, and McGouirk giving the Clerk of Superior Court his first case to enter into his brand new docket book.

The court battle went on for four years and went all the way to the Georgia Supreme Court. However, all of the legal wrangling and division didn't cause that much delay per Davis' book. County officials continued to organize the government best as they could.

Plans for the county seat at Skint Chestnut really took off once Young Vansant deeded 40 acres for the express purpose of creating the county seat exactly where the downtown Douglasville area sits today. Vansant deeded the property over on Jan. 9, 1871. Soon the elected officials, along with volunteers, helped erect a building east of the store at Skint Chestnut that would serve as a temporary courthouse for the next few years.

The deed where Young Vansant gave land was not recorded until April 9, 1874. It was one of the first recorded and can be found in County Deed Book A, page 235. Vansant gave no provisions or stipulations with the gift of land other than claiming access to the well on the property. The well was located in front of the Skint Chestnut store building facing Broad at the corner of Broad Street and today's West Courthouse Square. It was being used as late as 1920 when the city finally paved the sidewalk and the well was filled in.

The pending lawsuit against the commissioners finally came to a conclusion when the Georgia Supreme Court sent the legal action back to the Georgia General Assembly for review in 1874. The General Assembly then ordered a second election to be held that would hopefully finalize the location for Douglas County's seat of government.

Again, there were two choices–both near the railway right-of-way. Skint Chestnut, where the temporary courthouse had been built was a choice, and the second choice was Rueben Vansant Crossroads which was near today's Bright Star Road and Bankhead Highway. Skint Chestnut won with 149 majority votes.

It was finally official and legal. Skint Chestnut would be the county seat for Douglas County, and the Skint Chestnut name was replaced with the Douglasville name officially on February 25, 1875 when the Georgia General Assembly approved the act which incorporated the town of Douglasville.

On July 1, 1930, M.M. Smith wrote a letter to a county official where he discussed those days during the time the lawsuit was pending. He was 16 at the time the lawsuit was filed. Smith's father, Moses M. Smith was one of the original Plaintiffs in the lawsuit and had been a proponent of the center of the county being our county seat. Smith's letter confirms what I've shared with you here. He goes on to state the folks who wanted Skint Chestnut as the county seat were of course elated at the outcome of the second election.

From his letter:

"One thing that I might add, when the election showed that Douglasville was going to be the county site, there was a big celebration at which anvils with powder between them were used as big guns. Mr. Dorsett carried some powder out from his store to the place where it was to be used. This powder was in a paper, and it leaked and fell on some fire on the ground and ignited the powder in the paper which he still had in his hands, burning his eyebrows and hair pretty badly. I was sorry of that, but I must admit that some of the 'center' people were not."

See, sometimes history CAN make you smile!

Chapter 27

JOSEPH S. JAMES – DOUGLASVILLE'S FIRST CHEERLEADER

As I've mentioned before the city of Douglasville was built by men, many of them former Confederate soldiers, who were willing to follow the New South philosophy. Several key ingredients were needed to have a successful and thriving town.

The website for the City of Douglasville describes our town as an outstanding example of a turn-of-the-century railroad town. Stephanie

Aylworth, a former Main Street Manager for the city went one step further by stating, "Douglasville is a prime example of a postbellum rail town for several reasons including the orientation of the buildings to the railroad, the layout of the town, the types of businesses housed and their architectural features. All of these set the stage for a New South image campaign directed by Douglasville's primary booster [or cheerleader], Joseph S. James."

So, before I launch into an examination of Douglasville's early cotton mills I wanted to take a sidebar moment to discuss Mr. James since his name is all over every aspect of our early history. When I began my research into the history of Douglas County I quickly saw that I would need to devote more than one column to Mr. James since he was so involved with what appears to be every aspect of life in Douglas County. It has been a true joy to uncover various layers of his life, and the most exciting part to me is I know there are several things I haven't uncovered – yet.

Joseph S. James was born in Campbell County, Georgia in 1849. His father was very well known in the community and was one of the first settlers. A few historical sources print Joseph S. James' middle name as Summerlin, but other sources state the family has confirmed James' full name as Joseph Stephen James, and he preferred to be called Joe.

Some historical sources refer to James with the title of Colonel. Though his father and brothers served in the Confederate army, Douglasville's prime booster never did. As I've discussed in previous columns the title of Colonel is often given to attorneys as a sign of respect in the South and in the states of North Dakota and New Mexico. Georgia's governor can convey the honorary title per Georgia's legal code, section 38-2-111.

Memoirs of Georgia, a book compiled in 1895 with biographical details of people across the state advises, "[Around 1869 and] at this time being very poor and without a thorough education [James] was disqualified for the battle of life, but gathering all his strength and ability, he applied himself to the study of law." It was a custom at that time for young men wishing to be an attorney to merely attach themselves to a practicing attorney to learn the law.

Apparently he made quite an impression on folks because in 1881, at the age of 21, Joseph S. James was elected as the Justice of the Peace for Douglas County, and by the time the city was incorporated by the Georgia General Assembly on February 22, 1875 James was elected as Douglasville's first mayor along with five aldermen and a recorder.

James was also the editor and publisher of *The New South* paper and operated a general store in town with family members.

Following his term as mayor, James moved on to the Georgia General Assembly where he served as a state representative for two terms beginning in 1880 followed by a term as a state senator for the 36th district.

While serving in the General Assembly in 1883 James was able to assist the Pacific Railroad to locate sites for routes and stations in Douglas County, Villa Rica, Tallapoosa, and Temple. Some of this travels took him into Alabama and Mississippi.

In her historical account of Douglas County Fannie Mae Davis states, "[Joseph S. James] used [the entire] stratagem at his command in influencing renewed interest in the building of a railroad on the old right-of-way surveyed 30 years before, and when the Georgia Pacific Railroad became owners, James watched the progress with an eagle's eye."

James would actually go out on scouting expeditions with railroad officials. One such trip left him injured and crippled for life. Fannie Mae Davis explains how one day after looking over some railway sites the group was heading in after dark. They were traveling east towards Atlanta when they knowingly came upon a spot where a farmer had placed a barricade of oak rails on the track in protest.

There were some people who did not see the benefits of the railroad. Many farmers were upset the railroad was being built across their property. Eminent domain is never popular when it's your domain that is being taken, right?

James was sitting on a flatbed car with his legs hanging off the side. The engine was behind the flat car pushing it, and since it was dark the barricade could not be seen. The car hit the barricade breaking both of James' legs. Mrs. Davis reports Joe (as she referred to him) was about 30 years old at the time, and from then on had a noticeable limp and at times used a walking stick until the day he died.

James did what he could to continually promote Douglas County and Douglasville. In an article from *The Atlanta Constitution* dated May 5, 1888 James stated, "For the immigrant this region possesses many advantages especially for those intending to engage in agricultural pursuits…a lively, enterprising town, and that here is the center of an extensive and prosperous farming county…an industrious farmer, in a short time, can have an attractive home, and though starting poor, in a few years may become rich."

In 1888, he was very involved with the Piedmont Chatauqua, a major event in Douglas County where …close to 30,000 people poured into [the county] from Atlanta and from parts unknown via the railroad for a weekend of cultural and educational opportunities. James also owned the land in the downtown Douglasville area known as James Grove where Fourth of July celebrations were held beginning in 1886.

Georgia Memoir also reports that in 1892 James was chosen as a presidential elector-at-large for the state. During this time he made 102 speeches in 90 days all over the state with consecutive appointments being 100-300 miles apart.

President Grover Cleveland appointed James as the United States District Attorney for the Northern District of Georgia on April 3, 1893, and in 1897, James helped to establish a cotton mill in town, a move which would solidify Douglasville as a New South town.

When he wasn't serving as the number one cheerleader for Douglasville or in many of the other important positions he held Joseph S. James practiced law, was a member of the Odd Fellows, an altruistic and benevolent fraternal organization, was a member of the Methodist Church and helped to organize the United Sacred Harp Association. He was also a staunch Democrat, served on the Board of Directors for the Douglasville Banking Company and chairperson for the Democratic Executive Committee. He also helped organize a joint stock company for the purpose of building a large hotel in town.

Joseph S. James died on January 20, 1931.

Douglasville Lodge No. 289 F & A.M. honored Joseph S. James with a resolution in the *Douglas County Sentinel* soon after his death stating, "Brother James measured up to the highest standards…"

This may be true, but I've discovered Joe James was a very complex man, and not everyone looks on him favorably.

Stories are told how his daughter Eunice burned all of his papers and records, and that he was buried in an unmarked grave in Douglasville's City Cemetery. I have it on good authority he is buried west of the Pavilion, but why would she burn all of his papers?

Now, that just begs for another story, doesn't it?

Chapter 28

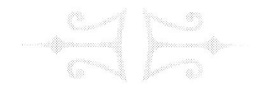

THE BUSINESS OF THE RAILROAD

For many today, the railroad running through Douglasville might seem a little outdated and an inconvenience. The blast of the train horns interrupt our conversations as we walk through O'Neal Plaza or while we have dinner or lunch along Broad Street. The train no longer carries us to Atlanta or west into Alabama. It merely blocks traffic as folks attempt to head home to Hiram and Dallas. However, there was a time when the railroad was premier in our thoughts and had it not run through Douglasville our past, and therefore our future would have been very different.

By 1850, Atlanta already had several rail lines, but until the Georgia Western Railroad was chartered in 1854, there was no line heading west. The concern was incorporated by Richard Peters, Lemuel Grant and other Atlanta businessmen.

Some sources state prior to the Civil War grading for the western line occurred from Atlanta to a point two miles west of Skint Chestnut/Douglasville, but I'm now a little skeptical of that since early railroad maps show the line passing through the southern portion of the county. There are stories that the right-of-way was used by farmers to move cattle from Birmingham to Atlanta for market. I haven't found any proof of this yet, but at any rate the Civil War interrupted the plans.

What I do know is that even after the war the western route for the railroad was still very much a point of discussion.

Maps from the time period clearly show a much different route out of Atlanta where the railroad would go through Carrollton and not Douglasville. Douglasville was not officially established until February of 1875 due to some legal entanglements and an election that had to be held twice, but the town fathers continued to set up the town, so it's no surprise to me that Douglasville was on the 1873 map. Not only did the town fathers have to convince the folks of Douglas County that Douglasville should be the county seat, they also had to convince the railroad to lay tracks through town as well.

On July 12, 1873 a railroad meeting was held at Chapel Hill to discuss proposed routes and issues surrounding stock subscriptions. Three days later a larger group met in Douglasville to consider the prospect of the Georgia Western Railroad passing through the county with W.P. Strickland as the chair and A.S. Gorman as secretary.

A committee was set up to create resolutions for those at the meeting to consider. John F. Glover, Dr. Poole, Ezekiel Polk, Captain Whitley and G.W. McLarty were appointed to the committee. They went into another room to devise the resolutions. While they met in the other room, John M. Edge entertained the crowd with what is described as his "fluent and impressive style describing the benefits to have the railroad pass through the county."

The resolutions were later published in *The Atlanta Constitution* stating:

> *Resolved – that the people of Douglas County want the Georgia Western Road; that the right of way be given through the county; the road to be the same width as allowed to other roads in this state.*
>
> *Resolved – that we recommend the company to cross the Chattahoochee River below the mouth of Sweetwater Creek, thence coming out by the great water power known as the old Sweetwater Factory site and the Merchant Mills on that stream.*

Resolved – that we are willing to subscribe stock under the form adopted at the railroad meeting at Chapel Hill on the 12th inst.

Railroad construction finally began eight years later in 1881. By that time the Georgia Western Railroad had become the Georgia Pacific, and fortunately, the final route included Douglasville.

The Weekly Star, Douglasville's paper at the time, advised on August 23, 1881, "On Tuesday, one hundred and twenty-five hands arrived here for the purpose of beginning work on the Georgia Pacific. Yesterday morning, they began preparing the graded portion of the railroad for the reception of crossties and iron. The men are from Virginia… This looks like business."

Business most certainly was the correct word!

Chapter 29

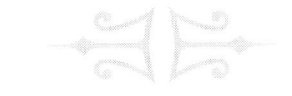

A FEW THOUGHTS ON THE RAILROAD

I was walking through O'Neal Plaza the other day as a train was rolling though the downtown commercial district. I stood there and watched it for a moment. All around me cars were coming and going and pedestrians were walking back and forth on the sidewalk. I seemed to be the only one that noticed the hundreds of tons of steel, power, and freight rushing past us. The only ones that might have had the train on their mind were the drivers in their cars along Campbellton and Broad impatiently waiting to cross the track and get on with their trip.

Seriously, do we as citizens of Douglasville think about the trains that roll down the nineteen miles of track from one end of the county to another each day? Yes, of course we had the train on our mind back in January when it derailed – for a few days. It made headlines, the mess was cleaned up and then other newsworthy items took over.   Occasionally, like me you might hear the sound of the train whistle late at night even if you live a few miles from town, but I would imagine the train is not on your mind often.

Forty-five years ago, however, trains were very much on my mind. My family had moved to a location along Highway 29 in Red Oak – a lovely

Craftsman style home with a huge front porch and a very clear view of the railroad tracks that ran through our front yard. Yes, a train ran through my front yard not more than seventy-five feet from my front door. Even at my young age I had seen trains before, and I realized what they were used for, but having one that close to where I played with my dolls and rode my bike was a little disconcerting.

Actually, the proper word to describe my feelings about the train was "terrifying". Back in those days children actually played outside the majority of the time, and I was no different. Within days of moving to that house I developed a keen sense of hearing. I could hear the three or four trains that barreled down the tracks during the day several miles off way before my parents or my sister. If I even thought I heard a slight whistle sound I would drop my dolls or hop off my bike and run at breakneck speed to get into the house. Once Mom and Dad realized why I would come tearing into the house their only reaction was amusement. They would smile and say, "Oh, I guess the train is coming." Within a few minutes sure enough they could hear the train and then experience it as the noise got louder and louder until it blared past the house shaking and rattling everything including the windows and even our hearts inside our bodies.

Gradually, I got used to the noise and the fear went away.

I remembered this as I stood watching the train rush through the middle of town, and I also couldn't help but think about Douglasville in the early days when the train was new, when the town was new, and how persuading the railroad company to complete the tracks through Douglasville was paramount to the town's growth and survival.

Let's go back in time to the year 1915:

The Georgia Pacific train headed west out of Atlanta bound for Birmingham, Alabama, one of the leading industrial centers in the South. About 27 miles west of Atlanta, passengers caught site of a relatively modern railroad town, stretched along both sides of the track. Horses pulled wagons filled with cotton bales on the road running parallel to the railroad, headed west to the cotton warehouses of the town…Slowing to stop at the…station, the train passed a large brick cotton mill to the left, and impressive two-story building with large windows. The loud clattering of spinning frames producing cotton yarn escaped the open windows, providing ventilation for the busy mill workers scurrying around inside.

The train stopped at the railroad station, located near the mill, stopping to release passengers and picking up new ones, loading freight to carry westward to Birmingham and beyond, delivering mail, and dropping off goods for residents of the town and countryside. Merchants sent men in wagons to pick up plows for farmers, ready-to-wear clothing and furniture for the town residents, and a variety of foods for sale at the local grocery stores. Once the train started up again, it began to gather speed as it passed by a solid row of brick store fronts to the left, several blocks long, featuring both one- and two-story buildings often with stylish wooden or corbelled brick cornices and even a cast-iron front.

Men stood outside the stores, visiting under the front porches that extended the length of the street façade and stopping ever so briefly to watch the train pass by. Women wandered the covered walkways shopping for their families headed to the grocery store to buy food and stopping by the millinery to check out the newest hats. Businessmen in the stores glanced out in expectation of the supplies that would soon be coming their way. After several blocks of brick commercial facades and ornate brick Italianate courthouse broke the pattern of the storefronts, with its tall clock tower dominating the town landscape. Soon, the train picked up speed and headed out of town, surrounded by the cotton fields, which fueled the town's industry.

The above explanation regarding how Douglasville looked and what was going on in the immediate years following the installation of the railroad was written by Stephanie Aylworth, a former Main Street Manager for the city of Douglasville, based on her extensive research regarding how our town was formed. Her description accurately shows how the unique combination of the railroad, a cotton mill and a group of men who followed the political and cultural ideology of New South boosterism helped to create our town.

Aylworth maintains the espousal of the New South creed reshaped villages into railroad towns, revitalized local economies, and resurrected the cotton mill industry. She states, "The promotion of the railroad and the textile industry served as a focal point for the New South brand of ideology that evolved in Georgia during the late nineteenth and early twentieth centuries…

The city of Douglasville, Georgia from 1880 to 1910, exemplified everything that New South boosters claimed to need to remedy the South's post-Civil War economic stagnation [including railroad access]."

Chapter 30

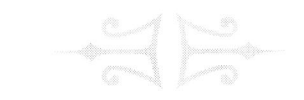

THE RAILROAD – MAKING CONNECTIONS

Last week I began to examine how the railroad running parallel to Douglasville's central business district came to be. The railroad was an important ingredient used by town leaders to create a successful business district per the New South creed. The espousal of the New South creed reshaped villages into railroad towns, revitalized local economies and resurrected the cotton mill industry per Stephanie Aylworth, former Main Street Manager for Douglasville.

In his book, *The Promise of the New South: Life After Reconstruction*, Edward L. Ayers states, The New South era began in the 1880s after the biracial and reformist experiment of Reconstruction had ended and the conservative white Democrats had taken power throughout the Southern states.

The Atlanta Constitution editor, Henry W. Grady is credited with the term 'New South' which represents an ideology that emphasized a new reliance upon railroads and industrialization to modernize the south.

Last week I quoted a *Weekly Star* article (see "The Business of the Railroad") advising the first Georgia Pacific Railroad workers arrived in Douglasville in August, 1881 to begin preparing the graded portion of the railroad for crossties and iron. Track laying for the railroad was begun in November, 1881 starting at the outskirts of Atlanta going in a westerly direction at the rate of one mile a day.

While many of the men working on the railroad were from out of town, Georgia Pacific Railroad tried to use the businesses in town for their needs when they could. A story in an October, 1881 issue of *The Weekly Star* discusses how two merchants in town, Price and Duncan, were contracted to furnish one hundred thousand crossties for the railroad. Douglas County historian, Fannie Mae Davis, explains in her book how the crossties were hauled to the rail line by ox wagon from the Jacks Hill – now part of Sweetwater Creek State Park – section of the county.

By January, 1882 the tracks had reached Austell and by May 10, 1882 *The Atlanta Constitution* announced the Georgia Pacific would begin a regular schedule to Douglasville.

The arrival of the first train in Douglasville was a grand occasion and major holiday, in April, 1882. Fannie Mae Davis advises over 2,000 people were on hand. She also advises many had never seen a train before. Today we find that fact to be absolutely amazing, but we have to remember until the Georgia Pacific line was completed there was no train in this part of the state and many of the people who had settled here had never traveled to Atlanta.

On the day the train was to arrive, women brought food for picnics. Horses were tied off a block or so away to keep them from being scared by the sound of the engines, but their actions were in vain. The horses heard the commotion when the train arrived and some broke free running for home. Mrs. Davis recounts a story that someone in the crowd yelled, "Look out, they are going to turn around here!" This only added to the over charged emotions of the throng of people.

Once service to Douglasville was established many people who lived in Atlanta bought tickets to travel to Austell Bridge, a popular picnic area located where Maxham Road and Sky View Drive intersect today.

The Georgia Pacific didn't stop in Douglasville. The tracks reached Villa Rica by July, 1882, and the last spike was driven at Cave Creek

Tunnel in November, 1883 linking Atlanta and Alabama. This meant the line was connected all the way to Columbus, Mississippi where the line connected to the Texas and Pacific Railroad.

Over the years several trains were scheduled connecting Douglasville to Atlanta and Birmingham including passenger trains. One such train was called The Accommodation or the Heflin Hustler. It made daily round-trips to and from Atlanta leaving Douglasville at seven in the morning and returning at six in the evening. It was perfect for those folks who worked in Atlanta. Many trains were simply known by their number including No. 40 which departed Douglasville each day at 11 a.m.

According to Fannie Mae Davis one of the "in" things for young people to do in Douglasville focused on the train. They would meet the train known as No. 39 each day and watch as the mail bags were unloaded. They would follow the bags over to the post office which was housed inside the Hutcheson Building where Gumbeaux's Cajun Café is located today. Mrs. Davis explained, "They crowded the small lobby and overflowed to the outside." It was quite the social event. We know that No. 39 was a westbound train because the railroad used odd numbers for trains heading west while trains traveling east were even numbered.

The original train depot was built in 1883 and lasted until January, 1899 when it was destroyed by a fire. Everything was destroyed but a few bales of cotton that had been left on the dock. J.I. Oxford, the former pastor at the First Baptist Church of Douglasville had moved to Atlanta the day before the fire. He had all of his families furniture stored at the depot to ship east. Unfortunately, he lost every stored item in the fire.

A second depot was built almost immediately and served Douglasville until 1916 when the third depot was built. Over the years as the roads improved, trucks began carrying more freight, and folks began to own more cars, they stopped depending on the railroad. The last depot was closed in the 1970s long after passenger service was done away with. The building was auctioned off for $1.00 to the Sword family in 1974 and moved to their Chapel Hill property where it remains today.

A few years ago I stumbled upon the old depot building when I stopped at the Sword property visiting a yard sale they were having. Seeing that old depot building through the trees reminded me – you just never know when history is going to pop up in front of you.

Chapter 31

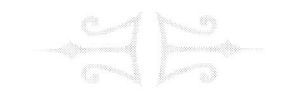

EARLY CITY ORDINANCES AND FINES

Well, television has the Emmys and the world of cinema has the Academy Awards, but one of my favorite awards is the Stellas. Not familiar?

The Stellas are given to people who file frivolous lawsuits. They are named after Stella Liebeck, the woman behind the words "Caution- Hot!" on each and every cup of McDonald's coffee. While I realize Ms. Liebeck, an elderly woman, was burned terribly, and McDonalds had been warned for years via customer complaints their coffee was too hot, there are other Stella award winners that are beyond reasonable and reach the bizarre and brazen category.

One Stella award winner was attacked by a squirrel outside a shopping mall and claimed her injuries could have been prevented if the mall had warned her that squirrels were living outside the mall doors.

Amazing.

I've never actually seen an attack squirrel. I have some that squeal their gibberish and peer over the gutters at me, but attack? Hardly. Perhaps it's the mall variety of squirrel that's the most dangerous.

Another plaintiff who won a Stella award blamed Mazda Motors for her injuries in a car wreck claiming the company failed to provide instructions regarding the safe and proper use of a seatbelt.

Seriously?

Perhaps each vehicle should come with its own private stewardess so we can receive the seatbelt, exit location, and life vest tour every time we venture from our driveway.

I really shouldn't be surprised. There are and have been all sorts of crazy laws throughout history.

Laws are necessary. You simply can't live with a group of humans and not have laws. While laws certainly don't prevent bad things from happening, they can serve as a deterrent and the consequences for breaking laws can eventually protect us from those who can't seem to follow laws.

But, sometimes laws are passed because someone wants to promote something or someone did something stupid. Also, from what I can see it's much more fun for our lawmaking bodies to pass laws than it is for them to repeal them, especially when they have become antiquated.

It's interesting to see what still remains on the books in some jurisdictions.

I've been told when you visit the City of Gainesville, Georgia, you must eat your fried chicken with your hands. Now, if you happen to know that Gainesville considers itself the chicken capital of the world then it makes sense they want to promote eating fried chicken with your hands, but a law? Any tried and true Southerner would know to eat fried chicken with your hands.

At one time in the city of Columbus, Georgia it was against the law to sit on your front porch in an indecent position. First of all, what I might consider indecent you might consider decent.

Second, I'd love to hear the story behind that little law.

It is also rumored the state of Georgia still has at least 75 laws on the books dealing with rice paddies.

Yes, rice paddies.

This dates back to a time when rice was the number one crop before the Civil War along the Savannah, Altamaha and Ogeechee Rivers. Later a hurricane damaged most of the coastal rice fields and they were never replaced, but the laws remain, just in case, I guess.

The City of Douglasville is no different. If you go back through the Douglasville city ordinances during the late 1800s some things stand out.

For example, citizens would be fined if they tied a mule, a horse, or a cow under a tree and left it there for any amount of time.

Since automobiles weren't around then it makes sense that folks would travel to town using animals, and if they had to go into the courthouse or one of the businesses along Broad Street the animals had to be hitched up somewhere, right?

The downtown parking lot didn't exist then, and at the time I write this it doesn't exist either due to construction, but that's another column for another day, so I would guess the appropriate place back then would have been the road outside the buildings. Apparently some folks wanted to tie their animals up underneath the trees around the courthouse or even James Grove. I guess with the animal droppings and the animals grazing on the grass and flowers the ladies had planted in James Grove, it would have become an issue.

Docket's for the Mayor's Court indicate Tom McElreath's horse, Julia Clayton's cow and George Gamble's mule were all found tethered beneath trees within the city limits.

Scandalous! All three were fined one dollar.

On the subject of animal droppings another early town ordinance called for all males between the ages 16 to 45 to work on the city streets for 15 days a year or pay $1.75, if they refused. I would imagine since the roads were dirt back then the road work would have consisted of filling in the constant mud holes.

I happen to know there was a large one at the intersection of Campbellton and Broad Streets. Folks finally named the hole because it couldn't be maintained due to the traffic. They called it Hog Wallow, if I remember correctly.

It would also take a regular crew of folks to keep the animal droppings off the streets. I don't guess folks were given baggies back then to keep the area around their horse or mule neat and tidy.

Some men were exempt from the road crews including men missing an arm or leg. The Mayor was exempt along with the councilmen and licensed ministers.

During the late 1800s men who were missing an arm or a leg were very commonplace as they were more often than not Civil War veterans. I can understand their exemption, but the other exemptions seem a little extreme to me. What about those men who were "filled with the Spirit" and "called to preach the Gospel", but were not licensed?

I guess they had to draw the line somewhere.

Also, why was the mayor and councilmen exempt? It wouldn't have been the first time a politician was known to shovel the…oh, never mind.

Traffic violations during the late 1800s were also recorded in the Mayor's Court dockets, but they didn't involve automobiles. Early research indicates two men were fined one dollar each for riding their mules on Douglasville's sidewalks.

In the early days Sundays in Douglasville were spent resting, visiting, and going to church, however, some early Douglasville citizens had a choice, and used the day to pursue other activities such as shooting craps, playing cards or making a little wager on a game of pool at one of the local saloons.

Bars in Douglasville dated back to 1877 when the first license to sell liquor was issued to G.R.Turner, Douglasville's City Treasurer. Four years later Mr. Turner would obtain a license that allowed him to offer a pool table for his customers to use.

Other saloons followed including one owned by G. G. Stewart. Licenses to serve liquor were $37.50 per year.

There were other entertainments, too.

In June, 1880 G.B. Stewart obtained a license to operate the first ten pin bowling alley.

During this time if city ordinances were broken citizens would appear in Mayor's Court. Most of the court cases involved fighting and failure to pay taxes. Back then taxes ranged from twenty cents to one dollar. Failure to remit your tax meant you might be sentenced to work on the city streets and/or pay a three dollar fine plus court costs, or a week in jail.

Fines for fighting were around one dollar.

Hmmm, I know some people I'd be willing to smack for a dollar fine. How about you?

Fines were also issued within the city limits for cussing (two dollars), for discharging a firearm within the city limits (two dollars or five days), for disturbing a meeting of the medical society (three dollars) and for getting on or off a moving train (one dollar).

Just like today laws were usually passed to solve a problem, so I have to wonder about the story regarding the disturbance at the medical society meeting. I wonder what went on there.

The more I find out about our amazing history, the more questions I have.

Chapter 32

DOUGLASVILLE'S FIRST SCHOOLHOUSE

Did you know that the very month and year Douglas County was birthed in October, 1870, our state legislature passed the Common School Act statewide?

Prior to 1870, the state allocated monies to academies in various counties. The academies were more like higher education institutions since they taught Latin, Greek, English literature and higher forms of mathematics. The students at the academies tended to be members of the wealthier families since tuition might be as much as $10.00 for the year, an exorbitant amount in those days.

Poor rural children rarely entered a classroom.

The Common School Act began to change that, but the change occurred slowly, and other forms of legislation had to be passed before large majorities of Georgia's children were being educated.

As far back as 1818 money from land lotteries was invested in bank stock and interest was used to pay the tuition of indigent children for a period of three years. In order to get the tuition, families had to claim pauper status.

Times were different back then.

Families shied away from a label like that, and many Georgia counties chose not to apply for monies since this early system made no provisions for elementary education. It wasn't until the Common School Act was passed in 1870 that the system began to straighten out, but again progress was slow.

W.A. Candler, President of Emory University, gave a speech in 1889 where he stated, "How far [the common schools] fell short of reaching all the people, may be inferred from the fact that in 1840 when they reached the number of 176, they had an aggregate attendance of only 8,000 pupils, though the children of school age then in the State numbered not less than 85,000."

Yes, there were children across the state not being served, but I'm so pleased to report that as early as our first year of legal existence the children of Douglasville were being served by a common school and the building is still standing today.

The first public school in Douglasville stands at the corner of Chicago Avenue and Strickland Street.

Today the building is a private home.

In 1870, the structure was built by the townspeople and bricks that were made right here in Douglas County covered the exterior of the building. Today the red bricks are covered with stucco and other changes to the structure include additional rooms, a second floor, and a porch.

There was no Board of Education in 1870.

Common schools would be organized in various neighborhoods by the parents. Fannie Mae Davis' history of Douglas County advises, "The parents of a community would acquire a site and construct, often by their own labor, a one-room schoolhouse. Parents routinely performed janitorial duties and maintained the building and grounds. As trustees of the school, they paid the teacher a salary based on a specified fee per child, per household. The 'contract teacher' often lived in the homes of students, spending a week at a time in each household.

The benefits of this system were mutual – the teacher received free room; the host household had a periodic captive after-hours private tutor, and no one family had to carry the economic burden of another mouth to feed.

Mrs. Davis also publishes a handwritten list of school rules from 1870 she found written by Mr. Lambert, a teacher somewhere in Douglas County in 1870. She published the rules just as Mr. Lambert wrote them including spelling and grammatical errors evidencing the fact that teacher education requirements were far different than they are now.

– Rules of the School, 1870 –

No laughing and talking in time of school

No rastling nor scuffing

No tagging or throwing rocks

No climbing trees

No cursing nor swearing

No nicknameing

No using by words

No lyeing in school

No telling tales out of school

No making fun of each other

No playing in the road to and from school

No fiting or quarreling

No student will be allowed to go out more than one time before recess and once after

No one is allowed to go out without my leaf

No play in the house nor on the benches

No playing about the [well?] Illegible

No student will be aloud to leave the play grown at Recreation without my leaf

No disputing about playing

I don't want any student to go inside of any other enclosures in going to an from school without leaf

While educators today formulate their classroom rules and procedures a bit differently, it would seem that at the most basic level children haven't changed that much since 1870. Most teachers today would recognize at least one scenario in their classroom that would fit Mr. Lambert's rules.

Chapter 33

THE ANATOMY OF A PICTURE – THE MCELREATH AND MCLARTY HOUSE

Close your eyes and think about a wagon wheel. Picture it in your mind. Notice the hub in the middle. Let's say the hub of the wheel is our starting point – or a topic I felt needed a bit of research this week.

Notice radiating from the wheel's hub is several spokes – all heading off in various directions.

The wheel is a great visual regarding my history research. I just never know where my focus or hub of research will take me, but one thing is certain, my research usually develops several spokes carrying me off in several different directions all at once, and then I get to decide how to put it all together.

The process is interesting, intriguing, frustrating, and delightful all at the same time.

My most recent research involves a home that used to sit on the east side of Campbellton Street between Broad and Spring Street directly behind today's Precedence building. The home was known as the McElreath House, and it was used as a boarding house.

A city parking lot sits there today

The house was most certainly a boarding house and might have been known as the McElreath house in later years, but the 1880 census indicates the house belonged to John Morris, and two important citizens of Douglasville reported living there in 1880. S.A. or Samuel McElreath and Robert Alexander Massey both reported living in the Morris "hotel".

During the 1870s and 1880s McElreath served as a city councilman. He was a partner with David W. Price in one of Douglasville's first businesses. In 1878, a business license was issued to Price and McElreath Drygoods and Groceries. The next year the business changed its name by adding the words "cotton warehouse" to the title.

The store was located where the Precedence building is today at the corner of Campbellton and Broad. The building is one of the oldest brick buildings in the commercial district, and I commend Greg Peeples and Allen Bearden for making the location a viable part of our downtown business district.

Samuel N. Dorsett was later brought in as a partner with Price and McElreath. Samuel McElreath was also involved with Mr. Dorsett in another business venture involving *The Weekly Star* newspaper.

Sadly Samuel McElreath died in 1886 still a relatively young man of 35. His widow, Sara "Emma" McElreath was given the job of postal attendant by her husband's former hotel-mate, Robert Massey.

My research indicates he had been a good friend of McElreath's. Massey had been appointed as postmaster in 1888 following a scandal involving the position that I'm still researching. Apparently Massey was too busy to oversee all of the duties, so he appointed his friend's widow to the position.

Within the year Emma had a new husband and father for her son, Glen. Yes, you guessed it – she married Robert Massey, and later they had a daughter named Louise. The couple settled on Price Street.

Per the City of Douglasville's well researched brochure titled "Founding Fathers", Robert Massey "was a local lawyer, devout Democrat, and was the first editor of *The Weekly Star*.

Are you beginning to pick up on the fact like I have that almost every mover and shaker in the City of Douglasville at one time or another was connected to *The Weekly Star*?

Robert Massey was also Mayor of Douglasville from 1880-1881 and was a county court judge from 1884-1886.

He was also the son of Robert Jehu Massey who can be found in the Index of this book.

Sadly, Massey passed away in 1890 leaving Emma alone again except she now had two small children.

Poor Emma.

Within five years she had given birth to three children. One had died, and she had had a child with each of two husbands. She also had buried both of the husbands.

I can't even imagine the stress, and apparently Emma couldn't handle it. Joe Baggett's research on file at the Douglas County Public Library indicates Emma became emotionally unbalanced and disappeared in 1891. Baggett states his source was the County Ordinary's minutes.

The Ordinary's minutes also indicate that a member of the McElreath family – John McLarty Morris – was awarded the guardianship of Glen McElreath in 1891 while a member of the Massey family took Judge Massey's daughter, Louise.

Getting back to my original focus – the house in the picture – it was torn down in the 1950s. At one point the property was home to Smith Motors, a used car lot owned by R.L. Smith.

For as long as I remember the space has been an empty gravel lot. Today we see a little more action there since it's the endpoint for the new Plaza East. Last year a *Douglas County Sentinel* article advised, "Plaza East is the final phase in a three-pronged project spanning 20 years and three mayors...The City of Douglasville's downtown area is intended to create a community identity and have a greater livability, mobility, and development alternatives, such as mixed use and walkability...When the plaza is complete, there will be connectivity to the main plaza [O'Neal Plaza] and Plaza West...." [per City Planning Director Michelle Wright.]

While people come and go and while progress marches on as it should, just remember, a gravel lot is never JUST a gravel lot, just as a picture is never JUST a picture.

Chapter 34

TAKING A MINUTE FOR THE MASONS

I hope you are having a great Labor Day so far. Today we tend to think of the day as summer's last hurrah with one more trip to the beach, barbeques, and parades, but there's more to it.

Early citizens of Douglasville would have known about the meaning behind Labor Day since it became a federal holiday in 1894, but it would be a few years before labor unrest touched Douglas County. The passage of legislation creating the official holiday was a political overture by President Grover Cleveland's administration. They were responding to public outcry after the U.S. military and U.S. marshall's fired upon workers during the Pullman Strike killing thirteen and wounding fifty-seven. The legislation creating Labor Day passed unanimously to reconcile the government and labor.

As I put this column together there is talk that the 48th annual Labor Day parade sponsored by the Sweetwater Shrine Club might be rained out. I know we need the rain, but it would be the first time the Shriners would fail to lead the parade down Broad Street since 1958.

Even if tropical storm Lee literally rains on our parade, the barbeque sponsored by Douglasville Masonic Lodge No. 289 will still go on at the

Hunter Park Community Center on Gurley Road. You can get a plate of Hudson's barbeque and all the trimmings for $7 from 11 a.m. – 6 p.m. The purpose of the event is to raise money for local charities. There will also be funnel cakes, snow cones and other kid friendly things including pony rides.

The involvement of Douglasville's Shrine and Mason groups for Labor Day festivities got me to thinking about their place in our history. One of the first questions I put to rest for myself happened to be the relationship between the two groups. They are two distinct groups, but Shriners have to be Master Masons in good standing before applying for membership.

Douglasville Lodge No. 289 F. & A.M. was granted a charter by the Grand Lodge of Georgia on October 30, 1873. If we go back as far as possible the Masons' original lodge was located on a 12 x 50 foot lot on Broad Street owned by E.H. Camp. In the 1880s, J.A. Pittman erected a 2-story building, and sold the upper story to the lodge, together with the stairway. Fannie Mae Davis's history isn't very clear if the Camp and Pittman properties were one and the same.

If you stand along Broad Street at the Campbellton intersection the building Mr. Pittman built is the third building towards the west from the corner.

At some point the first floor of the building was occupied by Thomas A. Duke Drug Company. Later Dorsett Drug Company was there and was owned by Dr. T. R. Whitley, a prominent doctor and surgeon in Douglasville.

The Sanborn Fire Insurance maps bear this out since the map for Broad Street for 1895 indicates a 2-story wooden structure on the lot, and by 1900, the revised map shows the building had been improved with brick as it is now. At some point the Douglasville Café was located there, and during the late 1940s the building burned. I have been told when the building was rebuilt the second floor was not replaced. I've also been advised this particular building was the location of Sim's Five and Dime during the 1960s owned by Jesse and Lamar Smith. One of the unique factors regarding Sim's was they had toy bins rather than packaging their items.

In 1909, Dr. James R. McKoy and R.E. James erected a new building at the corner of Price and Church Streets. Today, you would recognize the building as the one behind the Irish Bred Pub, and it is the building owned by Dr. Clark Robinson. When it was first built the Masons used the top floor as their meeting place, and the post office was located on the first level. The Sanborn map for 1911 lists the location as a lodge Hall, grocery and post office.

In her book, Fannie Mae Davis indicates, "In moving their furniture and regalia to the new place, Mr. Hiram Gurley, the [Tyler] of the lodge, drove a real goat (representing the legendary goat which the lodge was reported to have in those days) up the main street and around the corner to the new location."

I guess it could be argued the move could actually be the first sponsored Mason parade up Broad Street.

Can you imagine the spectacle of the goat being driven by Mr. Gurley moving up Broad Street and turning the corner at Price where O'Neal Plaza is today?

If you take a quick Internet search regarding goats and Mason history you find all sorts of speculation and myths mixed in with facts here and there. Eventually, the goat reference morphed from a malicious attack to something humorous. Many Mason groups embraced the humor hence the reason for Douglasville's Masons using a goat publically in their move.

Fannie Mae Davis also advises, "The [Tyler] of the lodge was a combination of doorman and custodian of the hall and, this same Mr. Gurley had a cow's horn which he blew like a bugle out through a window, about a half hour before each meeting to remind lodge members it was lodge night since half of the members lived within hearing distance."

It seems to me the Tyler of the lodge had the most interesting and fun-filled responsibility in those days. I guess today's members are reminded about meetings through text messages and e-mails though I'd enjoy hearing that horn!

Back in February I took a Sunday walk around the downtown commercial district taking pictures here and here. I zeroed in on O'Neal Plaza and the old lodge building. When you walk around it you can't help but notice the interesting brick work and of course, the Masonic imagery stands out as well.

The next time you are walking through O'Neal Plaza, notice the three links presented underneath the Mason symbol. The three links are not Mason symbols at all. The three links identify another fraternal service organization referred to as the Oddfellows, a separate organization. Some sources explain their name comes from the fact that ordinary folks could join where the Masons tended to be more professional in membership during the turn of the century. Fannie Mae Davis refers to the Oddfellows in her book briefly here and there and advises Joseph S. James was a member, and he certainly was no ordinary citizen.

The Oddfellows are still a viable fraternal service organization in the United States, but as far as I'm aware they are no longer active in Douglasville. I have to assume since their symbol is also on the building they also used it as a meeting location, but I have not verified the fact yet. The third symbol is also a mystery to me. I thought it might be the symbol of the Order of the Eastern Star, but it doesn't match up. At some point in my research I reach brick walls, but I'm always willing to climb over them and gather more information.

Later during the 1940s, Hoke Bearden and Dave Gurley operated a grocery store from the lower floor. Doctor Ralph Hamilton, a medical doctor, and Dr. R.B.Turk, a dentist had offices there as well at some point. When I first moved to Douglasville in the late 1980s, I remember a shoe repair shop in one of the stores along the O'Neal Plaza side.

Today, the Masons own a building located at 8519 Bowden Street on a lot purchased from F.M. Winn and continue to make productive contributions to our society here in Douglasville.

Chapter 35

CSI – DOUGLASVILLE, 1875

It was early morning on Sunday, November 7, 1875 when the body was discovered. It was found lying in the middle of a road one mile outside of Douglasville. Cries rang out and soon a crowd had gathered.

The body was that of a man. Later the scene would be described in the Atlanta papers as "ghastly" with the man "lying on his back, his clothes nearly all burned off down to his waist."

He had obviously been shot, and there were no signs of a struggle. The dead man was identified by those in the crowd as James Seals.

County officials were summoned, and Dr. C.C. Garrett was authorized to conduct an autopsy. Dr. Garrett (1850-1913) was a recent graduate of the Atlanta Medical College and had set his practice up in Salt Springs/Lithia Springs. He would eventually serve on the Douglas County School Board and also served as the first resident physician of the Sweetwater Park Hotel, but all of that would come later.

Dr. Garrett visited the scene and upon examining the body determined the ball had entered the chest in the direction of the heart. He ordered the body to be taken to the courthouse for the autopsy.

His goal was to find the ball and remove it from the body.

Once at the courthouse, Dr. Garrett opened the thorax and began to trace the direction of the ball. "He found that it had passed through the apex of the heart, entering the bowels through the diaphragm, and passing through the left lobe of the liver in the direction of the right kidney."

At that point it was a late hour, and the autopsy was suspended. Everyone agreed that it was unnecessary to proceed any further because the possible perpetrators had been identified, so the ball remained in the body.

James Clinton had been seen with James Seals leaving town just the evening before. Within hours two other names surfaced as possible accomplices – George W. Stewart and James F. Sisk.

Within five days of the murder James Clinton was arrested. The authorities felt they had a strong case, and predicted that Clinton would turn state's evidence against his two alleged accomplices.

Things weren't such a slam dunk, however, because the men told conflicting stories and pointed their fingers at each other.

Confronted with the conflicting stories, the authorities called Dr. Garrett back into the investigation for more sleuthing.

At this point Seals' body had to be exhumed because Dr. Garrett was set upon finding the ball from the murder weapon. Within just a few minutes the ball was located in the spine just above the right kidney.

Bullet/ball molds were made from the gun belonging to James Clinton.

You guessed it!

Not only did the ball found in the body match Clinton's gun, it also matched the remaining balls that were still in the gun.

Yes, Clinton was found guilty and sentenced to life in prison. James F. Sisk was acquitted, but the matter involving George Stewart drug on for a couple of years with his guilty verdict being appealed.

March forward in time to March 28, 1877 when an affidavit was submitted on behalf of George Stewart from someone named John Strickland who swore that on the night of the murder he was at the home of James Clinton all night. He swore that at some point Clinton got his pistol, left the house, and didn't return until at least one a.m.

I find it fascinating that in 1875 Dr. Garret was able to determine the ball that killed Seals came from Clinton's gun. I also find it a little frustrating that Mr. Strickland didn't come forward during the original trial, and – what was the motivation behind the murder of James Seals anyway?

Just some of those things that make you stop and say, "Hmmm…"

Chapter 36

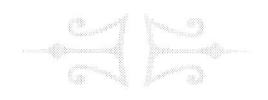

WELCOME TO THE FAMILY FEUD OR THE SAD TALE OF WILLIAM NOTTINGHAM

Humans attract each other, and that attraction leads to interaction. While the interaction can lead to wonderful things such as business ventures, marriages, and other various collaborations there can be a negative side.

Humans being humans we have a certain amount of vanity and pride with some of us having a smidge more than others. Sometimes we won't admit we are wrong, and we won't take any sort of responsibility for our actions.

Feuds usually begin over something very simple but often escalate to insults, violence, and even murder. Full scale wars have been fought over family feuds including Britain's the Wars of the Roses.

Feuds were so common during earlier times societies often instituted rules and laws to help settle them. The process of dueling actually came about to settle disputes. In 1804, Aaron Burr and Alexander Hamilton had different opinions regarding the direction our nation should take. Their differences developed into personal attacks and ongoing bitterness, and eventually led to a duel with Hamilton dying. Aaron Burr is mainly remembered as the man who killed Hamilton even though historians consider him to be a Founding Father, a New York state representative, a New York district attorney, a U.S. Senator and Vice President under Thomas Jefferson.

A larger feud in our history involved the settlement of the American West. During the 1880s The Pleasant Valley War was fought in Arizona between sheep herders and cattle ranchers over grazing land and property boundaries. The Tewksbury family had a large sheep ranch while the Grahams on the adjoining property had cattle. Their boundary dispute resulted in over 20 deaths and led to them employing mercenaries to do much of the dirty work including Tom Horn. By the end of the feud the Tewksbury family was extinct and only one member of the Graham family was left.

The most infamous feud in American History has to be the Hatfield-McCoy Feud between the wealthy pro-Confederate Hatfield family and the working class pro-Union McCoys. While the war certainly gave the two families something to squabble about the feud really picked up in 1878 when there was a disagreement over a pig.

Yes, a pig led to an all-out war including murder, beatings and kidnappings. Later on there was a Romeo and Juliet plot twist when Roseanna McCoy had an affair with one of the Hatfield boys. This led to more murders on both sides even though the relationship between the lovers was short-lived.

The feud finally reached its pinnacle in 1888 during what is remembered as the New Year's Night Massacre. The Hatfield faction attacked a McCoy cabin at night killing the children, beating the mother and burning the house down. The governors of both West Virginia and Kentucky called out the militia to contain the situation and several folks were prosecuted and received life sentences. By 1891, the families ended the feud with a truce, and today both sides actually attend reunions together.

Douglasville residents have also been known to have disagreements.
I mean, they ARE human, right?

One particular disagreement occurred early on in Douglas County history – eleven years after the birth of the county to be exact in 1881. The feud involved a family-neighbor fuss that had been going on for two years over a fence-line that resulted in each side chalking up one death and one injury.

Just like the Hatfield-McCoy feud a pig was also involved.

In 1881, the families of William H. Mitchell and James F. Cook lived along Burnt Hickory Road. There had been an ongoing property dispute that had been going on for ten to fifteen years. To further confuse the matter Mitchell's place was in Douglas County at that time while Cook was over the line in Paulding according to news accounts.

As ill will increased each man had his own separate fence, and it is said that Cook would shoot Mitchell's chickens when they strayed over the fence, and he would toss them back into Mitchell's field.

Neighbors tried to make peace between the two men, but without success.

Things escalated during the third week of September, 1881 when Mitchell's hogs managed to get into Cook's field, not once but twice.

Mitchell along with his son and William Nottingham tried to round up the hogs. Nottingham was from Macon and had only been in Douglas County for six weeks.

Cook, along with step-son, Joe Mahaffy let their dogs loose to chase the hog.

At some point Cook and Mahaffy met up with the Mitchell party in some nearby woods.

The men continued to quarrel. Cook was carrying a shotgun. He told Mahaffy to knock the younger Mitchell down. Nottingham advanced to step between Mahaffy and the younger Mitchell. Cook said later that Nottingham had his hand in his pocket; Cook ordered Nottingham to stop and then raised his gun and fired. Nottingham was hit dead center in his chest.

Without a word, Nottingham dropped. He died without a groan or a struggle. As Cook fired at Nottingham, Mitchell sprang on Cook, and Mitchell, Jr. drew a knife and stabbed Cook in the back twice.

When Cook dropped his gun, step-son Mahaffy picked it up and dealt Mitchell, Jr. a blow which caused him to relinquish his hold on the knife which remained in Cook's back.

Mahaffy then dealt the elder Mitchell a blow across the left temple, fracturing the skull with the butt of the gun.

At this point Cook, his small son who had joined them and Mahaffy started home. When they had gone about 200 yards Cook's small son discovered Mitchell's knife still sticking in Cook's back and drew it out.

Dr. Fred Cotton of Powder Springs and Dr. W.H. Poole of Douglasville gave medical care to those who required it, but Mitchell, Sr. died from his skull fracture a few days later.

William Nottingham was buried in Pleasant Hill Cemetery, but soon his brother, Warren D. Nottingham, a prominent attorney and judge in Houston County, arrived with a coffin to fetch his brother home to Macon.

It seems that the Nottingham brothers came from a very prominent Macon family. Their father, Curtis Bell Nottingham was a respected doctor known for having been a founder of the Georgia Board of Health.

As I state above William Nottingham had made his way to Douglas County six weeks prior to the fight. He came to teach school near the Mitchell property. In fact, the very day he died he was to sign the contract that would begin his new career. He was only 22 years of age, and died "in a difficulty not of his own seeking and with the merits of which he had nothing to do…"

Judge Nottingham swore a warrant out for Cook and an inquest was held. The grand jury here in Douglas County returned a decision in favor of Cook stating his actions were in self-defense, and apparently and so sadly – the feud was at an end.

Chapter 37

WILSON STEVERSON – GAME-CHANGER

Wilson Steverson was born in 1838 on the Stephenson plantation in Coweta County. Wilson was one of fourteen children raised by Archie and Harriet.

I can't even imagine trying to cover all the bases with raising fourteen children, but of course, Archie and Harriet didn't experience many of the things I had going on as parent. They didn't have any school activities, traffic, dinners out, money worries, etc.

All they had to worry about was keeping their master satisfied.

I'm being sarcastic because Archie and Harriet were slaves. They belonged to Moore Stephenson who owned the plantation.

Yes, Archie, Harriett and their children belonged to Moore Stephenson. Of course this means they were property. Think about the furniture you own, the dishes, the car, books, clothes – all of that is property, right? Archie and Harriet were on the same level of thought as your computer or the rug on your floor.

I can't even fathom that line of thinking.

At some point in my research I ran across an image showing the inventory journal Moore Stephenson had made in his own hand regarding property he owned. You can see nine year old Wilson is listed with the worth being $300.00.

I think you can buy some brands and sizes of flat screen televisions for $300 today, can't you?

Moore Stephenson had owned Archie and Harriet for many years. Archie had helped his master clear his land when it had been nothing but a frontier full of rattlesnakes and an Indian here and there according to family lore. There is also a family story that tells how the master saved Archie's life when a panther was close by and ready to attack.

I'm certain that there was some degree of feeling on both sides, but when everything was boiled down to the cold hard facts, Archie didn't really have a choice in helping Moore clear his property and Moore certainly didn't want to lose his property to a panther.

The master's family along with his slaves was thrown into a tailspin when Moore Stephenson died in 1849. The slaves along with all of the property were divided into equal lots for the survivors. The estate handlers worked meticulously to make sure each lot was equal monetarily, a dollar amount around $1600.00. Slaves were listed along with horses, mules, chickens and oxen.

Archie went to Linnah, Moore's wife, but later on Linnah Stephenson fell on hard times, and Archie was sold to a man named Brewster. Archie was fortunate in that he saw his wife and a few of his children on the weekends, and there was always a little time with them at Christmas. Most slaves who were separated from their wives, parents and children never saw them again.

While the manner of dividing Moore Stephenson's property seemed fair to his heirs, the process of dividing the estate had a huge effect on Archie and Harriet's family.

With the flick of a pen Archie and Harriet went to different owners and their children were divided as well. Wilson and his brother were given to Emily Stephenson, the master's daughter. At the time she was eleven.

Per the *African American Encyclopedia of History* edited by Paul Finkelman…"While some family members were merely hired out or rented, others were sold, mortgaged attached to satisfy debt or transferred to Texas with the expansion of the Cotton Kingdom."

A few years ago when I was still in the classroom students would invariably puff up and tell me that IF they had been living during slave times they would have run away, they would have revolted, they would not have put up with slavery at all, but it just wasn't that simple.

In an article from *The Herald*, Roland Barksdale-Hall who happens to be a great- grandson of Wilson Steverson says, "Wilson and his family never considered running away as an option. Because of strong family ties, a runaway slave feared retribution from his family as well as from his master….Slaves wanted to be free, but with their whole family."

So, life continued for Wilson and his new owner Emily Stephenson. A few years later when she married George R. Fambrough, Wilson followed his new master to the front during the Civil War in the capacity of a body servant.

With the passage of the 13th, 14th and 15th amendments Wilson and his family were finally free, and while they certainly celebrated that fact we need to remember that freedom in 1865, and at least the next hundred years, wasn't freedom as you and I would describe it. As soon as the 13th amendment was passed southern states passed Black Codes which basically kept former slaves under constant scrutiny of the white community.

As the family reunited Archie changed his surname from Brewster to Stephenson to reflect homage of sorts to their former master, and they encouraged their children to do the same. Most did. However, somehow Wilson went with the "Steverson" spelling.

After emancipation Wilson worked as a farmhand, logger and peddler in Coweta County. He saved 50 cents of every dollar he made to purchase 80 acres in 1885. The total cost was $600.

The land he chose lay along the Georgia Pacific railroad in Salt Springs/Lithia Springs.

Yes, I'm sure you were beginning to wonder where the Douglas County tie-in was going to come in.

The property had a two-story house and six 3-4 room cabins on it he could rent out or use to provide homes for family members who needed it. *The Encyclopedia of African American History* states, "The spacious grounds of Wilson Steverson's farm reflected a high standard of living with respect to the black family in the late 19th century." While it wasn't unusual for black men to own land at the time Wilson was certainly in the minority of his race, and according to Barksdale-Hall, Wilson had to keep an independent relationship going with certain whites in order to keep the Ku Klux Klan from forcing him off his land. It was also helpful that Wilson Steverson was a mulatto having bi-racial ancestors.

Wilson and his wife Rilla raised nine children in Douglas County, three of which would become educators. Over the years Wilson planted cotton crop after cotton crop, a very successful money maker for Douglas County farmers white and black alike for many years following Reconstruction.

Economically, things began to change in the 1920s.

While most of the country experienced a boom in the market place the price of cotton began to fall in Georgia. Boll weevils had arrived in the state around 1915, but by the mid-twenties farmers were feeling the full effects of ravaged fields.

Faced with menial jobs here in the south as the only alternative, Wilson sold his land and along with his daughter Mary and son-in-law Joseph he moved to Pennsylvania.

At the age of 80 Wilson became part of what we history types designate as the Great Migration, a period of time from 1916 to 1930 where over one million blacks left the South for better economic opportunities in the North.

Per his great grandson Wilson also left Georgia to experience real freedom, "He knew how to play the game, but he was tired of it."

Wilson worked for the Erie Paper Mill and American Sheet and Tin Plate Company in Farrell. He also served as the caretaker for the Church of God campgrounds while Joseph and Mary also had a stand at the Farrell Curb Market where they sold butter, fruit and port.

By 1921, Wilson's son Etainia and his wife and children moved to Farrell and suddenly there were three generations living in a three bedroom house, but isn't that what family does when they need to?

Etania had been a sharecropper and cotton picker here in Georgia. He got a job in the Farrell works of Carnegie Steel.

While Wilson and his children did find more economic opportunities in Pennsylvania, it wasn't all a bed of roses. The house they lived in which was owned by the steel company was in poor shape. The bathrooms on the upper floors leaked and urine often dripped down the walls. Blacks were given the lowest paid jobs at the steel mill and other places even when they had high school diplomas while their white counterparts had not finished school.

Before his death in 1948, Wilson Steverson was honored as one of fifteen centenarians in the state of Pennsylvania, at the time he was 109. Of the fifteen people honored he was the only one who had been born a slave.

Terry Harper, one of Douglas County's famous sons is the great-great grandson of Wilson Steverson!

Chapter 38

A FEW SNIPPETS FROM THE 1880S

Over the last few months I've periodically buried myself in newspaper research – mainly with *The Atlanta Constitution* – to see what was said about Douglas County and Douglasville during our earliest days.

We are mentioned fairly frequently, and it's fair to say by reading these snippets we can get a good picture of what our own paper at the time – *The Weekly Star* – was publishing since the text of their articles is what was published in the Atlanta paper.

Here are a few entries in chronological order printed in italics along with my reactions and explanations.

September 10, 1882 – The first new bale of cotton was sold [in Douglasville] today at auction by Dr. G.W. McLatry and was bought by Mr. M.B. Watson, one of the first merchants of the place. It will be shipped to J.M. Watson, Atlanta, and sold at Cumming's exchange next Wednesday at two o'clock as the First Bale of Douglas County for 1882, and the first new bale for the year shipped over the Georgia Pacific Railroad.

I've recorded the above entry from the paper just as it appeared, but I'm fairly certain the name "McLatry" was a misprint. It might be "McLarty"…and there was a George Wilson McLarty, but I'm unsure if he was a doctor. M.B. Watson would be Mathias Bates Watson. He was born in 1855 and married Lillie J. Vansant Watson. Her father was Young Vansant, the man who donated the land that would become Douglasville. Sadly, Lillie would be dead one year after her marriage.

Once the railroad was operational Douglas County cotton would be loaded on the train and sent to Atlanta for auction. "Cumming's" mentioned in the above article was J.F. Cummings & Company located at 37 Broad Street in Atlanta. The company dealt in cotton, grain and meat futures.

Along with several others J.F. Cummings was one of the incorporators for the International Cotton Exposition. It was similar to a world's fair and was held in Atlanta from October through December, 1881.

December 6, 1883 – From an article titled "Newspaper Change"…. *Dorsett & McElreath have disposed of the "Star", to W.A. Breckenridge, who will continue its publication. Mr. Breckenridge, is the proprietor of the "Fairburn News – Letter" and the "Dallas News Era", which with the "Star", makes him proprietor of three of the best weeklies in west Georgia.*

Dorsett & McElreath would be Samuel N. Dorsett and Samuel A. McElreath. Unfortunately, I've not been able to find out more about W.A. Breckenridge, yet, but it is interesting that ownership of the paper ended up in hands outside of Douglasville, though I'm sure the editors continued to be local citizens.

June 15, 1884 – From an article titled "Newspoints from Douglasville"...*Tom Edwards showed a blue sparrow [in Douglasville] this morning that he had caught. Dr. T. R. Whitley, who has lived in Atlanta the past five years, has moved [to Douglasville] to practice his profession. Mr. T. J. Smith, of Gadsden, Alabama, passed here today in pursuit of Joe Blalock, who had stolen his horse. W.J. Camp, of this county, has a field of cotton that will average two feet high.*

Catching a bird, the height of cotton, and a move from Atlanta to Douglasville seem like rather mundane news to us today, but the pursuit of a horse thief is rather interesting. Note that Mr. Smith is pursuing the thief himself. There is no mention of the police.

Those were the days, huh?

Once he moved to Douglasville, Dr. T.R. Whitley was very involved with various things including the establishment of Douglasville College which was located approximately where the Armory is located on Church Street today.

October 1, 1884...*The crop outlook in Douglas County is above average. The small grain crop is good, while there is an abundant yield of corn. The indications are that, while the cotton crop is late it will be much better than was anticipated...With a population of one thousand inhabitants [Douglasvlle] has about thirty stores, the proprietors of which [have] a thriving business. All of the merchants are classified as gilt-edged.*

Within the past year many improvements have been made. Notably among them being the three ...brick store houses by S.A. McElreath and Brother, J.M. and M.B. Watson and Selman, Smith & Co.

The cotton receipts of the past year were 5000 bales and this year they will probably reach 7500 bales.

There has been much immigration to this county of the smaller farmers from the "stock law" counties.

The taxable value of the property in the county has increased over two hundred thousand dollars as shown by the tax books during the past year.

In Douglasville there is no ad valorem tax and there is no source to ascertain the increase of the town. The entire revenue of the town is derived from the licenses exacted from bar-rooms. This is placed at such a high figure that it runs the entire expense of the municipal authorities. They now have under advisement and it will soon be a certainty, of establishing a complete system of water works that will furnish water for the whole town.

Douglas is a new county and has many resources that the completion of the Georgia Pacific will develop.

The most interesting part of the above article that jumped out at me was this particular sentence, "The entire revenue of the town is derived from the licenses exacted from bar-rooms."

Seriously!?!

What an interesting bit of history!

In the early days the city of Douglasville was funded almost exclusively by liquor licenses.

You might also be wondering what was mean by a "stock law county". Basically, it has something to do with fences and folks who might allow their cattle and other livestock to roam freely. A section of the law provided that land owners could keep any livestock that might wander onto their land if you were in a "stock law district". Apparently Douglas County was NOT a stock law county in 1884.

December 5, 1884 – *In Douglas County, West Summerlin is charged with the offense of committing an assault with intent to murder on the person of Tom Williams. Both are Negroes. Summerlin only has one arm. Yet the evidence shows that he made Williams "tote the fast mail."*

I've done some checking but have been unable to discover what "tote the fast mail" might mean, but considering Williams was assaulted Summerlin must have had the "upper hand" even if he only had one. He most certainly had the matter "in hand".

April 15, 1885 – *Real estate is being rapidly improved in [Douglasville], and is held at good prices. The population is being increased at the rate of about four per week – with new babies. The farmers are staying severely at home, planting, hence trade is dull. The merchants, however, say they had rather see them preparing for the fall payments than loafing around town now.*

In October, 1884, the population hovered at one thousand, and six months later four babies a week are being born.

Well, it would be easy to surmise what the folks were doing in their free time, right? They were most certainly planting seeds...of various kinds.

October 3, 1885 – *Douglasville with a population of one thousand has but one foreigner and two citizens born above the Mason and Dixon line. All are lawyers, merchants and physicians and were raised in this and the adjoining counties. We have an emphatically Georgia town.*

Oh my! Two Yankees...I think my research has identified them, but that's a story for another time, but seriously...a foreigner? I will keep my eye out for an identity.

April 18, 1886 – From an article titled "Improvements in Douglasville"....*The spring improvements have begun. A.W. McLarty has let out contract for the erection of two fine brick two-storied stores, while S.N. Dorsett will match them with one similar to them. This will give Douglasville a block of fine brick stores. Besides these there are five new dwelling houses in process of erection.*

Samuel N. Dorsett was one of Douglasville's first merchants and was a co-owner of Dorsett, Price and McElreath. He also co-owned *The Weekly Star* before it sold, was the city's second postmaster and was on the City Council in 1889. We also need to add Superior Court Clerk, County Treasurer, and he served on the committee to secure a bank.

February 10, 1887 – From an article titled "Douglasville's New Council"....*The new municipal officers were installed last night. J.C. Wright was elected mayor pro tem, S.M. Cash, marshall; W.T. Roberts, city attorney, and W.M. McElreath, treasurer.*

Messers. E.H. Camp, J.J. Haynes, A.R. Bomar and W.J. Camp are attending the state agricultural convention at Americus. There are two flourishing agricultural clubs in [Douglas County].

September 28, 1887...Can you imagine checking into an Atlanta hotel and it making the paper? Well, apparently in the 1880s *The Atlanta*

Constitution regularly published the names of people who were in town and staying at the local hotels. A blurb from the above date indicates S.N. Dorsett was staying at The Markham. Apparently Markham House was a very nice hotel in the 1880s located close to Atlanta's Union Station. The hotel had 107 rooms and central heat. The building was lost in a fire in 1896.

August 10, 1889…The headline read "Farmers Alliance Day"….*Today is a great one at Piedmont Chautauqua…The Piedmont Chautauqua held in Lithia Springs was in full swing.* The article goes on to advise the 8 p.m. address for that day would be given by Colonel J.G. Camp on "Woman and Her Influence". Mr. Camp is one of the most gifted orators in Georgia.

Joseph G. Camp was known as the orator of the south.

This advertisement states, "His splendid graceful periods are interspersed with enough humor to prevent a surfeit of beauty." Maybe so, but somehow I think Mr. Camp and I would have differing opinions on the subject of women and their influence.

Chapter 39

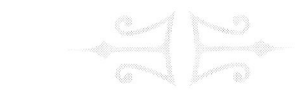

FED HUDSON AND THE MIDWAY SCHOOL

Every July my father's family gets together for a family reunion. At some point during the gathering I always take a moment and scan the room full of folks from Canton, Cartersville, Waleska, Atlanta and from as far away as Texas to realize that we all came from two particular people – my great grandparents, James William Johnson Land and Amanda Emaline Allred Land.

My family isn't alone. Many families across the nation get together for reunions including the Hudson family who meet in Villa Rica every year on the last Saturday in July. Like me, members of the Hudson family look back to one man and woman. In their case they trace their lineage to Fed and Amanda Hudson.

Fed Hudson's grave along with his wife's is located in a very small family plot located near the intersection of Liberty and Cole Roads in western Douglas County. The Douglas County Cemetery Commission has the family plot listed as Hudson-Dobbs Cemetery.

Most of the graves are unmarked, but Fed and Amanda's graves have a six foot marker with the words "gone but not forgotten".

While the Hudson family hasn't forgotten him, Fed Hudson has been lost in the Douglas County story and his contribution has only been known to a few.

Fed was born in 1839 according to the marker on his grave, but of course, it's hard to know for sure since records weren't always maintained where slaves were concerned.

Charles Hudson, Fed and Amanda's great-grandson indicates family research has led him to a ship leaving Sierra Leone in 1767 with 65 slaves. The ship was classified as a sloop named *Dove,* and the master of the ship was Harrison Hudson.

It may just be a wild coincidence that the captain of the slave ship was Hudson, but then again he could have been related to the man who owned at least one of Fed Hudson's great-grandparents.

Records reflect 51 slaves actually reached Savannah. It was very common for slaves to die along the harsh journey across the ocean since conditions were brutal.

The Hudson family believes one of Fed's grandparents was on that ship because the manifest lists the location of the slaves or their tribal names. Notations such as FEDr, FEDeyoh, LahFEDay, FEDay, etc. were made.

Of course, this could be a reason why Fed had such an unusual name, but again this is pure speculation.

It does seem plausible, right?

There has been no confirmation regarding the man who owned Fed, but due to census information from the year 1880, we do know Fed indicated he was born in 1839. Fed also indicated he was a mulatto. There is speculation that his mother was a slave and his father was his master, but to date there is no proof.

In 1864, Fed was freed along with millions of slaves across the south due to the Emancipation Proclamation followed by the 13th Amendment. The Hudson family believes upon receiving his freedom Fed was given $100 and 100 acres in the Bowdon area for him to make his own way, and it appears that he was successful!

By 1869, Fed Hudson decided the Bowdon area needed a school for blacks. He built what would become known as Fed Hudson High School on his property using his own timber.

In 1879, courthouse records indicate he paid taxes on 178 acres. By 1880, the land where the school sat was donated to the Carroll County School System and the "high school" became an elementary school by the same name in 1942.

A past West Georgia newsletter titled *The Journey* discussed the elementary school in Bowdon. It says:

> *Hudson [Elementary] was named in honor of a former slave, Mr. Fed Hudson, who organized Bowden's first school for African Americans in 1880 and donated the land for it. Mr. Hudson's original school was located on Highway 100 adjacent to New Hope Methodist Church.*
>
> *At some point between 1880 and 1900 Fed and Amanda Hudson moved to Villa Rica. Fed bought 101 acres in 1908 for $1,000, another 101 acres in 1910 for $1,000 and in 1912 he paid $500 more for the remainder of In the vicinity of Liberty and Cole Roads.*
>
> *Deed records at the courthouse indicate three acres of the total were excluded which means a school and/or church building might have always been school might have already been there.*

Last year the cemetery commission uncovered the foundation and bricks from the chimney for Midway School.

I want to thank the Cemetery Commission led by Sandy Whittington for their work at preserving and documenting the many family cemeteries around the county including the Hudson-Dobbs cemetery and the foundations for the Midway School. I also wish to thank Charles Hudson who was so kind to meet with Elaine Steere, a local genealogist, who is working with me to find out more about Fed Hudson.

The hunt for information will continue.

Chapter 40

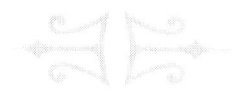

WHEN EAGLES WON'T FLY

Have you ever noticed how some people are like eagles? They seem to always make the right choices while others – the buzzards – tend to stumble from one poor choice to another. I tend to think the lines are a little more blurred between the two for most people, but for some reason the eagles tend to climb up on those pedestals we provide for them in our humanity, and we allow them to stay there.

Marion Barnett was one of those people who those acquainted with him thought him to be totally forthright and honest. He seemed to succeed at everything he attempted. James A. Watson, who would eventually manage the Sweetwater Park Hotel in Lithia Springs, hired Barnett to work at his dry goods store in Atlanta. Watson was so impressed with Barnett he made him a manager and later a full partner.

Of course, it's the people who seem to connect all the dots in their life so seamlessly who are the ones who might bear the most observation. Eventually, they misstep in some way, and Barnett is no different.

Barnett loaned a friend named Eubanks three or four dollars in half dollar coins. Eubanks used the money and was soon arrested for passing counterfeit coins. This in turn let to Barnett being arrested.

When the police searched Barnett's room they found several counterfeiting tools along with other items that pointed to his guilt.

Barnett, of course never confessed and told the authorities the items were left behind by a friend named Williams, but this Williams could not be located.

Of course there's a twist, right?

I wouldn't waste your time on a story at least one hundred and twenty years old if there wasn't.

It seems a farmer in Douglasville found a letter supposedly written by the elusive Williams that explained a plot had been hatched by the real counterfeiters blaming Barnett. The authorities never took the letter seriously. Barnett was found guilty and sentenced to four years.

End of story right?

No, there are some interesting coincidences that I think bear examination.

It seems that at some point in 1893 a few months before Barnett was arrested, the authorities in and around Douglasville knew some counterfeit coins were being used at local businesses. The coins had a flaw in the eagle that made them easy to detect as counterfeits.

Also, a group of four men from Douglasville – Bud Pilgrim, Ed Miles, James Jones, and Robert Hornebuckle – had traveled to Atlanta on Friday, November 24th to live the good life in the Gate City, as Atlanta was referred to in those days. Apparently, the money flowed as freely as the spirituous liquor. Saloons and other businesses in Atlanta weren't alert to the counterfeit coins being passed in the Douglasville area, but it seems once the men got to Austell on the way home they decided to have a meal. Once again those counterfeit coins flowed freely. Later the Austell merchant caught the coins as counterfeit and traced them back to the group of men.

Once again fingers were pointed at others. James Jones advised Bud Pilgrim was the ringleader along with his sons. Police questioned Pilgrim's wife, and eventually she took them to the yard and pointed to a freshly dug area at the base of an apple tree. Police recovered a bag of counterfeit coins along with molds. Pilgrim's wife declared Jones had placed the evidence at the base of the tree.

Overall ten to twelve men were involved with the counterfeiting. Most were eventually given prison sentences and fines of some sort. In an article titled "The Douglas County Mint" from the magazine *Looking Good Douglas County* from the late 1980s, historian and author John Bailey explores the Douglasville side of the story stating that it appeared many folks in the area of the county where these men lived knew what was going on or was involved in some way. Some of the neighborhood children were even wearing some of the coins around their necks.

The Atlanta papers never made a connection between Barnett's conviction with the group of men from Douglasville, but it would just seem to me that it was all part of the same story.

Moral of the story: Every eagle has a flaw.

Chapter 41

PUZZLE PIECES FROM THE NEWS ARCHIVES

When I'm asked about what I do I often use the puzzle analogy. I put together puzzles. Not the 1,000 piece jigsaw puzzles you find at Walmart, but puzzle pieces involving history.

The puzzles I put together involve missing pieces, torn pieces, sometimes pieces that are a little ragged, but all are important and all of them have their place in the story somewhere.

Today, I want to share some of my stray pieces of history. I'm not sure where they go. I hang on to them hoping that eventually I'll find the right place to fit them into the Douglas County story.

The resources I use in my research involve family histories, published scholarly articles, books, deed records, photographs, interviews, and newspapers. Sometimes I run searches through the Library of Congress database just to see if any mentions of Douglas County or Douglasville rise to the top in hopes I might find a missing puzzle piece.

The database contains hundreds of newspapers that were published all over the United States going back to the early 1800s. Of course, my target year for a beginning point with Douglas County is 1870 since that's when the county was born. It is always amazing to me to find a mention of the goings on in Douglas County published in some small town newspaper in Arkansas, South Carolina or even California.

Sometimes the news I find mentions things I'm already familiar with. From the *Marietta Daily Leader* published in Ohio comes this story from 1896:

> *Cotton Mill burned…Atlanta, Georgia, April 8: A special to The Atlanta Constitution from Douglasville says Eden Park cotton mills were destroyed by fire at midnight. Loss $125,000. One hundred hands thrown out of employment.*

The Eden Cotton Mill was in town before the cotton mill we are so familiar with that finally and sadly succumbed to fire last year. It was located on Factory Street – today's Church Street.

Sometimes these far-flung news stories have more information I was unable to find in the Atlanta papers. Take my post regarding the Italian peddler a few months ago –

From the *Austin Weekly Statement* in Texas on May 10, 1883 this story ran:

> "*In Douglasville, Georgia, about a year ago, the sheriff of the county, an ex-member of the legislature and several other prominent and enlightened citizens attacked a poor Italian image vendor, spat upon him, rolled him on the floor and then sat upon him, singing ribald songs and [telling] rude jokes. A jury recently gave the Italian $1,250 damages.*"

In my original post about this incident (see my chapter titled "The Italian Peddler"), I didn't get a clear picture of what had been done to the peddler, nor had I been able to ascertain if he received any monetary compensation

Here's a situation where a similar name leads to more mystery. The *Memphis Daily Appeal* dated August 25, 1873 stated that *the people of Douglasville, Georgia had succeeded in capturing and lodging in jail two noted desperados, murderers and horse thieves named James and Robert Seals. The article went on to note that Robert Seals "was supposed to be an escaped murderer from North Carolina."*

The name jumped out at me because back in January (see my chapter "CSI Douglasville – 1875 Style"), I wrote about a man who was murdered in 1875 by the name of James Seales. Had he gotten out of jail at some point, stayed in the area only to be murdered two years later?

Well, that's a story thread I'm holding open for sure.

Sometimes I find news we wouldn't consider news, but I don't discount any puzzle pieces. They are all important or might be.

From *The Hickman Courier* in Kentucky dated March 25, 1887 we discover that *Judge Massey of Douglasville killed eleven partridges at one shot* (See my chapter "The Anatomy of a Picture: The McElreath and McLarty House").

The Atlanta Constitution advised on May 10, 1882 via the *Douglasville Star*: *Ephraim Pray had a cow on his farm that gave birth to twin calves the week before. One was male and the other a female* (See my chapter "Ephraim Pray – An Amazing Man").

April of 1894 must have been a slow news month because someone in Douglasville figured out that there were 40 beautiful marriageable young ladies in town. The problem was that Douglasville was also the home to 28 ugly old bachelors and two men referred to in the article as "dudes." This bit of news reporting was also in *The Atlanta Constitution* via *The Weekly Star*.

Sometimes the news I find is just downright frustrating. *The Worthington Advance* for August 1, 1889 advised, *"Near Douglasville, Georgia a few days ago a man was arrested on a warrant for whipping his wife, when the case was called for trial he filed a plea that since their marriage, ten years previous, he had only whipped her once, and then with his left hand. The justice of the peace trying the case sustained the plea and dismissed the warrant holding that a husband has the right to whip his wife once in ten years if he does it with his left hand. This decision settles very important marital rights."*

I'm hoping the good judge in Douglasville who was not named was just being funny, but attitudes toward women were a bit off the mark back then.

Another story regarding a judge in Douglas County was published in *The Morning Call* published in San Francisco on June 20, 1891. The case in question involved a lawsuit for damages regarding a tobacco crop. The paper didn't advise how the crop was damaged, but did explain the judge took some of the weed and chewed it. He decided that it was damaged to the amount of 13 cents per pound and gave judgment accordingly.

In 1892, the *Edgefield Advertiser* from South Carolina ran a story involving the fastest courtship in history on September 15, 1982. The article stated *a quick courtship is chronicled by a Georgia paper. A man stopped at a house in Douglasville, Georgia and asked a lady for glass of water. When he had quenched his thirst he asked her if she was married or single. She replied, "Widow" on which the man said he was a widower in search of a wife. "Walk in" answered the widow and we'll talk the matter over. One hour later the twain were made one by the nearest minister.*

I'm still trying to figure out who the people were.

On August 14, 1887 *The Atlanta Constitution* captioned a story "Ten Rattles and a Button" which stated, *"Yesterday, Mr. S.W. Smith who lives here, brought to town a live rattlesnake six feet and two inches in length, and having ten rattles and a button. Mr. Smith captured the snake by throwing a noose over his head. The snake is now at Sweetwater Park Hotel on exhibition.*

Finally, from *The Atlanta Constitution* in December, 1883 is the notice that *English sparrows have become residents of* [Douglasville] *and their lively chirp can be heard at anytime.*

Think about that for moment – sparrows in December!

Chapter 42

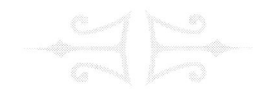

THE SOCIAL NETWORK ALONG SWEETWATER CREEK

Close your eyes and think back to the street you grew up on. If you grew up before the 1980s I'm thinking you would be able to tell me each and every person that lives along the street and possible some intricate details regarding what the inside of each house looked like down to the design of the kitchen counters.

Young people who have grown up from the mid-80s to the present have a harder time doing this because most people, even those who live in traditional subdivisions, no longer know their neighbors to the extent people did in the past.

Close-knit neighborhoods are a rarity. They do occur, but it's not the norm any more.

It would seem that during the 1800s it would have been difficult for folks to know their neighbors. In a world where transportation consisted of your feet or a horse, in a world where receiving a letter was an "event", in a world with no telephone, in a world where neighbors were several hundred acres apart or even miles down the road, it just seems impossible a close-knit community could be formed.

Yet my research indicates folks had no problem interacting with their neighbors, getting around, forming business partnerships, or finding folks to marry.

Take for example an article I found from *The Atlanta Constitution* dated May 4, 1882 titled "Sweetwater Scenes", an article that was supplied to the Atlanta paper more than likely by Charles O. Peavey, the editor of *The Weekly Star*, Douglasville's paper at the time.

This particular article is interesting in that it paints a picture for us regarding property owners along Sweetwater Creek during the early 1880s. It's almost as if we are on a tour floating down the creek and a tour guide is giving us information regarding the various property owners along the route.

The text of the actual article is in italics. I've added additional information in regular type.

After watching several years the cars have made their appearance in our county. They moved across Sweetwater Creek last Wednesday and moved into Douglas County last Friday, on the Georgia Pacific railroad, two and half miles west of the Sweetwater Creek. New life seems to take hold of our people at once.

Work to build a rail line out of Atlanta heading west had begun in the 1850s before the Civil War, but problems and a bit of apathy plagued the project. Numerous attempts were made in the 1870s to revive the interest in the railroad but the cleared right-of-way sat idle for many years.

Once the process had begun to set the tracks citizens understood the huge significance to the surrounding area and the papers reported new details of the railroad's process every day.

Sweetwater Creek is one of the best streams in any section of this state for mills and factories.

It's very obvious the tone of the article reads not only as a road map regarding the property owners along Sweetwater Creek, but as an advertisement for others to come to the area to make their home and to build their businesses.

Coming from your city to Douglasville by the Tallapoosa Road you will enter Douglas County at Love's Bridge, and you will pass through the farm of Colonel D.K. Love, which has been in cultivation many years. Indeed no small part of it was cultivated by the Indians.

You rarely see a tree or stump on the plantation and the land is still good and produces well.

Of course the Tallapoosa Road was the forerunner of Bankhead Highway today.

Colonel D.K. Love was David Kolb Love (1844-1892) who was born in Campbell County. He married Margaret Catherine Baker in December, 1861. She was the daughter of Absolum Baker (1811-1876) who ran the ferry – Baker's Ferry –that crossed the Chattahoochee River close to where Six Flags happens to be today.

Love operated a gin and grist mill along Sweetwater Creek at Salt Springs in the 1870s. During the 1880s when this newspaper article was written, he also had a mill and fertilizer store at Salt Springs with his brother, Charles B. Love (1847-1911).

Back of the residence of Colonel Love in a pine orchard old Sweetwater, the chief of the Cherokee Indians, is buried. Sweetwater Creek takes its name from him.

Near the grave of this Indian during the war a [Confederate soldier] stood and shot down a Yankee by the side of General Kilpatrick on the opposite side of the creek. The headquarters of Kilpatrick, on the farm of Colonel Love, were also the headquarters of Sweetwater.

Ray Henderson's book *The 100 Day War: The Western Front of the Atlanta Campaign* gives a good idea regarding the situation with Union troop movements around Salt Springs during October, 1864.

The next farm you pass is that of Judge J.C. Bowden, which a splendid place, containing several hundred acres.

On this place you will find the Salt Springs. You can take the water and boil it down to salt. The mine has never been worked to any extent. Denmead and Johnstone leased it and worked it a short time during the war, but were driven off by the enemy before they had worked it to any extent.

It is thought there is a good salt mine here.

You can read more about Judge Bowden in the chapter titled "Judge Bowden's Plantation".

This article was written prior to any of the water from the springs being bottled or sold and prior to the fabulous hotel and Chautauqua grounds being built. The book *On the Threshold of Freedom: Masters and Slaves in Civil War Georgia* by Clarence L. Mohr confirm Denmead and Johnstone leased the property during the war (1862) with a labor supply comprised of slaves.

The next place is the farm of H.P. Howell, or Humprey Posey Howell (1819-1891) who partnered with D.K. Love with the gin and mill. The article states...*On this place Mr. Howell and Colonel Love have a cane mill and cotton gin and a supply of water power enough to run four times the machinery they have.*

Howell's daughter, Lula Howell, died a tragic death drowning in Sweetwater Creek in 1883 at just fifteen years old.

The next place, going south is the farm of J.A. Watson – James Anthony Watson – *He has just purchased this place containing one thousand acres on both sides of Sweetwater Creek and from the way he moves things around, it appears he will make as good a farmer as he does a merchant. He has 500 acres sown in oats, which are looking fine.*

Records indicate Watson operated a dry goods store in Atlanta from 1870-1896 at 20 Mitchell Street. During the 1880s he also had a store in Salt Springs, and in 1894 he served as the mayor and later a councilman at the springs.

Watson is best known for partnering with E.W. Marsh, S.M. Inman, Henry W. Grady and several others in the development of the Piedmont Chautauqua.

Going on down Sweetwater you pass the splendid farms of Cooper, White, and Columbus Blair, who has one of the best places in our county and is one of our most successful farmers.

I'm still researching the names Cooper and White, but Columbus Blair (1836-1901) was a state representative for Douglas County in 1895.

His children include Judge Daniel Webster Blair of Marietta and Ruth Blair director of the Georgia Department of Archives and History and Georgia historian for many years.

After leaving Blair's, the next place is the farm of Angus Ferguson. On this place the shoals properly begin.

Mr. Ferguson owns a fine mill on this place and water power to run a large factory.

Ferguson moved here from North Carolina and set up a mill at Factory Shoals that was operational during the Civil War. While the New Manchester Mill was destroyed there are conflicting stories in the research that Ferguson's mill was not touched. Ferguson is an interesting man, and I continue to collect information on his life and property. I hope to be able to devote a full column to him. His grave lies within the boundaries of Sweetwater Creek State Park.

One mile below this mill is the mill site of the New Manchester factory. This factory was owned principally by ex-governor Charles J. McDonald and was a successful operation up to and during the war, until a few weeks before Atlanta was taken and was burnt by order of General Sherman, which was a great loss to this section of the country. The old brick walls are still standing.

…and they remain standing even today.

The property has been sold and is now owned by A.C. McIntosh of Powder Springs and S.N. Dorsett of Douglasville and is for sale.

Dorset was very involved with business and politics in Douglasville. He served as the first Clerk of the Superior Court, and I hope to be able to post about his most interesting relationship with A.C. McIntosh very soon.

From this place to Aderhold's Ferry there is 190 feet of falls and water plenty to run six or seven factories as the old New Manchester factory. This is a field for persons wishing to run cotton mills by water power.

This is a good country for capitalism. It is undeveloped. About two-thirds of our land is original forests. With railroad facilities we are bound to prosper. Land is cheap and plenty for sale.

Aderhold's Ferry was located where Riverside Parkway crosses Sweetwater Creek.

Getting back to my original thoughts, we like to think about how advanced we are today with various communication devices, various forms of media outlets streaming news to us twenty-four hours a day, yet, the people who lived along Sweetwater Creek in 1882 seemed to have a great social network themselves.

They supported one another, went into business together, married into each other's families, and formed a thriving community yet they did it in a very simple way.

I have to wonder – we may be advanced technologically, but are we any further along socially?

Chapter 43

CONTENTIOUS POLITICS

I've been looking through several old newspaper clippings this week concerning Douglasville and one thing is clear. Interesting political seasons are nothing new no matter the office involved.

The following article titled *Gartrell at Douglasville* appeared in *The Atlanta Constitution* on September 21, 1882. This article or one similar to it would have appeared in the local paper, *The Weekly Star*, and would then be submitted to the Atlanta paper similar to the way news stories are handed off via the Associated Press today.

The Atlanta Constitution regularly carried items involving Douglas County and Douglasville back then. Yes, I know it's hard to believe since we aren't mentioned nowadays unless the situation involves scandal, murder, floods, mayoral vetoes, fires or some other sensationalized story.

We must remember, however, back in the 1880s the leading movers and shakers in Douglasville were fast friends with Henry W. Grady, the editor of *The Atlanta Constitution*, and many of Douglasville's families had close ties to the business elite in Atlanta. For this very reason alone Douglasville was mentioned and mentioned often.

I'm presenting the contents of the clipping below in italics with my notes of explanation as well to help set the context of the event.

Yesterday was a lively time in this usually quiet town. It had been announced for several days that General Gartrell would speak here on his claims to the governorship, and it was also well known that D. Pike Hill, of Atlanta, would be present to reply to him.

The Georgia governor's race in 1882 was an interesting one pitting two former Confederates against one another.

What's interesting regarding this article is the fact that General Gartrell's actual opponent was not present to counter his remarks. D. Pike Hill was not running for governor. He was a well-known Atlanta lawyer who was very active in Democratic politics. I assume he was in Douglasville to represent the Georgia Democratic Party, and to speak for the actual candidate, Alexander H. Stephens, the very well-known vice president of the Confederacy.

The newspaper article continues:

The prospect of hearing a lively discussion brought a good crowd to the town, and by 11 o'clock there must have been nearly four hundred people in and around the courthouse.

Those people would have been gathered on the same grounds where the Douglas County Museum of History and Art sits in downtown Douglasville today. To date, I have not located any pictures of the building that would have existed in 1882. It was constructed in 1880 and is described as a two-story brick courthouse. The building was abandoned in 1884 and taken down due to faulty bricks and mortar. Apparently the building was literally crumbling and was a danger to citizens.

The fact that approximately four hundred people had gathered to listen to General Gartrell is interesting since a ride to town wasn't as easy as it is now. Even if the majority of the people who had gathered lived in the downtown area this would mean nearly half the town turned out since the population of Douglasville hovered around one thousand people during the 1880s.

General Gartrell refused to divide time with Mr. Hill, saying he would discuss in this campaign with Mr. Stephens only. Mr. Hill then demanded that the general should tell the people he meant to speak. This General Gartrell did, and then proceeded to make his regulation stump speech. He met with little encouragement, and was rewarded with little applause.

At first read General Gartrell really comes off as a rude individual, however, I'm sure it was frustrating for him to campaign against a man who decided to run his campaign in what is described by historians as "casual."

Stephens only spoke in larger cities such as Macon, Columbus, Augusta, and of course, Atlanta. He was well known and well liked. Stephens had served the state of Georgia as a United States Representative prior to the war, and served the citizens of Georgia in Congress during Reconstruction, as well.

However, Stephens appeared to be in poor health most of the time and generally weighed less than one hundred pounds. I've read his voice was shrill and unpleasant. Perhaps that is why he didn't travel to smaller towns to debate his opponent.

However, for all his frailty Alexander Stephens was considered one of the strongest men in the South mainly due to his intelligence, judgment, and eloquence.

General Gartrell was no slouch either. Prior to the war Lucious Gartrell had served in the Georgia House of Representatives. He spent his time during the war bouncing between the battlefields and serving in the Confederate Congress.

He helped formed the Seventh Regiment of the Georgia Volunteer Infantry where he saw action at First Manassas. He was approached as early as 1863 to run for governor, but declined. After the war, in 1870, Gartrell had his sights on the U.S. Senate, but when he found out Alexander Stephens planned to run for the seat he stepped aside.

Once Gartrell spoke, it was Hill's turn.

When he had finished Mr. Hill arose and said he would say some very plain things about General Gartrell, and was sorry he could not stay to hear them. The general went outside the courthouse, ...where he lingered about... He then came in and heard all Mr. Hill's speech, which may be termed a "rattler." He frequently brought a hearty cheer showing that he had the sentiment of the people with him.

After he concluded R.A. Massey made a few remarks in reply, but Mr. Hill corrected some of his statements in a very amusing way, and threw in another good stroke.

R.A. Massey would be Judge Robert A. Massey. He was involved in politics and business here in Douglasville as an attorney. By 1888, he was also serving as postmaster.

The crowd then dispersed to discuss the events of the day and the probable majority for Stephens in Douglas. General Gartrell had some personal friends here, but the mass of the people prefer Mr. Stephens for governor, and will so express themselves on the fourth of October at the polls.

In fact, General Gartrell only carried eleven of Georgia's one hundred and thirty seven counties that October. Thomas A. Martin who wrote the book *Atlanta and Its Builders: A Comprehensive History of the Gate City* explains, "...Though [Gartrell] felt that he had little hope of success at the polls, it was an evidence of [a] fidelity to principle that he was willing to oppose such an idol of the people as [Stephens], and he accepted his defeat with heroic magnanimity, knowing that it was to an appropriate sense of fitness on the part of the people of Georgia that the career of Mr. Stephens should be closed with gubernatorial honors."

As for Governor Alexander H. Stephens, he finally succumbed to his frail health and died after being in office for fourth months.

I'll end with a little interesting fact I picked up from Franklin Garrett's *Atlanta and Its Environs,* Gartrell had lived since the 1850s in a grand home in Atlanta on Decatur Street between Jackson and Yonge Streets. In 1893, following Gartrell's death the home was sold. The new owner was none other than Douglasville's own Dr. T.R. Whitley.

General Gartrell is one of a handful of Confederate generals buried at Atlanta's Oakland Cemetery.

Chapter 44

MARONEY'S MILL

When you look back into Douglas County's history you can't emphasize enough the impact various mills that dotted the county had on sustaining and growing the population. Douglas County had several mills for all sorts of purposes including lumber mills and mills that ground all sorts of grain. Every single mill was vital to the area it served; however, one mill stands out because to date it's the only mill I've found that was mentioned in *The Atlanta Constitution*.

An article titled "A Wheat and Corn Mill" from April 10, 1883 states "Messrs. W.P. Strickland and Alfred Maroney are erecting a wheat and corn mill on Mud Creek, two miles north of Douglasville."

The property lying in the Beulah Community belonged to Mr. Maroney being the namesake for the mill as well as Maroney Mill Road. In fact, other sources verify that Maroney had a mill in operation on Mud Creek as far back as 1864, and once his son, Benjamin was old enough they operated the mill together.

W.P. Strickland (William Parks) is best remembered as being a city councilman in the 1880s and lived in one of the first homes along Strickland Street. There's a reason it's called Strickland, you know?

The newspaper article also relates "the millhouse has just been completed. They have received their mill rock (they are French burr...) and machinery from Atlanta and are now engaged in putting them up."

Millstones worked in pairs to do the grinding with a bed stone and a runner stone. The two never touched and depended on the sharp grooves worked into each stone to do the work. The website titled *The Art of Millstones, How They Work* by Theodore R. Hazen advises French burrstones were used for fine grinding and were purchased directly from the manufacturer in France or from milling concerns in England.

The millstones were not cut from one piece of stone because it was hard to locate chunks that were large enough to make an entire millstone. They were built up from sections of quartz, cemented together with plaster of Paris and bound by iron bands to help reinforce them.

Burrstones are generally a very hard type of gray colored quartz mined at just one quarry located outside Paris, France.

Millstones would wear down over time so the miller had to be knowledgeable in how to redress and sharpen the stone.

The top runner stone had to be lifted off and turned upside down. The miller then used a hammer like tool to redress the stones called a millpick. Dressing the stone consisted of re-cutting a pattern of grooves in the stone's surface.

Getting back to Messrs. Strickland and Maroney, I would imagine since other sources state Maroney already had a mill in operation prior to the newspaper article, Mr. Strickland got involved as a partner to fund the purchase of a new pair of stones and other equipment. Both gentlemen were involved in various concerns for the town of Douglasville. Alfred Maroney was on the committee that oversaw the original formation of the pauper farm on Chicago Avenue. An article in *The Weekly Star* published on January 30, 1883 mentions Maroney was paid $1.50 per day for four days work on the committee. W.P. Strickland was also involved in town business as a city councilman.

Therefore, since both men were involved citizens I don't find it surprising that *The Atlanta Constitution* article ends by giving a quick little plug for Douglas County advising such things as a "great climate, waterpower and wood as resources and states further we would be very glad to have some of the many persons who are looking for places in Georgia to locate manufacturers. Visit our county before locating elsewhere."

Alfred Maroney kept his mill in operation through 1894 when he passed away handing over the operation to his son, Benjamin. The millstones finally stopped grinding when Benjamin went on to his heavenly reward in 1900.

Chapter 45

GROVER CLEVELAND AND THE ELECTION OF 1884

As I write this it is exactly 48 hours until the polls will close here on the east coast Tuesday night. The pundits are all squawking filling up the airwaves with their poll numbers, commentary, and spin, and once the polls close it won't get any better. Those next few hours will be a never-ending series of maps, numbers and election tidbits until we know without a doubt that we have a winner.

I'm not sure how you feel about the matter, but I'm a little weary of the election slug fest, and I long for Wednesday to get here, so the suspense will be over, but will it really be over?

Yes, by Wednesday we will know who the next occupant of the Oval Office will be. Some of us will be celebrating because the current resident, President Obama will remain in office or some of us will be celebrating because a new guy, Governor Romney, will be making arrangements to move his family into the White House come January.

No matter the winner, one thing we can count on will be the reactions. The news media will keep talking, and you will see all sorts of reactions good and bad via social media like Facebook.

You didn't really think the election would actually end all of that, did you?

With possible reactions in mind I did a little digging regarding past elections and how folks in Douglas County reacted to the news. I found an interesting reaction from the election of 1884.

The election of 1884 pitted Grover Cleveland for the Democrats up against James G. Blaine representing the Republican Party, and it is one election year remembered for its extreme bitterness including personal slurs, casting blame to the other side, and just downright nastiness.

Hmmm…

I really don't have to voice the obvious here, do I?

This was also one of the first presidential elections where the candidates had to try a little harder to get before as many citizens as possible to make the case why they were the best person for the job. The news media also realized hawking sensationalism could sell a few more papers. They picked up on drama on both sides and kept it churning throughout the months of campaigning by both candidates.

Again, do I need to bring up the obvious here?

Cleveland was accused of having an illegitimate child and Blaine carried around the nickname "Slippery Jim" due to several questions regarding ethics violations as Speaker of the House.

Cleveland won, but just barely in what is described by historians as one of the closest elections in United States history. Cleveland's election was also notable because it broke a 25-year losing streak for the Democratic Party.

So, the reaction?

Well, as far as Democrats go they were ecstatic, and southern Democrats were beyond ecstatic. They were downright giddy as they had endured years of Reconstruction and Republican rule not only with national offices, but within their own states as well.

Douglas County Democrats were among the ecstatic bunch per *The Weekly Star* newspaper:

A number of Douglasville boys went down to Atlanta last Friday night to participate in the jubilee over Cleveland's election.

Some of them" jubilated muchly".

I have my own personal opinions regarding what "jubilated muchly" might mean, but I'll keep them to myself.

The boys painted the town red last Friday, when the news of Cleveland's election was received. Amid the firing of anvils, whooping and rejoicing, Captain C. P. Bowen made his appearance on the smallest mule in the county and rode up and down the sidewalk and all over town, with little Joe Johnson behind him. He had placed on the mule's forehead a placard which had written on it in large letters, "Cleveland and Hendricks".

Hendricks was Cleveland's running mate and our 21st Vice President, Thomas A. Hendricks.

Bowen was followed by half the town, some holding to the mule's tail, some its ears, and all hollering at the top of their voices.

Before the election, the Captain had pledged himself, that if Cleveland was elected, to ride a bull all over town. He was not able to find a bull and substituted this little mule.

Well, the occasion justified the behavior.

Unfortunately, I'm not aware which Douglas County citizens made their way to Atlanta and "jubilated muchly" following the Election of 1884, but as far as Captain C. P. Bowen goes I do have a little more information.

Captain Bowen was known to his mama as Caleb Perry Bowen (1827-1907) and his mama was Nancy (Yarbrough) Bowen. Captain Bowen's father was Major Thomas J. Bowen who moved to Campbell County (later Douglas County) from Jackson County, Georgia. Major Bowen received his rank while serving during the War of 1812.

Bowen earned the title of Captain during the Civil War when he was with the Campbell County Sharpshooters, Company F of the 30th Regiment. Originally the group of soldiers was known as Company C, but after being sent to Camp Bailey in April, 1862 the group was reorganized and they were referred to as Company F throughout the remainder of the war. Per Douglas County historian Fannie Mae Davis, Company F was with the 30th Regiment throughout the war in all the engagements in which the regiment participated in including Vicksburg and Missionary Ridge.

Captain Bowen was wounded at Chickamauga, but still stayed on the battlefield for five days following the engagement to help bury the dead. He was captured at Nashville in December, 1864 and sent to Johnson's Island.

Bowen came home to Campbell County after the war and soon got involved with the efforts to create Douglas County. He was a member of the contingent who traveled to Atlanta when Dr. Zellar's bill was presented to the state legislature along with Ephraim Pray and several others

Captain C.P. Bowen served as the first treasurer of Douglas County, was a state representative in 1876 and also served as postmaster from 1893 to 1897. He was also an investor in the canning plant that was established in 1887.

Further checking regarding the mention of little Joe Johnson who followed closely behind the Captain and the mule revealed little. At the time the pastor of the First Baptist Church of Douglasville was named Thomas J. Johnson and he did in fact have a son named Joseph, but I was unable to get an exact verification of this.

Chapter 46

THE GLORIOUS FOURTH

So, here it is – another Fourth of July! How are you spending it? Did you make it to the parade this morning down Church Street? Did you stop by the SHARE Festival going on all day at Hunter Park? Perhaps you had a bite to eat at the American Legion Post 145 BBQ, or maybe you headed off to Sweetwater Creek State Park to fish a little. Then again if you are like me you just stayed close to the house to grill some burgers and take a dip in the pool.

No matter your choice of activities to celebrate the Fourth most folks who live in Douglasville and the surrounding area head out when the day is done and dusk is rapidly turning to night in order to claim a prime location to view the annual fireworks display sponsored by the City of Douglasville.

Say what you want about the fireworks including complaints about the traffic afterward, but I think you really get a sense of the Douglasville community as people fill up parking lots, grassy areas on the side of the road, and any other spot you can think of to see the lightshow. The annual fireworks are one of the few events I think can be correctly termed as a community-wide event.

You might think such gatherings are something new, but they aren't. Fourth of July celebrations have been a big deal in Douglasville going all the way back to 1886 when the town was a mere twelve years old.

Beginning in the late 1800s Douglasville was one of THE places to be in the Atlanta area to celebrate the Fourth. In fact, a large number of folks from Atlanta would trek to Douglasville for the festivities, and according to historian Fannie Mae Davis special rates were secured for the day so that the event was open to more people. *The Weekly Star* estimated the crowds in 1886 ranged from three to four thousand people. Mrs. Davis states, "The morning trains brought into town well known political leaders who occupied a speaker's platform for the day. A politician of Tom Watson's or Hoke Smith's stature could hold the attention of an audience for two hours regardless of the heat and crying babies."

One of the areas of town serving as the main focal point for the celebration was a grove of trees east of today's historic district.

Yes! A grove of trees along Broad Street!

I can't even imagine it – a small grove of virgin oak trees…located directly east of, and adjoining today's Hartley, Rowe & Fowler building, extending about 300 feet east and west and running north and south from Broad Street to Church Street.

The trees were the remnant of the great forest that had covered the ridgeline where Douglasville's historic district stands today. Eventually, the stand of trees became known as James' Grove since Joseph James was the owner of the land.

If you really want to get back to Douglasville's Fourth of July roots then that plot of land east of Hartley, Rowe & Fowler is where you need to focus your attention. From Douglasville's earliest days Joseph James allowed the town to use the grove of trees for picnics, political meetings, and of course, Fourth of July celebrations.

In 1886, the Fourth of July that year fell on a Sunday, so the bash was scheduled for Saturday, the third. Serving as a kick-off on Friday night was a balloon launch. The balloon was so large it could be seen eight to ten miles away. An "amateur musician's festival" was also held that night.

The next morning prayers were offered up, an address of welcome was made and then W.T. Roberts, read the Declaration of Independence. It stirred the crowd and from that point on the reading of the document became a tradition for Fourth of July celebrations, and why not? It's the whole purpose of the holiday in the first place.

The main speaker in 1886 was Colonel P.L. Mynatt, candidate for the nomination for Congress for the Douglasville area. A comedian followed Col. Mynatt and then a mid-day meal described as a "free-for-all-feast" was served in the shady grove.

Photographers from Atlanta were available to take pictures, so people could have a memento of the day's festivities, and in the afternoon there was plenty of time for courting, dancing, baseball, horse racing, foot racing, a wheel barrow race and in the evening another balloon launch.

In 1915, a group of ladies took on the grove of trees as a service project. They cleaned up the area and installed swings, benches, tables, planted flower beds and enclosed the grove with a fence. They bestowed a more formal name on the grove calling it Civic Park.

By 1920, the celebration was just as big and as grand as the first one. It must have been quite a party because the festivities that year started on Saturday and didn't conclude until Monday. *The Douglas County Sentinel* advised 5,000 people attended, and stated, "It was one of the biggest events in the history of Douglasville, and one that will not soon be forgotten by those who attended, and the fellow who failed to come will be kicking himself the rest of his days for missing the great affair."

A ballgame and dinner served by the ladies of the Methodist Church was held on Saturday followed by an all-day singing on Sunday. On Monday a baseball game was held between the city of Douglasville and the city of Acworth with Acworth coming out on top with a score of 10 to 6.

Hon. Thomas W. Hardwick, a U.S. Senator who would go on to be Georgia's governor from 1921 to 1923, spoke in the grove and Dr. T.R. Whitley announced he would be candidate for representative. J.L. Selman & Son provided ice water for Sunday's crowd free of charge.

1920 was the last year the grove was used as a venue for the Fourth of July celebrations because Joseph James sold the stand of trees to R.E.

Edwards and "the tract was cleared of the fine old oaks and the haven-like park was no more."

While we don't have the stand of oak trees anymore to use as a meeting spot to celebrate our nation's birth as a community, we still understand the importance to gather somewhere and make a statement with our exclamations over parade floats and the red, white and blue fireworks. No matter the current political climate the need to gather and celebrate together is one of the reasons I'm proud to be an American and proud to make my home in Douglasville.

Happy Fourth!!!!

Chapter 47

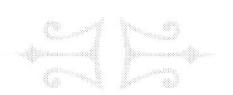

SHORTENING ON THE PLAZA

The D.H. Gurley grocery ad featuring Snowdrift Shortening at O'Neal Plaza provides an iconic view of Douglasville. The vintage ad is part of the plaza's charm taking us back to the turn of the century and our earliest roots when Douglasville's commercial district had several grocery stores. As we can see D.H. Gurley had "fine" and "heavy" groceries, and he delivered, too!

The main focus of the ad is Snowdrift Shortening, and to understand some of the history behind the product, we need to look to cotton.

Not only was cotton king throughout Georgia and the rest of the South prior to the Civil War, it continued to be king for years afterward until the boll weevil arrived in 1915. I've read where cotton fields surrounded Douglasville in all directions during those days. In fact, you only had to drive as far as Douglas County High School and the fields of white would begin.

Most people are unaware cotton and shortening have a connection. Both are snowy white, but the connection goes much deeper than that.

Once cotton is ginned and the fluffy white fibers are separated from the seeds, the cotton farmer ends up with a lot of seeds.

The cotton gin owners were drowning in seeds and figured there had to be some uses for them and make the gin owners a few extra dollars.

The hull from a cottonseed can be fed to animals for roughage. Ground cottonseeds can be used for fertilizer. They can also be crushed for cottonseed oil. Thirty million pounds of cotton has the potential to produce tons of seeds and gallons of cottonseed oil.

Crude cottonseed oil is dark red in color and has a very distasteful flavor and odor. Several industrious people decided there had to be a use for the oil and began working on a way to work around the color, flavor and order issues. There was also a more dangerous outcome to work around. Untreated cottonseed oil can become a paralytic pesticide.

Enter the Southern Oil Company formed in 1887. They took on the cottonseed oil in order to create viable consumer products. There had to be a way to make cottonseed oil more appetizing and safe. They hired David Wesson, a food chemist who was a graduate as well as faculty member at MIT.

It took Doc Wesson, as he was fondly called, 16 years to develop the process to deodorize cottonseed oil. The process he finally hit upon involved a high-temperature vacuum process that became known as the Wesson Process.

If you haven't guessed by now, the resulting product was Wesson Oil, a product currently owned by ConAgra, but when it first hit the market, Wesson Oil was created by The Southern Oil Company.

Several forms of Wesson Oil exist today, but in the earliest days, cottonseed oil was the only basis for Wesson Oil.

The company also wanted to develop a product that would be an alternative to hog lard. Doc Wesson used the process of hydrogenation with the cottonseed oil and created a product the Southern Oil Company marketed as Snowdrift Shortening.

Hydrogenation involves adding a little hydrogen to help convert liquid oil to solid fat and then it is chilled.

But the marketing department at Southern Oil Company had a problem. Cooks were used to using hog fat and were fairly stubborn regarding changing to an all-vegetable shortening. They had to utilize a heavy advertising campaign.

Snowdrift was advertised all over the South. Several outdoor advertisements still exist including our advertisement featured prominently in O'Neal Plaza.

Not only does the outdoor advertisement harken back to past times, it actually connects us to a crop that helped support Douglas County for many years.

Chapter 48

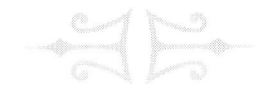

DOUGLASVILLE'S CANNING AND PRESERVATION COMPANY

Dear Daughter occasionally goes to the trouble to post something on my Facebook wall. It's always a moment of anticipation mixed with dread when Facebook notifies me. I log on thinking, "Oh, she was thinking of her mama "and then my mind turns to "Uh-oh…what did she put on there for all to see?"

Last week I found Dear Daughter had left me a link regarding reusable Swiffer covers on my wall along with a question that read, "Do you know how much money you would save not buying the refill packets?"

Let me clarify here that Dear Daughter is 18 and away at college.

She continued in her comments, "I have learned so many do it yourself things over the weekend. For real!!! I think I can seriously save our family so much money when I tell you all my ideas."

I think she was using the DIY online videos to distract herself from the mountains of homework college life has suddenly dumped in her lap, but I am for saving money and finding new and different ways to do things. However, my Swiffer mop and I are having quite a little love affair, so I don't know if I can get rid of it anytime soon, but I'm willing to listen to Dear Daughter's ideas.

Yes, I'm guilty of using various use it and throw it away type convenience products including food stuffs that I can utilize to save time – the already roasted chicken, the pre-cut fruit, bagged lettuce, etc., but if the situation was forced on me I can roll up my sleeves, gather the produce and actually can and preserve things.

Yes! I know how to use a Mason jar for its original intention. You didn't think those jars were something trendy to drink your iced tea out of, did you? If I wanted to I could fill up a freezer in nothing flat with a garden full of produce.

The key words there are "if I wanted to."

Growing up I never saw the shelves on my grandparent's back porch empty. They were filled with canned green beans, okra, squash and the freezer was full as well with dried fruits, frozen peas and corn. My grandparents ate from the garden all summer and ate from the freezer and from canned goods the rest of the year.

My father continues that tradition and to be honest about it he never does anything small and that includes gardening. He has a garden on my family's place that has been "the garden" for over 100 years. Five generations, including my children, have worked that land planting, plowing, picking up rocks, pruning and picking things from green beans to potatoes. Currently the garden spot covers a half acre of land and at 83, Dear Daddy continues to work it each day during the spring, summer and into the fall during collard season.

The summer I was 18 we had a huge crop of corn that once harvested filled my dad's truck bed completely. My mother, grandmother and I worked around that truck for three days preparing the corn for freezing.

We worked in assembly line fashion. My grandfather and father shucked the corn, removed the silk tassels, and broke off the knobby end of the stalk. They handed the ears of corn to my mom and my grandmother who set about slicing the corn kernels from the cob before stacking the cobs up for me to finish.

I found myself standing at the end of my dad's truck bed with a sharp knife running the knife blade along the cob of the corn making sure every ounce of corn was extracted from the cob. We worked fast. My knife flew over the surface of each corn cob raking the remainder of the kernels from the husk causing milk from the corn to fly everywhere – on my hands, in the bucket, around the bucket, and face and in my hair.

We worked for hours, and when we took a minute to eat something I took a look at myself in the mirror and discovered I even had corn on my eyelashes. It was exhausting labor. My arms screamed in pain for days afterward.

NO, I have never frozen creamed corn ever again, and have no desire to do so, but the work I performed over those three days was just a sample of the labor performed in so many households during the past here in Georgia and across the country.

An article titled *Canned Goods for the Greater Good in Georgia* from the "Blog of the Digital Library of Georgia" states, "Georgia boasts a history of industrious people who not only generated vast quantities of preserved goods, but whose canning efforts fortified the land that they farmed from, secured educational opportunities that had not previously existed, and supported national defense efforts."

This is so very true. I'm sure if you look back just to the last generation in your family you have relatives that can tell you about canning clubs, 4-H Clubs and state and local fairs where folks showed off their gardening, preservation, and cooking skills. These activities do exist today but on a much smaller scale than in the past.

The DLG article continues, "In Georgia, canning clubs became extremely popular; thousands of girls were instructed and supervised by home demonstration or "canning" agents across the state's participating counties."

"Georgians had embraced home canning as a common household practice by the mid-to-late nineteenth century. Most kitchens, both on the farm and in town, likely contained some version of an airtight screw cap and glass jar: either one that was patented by John Mason in 1858, or any number of similar jars that were patented shortly afterward."

In the late 1880s the citizens of Douglasville successfully worked together to create a business concern that would be a win-win for area farmers, businessmen, and non-farmers alike.

The Douglasville Canning and Preserving Company was established in 1887 with capital stock of $25,000. There were over 35 Douglasville businessmen who were the original stockholders including Joseph S. James, Dr. Thomas Whitley, J. Penn Watson, A.W. McLarty, C.P. Bowen, Dr. J.L. Selman, J.T. Duncan, J.M. Abercrombie, J.K. Edge, E.A. Morris, Henry Ward, C.W. Weddington, and W.C. Hodnett.

The first president of the company was C.C. Post who is such an interesting fellow I'll be giving an entire column to him as soon as I get all of the research I've compiled in some sort of order. In 1887, Mr. Post was a very recent addition to the city of Douglasville moving like a meteorite across the landscape. By 1893 he and his wife were gone having worn out their welcome, but in 1887 folks thought enough of him to appoint him as the canning company's president. C.C. Post hailed from the great beyond about as far above the Mason-Dixon Line as you can get – Chicago, Illinois. In fact, Mr. Post is the reason why Douglasville has a street named for the northern city. His home was located along Chicago Avenue.

The goal of the Douglasville Canning and Preservation Company was to provide a market for area farmers plus provide an incentive for the farmers to plant more fruits and berries. The company handled wild grapes, muscadines, wild strawberries, blackberries, and huckleberries. During the company's heyday many peach orchards were planted in Douglas County to feed the canning business.

The business operated on a seasonal basis for many years with up to 15 employees. Fannie Mae Davis states there are indications up to 50,000 cans of fruit and vegetables were preserved each season.

The cans carried a label with Amakanasta, the Indian leader, and bore the name Sweetwater which is said to be the English translation of his name. Mrs. Davis also explains how the company meant added income to local farm families.

Many of the berries grew wild all over the county and many farm wives and their children scurried out along the countryside during berry season to gather product for the canning company since they could earn 5 cents for each gallon of berries. Buckets of them would arrive at the cannery daily during berry season.

The Douglasville Canning and Preservation Company existed until the early 1920s. Mrs. Davis indicates in her work that she was unable to find a reason for the cannery's demise, however, in another section of her work she indicates hard times came to the county in the 1920s. I am making an educated guess the county could no longer sustain the business.

Today, many in our community face economic hardship and everyone is looking for ways to cut corners growing their own fruits and vegetables and cutting costs with cleaning materials as Dear Daughter was suggesting.

The DLG article advises, "Home canning has regained popularity with Americans sharing a renewed interest in locally-grown food, handmade goods, and household thrift. Canning equipment sales are booming despite lean economic times, canning parties and can swaps are sprouting up throughout the country, and delicious recipes designed for storage in glass jars have recently shown up in cookbooks and food blogs everywhere."

Recently we have seen a surge towards family farms, locally-grown food, and handmade goods right here in Douglasville with the Main Street Farmer's Market on O'Neal Plaza.

The market features fresh produce, organic meat, goat cheese, handcrafted items, baked goods, specialty items. All local growers, artisans, and crafts people are welcome to participate.

Chapter 49

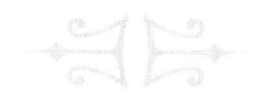

PROMOTING DOUGLASVILLE

Back in the fall of 2012 I had the honor or being asked to write a short historical overview for the city of Douglasville that would be included in the new visitors guide for 2013 published by the Douglasville Convention and Visitors Bureau. If I was new to the area needing a place to stay, a place to dine or even a place to hold a special event it would tell me everything I need to know about the city and a little about the county, too.

Promoting Douglasville and Douglas County is nothing new. It's been done since the minute the county was created in 1870 and when the city of Douglasville was birthed five years later.

The formation of Douglasville coincided when New South ideals were gaining momentum across the South – when small villages were reshaped into railroad towns.

In the case of Douglasville the town's leaders had the opportunity to build a New South town from the ground up, and they worked diligently to include all the ingredients necessary for a thriving town for that period which included a railroad, cotton mill, hotel, bank and a commercial district, but the most important ingredient was people.

They needed people to move to Douglasville to make all the other New South ingredients work, so they wrote articles published in the local paper that were eventually run in the Atlanta paper and other papers across the country explaining and sometimes exaggerating how wonderful it was to live here.

In January, 1889 the following piece was run in various papers. Notice the extended invitation to folks in the North and the claim that mosquitos were almost nonexistent here. After our recent heavy rainfall I find it quite humorous.

Our town has 1200 people in it. It is on the line of the Georgia Pacific Railroad. We have two mails a day. It is 27 miles from Atlanta, the capital of the state. There are already quite a number of Northern families here. The Southern citizens are genial and kind and give a most cordial welcome to Northern and Western immigrants.

Three months will include all the cold and windy weather we have here and even that is not very cold. The summers are long – not excessively hot – breezy and delicious. Never in the world have I seen a country so well-watered; there are natural springs everywhere. The water is soft and cool.

And now, listen to me O, housewives, and I will tell you something that will make you glad. There are neither fleas nor mosquitos here, and the flies are less numerous than elsewhere. Snakes and poisonous insects are scarce; and then again there is hardly any mud; owing to the character of the soil and the rolling nature of the surface; the hardest and longest rains scarcely leave a disagreeable trace for more than a few hours.

I cannot end this article without speaking of the wild fruits and nuts. The blackberries are very numerous, large and delicious. Hundreds of bushels of wild grapes are found in the woods, amongst which some varieties are as large as the immense flame colored Tokay of California, and when in season there seems to be literally no end to them. They make the best jelly and sauce; they are also excellent eating as they come from the vines. The woods are covered with huckleberries at one season of the year…We have persimmons and various kinds of nuts.

But I have told you enough. If you want a home, come to Douglasville, Georgia.

From reading this, of course, it's evident our priorities have changed greatly in the last 124 years, however I think Douglasville's founding fathers would be pleased. Douglasville has entered the 21st Century as a vibrant city with a thriving historic downtown district.

Section Five

SALT SPRINGS – THE RESORT TOWN

Chapter 50

IN THE BEGINNING – THE SWEETWATER PARK HOTEL

One hundred and twenty-eight years ago this very summer excitement was at frenzy level as the Sweetwater Park Hotel was going to open.

For months the building's progress was given in the Atlanta papers. Reporters likened the construction to the magic of the Genie from

Arabian Nights who "in a twinkling built palaces in the deserts and made grand courts in mere wastelands."

What was described as magic actually took 200 men (by some accounts) to erect the huge hotel on the property located on the western corner of Veterans Memorial Highway (Bankhead) and S. Sweetwater Road.

Just a few weeks ago I shared some information about Edwin W. Marsh and Samuel M. Inman who were wealthy Atlanta businessmen. They were the primary investors with the hotel project along with James A. Watson who had ties to Douglasville.

The hotel would open in the summer of 1887 boasting 250 rooms besides parlors, offices, and billiard rooms. Piazzas stretching for 700 feet with widths of 14 to 28 feet surrounded the hotel with wide halls dividing the rooms. One description states, "It [was] built with wings of open courts of wood and grass enclosed, so that there [was] not an inside room in the house."

The third story contained open balconies 40 feet square, handsomely finished from which guests could look towards Marietta on one side and Atlanta on the other with the Blue Ridge Mountains in full view.

On top of the main building was a handsome covered court for observation. There were reading rooms for gentlemen, parlors, billiard rooms and every possible convenience of the best hotels.

The building had electricity and the halls were heated by steam though most of the rooms also had open fireplaces. There were electric call bells in every room and most had private balconies. Bathrooms had hot and cold water as well as shower baths.

The baths were supplied with salt water from the springs, of course.

The dining room was 50 by 86 feet finished with enormous plate glass windows and decorated inside with 8 huge mirrors of the finest French glass.

E.W. Marsh and James A. Watson wanted the best man possible to run the hotel. They traveled to Traverse City, Michigan to observe John B. Billings, the manager of a large hotel there. After two or three days they were satisfied enough and made Mr. Billings an offer, however, Billings refused until he could travel to the Sweetwater Park Hotel and take a look around.

The hotel must have met his approval because not only did he accept their offer to run the hotel, he set out on a trip to New York with them to buy furniture and other appointments.

They purchased the finest pianos that could be bought, plush Brussels carpet and the same furniture that could be found in Fifth Avenue hotels.

Silverware was purchased from Rogers & Sons, a company which eventually became known as International Silver, and the crockery was made especially for the hotel by the Dobbs & Wey Company.

The bathhouse was constructed of brick with a tower of ornamental design. A parlor was on the right with ladies bathing parlors and the left side was for the gentlemen. The building was decorated with fine engravings, sofas, and "every convenience and comfort."

The workmen were working around the clock down at the springs, too. A pavilion was being built over the springs and was "ornamental to the highest degree…with an arched roof that was finished in exquisite taste." The pavilion floor was a sheet of solid marble that measured 65 by 50 feet. Today, a piece of that very floor is on display at the Douglas County Museum of History and Art.

Tragically, the Sweetwater Park Hotel burned to the ground in 1912.

It came "as if by magic" and left us in much the same way. Today, there is little evidence it ever existed, and though there was no loss of life, I consider its loss to be one of Douglas County's greatest tragedies.

Chapter 51

INMAN AND MARSH – THE MEN BEHIND THE SWEETWATER PARK HOTEL

A few investors were behind the magnificent Sweetwater Park Hotel in Lithia Springs, but Edwin W. Marsh and Samuel M. Inman were the primary figures.

I felt it was time that I found out more about them.

Edwin W. Marsh is remembered as an extremely successful dry goods merchant. He was born in North Carolina in 1824 yet spent time for several years as a merchant in Chattanooga, Tennessee. He transferred his business to Atlanta in 1863 when he was 39.

Besides his efforts at the dry goods trade, Marsh also had controlling interest in the newspaper, *Southern Confederacy*, which relocated to Macon during the Union occupation. Following the war, Marsh's dry goods store was the first one to re-open in the city. He developed an extremely prosperous business and invested heavily in real estate.

I could go on and on regarding his accomplishments as there are many including the first cotton factory established in North Georgia at Trion.

He was unbelievably wealthy, so it's no surprise he would invest his time and dollars in resort in Douglas County.

Samuel M. Inman was born in Tennessee to a wealthy planter family. He attended college at Princeton, and fought in the Civil War. Like many, the Inman family was hit hard by the war and found it necessary to relocate. They headed to Georgia where they acted as bank agents, merchants, and they owned a cotton factoring concern called the S.W. Inman & Son Cotton House.

Like many former planters, the Inman family took the changes the New South brought head on and went into business. Eventually, the Inman family became very influential and powerful again. Samuel M. Inman's brother was John H. Inman, the head of the company Inman, Swann, & Co. of New York and president of the West Point Terminal Company which controlled 11,000 miles of track and $4,000,000 in steamships. Another brother, Hugh T. Inman, owned the Kimball House Hotel in Atlanta.

Samuel M. Inman entered into a partnership with Joel Hurt in the 1880s to form the East Atlanta Land Company. Their main venture was to develop Inman Park, the beautiful Atlanta neighborhood that still exists today. A second venture included the Atlanta & Edgewood Street Railroad. While today we think of Inman Park as a downtown neighborhood, it was originally outside of town. The railroad provided a way in and out of town for residents, a huge selling point.

By 1889, Inman was involved with the Inman System, a group of nearly all of the railroads across the southeast. He was also involved with the beginnings of the Georgia School of Technology or Georgia Institute of Technology as it is known today. His put up his own money to get the ball rolling plus was able to secure other money donated by investors and the city of Atlanta.

At one point it is thought Inman was worth around $750,000 to $1,000,000. He was on many boards and gave much of his money to charity.

Like Marsh, it's no wonder that Samuel M. Inman had a few extra dollars to invest in a resort hotel in Lithia Springs.

They didn't even miss the money.

Chapter 52

LET'S GO TO THE CHAUTAUQUA GROUNDS

While many have heard about the Sweetwater Park Hotel that brought such notables to Lithia Springs as Thomas Nelson Page, Joel Chandler Harris, and President William McKinley while he was still a congressman, few know about the Piedmont Chautauqua.

The Chautauqua began in New York in 1874 as an adult education movement.

In March, 1888, Henry W. Grady, editor of *The Atlanta Constitution,* New South booster and friend of many of the movers and shakers in Douglas County, held a meeting in Atlanta to pitch an idea involving an effort to bring the Chautauqua Movement to the Atlanta area consisting of summer educational seminars, lectures, and classes for adults. Grady had found the perfect location just west of the Sweetwater Park Hotel along today's Bankhead Highway. Grady had become a national figure overnight when he spoke on the New South before the New England Society of New York in 1886 and felt his many Northern contacts would be a resource the Chautauqua and Georgia could rely. Grady advised approximately 200 Atlantans at the meeting that he wanted to create the "Saratoga of the South". Grady realized that success was hinged not upon the small number expected to register for educational classes, but upon the size of crowds coming out for the special attractions at night and the Sunday sermons. He encouraged those in attendance to invest $100 a piece to get the ball rolling, and they did.

By May, 1888, construction was underway to turn the barren and rough land into a showplace. Weekly and sometimes daily accounts of the progress at the Chautauqua were given in *The Atlanta Constitution*.

A huge grand opening celebration occurred on July 4, 1888 with grand speeches and a barbecue. Visitors saw an amazing place reminding them of scenes they had only read in "Arabian Nights". One writer describes a "tabernacle vast in size", but apparently built in such a way that the acoustics were perfect. Another building was also "colossal in size" and "crowned with a Moorish dome". Another building sent "up a slender minaret above the forest growth into the blue southern sky".

There was a man-made lake covering a few acres along with "flower beds, emerald green lawns…and fountains". One portion of the ground included a mound 42 feet high and 100 feet at the base. It was covered entirely in roses. Opposite the mound was a sunken garden sodded with blue grass and watered by many fountains. Paths wound from the sunken garden to the top of the mound.

It really must have been something to behold.

Advertised to the hilt, the Chautauqua never quite became all that Grady had hoped. He personally invested $5,000 of his own money for the grounds and buildings and another $2,000 to pay for staff. Grady's friend, Joel Chandler Harris wrote Grady continually wanted to protect investors who had gone "into the enterprise on his account, and as usual in such cases, the capitalists were perfectly willing to be protected.

Grady passed away after the second Chautauqua season in 1889. The company went on for a time, but without Grady's vision the desire for the Chautauqua eventually faded. By 1902, visitors at the Sweetwater Hotel were referencing the Chautauqua buildings as abandoned and deteriorating. The Piedmont Chautauqua lives on though in the history books even if the buildings are a distant Douglas County memory

Chapter 53

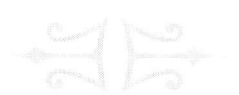

SENATOR MCKINLEY'S VISIT TO SALT SPRINGS

July, 1888 was an important month in Salt Springs (today's Lithia Springs). The Piedmont Chautauqua opened in grand style with a huge barbecue, fireworks, and speechmaking by the likes of Henry W. Grady who brought the Chautauqua to Douglas County.

During the late 19th and early 20th centuries people were hungry for cultural and educational opportunities. The Chautauqua caught on because the events included a mixture of instruction with play. Take the atmosphere of the fair and mix in speakers, teachers, musicians, entertainers and preachers for a couple of months, with a dash of fireworks, and you get the idea.

The Piedmont Chautauqua Association had been working hard extending invitations to all sorts of people to speak during the Chautauqua season including an invitation for Senator William McKinley.

McKinley's invitation set tongues to wagging because Georgia happened to be a state controlled by Democrats in 1888, and Congressman McKinley was not only a Yankee, he was a Republican Yankee.

At this point you should have a mental picture of Scarlett O'Hara's Aunt Pittypat exclaiming, "Yankees in Georgia!!!"

During the weeks leading up to McKinley's appearance at the Chautauqua on August 21st there were all sorts of rumors flying about that he would be snubbed. Some folks made accusations against the Chautauqua accusing it of bringing politics into what should be a non-political venue centered on education.

However, the rumors turned out to be just a bunch of drama to sell a few more papers.

Imagine that!

The day after McKinley's appearance at the Chautauqua, *The Atlanta Constitution* used one word to describe McKinley's visit – REMARKABLE.

The notion that Senator McKinley might speak at Salt Springs was remarkable – a great leader of one political party coming to Georgia to address an audience comprised mainly of folks from the opposing political party.

McKinley's subject was the protective tariff – the very subject that party lines were drawn upon, and if anyone had the right to discuss the tariff it was McKinley. He was considered to be the nation's go-to-guy regarding the issue in 1888.

Come on, you remember the tariff, right?

It was that one thread woven through your early American history course in high school, but in case you don't remember, a tariff is a tax, and the protective tariff would protect American business. The tariff was a tax on the importation of foreign goods.

Some argued that a protective tariff hinders free trade while others pointed out a protective tariff would prevent inexpensive imports from destroying local business.

In his biography of McKinley, Oscar King Davis states the senator's Chautauqua address was one of the more notable speeches he made during that year.

McKinley told the crowd, "One third of the cotton crop of the South is consumed at home. Who would not wish that all of it might find a market in the United States? We of the North would be better off; you of the South would be better off. The country at large would be the gainer if the whole cotton crop was fabricated in our own mills by our own people…"

The second reason why *The Atlanta Constitution* felt McKinley's speech was remarkable had to do with the crowd's enthusiasm. The article continued,"…when Major McKinley entered the hall, his appearance was the signal for that hearty welcome which Georgians know how to give so well. There was cheering and applause from all parts of the immense building. Half the audience rose and, waving hats, handkerchiefs, anything they had in their hands."

Notice how *The Atlanta Constitution* refers to McKinley as a major and not as president. That's because in 1888 McKinley was a United States congressman. He would not be president until 1898. The paper referred to him as Major because that had been his rank in the United States Army during the Civil War.

In fact, McKinley's experience during the war was one of the icebreakers that existed during the trip to Atlanta and then on to the Chautauqua Grounds. Even though he had served on the opposite side during the war, the men had common ground and shared their Civil War experiences.

Sometimes, that's all opposing parties need to move ahead – a little common ground.

But the most remarkable thing about the visit per the newspaper had to do with the quality of those present in the hall. There were prominent Democrats from all over the state as well as Alabama and Tennessee. There were professional men, manufacturers, merchants, and – gasp – leading Republicans, too.

The *Atlanta Constitution* stated, "The audience was thoroughly representative of the best elements of southern life."

Well, I guess it depended on your opinion, because not all of Georgia's Republicans were in the hall to hear McKinley's speech.

You see, most of Georgia's Republicans in 1888 were Black, and my research indicates they would not have been allowed admittance.

Chapter 54

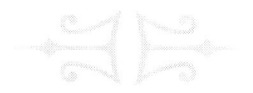

GARRETT'S VIEWS OF THE CHAUTAUQUA

Students and friends alike have often asked me how I became interested in history. Was it a special teacher?

Was it a family friend?

Perhaps a grandparent was a history buff and ignited this flame that basically rules my life these days.

Actually, it's a combination of many things including family members sharing stories, old buildings on a family farm, and books on the Civil War given to me as a child and hearing Franklin Garrett on local television discuss Atlanta's rich history.

Franklin Garrett is the only official historian the city of Atlanta has known. Garrett spent 28 years as the historian of the Coca Cola Company and researched various aspects of Atlanta's history as well during that time.

His book, *Atlanta and Its Environs* is one of my most favorite go-to resources regarding the history of the metro area and Douglas County and Douglasville does have a mention here and there.

During the 1880s one of the largest events held in Douglas County and perhaps never equaled since happened to be the Piedmont Chautauqua.

Franklin Garrett included a section about the Chautauqua in his book mainly centering on Henry W. Grady, editor of *The Atlanta Constitution* and cheerleader for the New South and Marion C. Kiser, Grady's partner in the Chautauqua.

Mr. Garrett provides an interesting view of the Chautauqua as well as a humorous remembrance from the opening remarks of Mr. Kiser. Here's what he had to say:

During the summer of 1888, [Henry W. Grady] was engrossed in his plans for the Piedmont Chautauqua…

The institution of the Chautauqua had attained great popularity in the United States since 1874, when the first Chautauqua Institution was founded on the shores of Lake Chautauqua, New York, to promote the training of Sunday school teachers. Since then some 42 other Chautauqua's had been organized in various parts of the country.

The Piedmont Chautauqua, patterned after the original, was largely the inspiration of Grady. In March, 1888, he called a meeting to explain the movement to a group of Atlantans.

A plan was evolved by asking 200 citizens to subscribe $100 each toward the undertaking, after which the Piedmont Chautauqua was incorporated, with Marion C. Kiser, wealthy wholesale shoe and dry goods merchant as president, and Grady as vice president.

The site selected for the new enterprise was the little resort town on the Georgia Pacific Railroad, then known as Salt Springs, though now and for many years past it has been called Lithia Springs. A spring-fed stream offered possibilities for an artificial lake and other attractions.

Salt Springs already had one resort hotel, advertised as "the most sumptuous summer hotel in the South," and the promoters of the Chautauqua proposed to erect two smaller hotels. In addition, plans called for a classroom building, a restaurant accommodating one thousand persons, and a tabernacle seating seven thousand.

Yes, you read that right. The tabernacle could hold up to seven thousand people.

Lots for summer cottages were staked out and offered for sale, space was provided for various outdoor sports, and the stream was dammed to provide boating and swimming facilities.

The Georgia Pacific promised to run special trains, making the 21-mile run from Atlanta to the grounds, three miles west of Austell, in 35 minutes.

The Chautauqua announced that it would have instructors in Bible, English, foreign languages, the natural sciences, the fine arts, physical education, and 'every chair of a first-class university'. The entire curriculum cost $10. Any single department was open for a $5 fee.

Grady realized that the success of the Chautauqua hinged, not upon the relatively small number expected to register for classes, but upon the size of the crowds coming out for the special attractions at night and for Sunday sermons.

A number of celebrities were signed up for the program. Congressman William McKinley and Roger Q. Mills came down from Washington to give Georgians contrasting views on the tariff, then a particularly warm issue. Dr. T. De Witt Talmadge delivered his lecture on "The Bright Side of Things"; and Thomas Nelson Page gave a reading of his "Unc' Edinburg's Drowndin'".

There were sermons, chalk talks and scientific demonstrations by lesser personalities. A "Hungarian orchestra" gave daily concerts, and several large bands appeared from time to time. Four leading manufacturers of fireworks produced striking displays in competition for the "Chautauqua championship" and a $1,000 prize.

July 4, 1888, was selected as the appropriate day upon which to open the Chautauqua grounds. The featured event was a barbeque and Chautauqua president, Marion C. Kiser was slated for an address of welcome. [Even though he was a successful businessman, sterling citizen and civic leader, Kiser was no public speaker nor did he profess to be.] Born and reared on a Fulton County (old Campbell) farm, he had had limited educational advantages. As a young man he had lived at Powder Springs, not far from Salt Springs, and had, in fact, begun his mercantile career there in a store owned by two older brothers, W.J. and M.P. Kiser [located at the corner of Pryor and Wall Streets].

Henry W. Grady, Jr., and his young friend and future [brother-in-law], *Eugene R. Black, were ticket-takers upon the occasion of the Chautauqua opening. Both recalled an incident in connection with President Kiser's address of welcome.*

The speech had been written out in advance by Grady, but when Kiser rose he fumbled around in his pocket without being able to find the manuscript. Finally, he looked out upon the crowd and began hesitatingly by saying, "Right down thar is whar I used to hunt foxes."

Not being able to think of any further extemporaneous remarks he turned to those closest to him and asked, "Whar's Grady?"

The Atlanta Constitution of the next morning reported that "President Kiser's speech was a model of good sense and good humor, well and briefly expressed. It was just such a sensible talk as was to be expected from so sensible a man."

The Chautauqua's largest crowd assembled on August 28 to hear the closing address by its impresario, Grady, on the subject of 'Cranks, Croakers, and Creditors'. The "cranks" were identified as those who started the enterprise, the "croakers", the fault-finders who predicted failure and the "creditors" those whose patience and cooperation enabled the Chautauqua to weather a successful season.

The primary purpose of the Chautauqua was the diffusion of knowledge. Grady believed so firmly in this objective he personally advanced $5,000 to complete the buildings and $2,500 towards making up a deficit on the teacher's salaries.

Certainly the idea for the Chautauqua in Atlanta was sound, though the directors erred in locating it so far from the city because some of the backers happened to own land there. In spite of this handicap, however, the Piedmont Chautauqua continued for many years to carry on the work Grady had started.

Chapter 55

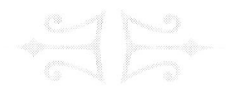

VIEWING THE SWEETWATER PARK HOTEL THROUGH A WRITER'S EYE

The website *WikiAnswers* advises that we spend approximately six months of our entire lifetime waiting at traffic lights.

Sitting – waiting – bored – even though there are several things you can do to pass the time. You can return a phone call, check your e-mail, send a text, check your list of things to do, or my personal favorite – I just sit and think.

More often than not I sit and think about my surroundings and contemplate how those places have changed over time. It seems natural that you would try to visualize certain areas regarding how they looked fifty to one hundred years ago, and I do try and do that. I guess it's just a symptom of researching and writing about the history of certain areas.

Some locations are fairly simple. As I head up Broad Street from Fairburn Road towards the Old Courthouse Museum I can easily visualize the look of the town in 1940 or even back to 1900.

The buildings are basically the same, and several landmarks such as the railroad are still there. It's actually very easy to visualize the spires of the once grand courthouse that stood up on the ridge rising up above the various businesses along Broad Street.

There is a well-published image of the Sweetwater Park Hotel that was located in downtown Lithia Springs at the turn of the century. When I sit at the red light at Veterans Memorial (Bankhead) and S. Sweetwater Road I try to visualize the hotel and how my surroundings looked back then.

I try.

It's hard.

The Sweetwater Park Hotel was located just southwest of the intersection of Veterans Memorial and S. Sweetwater covering many acres where there are now residential areas. It's amazing to think such a complex of buildings and beautiful grounds were ever located there, but it did exist.

The Sweetwater Park Hotel was trendy for the times. It was the place to be and be seen. Some very important folks including a president or two all enjoyed the many amenities of the resort which included rooms with electricity and individual baths, wide verandahs, excellent meals with European wines, and a train schedule that allowed guests to visit Atlanta for shopping or matinees and be back at the hotel by bedtime.

Thankfully, we have a few pictures of the hotel and grounds that have survived through the years, but I've also been able to locate a written description to help us appreciate the beauty of this long departed Lithia Springs landmark.

Madison J. Cawein was from Louisville, Kentucky. During his career he published 36 books and wrote over 1500 poems. His efforts earned him the nickname "the Keats of Kentucky." He is touted as having a lyrical way of describing nature and after reading his descriptions of the hotel grounds and surrounding areas I would have to agree.

Cawein, like many visitors to the Sweetwater Park Hotel, was in poor health and was hoping the famous Lithia waters would cure him. Cawein wasn't alone. During the late 1800s and into the turn of the century hundreds of people visited the hotel for health reasons as well as for recreation.

The book, *The Story of Madison Cawein: His Intimate Life as Revealed by His Letters* by Otto Arthur Rothert contains a few letters Cawein wrote during a stay at the hotel during May, 1902.

In a letter dated May 8, 1902 written to a Presbyterian minister by the name of Lucien V. Rule. Cawein described the hotel and grounds stating," ...It is very picturesque and romantic around Lithia Springs, whose waters are doing me a great deal of good, I think. I am also taking the baths...The woods here are overgrown with wild flowers; wild honeysuckle, wild phlox and calcanthus; and ferns! – in masses, sometimes above your waist. The brook bubbles over beds of crystal, honestly and virtually speaking, - not figuratively, - for everywhere, in the fields, on the roads, in the woods and scattered boulders and pebbles and pieces of sparkling white spar, which is crystal of some sort. I have seen lots of it and the creeks ripple and babble musically over it."

Cawein continues, "Near the [Sweetwater Park Hotel] is a place going absolutely to ruin now; in its time it was the Chautauqua, where revivals were held, meetings of all sort, for pleasure, religion and politics. Vast buildings, built in a forest, ...and of fantastic yet beautiful architecture of the Moorish order, with towers and turrets and loggias; also a large amphitheater capable of seating thousands are slowly moulding to decay here. What was once an artificial lake, covering several acres, is now merely a frog-pond filled with mud and weeds in whose center an old boat is slowing rotting...in one spot there is a mound some twenty to thirty feet high up [which all around winds a road]. The road is scarcely discernible now, for the entire mound is overgrown with tame honey-suckle vines, commencing to bloom, and forms a fragrant tombstone for the dead-body of the old place lying mouldering there. I love to climb to the top of this green and fragrant monument and stand there and watch the sunset in the west, and listen to the wind in the pines that seems mourning something lost and never to be found again – Never! Never! It is a lovely place, altogether, this hotel, with its charming people and its beautiful grounds filled with flowers and trees, the holly, the roses and fountains, syringe bushes and mountain laurel in full bloom and over it all the blue sky of Georgia vibrating with the melody of birds, the mocking bird and the thrush, whose note is the sweetest I ever heard."

The grand Piedmont Chatauqua was held in 1888. I find it rather sad that just a few years later the buildings were abandoned as Mr. Cawein reports in his letter.

The next day Cawein wrote Miss Jenny Loring Robbins. Ms. Robins lived in Louisville at one point she was the guiding force behind Louisville, Kentucky's Speed Art Museum, a museum begun by her aunt.

Cawein described the mill at New Manchester to Miss Loring Robbins stating, "...I am falling more and more in love with the hotel, its grounds, and the people in and around them, to say nothing of the woods and the waters, the latter of which I am drinking with much gusto and, I hope, benefit.

I have found a number of old mills here – all dilapidated or going to ruin; one a total ruin. One on Austell Run is supposed to be still in operation, but I have been there twice and neither time have I seen a soul. On the Sweetwater Creek, six miles from here, I found an old grist-mill, below a rushing and roaring dam. It is a great gaunt thing of frame, weather-beaten and old, but still in operation.

A half-mile below it, under a wild hill-side, on which the dogwood was blooming in profusion, together with the wild honey-suckle, the other mill, built of rock and brick, towers five stories high. It was burned by General Sherman during the war and stands a sad relic of that time. It was a cotton mill, and the workers in it lived on the hillside in their cottages, but their homes were burned also and not a vestige of them is left."

Cawein continued, "Only the ruin – here is a wilderness of trees, great trees, grown up in its gaunt interior, crowding its crumbling walls, and the wild vines and creepers trailing over and covering its rocks and bricks – stands pathetically looking out upon the tumbling waters beneath and the projecting pines around. The creek, wooded on both sides, foams and roars past it, over huge rocks and boulders, upon which it stares with its one mighty arch of stone, in which the mill-wheel once rushed and sounded and its empty windows like hollow eyes in the face of death."

This was written 112 years ago, yet it is a description that still applies today, don't you think?

On May 11, 1902 in a letter to James Whitcomb Riley Cawein wrote, "Your note did me lots of good, coming just in the nick of time when Mr. [Robert W.] Geiger was visiting me at Sweetwater. He and the rest of the literary clan, Harris and Stanton [Evelyn Harris and Frank L Stanton who called on Cawein] want you to come down here. Well, here I am and delighted am I with the hotel and everybody in it. But I can't say that am getting well rapidly…I am not much better for all the water I drink and all the baths I take. And so, about Friday or Saturday next will find me wending my weary way home again to commence the nauseating round of medicine taking once more. I don't know where it's going to end. Nothing seems to benefit me. Things that benefit, that cure, other people don't have any effect on me.…will probably see Joel Harris Wednesday. He is still ailing, but sends me word he wants to see me."

At this point I think it's necessary to identify the folks Cawein mentions. I'm almost certain Geiger is a railroad executive who happened to live in Atlanta at the time. Evelyn Harris is the son of Joel Chandler Harris who we remember as "Uncle Remus", and Frank L. Stanton was a columnist for *The Atlanta Constitution* and was a famous American lyricist. During the 1920s he would serve as Georgia's poet laureate.

James Whitcomb Riley, who the letter was addressed to, was also a very famous writer and poet and was very popular with children.

Eight days later on May 19, 1902 Cawein writes again to James Whitcomb Riley saying, "I saw Uncle Remus [in Atlanta] last week and enjoyed an hour-or-so talk with him at his beautiful home in the West End. Stanton was with me, also Evelyn Harris [son of Joel Chandler Harris]. Joel Chandler Harris looks poorly. He is still a very sick man. I am sorry to say. Mr. Geiger and Stanton were out to see me last Saturday, stayed to supper and we had quite a walk and considerable talk."

Cawein continues, " I am returning home today. Shall go to Atlanta as the guest of Mr. Geiger for a day or so, then home once more. My condition is about the same as it was when I came here. However, I have enjoyed myself greatly wandering around the country and setting on the verandah or under the trees meeting people or watching the roses bloom. My English volume of "Kentucky Poems", with an introduction by Edmund Grosse, will be out sometime next month, I think, so look out for a copy; I am going to fire one at your kindly countenance."

Cawein mentions Joel Chandler Harris's "beautiful home in the West End of Atlanta". It is of course, The Wren's Nest which still stands.

Madison J. Cawein earned approximately one hundred dollars a month from his writing, a comfortable sum at the turn of the century. Unfortunately, poor investments and the Stock Market downturn in 1912 meant his savings simply evaporated. At some point between 1912 and 1914 Cawein was placed on the relief list with the Authors Club of New York City.

Over the next five years Cawein's health worsened, and he died on December 8, 1914.

It would seem that the end of the story for Cawein is just as sad as the end for the Sweetwater Park Hotel and the Piedmont Chautauqua.

I'm grateful, however, that Cawein's letters survive giving us a little insight into how wonderful the Lithia Springs resort area was for folks to visit!

Section Six

THE COTTON MILL

Chapter 56

THE COTTON MILL – AN IMPORTANT NEW SOUTH INGREDIENT

LOIS COTTON MILLS, DOUGLASVILLE GA.

The Georgia General Assembly approved Douglasville as our county seat about the same time New South ideals were gaining momentum across the South, so business and political leaders had a unique opportunity to set up each facet of the town to fit the New South image.

The main commercial district was positioned to run parallel along the railroad track so that it could be seen by travelers who might be looking to move to a vibrant city. The railroad was also in close proximity for moving and receiving freight. Within a few years buildings went from being wooden structures to permanent brick buildings with all types of architectural elements that were innovative and pleasing to the eye not to mention promoting productivity and wealth. Stephanie Ayleworth, Douglasville's former Main Street Manager has conducted exhaustive research into the city's New South beginnings and advises Douglasville had sixty-two buildings in 1895, and by 1911 that number had jumped to eighty-four.

So, the town fathers had a growing downtown commercial district and a railroad. The next ingredient they needed was a way to revive the devastated economy following the Civil War and Reconstruction. It is only natural they looked to the cotton fields because they knew cotton was king.

Cotton is king!!!

Isn't that what every student learns about the South as they advance through each level of American History?

Don't worry. I'm certainly not going to lead you down a path pretending some other commodity was on the throne. I'm a history teacher for goodness sake! It's true. Prior to the Civil War cotton was the major ingredient to the southern economy.

Cotton was king, but what isn't taught generally is that cotton continued to be king and drove the economy for some time. Usually, most of the content that is taught after the Civil War leaves cotton behind overshadowing it with the events involving Reconstruction, and moving on into the Gilded Age. The importance of cotton is rarely mentioned in postbelllum studies unless you are sitting in an eighth grade Georgia history classroom with a very content focused educator.

Just because the Thirteenth Amendment emancipated the slave that doesn't mean the cotton fields went fallow. In fact, one of the tenants of the New South philosophy had everything to do with cotton and reviving the southern economy.

It wasn't just about getting cotton production up. The New South philosophy was all about getting the cotton mills to the cotton fields.

Douglasville's leaders knew they had to have a cotton mill and set about raising the money. In fact, Douglasville wasn't alone in their quest for a cotton mill. Every little town across Georgia and across the South were vying to build their own mill mainly through the investments of Northern manufacturers, but it was also key for citizens of the town to invest in building a mill.

In her history of Douglas County, Fannie Mae Davis writes that town leaders called a meeting to appeal to local citizens to get Douglasville out of what they identified as "the doldrums". They discussed how to best develop the town and committees were formed to pursue a bank, a hotel, and cotton mill. Mrs. Davis quotes an article in *The Atlanta Constitution* describing how several people gave short talks. Joseph S. James concluded with an appeal to the people to open their hearts and purses in giving. One of the items everyone agreed upon at the meeting was a town slogan proclaiming, "People make the town!"

Have you ever heard the saying, "Location, location, location"? If a postbellum town was seeking to build a cotton mill the location was very important. The mill had to be close to the railroad, and it had to be near cotton warehouses.

Back in the early days of Douglasville Church Street was known as Factory Street per Fannie Mae Davis's county history and early insurance maps. By its very name town fathers hoped Factory Street would indicate to investors that the town recognized industry was important, and it was welcome.

The strategy worked because Douglasville's first cotton mill was Eden Park Mill, and it was located along Factory Street. An article published in *The Atlanta Constitution* indicates the capital needed to build the factory was $50,000. The majority of the stock was held by a northern investor named Simon Baer and Joseph S. James, Douglasville's first mayor and prime New South booster. The paper also advised about 4,000 spindles were operated and over one hundred employees secured work at the mill.

Unfortunately, the Eden Park Mill was consumed by fire around midnight on April 7, 1895, and it was a total loss. The design of the mill turned out to be the culprit. The furnace had been placed directly beneath the spinning rooms and a spark from an engine caused the fire.

The pride of Douglasville was gone.

So, James and his Yankee partner, Baer set about to build another mill. This time they chose a location one-half mile east of the central business district on a parcel of land then totaling fifty acres. This location was actually better since it was parallel to the railroad just like the central business district.

You've seen it.

You've driven past it.

It's still there.

It is the white brick abandoned and dilapidated building along U.S. 78/Bankhead Highway between Courtland and Hagin Streets.

Within two years following the New Eden fire, *The New South*, a paper published in Douglasville, announced a contract for the construction of the Georgia Western Cotton Mill. Later the mill would be known as the New Century Cotton Mill and then the Lois Cotton Mill, named after one of Joseph S. James' daughters. The anticipated completion date for the building was January 1, 1898.

The Cawhern Building Company out of Atlanta would oversee the construction using local labor and bricks that were created right here in Douglas County. The total cost for building and equipment would be approximately $430,000 and James and Baer anticipated hiring 450 employees.

It would be a major force in the economy of Douglasville and Douglas County as area farmers would have a local source to purchase their cotton and to feed the 20,000 spindles the mill would spin.

The Atlanta Constitution finally announced on November 15, 1908 the Douglasville mill had begun operating the day before, but it was approximately ten years after the construction had been announced.

There were several reasons for this. First, James and Baer had not received an insurance settlement for the Eden Park fire. Second, business that supplied the Eden Park machinery had filed a law suit in 1897 indicating they had not been paid. James held off the creditors for a while by claiming the shipment of equipment had never arrived.

Then to make matters even more complicated Simon Baer severed his business relationship with James. It wasn't until 1907 when James was able to secure a primary investor for the second mill by joining ranks with a South Carolina mill owner by the name of M.E. Greer per an article in *The Atlanta Constitution* dated October, 1907.

As far as cotton mills built during the New South time period go the mill in Douglasville was and still is very unique. It is only one of five mills built in the South using Charles Praray's innovated design for mills patented under the name "Praray Improved Construction for Mills", and is only one of two where the tale tell zigzag walls are still standing.

Ayleworth's research indicates according to the patent, Praray's striking design is best identified by the zigzag appearance of the exterior walls and windows. The mill is an excellent example of Northern architecture adapting to the New South economy. The unique architecture of the mill was a cost saving device.

The mill was built on two separate foundations. The inner foundation housed the equipment, while the outer foundation and walls were for the vast window casings. This construction technique made the walls cheaper to construct and, in case of fire, they could be more easily removed and less costly to replace. The walls were entirely free from strain. The outer walls allowed for more windows, thus allowing more light and ventilation and facilitating longer hours of operation."

Over the years the windows were removed and bricked over as air conditioning and electric lighting was improved.

By the early 20th century Douglasville had evolved into a modern town prophesied by New South visionaries such as Henry Grady per Fannie Mae Davis mainly due to the New Century Cotton Mill, and when it opened the mill became the greatest economic success in the history of Douglasville.

Sadly, the 104 year old structure stands abandoned yet it remains a symbol of Douglasville's pioneering father's vision made manifest per Stephanie Ayleworth.

Unfortunately, its unique design gives the building a deceptively modern appearance which ultimately was its downfall regarding identification for National Register status. It wasn't the only reason for not being recognized, but I'll address that issue in a future column.

Chapter 57

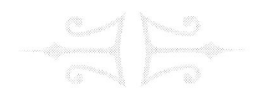

MR. GEER AND THE GRANITE

I know it's easy to fuss about the downtown business district in Douglasville. Some of the buildings are crumbling away and many remain empty, but the buildings are protected. The buildings aren't going to disappear from one day to the next unless some act of nature occurs or without many people knowing about it first.

It's a different story regarding our late 19th century to turn-of-the-century homes. With the exception of the Roberts Mozley House which is headquarters for the Cultural Arts Council of Douglasville/Douglas County, our older homes are all privately owned and have no historic designation. It's a personal choice regarding National Register status, and many owners don't want to follow the criteria to keep it. I certainly understand this, but so many our earliest homes are gone. They were taken down for one reason or another over the years and replaced with other buildings or blankets of asphalt.

The homes that remain are treasures. Many of the people I meet who live in Douglasville's oldest homes realize the importance their residence holds within our collective history, but so many other citizens don't realize, know, or even care.

My hope is by educating more and more people regarding these structures – who lived in them and their contribution to Douglasville history – we can make more people begin to realize the importance of preserving and saving some of our older structures.

One important home sits at the corner of Colquitt and Strickland.

It's easy to drive right past it without much notice mainly because a business has taken over the former home. There are no flowers or furniture on the porch or toys to signal someone lives there, but for over half a century the structure was a home.

This home was built by M.E. Geer during the first decade of the 20th century though today it is home to Douglas County Resource Alliance – an organization that advocates for and provides services to individuals with developmental disabilities.

Mr. Geer's grandson, Richard Geer Morgan, has been in touch with me and has advised his grandfather was never called by his legal first name – Major. If anything besides "Mr. Geer", it was "M.E. Geer" or "Ernest Geer".

Mr. Geer was born in Belton, South Carolina which is in the Anderson area. On April 23, 1902 an issue of *The Anderson Intelligencer* stated... *There was a reunion of the Geer family at the residence of Mrs. Mary Geer in this town, Sunday, April 20th, at which were present her children and their families as follows: President John M. Geer of the Easley Cotton Mills and family, D. Aaron Geer, merchant of this place,...M. Earnest Geer merchant of this place and Professor Ben E. Geer, Furman.*

Mary Geer had repeatedly told her sons they needed to move out of Anderson since they could not make anything of themselves raising cotton. Well, they didn't exactly raise cotton, but at one time or another all four were cotton mill presidents.

By 1907, Earnest Geer was no longer a merchant in Anderson. *Textile World Record* (volume 34) advises he had taken a position as vice president and manager of the Lois Cotton Mill in Douglasville under a section titled "New Mill Construction". By taking the position in Douglasville, Geer had followed his mother's advice and joined what would become the family business, of sorts.

John Mattison Geer was president of Easley Cotton Mills in Easley, South Carolina – a 68 acre complex that today is protected by National Register status. His brother Ben took over for John in 1911 when he became ill and passed away. Later, in 1933 Ben E. Geer returned to Furman University where he had been a professor and took over as president of the college.

Getting back to the house on Strickland Street – it seems that while the cotton mill was being built and during the process of digging a well on the property a vein of granite was discovered. The granite was extracted and cut into blocks. Ernest Geer was in the process of building his home on Strickland Street and needed a foundation.

You guessed it – the granite from the mill site became the foundation for the Geer home. As soon as I read Mr. Geer's grandson's e-mail advising me of this I couldn't wait to head over there to the house and see it for myself.

I began snapping pictures as soon as I got out of the car noticing that the home did indeed have a foundation of granite as well as granite front steps.

And then I remembered I was on private property.

I walked into the office, and handed the folks my business card and asked, "Did you know the foundation of this home came from the cotton mill property?"

I'm sure they thought I was crazy, but they were very gracious, and I was happy to discover there were employees who did realize they worked in a home with some history behind it.

They allowed me to walk around on the first floor and take pictures.

Yes, it seems Ernest Geer didn't really have a choice regarding his profession and found himself in Douglasville where he would manage our cotton mill into the 1930s, but unfortunately, the Depression was too much and eventually the mill was sold to what would become a string of owners through the 1970s.

Mr. Geer's grandson tells me the people of Douglasville had confidence in his grandfather, however. He stayed on in town raising his family, and served as mayor of Douglasville and even served as a Justice of the Peace.

I'm going to keep M. E. Geer's name on my mind as I continue to research Douglas County history including *Sentinel* and county records research. I'm sure I'll be writing about him again real soon!

Chapter 58

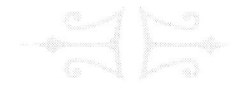

DEMOLITION BY NEGLECT OR HOW DOUGLASVILLE LOST ITS MOST IMPORTANT HISTORIC ASSET

This past week I performed a little experiment. I threw the word "history" out at various people – friends, waitresses, store clerks, even a couple of surprised strangers – and asked them to tell me what immediately popped into their minds.

Various words were thrown back to me – events, dates, maps, wars, battles, – and the list goes on.

None of the responses really surprised me, but there are other words to parallel with the word history. Words like preservation, remember, and trust come to mind and unfortunately, the words failure, greed, demolish, surrender, neglect, and ignore are on the flipside as I continue examining the winding path of history our cotton mill in Douglasville has taken.

I shared the story last week regarding how Douglasville ended up with the cotton mill and how important the mill was to our economic health over most of the last century.

Now I want to share the rest of the story regarding how history can be neglected and forgotten by the very people we trust to preserve it. Sometimes in their attempts to improve the lives of citizens in the here and now they actually betray the trust handed to them by citizens who took their leave a long time ago. They also end up cheating future generations regarding our historical record.

History can also be used by folks who are just looking for easy outs in business in order to leverage property or satisfy some misguided need to collect historic properties, and then allow them to die a slow death of neglect for some strange reason I simply cannot fathom.

It's a shame that a unique and proud cotton mill with such a rich history ended up as a sad and lonely piece of Douglasville history slated to be sold on the courthouse steps in just a few days.

Construction for the mill began in 1897 and over the years mill housing was built for employees. The mill village also included a company store, athletic fields and churches. In 1934, the mill was involved in the Textile Worker's Strike of 1934, the largest labor strike in the history of the United States, with over 44,000 mill workers across Georgia on strike regarding various issues of discrimination and evictions. In 1953, sources indicate the cotton mill was Douglasville's largest employer with 3,000 workers or one-fourth of the county's population.

It was during the late 1990s that the Douglasville Historic Preservation Commission and Douglasville City government became involved with the cotton mill property due to a proposed widening project for Bankhead Highway that is still on hold to this day. In case you aren't aware when the Georgia Department of Transportation or GDOT wants to make any changes regarding our roads they have to conduct various studies including one that determines how any historic sites in the proposed area will be impacted by the road changes.

At first all GDOT did was a quick assessment referred to in a later document as a "windshield survey" meaning they didn't even get out of the car. An article published in the *Cultural Resource Management* magazine presented by the National Parks Service indicates, "Local historians were unaware of the patented design for mills in …Douglasville, Georgia", and since the windows had been bricked in "the mill in Douglasville was deceptive in appearance causing it to be overlooked [initially] in a [GDOT} survey of historic resources."

On November 13, 1997, the United States Department of the Interior issued a letter to the Georgia Department of Natural Resources, Historic Preservation Division noting GDOT had not designated the cotton mill as historic and sited their own research DID indicate the structure had historic value even though it had been "altered on the exterior". The letter further stated, "This mill IS certainly worthy of additional examinations."

Finally, on January 30, 1998 officials with GDOT, the City of Douglasville, as well as officials from the Georgia Historic Preservation Division met and all were in agreement the cotton mill site was eligible for listing on the National Register of Historic Places under Criterion C for its distinctive method of construction.

Now, here is where I need to make a clarification. The agreement between all of the government entities regarding historic status does not mean the property was automatically protected. Anyone can fill out the paperwork and nominate a site for National Register status but the owner of the property can turn it down.

I also need to note that National Register status does not protect a property from neglect or demolition.

Yes, it can't be forgotten that during all of the to and fro between all of the governmental agencies and officials the mill property was privately owned. The wrangling over historical status merely had to do with the GDOT project and the hoops they are required to jump through when trying to get a project off the ground. During the initial wrangling over historic status the mill property was owned by Kenneth Farmer and then in August, 1999 the property was transferred to Fellowship Christian Center, Inc.

If the Bankhead widening project had happened the way it was initially proposed the outside wall of the mill would have had to be removed if not the entire structure, so of course the situation had to be fully examined. The widening project could have been very beneficial to the property owner as a selling point, but historical status could hinder GDOT with their plans as they were.

Eight months prior to Fellowship Christian taking over the property the Douglasville Historic Preservation Commission prepared a document titled "Report for Nomination: Proposal for Historic Designation Georgia Western Cotton Mill containing the information noted above. In fact, I've been told the cotton mill was one of the first properties the Commission identified formally as a historic site.

Sadly though, I have been advised the City Council pressed the commission to remove the listing a couple of years ago after being convinced by a developer that the historic designation limited development options. Rather than take steps to prevent deterioration and market the property as an asset, the Mayor and Council for all intents and purposes promoted its demise.

An undated letter from the City of Douglasville to the Douglasville Historic Preservation Commission requests the Commission to remove the cotton mill property from the local historic registry. The letter advises "the buildings are in a state of disrepair and it is unlikely they can be returned to a state of historic significance".

I have a problem with that. Historical significance does NOT disappear simply because a site is not in pristine condition.

The letter goes on to state, "the buildings are unsafe to occupy and are a hazard to the community. We need to pursue condemnation procedures and are unable to do so due to its historic affiliation."

First, it bothers me that the letter is not dated. Second, it bothers me that if condemnation was on the City's mind why has the property not been condemned? It seems to me the "historical status" of the property was the hindrance.

Inman Park Properties took ownership of the mill property over in 2001, and here is where the ride gets even bumpier.

Let me introduce you to Jeff Notrica, the person at the helm of Inman Park Properties, hereafter referred to as IPP. Do a quick look across the web and you can quickly see several adjectives that describe Mr. Notrica – businessman, property developer, landlord, deadbeat, slumlord, scum of the earth, innkeeper, crook, and hoarder. Hoarding is defined as the excessive acquisition of possessions and failure to use or discard them, and I think the shoe fits.

Under the guise of IPP and various other LLC businesses Mr. Notrica spent the1990s and the first few years of the last decade buying up property after property in Atlanta, Birmingham, and Savannah.

As I continued with my research I noticed a pattern.

The majority of the properties IPP acquired were interesting or significant in some way. IPP acquired the properties and generally did nothing to improve them even if they had tenants. Apparently IPP charged high rents, but the buildings were in poor shape and remained that way so they could be tax write-offs. In some cases IPP even told prospective tenants THEY had to pay for property upgrades. Then of course, IPP would take out mortgages on each property for up to four times the actual value of the property. The borrowed money would fund the purchase of more properties and the process would begin anew.

For example, IPP bought the Gordon School property in the East Atlanta Village for $200,000 and then placed over $4 million in debt against it.

Improvements?

No, at one point there were trees growing on the second floor of the structure.

There was also a small parking lot in IPP's portfolio bought for $127,000, but was quickly mortgaged for $600,000. Guess there was yet another historic property for IPP to snap up.

The whole business model (if you really want to call it that) harkens to one of those late night infomercials where the announcer repeatedly tells you, "Yes! You too can get rich quick in real estate!"

Even our own cotton mill property was purchased by IPP for $195,000 in 2001. In November, 2004 a mortgage was issued from Omni Bank (it has since been assigned to another company) for $1.2 million dollars.

Was the money used to improve the property?

No.

Of course during the time IPP has owned the cotton mill property the property taxes have run behind. The last delinquency is for 2008, 2009, and 2010 leading to a Sheriff's Sale.

The now defunct website for IPP stated the company motto was "Preserving the future by saving the past".

Really?

Sad.

Many links across the Internet discuss IPP's holdings in the East Atlanta Village explaining how many of them were in a state of neglect including huge piles of garbage and tires. One article details IPP's ownership of the Kreigshaber House which you might recognize by the name Wrecking Bar (now saved by someone else and open), and The Clermont (the lounge is still open), as well as other very historic Atlanta properties.

A Birmingham news article from 2009 details how IPP began buying up historical properties in Birmingham tying up as much as $10 million with at least 11 properties that were allowed to decay.

Of course foreclosures began to plague IPP around 2008 and 2009, and I would imagine they are continuing to this day. While the current economic downturn did hurt Notrica and IPP, his past history clearly shows today's commercial real estate climate is not the cause of what can only be termed "a mess."

And through this whole thing one has to wonder where the cities and counties are? Why are they not enforcing their regulations and accountability regarding code enforcement? What about the tax delinquencies?

Yes, there are several reasons why I'd like to kick Mr. Notrica but in an attempt to be fair I would like to mention that at one point he was appointed to the board of The Atlanta Preservation Center. It would seem, however, it was a move by the group's leader just to keep IPP/Notrica close, and it was a very controversial issue among group members.

In 2003, the preservation group placed the Trust Company Bank at Monroe Drive and Fire Station No. 11 on the "Most Endangered Historic

Places" list. Both were owned by IPP/Notrica and magically the two historic spots were turned around earning Notrica awards and accolades. A quick Internet search also advises success with properties in Little Five Points where Front Page News and Tiuana Garage are located.

And today?

Mr. Notrica lives in Savannah where he promotes himself as an innkeeper at the Dresser Palmer House. The website advises, "Don't be surprised to see him checking you in when you arrive or fixing drinks at the evening social." His bio at the website only mentions he owned a small inn in Atlanta. I didn't see a single word about his status as a land developer.

While I do enjoy historic inns somehow I don't see myself ever allowing Mr. Notrica to pour me a drink.

Chapter 59

A PRIMER REGARDING BROWNFIELDS

Word of warning – this is not my typical column, but it does fall into the realm of history since so many historical properties are also classified as brownfields due to their past use.

A brownfield isn't what you might think at first. They don't necessarily refer to fields, and they are necessarily brown, but brownfields do concern real estate.

The first instance of the term "brownfield" being used in any way was during a U.S. Congressional hearing in June, 1992. That year also saw the first detailed policy analysis regarding brownfields by the Cuyahoga County Planning Commission for the Cleveland, Ohio area. Cuyahoga's Sunar Houserman project was the first brownfield pilot project in 1992. The Sunar Houserman focused on redeveloping an industrial plant that had been in business since 1913. Once the project was completed the site became home to several businesses, created 181 new jobs and generated more than one million in annual revenue.

One of the largest brownfield sites in the United States that has been successfully redeveloped is Atlantic Station in Atlanta. The site originally saw light industry when the Atlanta Hoop Company produced cotton bale ties and barrel hoops as early as 1901 and then more heavy industrial use and contamination by Atlantic Steel. The EPA awarded the Atlantic Station project their Phoenix Award as the Best National Brownfield Redevelopment in 2004.

The Environmental Protection Agency (EPA) defines a brownfield site as "real property, the expansion, redevelopment, or reuse of which may be complicated by the presence of a hazardous substance, pollutant, or contaminant." Today, the National Brownfield Association estimates between 400,000 to 1 million properties across the United States might classify as a brownfield site. They estimate up to $2 trillion in real estate is undervalued due to the presence of contamination.

Typical contaminants include hydrocarbon spillages, solvents, pesticides, heavy metals such as lead based paints and asbestos. Brownfields also include properties that are underutilized for various socioeconomic reasons such as abandonment, obsolescence, tax delinquency and/or blight.

In 2002, Congress passed a bill to put an end to excessive regulations and litigations many entrepreneurs incur when revitalizing dilapidated fields called the Small Business Liability Relief and Brownfields Revitalization Act. The Act provides for is funds to assess and clean up brownfields. Financial incentives and regulatory requirements are included in other related laws and regulations.

Per the EPA the Brownfield Program has increased residential property values by 2-3 percent when nearby brownfields are addressed, leveraged 72,434 jobs nationwide, and promotes area-wide planning.

Think about sites that have been abandoned or underused industrial and commercial facilities that might be available for reuse. Think about old textile mills, industrial plants, gas stations, drycleaners, places that look like illegal dumping grounds, junkyards and other abandoned commercial or industrial properties. The key to remember is sites do not have to be identified. They only have to have the potential of meeting the brownfield descriptors to be included.

So, do you think we might have a few brownfield sites in Douglasville?

Well, of course we do!

I wasn't surprised at all when I received a notice from the City regarding a community meeting to discuss their brownfield program last week.

The notice I received from the City advised, "Douglasville has many brownfields that offer an opportunity for redevelopment. The City is working on a strategy to redevelop these properties. The first step in that strategy is to apply for grant funding from the EPA to assess these properties and determine if contamination is indeed present. The grant application is being prepared and will be submitted to the EPA for consideration in November, 2011." The EPA will announce the communities who will receive grant money during the Spring or Summer, 2012.

The meeting I attended was led by a Joe Morici, a consultant with CTC Public Benefit Corporation. The City of Douglasville is using CTC to assist them with the grant application process. CTC specializes in EPA brownfield grants and has handled 50 such grants since the program began in the mid-1990s.

The application is for up to $200,000 regarding hazardous substances, pollutants, or contaminants and up to $200,000 regarding petroleum contaminants. The process is very competitive, and I've been told community involvement is the main component the EPA looks for when reviewing applications.

Initially the City is looking at the Lois Cotton Mill site and the County Jail that will be vacated soon as locations to include with the application. Other properties can be included as well, and suggestions from citizens would be most appreciated.

As many of you know the cotton mill site is most certainly on my radar as a missed and ignored historic site for our city. In my view it is THE most historically significant location in the City of Douglasville. As I stated in August in my column titled *Demolition by Neglect,* "It's a shame that a unique and proud cotton mill with such a rich history ended up as a sad and lonely piece of Douglasville's history."

The mill site was sold on the Courthouse steps days in September, 2011. The City of Douglasville now retains control of the property, and

I strongly agree that by including the mill property on the EPA grant application it is the best course of action to move forward.

While contamination and deterioration has made the structure of the mill impossible to save it is still my FERVENT hope that the unique and historic Praray wall – or just a section of it – that is still standing can be saved in some way and not merely ground up to serve as filler for the road bed for the Highway 92 realignment project as some officials have suggested.

Several dozen of you recommended my original column regarding the tragedy of the mill site on *Facebook*, some of you commented here at *Patch*, and I know the column inspired many of you to e-mail me and others regarding the situation. Please get the word out regarding the brownfield application. The application process isn't just about the mill property, but is about identifying other sites within the City of Douglasville that might fit the descriptors I provided above.

So, do you want to help shape Douglasville's redevelopment? Do you want to have input in transforming abandoned or underutilized property into new uses that benefit the community?

There are several things you can do to help. You can attend future community meetings, voice your concerns, ask questions, spread the news, and participate in the redevelopment plan once it's in place.

Chapter 60

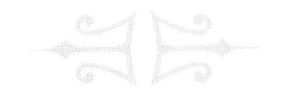

MOTHER'S DAY, THE MILL, AND MEMORIES

One of the hardest things I have ever done – and there have been many hard things – was walking away from the hospital room where my mother lay dying. I'd been at her bedside alone with her all day. I had been grateful for the time I could spend with her, just she and I, but once my sister arrived I felt she needed her time alone with mom, so I made ready to leave.

Still when I told Mother I would see her later our eyes met and she smiled in that little knowing way she had. We knew we would not see each other for a long, long time, but we didn't acknowledge it, being strong for each other. What I really wanted to do was jump up on the bed next to her tiny, frail frame, wrap my arms around her and demand that she stay, but I didn't, and it wouldn't have mattered at all.

My selfish demand wouldn't have changed anything.

Mother had a date to keep with my memories.

I told her I loved her, and she told me she loved me, and I walked out.

Mother died early the next morning as my sister brushed her hair.

Things change.

People pass.

Buildings burn.

But the memories remain.

Sometimes we don't want that exchange.

It doesn't seem fair exchanging memories for the real thing or for the real experience, but it happens whether we want it to or not.

So, as of today – May 12, 2012 – our mill is gone, but if we are really honest with ourselves it was gone when the mill ceased to operate and the doors were padlocked. It ceased to exist when the first awning sagged. It ceased to exist when the fence surrounding the property developed a patina of rust.

Our mill ceased to exist when Inman Park Properties purchased it and wound it up in their little scheme to allow dozens of properties across the Atlanta area to be demolished by neglect.

As I've discussed before the property was doomed once Inman Park Properties purchased it, and once the city failed to hold their feet to the fire regarding code violations as well. The property was doomed when the Douglasville Historic Preservation Commission was pressed to remove the mill from a list regarding historic designation. As I mentioned in my article in August, sources indicated to me the City Council pressed the commission to remove the [historic designation] a couple of years ago after being convinced by a developer that the designation limited development options, and because no one held the property owner's feet to the fire regarding code violations the minute the property began to slide down into despair.

We ended up with a derelict eyesore.

However, while those who control historic properties ultimately have the final say, memories don't fade. Memories don't die. Memories don't rust away or cave in, and they certainly don't perish in a fiery stroke that wiped the mill away Saturday night.

In fact, if you stop and think about it fire is often used to refine things, to make things stronger, even our memories.

I was heartened Saturday morning to see so many Douglas County citizens being interviewed on television regarding the mill, as well as comments I saw on *Facebook* regarding the building's significance to their lives. Our people built the mill, our people worked at the mill, they met and married because of the mill and they supported their families as well as Douglas County's economy.

Most citizens in Douglas County had a connection to that building in some way or another.

You can neglect a property into despair, you can formally decide a property has no historical value, but you can't erase the memory or the connections citizens have to the property. Many spoke of grandparents and parents who worked at the mill. Some mentioned the traveling ball team. I've heard they were considered to be the best traveling ball team in the state. I've heard stories of young adults who walked Fairburn Road daily to deliver a dinner pail to their parent working away in the mill. All great memories to hold onto, even though the building itself was in dire need of a meeting with a wrecking ball.

I was up early Saturday morning around 1 a.m. when the Douglasville Police posted a picture of the fire on their *Twitter* account which also posts to *Facebook*. I immediately posted something about it on my wall and immediately assumed a group of kids had probably gotten inside the fence and a fire had either gotten out of control, or it had been set deliberately in some macabre pretense of having fun.

A young man, a neighbor of mine named Tyler Rowan, instantly commented on my post and his words regarding the mill gave me instant pause. Now, I'm not that naive. I know that over the years photographers have gotten in the mill and kids had gotten in as well, and not necessarily to take pictures, but Tyler gave me a different perspective regarding the fence jumpers when he told me, "I can't tell you how many nights we spent just exploring and enjoying that place. So much history. The place was stuck in time. There were fire extinguishers on the ground still in place from where they were left when the place caught fire in the 1980s. Dated papers scattered around. Not to mention the top of the water tower had to be one of the best views in Douglas County. You could see Atlanta, Downtown Douglasville, Hiram, and a little of Villa Rica."

I expressed to Tyler my own desire to have explored the mill, but I knew that after the last round of tornados through the middle of town the building was just too unstable. I had only explored on the correct side of the fence with my camera's zoom lens.

Tyler continued, and his point really hit home with me. He said, "I will legitimately miss the mill…They wouldn't preserve it, so we had to admire it and enjoy it for ourselves risking a slap on the wrist. The mill was something to be proud of. It was such a unique and vast structure. I'd been there many a night with either myself or just a couple of others, and it was pretty creepy. The office section had a long dark hallway with about 40 rooms to the end, so shining a flashlight down to the end was almost nerve racking. And yes, just because the City of Douglasville wouldn't cowboy up years ago and recognize it as a historical building, it didn't mean the building didn't have historical value to us. I feel lucky enough that we had something like that so close to us, and so did many others my age. I just wish I had taken more pictures. I never really thought that it would be totally gone one day."

We love and admire people in lives. We love and admire various things. Those people, those things, all have deep rooted meaning for us in so many various ways. Yet, we are so busy loving and admiring that when the time comes to exchange those people and those things for memories, it can be a very defining moment.

The old mill burning to the ground is one such moment for the City of Douglasville and for the citizens of Douglas County as whole.

Now we have the job of gathering the memories, and learning from the mistake of taking things for granted.

Chapter 61

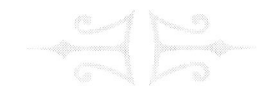

THE COTTON MILL – ONE YEAR AFTER THE FIRE

Today is the one year anniversary of the fire that finally put our cotton mill out of its misery. We had watched the building die a long lingering death, but somehow it managed to stand as a testament to our town fathers who knew that the economy of Douglasville and Douglas County would survive only if they could bring a cotton mill to the many cotton fields that covered the countryside.

After several fits and starts and ups and downs including a fire, a revolving door of business partners, and a lawsuit or two, the mill along the Military Road, as it was known way back when, was finally operating in full swing by November, 1908.

Over the years the mill became a town within a town including a village for workers to live, a store to shop, athletic fields for recreation and a church to worship.

Early names for the mill included Georgia Western, New Century and Lois Cotton Mill. The name Lois came from Joseph S. James, Douglasville's first mayor and main champion for the mill. James attached the name to the business to honor his daughter.

In 1924, Martel Mills, an outfit from New York bought the mill and changed the name again to Beaver Lois Mill.

By the 1930s and 1940s the mill had become a major employer making pants and dresses.

In the 1950s Glendale Mills purchased the property for their parent company, J.F. Stifel. Stifel propelled the mill to be the top employer in the county – at least 800 men and women worked there.

The 1970s and 1980s saw the DeSoto and the Douglasville Spinners before the doors were locked forever.

Douglasville's mill was unique not just for the community of workers it created through the years, but the building itself was extremely unique in design.

Prior to the fire it was one of two mills designed by Charles Praray that still had the tale-tell zigzag walls standing, and one of only five that Praray built in the South.

Stephanie Ayleworth, former Main Street manager for the City of Douglasville and I have had numerous conversations regarding the cotton mill. She tells me her research indicates Praray's striking design is best identified by the zigzag appearance of the exterior walls and windows. The mill is an excellent example of northern architecture adapting to the New South economy. The unique architecture of the mill was a cost saving device.

Ayleworth also advised the mill was built on two separate foundations. The inner foundation housed the equipment, while the outer foundation and walls were for the vast window casings. This construction technique made the walls cheaper to construct and, in case of fire, they could be more easily removed and less costly to replace. The walls were entirely free from strain, the outer walls allowed for more windows, thus allowing the light and ventilation and facilitating longer hours of operation.

Over the years the windows were removed and bricked over as air conditioning and electric light was improved.

Sadly, National Register designation for the cotton mill never happened. The mill fell victim to a greedy owner who made grand promises while his real intention was to leverage the property into more loans to buy up more historic properties that would also just sit idle and waste away. The mill also fell to various government entities who looked the other way and ignored code violations and thousands owed in property taxes not wanting to have to deal with the inconvenience of the property. This is a little ironic since the act of four teens plopped the property right into the city's lap. Even more tragically we the citizens turned our backs on the property not getting involved and thinking others would do the right thing years and years ago.

How many times did you drive by and think, "Gee, someone should really do something about that?"

Somehow there's a lesson to be learned in the tragedy of our lost cotton mill, but I don't know if we can grasp it.

When are we going to realize we – all of us – represent "someone"?

We are the "someones".

Section Seven

A PROGRESSIVE TIME

Chapter 62

IN THE POOR HOUSE

When I was growing up my daddy always seemed to have some money in his pocket. He would pull out his "folding money" and peel off a ten dollar or twenty dollar bill when my sister or I would hold out our hand for something we needed, but I seriously doubt if he ever knew at any given moment the exact amount he and mother had in the bank. Mom handled the day to day bill paying, the checkbook reconciliations, and overall handling of the money once Daddy gave her his paycheck. She knew on a daily basis how much money was in play and watched it like the mother hen that she was.

We could usually gauge how things were going in the finance department with Mother's references to the "poor house." Statements such as, "We are going to end up in the poor house at the rate we are spending!" or "We can't do that! It will put us in the poor house!" I didn't know what or where the poor house was, but I can assure you from my mother's tone I knew it was a place I didn't want to go.

You might have heard someone in your past refer to the poor house. In fact, "in the poor house" is listed in most reference books as an idiom — words and phrases that are grammatically unusual or cannot be taken literally such as "It's raining cats and dogs."

Today, the phrase "in the poor house" can't be taken literally, but prior to the Great Depression and the advent of Social Security poor houses were real places set aside by local governments for dependent or needy persons. They were very common in the 19th and early 20th centuries. Anne Sullivan – Helen Keller's teacher, Calamity Jane and Annie Oakley all resided on a poor farm at some point in their lives.

Here in Douglasville the poor house was referred to by citizens as the poor farm, but official records used the term Alms House to refer to a type of welfare program before Social Security and welfare as we know it today came into existence.

Paupers made application to the county commissioner or county Ordinary – today's Probate Judge. State law defined a pauper as someone who was unable to support themselves by laboring. Census records indicate most of the inmates (a term used in public records) were elderly people who had nowhere else to go and in most cases were women over the age of 50. The liability of relatives to support the poor only extended to parents and children, so this meant it was possible for extended members of a family to be out on the street once a spouse died if there were no children or parents around.

Prior to the poor farm local residents who were found to be indigent or were caught begging on the streets were often auctioned off where the pauper was sold to the lowest bidder. The bidder would agree to provide room and board paid for by the county for a specific period of time. In return, the pauper would provide some type of labor basically making the situation a form of indentured servitude. Reference is made to this in the 1883 Grand Jury Presentments for Douglas County recorded in *The Weekly Star* where it states, "Further that Anderson Wheeler and his wife, paupers, be let to the highest bidder. It is also recommended that said Anderson Wheeler and his wife remain with John M. Haines until let to the lowest bidder, and that said Haines be paid twenty-five dollars per month for keeping them."

The poor farm in Douglasville was located two miles north of town down Chicago Avenue. It was first organized in 1882-1883 when 65 acres was purchased by the county in response to a Grand Jury recommendation stating "It is recommended that the Ordinary build an Alms House for the care of paupers and that J.B. Daniel, T.H. Selman, J.W. Brown, and A.L. Gosline be appointed a committee to [work] with the Ordinary in selecting and purchasing site for same…"

Found within those same Grand Jury Presentments for 1883 is a review of the Ordinary's books for that year. Their findings indicate "extravagant expenditures since the last term". Those extravagant expenditures might be the reason why the recommendations for an Alms House were made. The report indicated "an order for a pauper's coffin, $20.00; burial expenses of John Hawkins, not a pauper, $12.85; burial expenses of Reece Stewart, a pauper, $21.50; medical expenses to J.L. Williams, not a pauper, $70.00."

In setting up a poor farm most local governments required the inmates raise their own food and raise crops that could be sold to off-set the cost of maintaining the farm. State laws governed the poor farm where rules were strict and accommodations very minimal.

By 1884, the farm in Douglasville was in full operation with a vegetable garden, fruit orchard and a few cash crops as well. George M. Souter, a former Douglas County sheriff, was the poor farm superintendent until his death in 1902.

Once the poor farm was up and running it was inspected once a year by the Grand Jury to access the health and care of inmates as well as review how productive the farm had been during the last year.

In 1897, the poor farm reported to the Grand Jury they had a total of eight inmates and the total expenditures for the farm including the superintendent's salary were $403.08.

Fannie Mae Davis indicates in her history of Douglas County, "In the early years of the 20th century, the state allowed prison labor to be used in building and maintaining public roads. At which time Douglas County located a prison camp on the farm at a site near the residence of the paupers and as the county acquired heavy road machinery that too, was parked at the prison site when not in use." This was a common practice across the state. You can still find the county's maintenance building and heavy equipment parked on the site close to the corner of Chicago Avenue and Cedar Mountain Road.

The 1903 Grand Jury Presentments include a lengthy report from George Souter's son since Superintendent Souter had passed away in 1902. The report indicated total cost of maintaining the farm and the inmates for a seven month period was $107.95. There was also a notation that two of the chimneys at the farm needed to be repaired. Cash crops were also mentioned – rent cotton had been "gathered and marketed for $68.00" with the money being deposited with the county treasurer at the Douglasville Banking Company". Other crops mentioned was "rent corn at 100 bushels; rent fodder at 1200 bundles; rent forage at 2 loads; rent cotton seeds at 50 bushels and rent sweet potatoes at 15 bushels."

The report also makes mention of two cows giving milk and butter as well as a garden full of collards and turnips.

The farm phased out in 1932 once Social Security began as part of President Theodore Roosevelt's New Deal. The last burial in the poor farm cemetery was that same year. The county finally sold the land to Will Morris, a dairy farmer, in 1945. A land developer took possession of the property in the 1970s and a few duplexes were built. Fannie Mae Davis indicates the developer had "little regard to the long forgotten and barely recognized old [poor farm] graveyard."

Sadly, it seems some of the newer buildings were built over the cemetery as Mrs. Davis continues, "However, it was as if an ancient city had been discovered, when in 1980, a new home owner found that his yard was a cemetery and his house was built in the middle of it. The case was fairly resolved, but not before the Atlanta television stations and the Atlanta newspapers gave space and time to the story for a few days."

I ventured down Chicago Avenue this past weekend to see what I could find. The county maintenance buildings are still there, along with some heavy equipment. There is a Shell gas station and a subdivision adjoining the property, but I never could determine exactly where the cemetery is. I asked the man behind the counter at the Shell station, a couple of customers and a couple of folks who were out in their yards in the subdivision about it, but no one knew about the pauper's graves. I checked with the county cemetery listings at *Celebrate Douglas* and the poor farm cemetery is not listed.

I have to wonder – Is the poor farm cemetery lost again?

Chapter 63

THE ITALIAN PEDDLER

When I realized I would be diving into Douglas County history and publishing my research I had to make myself a couple of promises. I never wanted accuracy to be an issue. I've had a couple of situations here and there – one biography piece I know I need to go back and properly label the sections that are backed up by historical sources and the sections that are admitted family embellishments, but overall I work hard to use more than one source wherever possible, and I constantly wring my hands over the facts.

The other promise had to do with sugarcoating history. I've been researching and writing about history since 2006, and I print the good with the bad. If you only want the "pretty" side of the Douglas County story then you might not want to stay tuned.

I know this is fairly obvious, but history ISN'T pretty. History is the human story, and humans are rather flawed, right? They make poor choices, they often react without thinking, and group thinking often trumps individual thought leading to all sorts of ugly history.

Take the time period known as the Progressive Era – those years between the 1890s and the 1920s. It was a time of social activism and political reform. Corruption was exposed especially in government. The time period also had some ugly aspects such as efforts to restrict immigration.

Now you might be saying to yourself what in the world does immigration have to do with Douglas County, especially in the early days of this place we call home, but one hundred years ago sentiment towards immigration impacted a group of men right here in Douglasville. The men made poor choices, reacted without thinking, and let their group mentality get the better of them.

In the book *Race and the Atlanta Cotton States Exposition of 1895* Theda Perdue examines Atlanta and race relations as the Exposition was being planned and held. The Exposition was a world's fair held in Atlanta to stimulate foreign and domestic trade. The event was very important to the region since an economic depression had a firm grip on the area.

Perdue advises….*Nativism, the intense opposition to immigration, is a hallmark of late nineteenth-century America. In the 1890s four million people immigrated to the United States. Many were from eastern or southern Europe, and native-born Americans viewed them as poor, unskilled peasants who clustered in urban neighborhoods and resisted assimilation…[Most people felt immigrants] were linked to immorality, crime, political corruption and labor unrest and moved to stem the tide of immigration.*

Southerners took pride that few immigrants had found their way to this region. The Atlanta Constitution concluded that it was "a blessing in disguise that the tide of immigration went west and not south" and reported with relief that "fifty more Italian laborers employed on the sewage work [in Atlanta] were shipped back to New York today by the contractors.

In his keynote address at the opening of the exposition, Judge Emory Speer contended that "multitudes of those who seek our shores to better their condition have no conception of the character of our government, and therefore, no devotion to the institutions of free men and this is one of our greatest dangers.

….and lest you think it the white population who had that attitude against immigrants consider Booker T. Washington's remarks at the exposition. He urged the audience to look to African Americans for achieving "the prosperity of the South" and not to "those of foreign birth and strange tongues and habits.

Since these attitudes towards immigrants at the turn of the century were so prevalent in Atlanta it should not be surprising that the same attitudes existed here in Douglasville.

Buried within a section regarding Fairburn news titled "Fairburn Facts" in the June 13, 1882 issue of *The Atlanta Constitution* I found this:

Fairburn, Georgia…June 11….It is reported here upon good authority that a poor Italian peddling his wares in Douglasville, was set upon by some of the county officials and the authorities of the town and beaten almost to death.

By June 16, 1882 the matter was more prominently displayed with a headline that read "A Douglasville Outrage", but the outrage wasn't so much against the beating, but that another official had been linked to the beating….an official by the name of S.N. Dorsett.

The article reads:

Douglasville, Georgia…June 15….In the post appeal of the 13th instant we find that the name of S.N. Dorsett, clerk of the Superior Court of this county, is charged with being in the party who outraged the young Italian. We desire to state in behalf of Mr. Dorsett that he is not charged with nor did he have anything to do with, the unfortunate affair, and no such rumors have ever prevailed in this community.

Mr. Dorsett is a most perfect gentleman in every sense of the word and the assault upon his character is very unjust and positively false.

He is a faithful officer and performs his duty as such. We think that when the facts of this whole affair are known will show that there has been a great deal more important attached to it than the means by this to say there has been one and a thousand rumors circulated about this unfortunate affair that are untrue.

Signed…John I. Freely, J.P. and M.B. Watson, J.A. Pittman, J.S. James, W.J. Abercrombie, J.W. Westmoreland, M.D. and W.G. Hanson, J.L. Selman, M.D. and W.H. Malary, H.L. Baggett, A.W. McLarty

Ten months later the case was being heard in the United States Circuit Court. *The Atlanta Constitution* dated April 18, 1883 carried a headline advising "The Italian Peddler" with a smaller heading…"The man who was mashed up asking for ten thousand dollars damages…"

The article advised…*Yesterday an interesting case came up for trial in the United States Circuit Court. It was a suit for ten thousand dollars damages instituted by an Italian named Michael Burney against W.T. Lindley, John V. Edge, C.P. Vandergriff and C.P. Camp of Douglas County. The Plaintiff alleges that the Defendants have damaged his pocket and he will doubtless recover something on his claim as he was considerably used up.*

One day last year, the young Italian while peddling plaster of Paris images passed through Douglasville. He could not speak English and was only able to name the prices of his wares.

At Douglasville he "fell into the hands of the Philistines" who took him into the courthouse and after smashing his toys proceeded to smash the Italian. They threw him down and sat on him and so roughly used him up that he stayed in the bed 16 days and at the end of that time was able to get to the train to come home only by being transported in a chair borne by two stout Negroes.

The Italian employed counsel to bring suit against the persons named and the case came up in the United States Court yesterday.

…The Defendants set up their defense that if they did as charged they were too drunk to know what they were doing.

Pending the argument court adjourned.

Well, I told you history was ugly sometimes.

The men named in this lawsuit were all important leaders in our community at the turn of the century. They all did great things and did their part to build the county, but based on prevailing thoughts at the time it would appear they made some terrible choices and then had the temerity to use being drunk as an excuse.

Did you notice the Italian's name? Michael Burney. It doesn't seem very Italian, does it? However, foreign sounding names were often Americanized at Ellis Island and other entry points into the United States.

At this point I'm sure you are asking yourself what type of remedy the young Italian received through the verdict of the court.

It took several months but I finally came across a story in the *Austin Weekly Statement* from Texas dated May 10, 1883 that stated, "In Douglasville, Georgia, about a year ago, the sheriff of the county, an ex-member of the legislature and several other prominent and enlightened citizens attacked a poor Italian image vendor, spat upon him, rolled him on the floor and then sat upon him, singing ribald songs and [telling] rude jokes. A jury recently gave the Italian $1250 damages."

Chapter 64

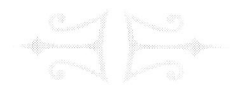

THE BROCKMAN BOYS OF DOUGLAS COUNTY

During my years as a fourth and fifth grade teacher I managed to have my fair share of parent conferences. One thing remained the same no matter the needs of the child – every parent wants their children to achieve and experience certain goals and dreams.

Some parents want their child to maintain As and Bs while others have a particular college in mind and begin planning early. Some parents have smaller goals such as getting through the week without receiving a bad behavior note from the teacher.

Other parents seem to be very comfortable planning out the lives of their children including which career path they will choose. Yes, I had my fair share of parents tell me little Johnny was going to be a doctor or little Susie would be an attorney one day, and the wants of the child rarely figured into the picture.

I always had to wonder how those goals would turn out. What would happen if the child inevitably rebelled and went his or her own way? However, there are plenty of people who have their careers foisted upon them or want to please their parents so much they follow the plan. Those children seem to do just fine including the Brockman boys of Douglas County.

You probably aren't familiar with them – they all moved away many years ago.

All three of the Brockman boys followed their mother's fervent desire – they all became missionaries.

The Brockman story begins before the Civil War when Rev. Henry D. Wood of the Virginia Methodist Conference came to Georgia with his wife and daughter. They took possession of Glennwood, a plantation along the Chattahoochee River which encompassed the land across from the Bullard-Henley-Sprayberry house along Route 92. I've also seen references as the place being called The Oaks. Basically the cotton plantation lay on the left side of Route 92 as you head towards the river.

Unfortunately, Rev. Wood passed away in 1863 before the war's end leaving his daughter, Rosa Emory Wood to run the plantation. His grave can be found at Campbellton Methodist Church across the river.

During July, 1864, as Sherman's men approached Glennwood to cross the river, Rosa and her mother decided to head to relatives in Virginia for the duration of the war. Rosa road out to meet Sherman's men and explained her plight. She requested an escort to help her get to the train in Atlanta so she could leave.

My source for this story was the excellent book regarding Douglas County history compiled by Fannie Mae Davis, however, she identifies the mistress of Glennwood as "Rossleigh". My recent research including the birth records of her children indicate her name was Rosa Emory Wood.

She spent the end of the war and the early years of Reconstruction in Virginia only returning after Glennwood had become part of Douglas County in 1870. Rosa brought along a husband when she returned named Willis Allen Brockman who had been born in Albemarle County, Virginia. His family had been long associated with the families of Presidents Washington, Jefferson and Madison.

Mr. Brockman "purchased the farm from the Wood estate and added land to the holdings." The Brockmans proceeded to live life and raise a family. The Brockman children – Fletcher, Whitfield, and Francis – were educated on the farm.

Times were naturally hard for large landowners following the Civil War and most sources describe the Brockman boys as having grown up on an impoverished Georgia cotton plantation, but all three achieved their mother's dream. They were all educated at Vanderbilt University and all three became well-known missionaries in China and Korea.

In a book titled *Pathfinders of the World Mission Crusade* by Sherwood Eddy, Fletcher Sims Brockman is described as "a country boy from a cotton plantation in Georgia hindered in his youth by impoverishment after the war." Eddy explains how Brockman remembered as a boy traveling along Douglas County roads with his father who would lift his hat to whites and blacks alike telling his son, "I can let no man excel me in courtesy."

Fletcher Sims Brockman graduated from Vanderbilt in 1891 and through the Young Men's Christian Association or YMCA he acted as Field Secretary and served as a missionary. Fletcher reached China in 1898 just in time for the Boxer Rebellion, when the Righteous Harmony Society led an uprising opposing foreign imperialism and Christianity.

During the 25 years he spent in China, Brockman and his wife, Mary, collected various relics and artifacts. Recently Vanderbilt University opened an exhibit titled "Fletcher Brockman's Missionary Life in Asia" showcasing many of the hundreds of items the Brockmans collected including "ancient coins, a bronze mirror, Japanese woodblock prints, and a Korean horsehair handbag."

Whitfield Brockman and Francis Brockman were missionaries as well. Whitfield served in China along with Fletcher while Francis held the position of Secretary of the YMCA in Seoul, Korea.

Willis Allen Brockman passed away in 1898 at Glennwood. He is buried beside his and and Rosa's children who did not survive to adulthood at Campbellton Methodist Church. Rosa ended up overseas with her boys heading to China in 1904. She died at the age of 75 and is buried alongside her son Francis in Seoul, Korea.

Glennwood Plantation continued to pass into the hands of others – Herman Harper in 1921 and the more recent owners were Henry and Sally Rawlins.

Chapter 65

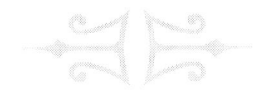

BAPTISTS VERSUS METHODIST – DOUGLASVILLE'S DEBATING PASTORS

Two ministers, one Baptist and one Methodist, walk into a church… Almost seems like there should be a joke in there somewhere, but there isn't.

While the Baptists and Methodists do disagree on various propositions of their faith, I think we get along fairly well here in Douglasville. Both churches have always been close to each other in location whether it was on Church Street or out on Prestley Mill Road. Both congregations get along well, though there is that running gag about who is going to beat who to the restaurants for a meal after church, but for the most part, both churches work to provide places where citizens can go if they are religious and want to feed their faith.

In 1891, however, Douglasville's Baptist and Methodist communities became caught up in a war of words between two pastors. The preach-off was fought nightly in the sanctuary of the Methodist church in Douglasville and splashed all over the papers daily in Atlanta.

The parties involved were Dr. E.R. Carswell, Jr. who ministered to the flock of the First Baptist Church Douglasville and Dr. W.S. Armistead, who was famous for speaking out on behalf of the Methodist Episcopal Church South throughout Georgia. For clarification the Methodist Church as a whole would not be known as the United Methodist Church as it is now until 1968.

Dr. Carswell was known for being aggressive with his doctrinal points and liked to claim during his career he had saved over 3,000 souls. Apparently, Dr. Carswell was so persuasive in his delivery of the Gospel that he manage to convert Mr. Harris from Elberton. Many Methodist throughout Georgia were upset over this because Mr. Harris had been a very popular Methodist minister up to the point he was converted. To add further insult to injury Mr. Harris began pastoring a Baptist church.

Joseph S. James, attorney, a former mayor of Douglasville, and general "finger stuck in every pot" type of citizen concerning Douglas County, wasn't a fan of Dr. Carswell since he followed the Methodist faith. He considered Dr. Armistead an expert controversialist, or to be more exact James felt Armistead would be the perfect person to take a few jabs at the Baptists and hurt their pride a little. He promptly sent Dr. Armistead a letter and invited him to visit Douglasville and challenge Dr. Carswell to a debate.

As men tend to do they all had their own agenda regarding the debate. The Methodist church as a whole wanted to put Dr. Carswell in his place for converting one of their best ministers, Joseph S. James thought the debate might get some attention for Douglasville in the Atlanta papers, and he wanted to take the Baptists down a notch or two here in town, and Dr. Carswell? Well, I've already stated he was aggressive about sharing his faith and proving his point.

Another underlying cause had to do with the Douglasville College, a school that was set up in town in 1888 along Church Street close to the spot where the armory sits today. The school included what we consider to be elementary, middle and high school grades today even though it was referred to as a college. Children from other towns were accepted and boarded with local families.

It seems that there was a controversy regarding which faith – the Methodist or the Baptist – would end up controlling the school. I'm still trying to piece together the whole dust up, but folks here in town were afraid the Carswell and Armistead debate would bring that controversy up all over again.

One Douglasville citizen was quoted in the paper saying, "These people [such as Armistead] may come and go and feel none of the bad effects of a controversy, but we must stay here and fight it out." Even Pastor Moon of the Methodist church here in Douglasville was against a debate stating he had never known a single soul to be saved due to a debate regarding which church was correct in their interpretations of the faith.

The debate was scheduled to run each night for three hours over a thirty day period.

Yes, you read that right.

Dr. Armistead arrived in Douglasville, but before the first speech was made ground rules regarding how the debate would take place had to be debated.

Right – a debate concerning the debate.

Several days were spent ironing out the debate rules.

The pastors agreed the Bible would be their only source to support their arguments. Points that would be discussed during the debate would be the formation of the Christian church, baptism, and the Holy Ghost. Each pastor could have a moderator from their respective churches, and finally during the course of the debate they would refer to each other as "Brother".

The debate began on December 30th and 31st with a lecture given by Dr. Armistead followed by a discussion where both pastors participated. Folks in Atlanta were so interested in the nightly debate that *The Atlanta Constitution* sent a sketch artist to record the participants and members of the packed audience to enhance their coverage.

On January 4th, a rumor went out that the joint debate might be suspended due to Dr. Carswell being ill. He had catarrahal fever which is the 1890s way of saying he had Influenza.

The cold weather and the fact that one of the participants was missing didn't keep people away. Many of the Baptist brethren continued to attend. They took careful notes to support Dr. Carswell upon his return while Dr. Armistead argued John the Baptist was a Methodist minister.

By January 5th several pastors in the Atlanta area were speaking out regarding the spectacle. Pastor J.W. Lee of Park Street Methodist in Atlanta's West End said no good would come from the debate regarding an issue that was not key to salvation and characterized the Douglasville debate as the work of cranks. Dr. Armistead countered by inquiring, "Who is Dr. Lee, and where is West End?"

On January 13th, Dr. Carswell was still missing, but Dr. Armistead continued to talk for three hours each evening. By January 15th, he had finished his discussion regarding baptism ending with claims he was the second John Wesley of Georgia.

Once he had finished his lectures around January 16th Dr. Armistead turned his attention to his naysayers by sending a letter to *The Atlanta Constitution* stating he wasn't accustomed to "paying attention to yclps of a cur, the braying of an ass, the gibes of a buffoon and…..there would be no issue except folks from other places were interfering with the great debate."

It was also at this time that Dr. Armistead made an announcement that he wouldn't preach or lecture further until his book titled; *History of the Church in All the Ages* was complete.

Dr. Carswell retorted from his sickbed that he could tear the book down before it was even written, but he never returned to the debate as far as I can tell from the newspaper accounts.

In fact, the last mention I located regarding the debate was on January 19, 1891 where it was related that people across Atlanta were more up in arms over the debate than the folks here in Douglasville. It seems the debates which had actually become a nightly performance by Dr. Armistead had been well attended by citizens here, but there was no great divide between the religions here in town.

At the beginning of the debate *The Atlanta Constitution* asked, "If there is to be no judge, how will we know who won?

One hundred and twenty-three years later it looks like there was no winner other than the citizens of Douglasville who didn't let two egotistical pastors divide them.

Chapter 66

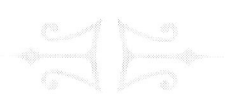

A LITTLE BACKGROUND REGARDING MR. AND MRS. POST

I've been hanging onto this story for quite some time mainly because I wasn't sure how I wanted to present it. When I first became aware of Mr. and Mrs. Post I knew their story had value and should be included in the history of Douglas County, but I also knew I needed to verify facts and try to add to the story where I could.

I just didn't know in order to verify facts and add to the information I would be creating a story several inches thick and several miles wide with interesting "stuff."

This story has a little of everything – women's rights, healing powers, mining in California, a woman asserting her independence and following her dream, third party politics, mail fraud, and fights in the middle of the street.

Be patient. There is a payoff to meandering through each of the four parts of the story, so hang in there with me as I begin by examining the early life of Helen Post, one of the stars of the story.

She was born in Fairfield, Illinois on June 14, 1831 to fairly well-to-do folks. She was well educated for the time period including some college. She was considered by many to be a spinster when she eventually married Dr. John Caldwell Baker in 1856 at the ripe old age of 25.

Instead of taking her expected position in society as a doctor's wife in some Midwestern town, Dr. Baker moved Helen to Texas – Solano, Texas to be exact. The 1860 census shows the Bakers living there, and by 1870 four children were added to the census rolls – Florence, Ada, Claude, and Jennie.

Later records indicate the family moved to Lake County, California near Soda Springs where the family had a farm and a quicksilver mine.

Unfortunately, the family lost money each year, and the place was heavily mortgaged. Dr. Baker eventually lost the property.

Not only had Helen given up the life of a doctor's wife she thought she was going to have, she had always wanted to make her living with a pen, and it just wasn't happening.

As she worked from daylight to dark cooking, washing, ironing, sewing and tending house for her family and the men who worked for her husband, at times as many as twenty-five men per some sources, she dreamed of being a writer.

She was in pain constantly, and her husband refused to hire any help for her. She is quoted as saying, "[Dr. Baker] seemed to consider me a machine with power to run day and night. He had consideration for his men and for his horses, but none for me."

She tried to break away in 1875, but when Dr. Baker found her in San Francisco she returned to the farm with him and attempted to reconcile.

Soon after, her youngest daughter, Jennie, died at age nine. Seeing that things hadn't changed on the farm Helen finally had enough.

The year was 1877.

She wasn't getting any younger. The older children were nearly grown and away at school in San Francisco.

One morning Helen prepared her husband and his crew breakfast as usual, packed a bag and then headed for San Francisco never to return. Their divorce was final in 1879.

In San Francisco she found a job writing a four page weekly paper devoted to the sale of various medicines. Later she moved from paper to paper until she landed a position with *Overland Monthly*, a paper dealing with reform issues, and during the 1870s, 1880s and 1890s there were several reforms to write about – women's suffrage, corporate monopolies, poverty, immigration, labor reforms, and many more.

In 1880, she moved to Chicago and took a position with *The Chicago Express*, a paper Helen described as the leading reform paper in the world. Over time, she became bored with labor reform issues stating that most laborers simply wanted to trade places with their employers, not really wanting to end their practices and have true reform. Plus most in the labor movement weren't in favor of woman's suffrage, and it was an important issue to Helen.

She quit the paper and struck out on her own beginning a paper called *The Woman's World*. The paper covered such topics as forced maternity, women's suffrage, financial independence, and even praised efforts for women to become ministers.

Yes, her views were extreme for her time period.

An online biography page by Cornerstone Books regarding Helen states, "A woman of middle age, living among strangers, torn by sorrows and worn by worries, having no capital whatsoever, no experience in managing a business, and no money to pay her board bill, founding a publishing concern that made money from the start and put her on her feet within a month after went into business by herself."

Helen stated in her book *A Homecourse in Mental Science*, "I went to my room and began to type; and that article was the most emphatic declaration of the right of the "I" that ever put in type...It said [for people] what they wanted to say but dared not. Hundreds of journals copied it and it ran through public feeling like wildfire."

She further stated, "...no man will ever be the magnet to attract success until he can stand alone, straight and tall as a liberty pole, glorying in the position; free from fear; independent of public opinion and daring to be himself."

I guess in our way of thinking Helen's article went viral and was seen by many people which is just what you want to happen as you are seeking subscriptions for a new publication.

Helen was married again by 1883.

She had met Charles C. Post also known as C.C. Post while working at *The Chicago Express*. Post, fifteen years younger than Helen, was an experienced journalist and was heavily involved with politics. At the time they married he was writing his first novel, *Drivin' from Sea to Sea or Just Campin'*.

He also ran his own journal titled *Roll Call*.

His political maneuverings would play a heavy hand in Douglas County politics during the 1890s.

Their marriage cost the happy couple a whopping two whole dollars, and it severely depleted their joint savings account. During those early days of wedded bliss they tried to live on five dollars a week.

Between 1882 and 1886 Helen struggled to keep her paper afloat. It was hard for her to find the right niche to support her.

In the book, *Each Mind a Kingdom: American Women, Sexual Purity and New Thought* the author, Beryl Satter, scrutinizes Helen's writing over those years advising her various opinions and how those opinions seem to lose focus and change over time.

Specifically between 1882 and 1884 *The Women's World* would publish sporadically due to a lack of resources.

Another issue that kept Helen from publishing was her granddaughter's illness. Helen and her husband lived with her daughter Ada and her children. At some point one of the granddaughters was very ill, and Helen went into debt trying to care for the girl. Eventually the baby died in March, 1885.

During the financial and health crisis the content of *The Women's World* began to change as Helen began to play with the idea of using her readers as a source of money.

In February, 1885, Helen published a story about a girl named Rose, a girl who had been impregnated and abandoned by her employer. Helen asked for her readers to send "Rose" some clothes for the child.

Packages poured in.

Another time Helen wrote about a girl named Mary and asked readers to send her cash.

Cash poured in, and yes, it went into Helen's pocket.

Helen kept "Mary" alive for six months until she wrote in September, 1885 that "Mary" had finally passed and provided a tear-jerking description of her death.

While the money for "Mary" was still pouring in Helen also posted an article in June, 1885 titled "A Talk to My Reader" where she confessed her financial troubles and advised she would begin accepting advertisements from that point on.

The ads were for such things as compound oxygen which folks in the Victorian era inhaled, and there were ads for magnetic undergarments.

Yes, magnetic undergarments.

Think "personal massager" and you get the idea.

The advertisements were always paired with a written endorsement by Helen, and they took up most of the newspaper.

Yes, Helen was an interesting "reformer."

As Beryl Satter stated, "Helen wrote that womanly love would end poverty while she herself lived at poverty's brink. She attacked corrupt male intelligence that used sharp business dealings to fleece the public while it was only her own such dealings that kept Helen and her family afloat. She was a reform journalist who started her career praising the women's era and concluded it asserting that wealth, the product of bloody corruption and unleashed desire was the "birthright" of all."

Helen issued the paper's final edition on May15, 1886. By June, she had signed up for a course conducted by Emma Curtis Hopkins regarding Christian Science.

She didn't know it, but Helen had reached a turning point in her life.

During this time per Beryl Satter, "[Helen] learned ambiguous doctrines concerning the power of thought and power of women, the necessity of selfishness and the godliness of desire as well as the problem of poverty."

While she was taking the Christian Science classes her husband, C.C. Post fell ill.

Later Helen would claim she had cured him with her "powers", and those claims of healing people would bring the Posts to Douglasville.

The town would be turned upside down.

Chapter 67

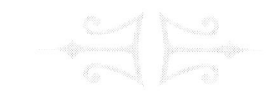

WHEN MR. AND MRS. POST CAME TO TOWN

Charles C. Post and Helen Wilmans Post entered the Douglasville scene in the late 1880s.

The late Douglas County historian, Fannie Mae Davis used the words visionaries, social reformers and even eccentric to describe the Posts, and it's clear from my research they brought Douglas County to the forefront of a very tumultuous time in Georgia's political history.

Personally, I'd like to add the word nefarious as well to the descriptors.

When we last left Mr. and Mrs. Post she had decided to take classes regarding Christian Science with Emma Curtis Hopkins, and while she was doing so poor Mr. Post suffered from what has been described by some sources as a weak physique while other sources mention the word "consumption".

In case you are not aware consumption refers to what we know today as tuberculosis.

Helen promptly introduced her future husband to Christian Science doctrine. Afterwards she advised anyone who would listen that she had cured him. Mr. Post agreed with her and encouraged her to share her healing powers with others.

At this point the story shifts from Chicago, Illinois to Douglasville, and if you are like me you have to wonder what prompted the Posts to move from a large city such as Chicago to little old Douglasville.

In fact, an article in *The Atlanta Constitution* concerning the background of Mr. and Mrs. Post refers to Douglasville as a mere hamlet, possessing but one grocery store and a blacksmith shop.

Indeed.

Douglasville doesn't seem to be spot where a muckraking political journalist/novelist and a newspaper/healer might end up.

Mrs. Post advises in her book *The Search for Freedom* concerning the move south saying, "Some three years after my marriage to Mr. Post we came south. We were on a search for conditions. We hardly knew what the conditions would be; but we had worn out the old ones, and had been worn out in them until a complete change became imperative. Indeed, Mr. Post was a very sick man. He had worked too hard at the desk, and death threatened him in the shape of consumption. When we left Chicago not one of our friends expected to see him alive again...We went to Douglasville, Georgia and there, in a little country hotel, we fought the battle with death, and won the victory. As health began to be established in Mr. Posts' wasted frame..."

I'm thinking the Haymarket Riot in Chicago might have prompted their move. The riot occurred in May, 1886 – six months before the Posts arrived in Douglasville.

The whole affair started out as a peaceful march by workers demanding an eight hour day. However, when police tried to get the crowd to move along someone threw a bomb into the crowd. After the blast and the gunfire that erupted several policemen and civilians were killed or wounded. The eight organizers for the march were prosecuted and convicted of conspiracy. They were branded as anarchists and sentenced to death. During the eight weeks after the riot a red scare ensued.

The Posts were known supporters of the labor movement, and Mr. Post's co-workers at the paper didn't take kindly to it when they learned Helen Post had sent money to those on trial to help with their legal bills.

It could just be that Chicago had gotten a little uncomfortable for Mr. and Mrs. Post. She did mention "a complete change was imperative."

At any rate, Helen sold her paper, *The Woman's World*, to fund the move. She wrote, "I soon grew tired of the whole matter, especially as it took up my entire time and there was no money of any consequence in it; and we needed money...Mr. Post had been unable for months to earn anything with his pen. It was quite a long time before he recovered his mental vigor sufficiently to enter the field of literature again."

The Posts arrived in Douglasville in January, 1887 with what probably amounted to the clothes on their backs and two hundred dollars between them.

During the move C.C. Post had encouraged Helen to figure out a way to share their experiences with Christian Science and his "cure" with the public. After thinking on it a bit Helen decided she could fashion the philosophy into her own dogma stating in her book, "It's hallmark was the claim that humanity was nourished by an inferior fountain of thought and will which represented one's inner divine power."

She improved upon the "one's inner divine power" principal and became the self-appointed founder of "Mental Science".

Please understand I am in no way discounting Christian Science in any way, and don't wish to make a judgment on it. The problem has to do with how Helen Wilmans Post perverted the thoughts behind Christian Science and eventually twisted her "Mental Science" to such an extent she was committing fraud.

While in Douglasville, perhaps during their stay at the hotel in town on Strickland Street, Helen Post wrote her series of lessons. Between herself and her daughter Ada, Helen handwrote six copies of the lessons, placed an ad in *The Woman's World* and upon receipt of $25 a copy of the lessons would be mailed to the customer. The customer then produced their own handwritten copy of the lessons and mailed them back to Helen.

Later, Helen was able to print the lessons, and the cost was reduced to $20 for each client.

Apparently, Mr. Post had recovered enough by March, 1887 to get out and about. Helen writes, "...He wished for some ground in which to dig and plant. He had been brought up on a farm, and it was strange to see how he really longed to come into close relationship with old mother earth once more."

Mother Earth was the last thing on C.C. Post's mind. He missed politics and had set about working on his way into making the right friends in Douglasville.

By March, 1887 Mr. Post had become very friendly with Joseph S. James and Dr. T.R. Whitley, and was named the president of the Douglasville Canning and Preservation Company. The goal of the [company] was to provide a market for area farmers plus provide an incentive for the farmers to plant more fruits and berries.

It wasn't just about providing a market. The business was a farmer co-operative and a main tenant of the Farmer's Alliance – a political concern Post was heavily involved with before he ever reached Douglasville, and that eventually would turn the town's political structure upside down.

The Posts eventually bought some land described as "adjoining the town", and "began to improve it."

The land in question happened to be four lots belonging to Dr. T.R. Whitley. They set about using some of the money Helen had earned from her mail order business building a home, a home Fannie Mae Davis advises was so fine and impressive the street it was on became known as Chicago Avenue since the Posts were from that city.

An article from *The* Atlanta *Constitution* from 1891 states, "...just on the outskirts of Douglasville....is one of the handsomest residences in the state. There lives Colonel C.C. Post and his wife...The home is one of elegance, unsurpassed by many city palaces."

Some may still remember the home with its unique tower. Joseph S. James eventually bought the house and was living in it at the turn of the century. As the years rolled by a few others lived there and later the home was a nursing home before it was torn down.

Apparently, the venture was an immediate success and started gaining Helen Post attention as well as a fat bank account. She and Ada began work on their next project, a paper clients could subscribe to called *Wilman's Express*.

Four years later Helen advised in an article published in *The Atlanta Constitution* (February 15, 1891) her paper was printed by *The New South* in Douglasville and brought in close to twelve to fourteen thousand dollars a year in subscriptions. She advised that the paper had circulation of 30,000, but close to 50,000 were printed each month.

During those years when Douglasville's population was around 1,000, I venture to say that Helen Wilmans Post was the number one customer at the downtown post office!

By 1891, there were two "Mental Science" courses offered, a beginners and an advanced course. Mrs. Post estimated that over 5,000 had been sold. This means that in the four years she had been living in Douglasville Mrs. Post had made close to $100,000 with her course, and let us remember that this was prior to income tax!

Fannie Mae Davis advises the Posts were "promptly welcomed in the social and power structure" of Douglasville.

Helen Post advises in her book…"a wild curiosity was manifested find out what cured [Mr. Post]. It was believed I possessed some se power that was denied to others, and I become a marked individua the community. Especially the Negroes were affected by Mr. Post's c and they came to me with their complaints and begged to be cured a

Some of her words might offend us today, but we need to reme this particular book was written in 1898, and opinions and the man which they were expressed were much different.

Helen continues, "But soon there was another class [who Southern society is divided into three classes; the Negroes, the class of white people who are tenants on the land they planted, a upper classes who are property owners, and in every way superio others. I only had a short experience with the middle class when t intelligent and refined people began to crowd all the others out."

Chapter 68

MR. POST AND THIRD PARTY POLITICS

During the 1890s the following ad/article appeared in *The Sun*, a paper in Kansas City.
Driven From Sea to Sea!
A real story of today, illustrating the fate of the disinherited, by C.C. Post, ex-editor of the Chicago Express...The author of the above book is now sojourning in Douglasville, Georgia, where he went after inspecting the over-advertised land of Florida and he is so well satisfied with the climate, the price of land, the water, the scenery, the products, the people and the prospects in general that he is naturally desirous to see a nucleus of his northern friends gathered about him.

So, C.C. Post was sojourning, was he?

To sojourn means to stay somewhere temporary, but for someone who intended to stay in Douglasville temporarily Post certainly stirred things up.

By the time he and his wife, Helen Wilmans Post had fled the town he had the place turned upside down, and made Douglasville the hotbed of third party politics.

293

Post wasn't just a muckraking journalist and novelist. He had been involved in politics for some time before arriving in Georgia, and he was hardly the sort to let a little thing like being a Yankee in the Deep South keep him from dabbling in politics again.

However, he underestimated the good people of Georgia, and the even better folk of Douglas County as Joseph S. James was quoted in *The New South* in 1902, "[The Democratic Party] has in the past withstood all assaults upon it. If you are a friend to it you will do well to try to reform your own actions to its policy or, at least, stay in its lines. The history of it is all those who undertake to burst it usually get bursted themselves."

In other words what Joseph S. James really meant was don't trifle with the party – the ONLY party in Georgia per the time period, and whatever you do, don't try to split the party by instituting a third party.

Here's how it all went down –

When we last left Mr. and Mrs. Post she was busy with her "mental science" making living selling information that more than like was simply not true, while her younger husband, C.C. Post, busied himself by becoming involved in the power structure of the town. During the late 1880s and through the turn-of-the-century the power structure was headed up by Joseph S. James and Dr. T.R. Whitley. Mr. Post had several business dealings with both men and had bought some land from Dr. Whitley where a grand mansion was built along Chicago Avenue.

So, when did the love affair with the Posts begin to go sour?

Things took a nasty turn as C.C. Post returned to politics. He soon became involved with the Farmers' Alliance which originally came to be in the mid-1870s starting out in Texas and eventually moved across the South. It was an organization of white farmers and many others including teachers, ministers, and doctors.

Farmers' Alliance members were concerned with the growing plight of farmers by forming cooperative purchasing and marketing enterprises. They also introduced the sub-treasury plan which called for federal farm credits and other marketing tweaks. By the 1890s the movement had birthed a political party known as the People's or Populist Party as well as the Third Party.

Farmers did have a legitimate gripe. The landowners were getting wealthier while the farmer was getting poorer.

But wait, weren't the landowners and the farmers the same people?

No, not necessarily. Since the economy had been destroyed following the Civil War many planters could no longer work their fields. They divided their land and allowed others to work their fields for a fee – a fee based on the production and sale of the crops. What developed was basically another form of slavery as small-time farmers owed larger and larger amounts to the landowner and often also ran up huge bills with merchants for supplies and staples. Sometimes the merchant and landowner was the same person which meant they had even more leverage over the farmer.

Post used his prior experience with the Grange movement in Indiana to become a lecturer for the Farmers' Alliance. In her book *From Indian Trail to I-20*, Fannie Mae Davis advises Post had convinced ten of the twelve members of the Douglas County Democratic Executive Committee to defect to the Farmers' Alliance by 1891. Only J.B. Duncan and J.H. McClarty remained Democrats, and they were referred to as the 'Lone Fishermen.'

Soon Post was traveling the state, and he soon moved up in the ranks of leadership in the Farmers' Alliance.

Now, in the beginning staunch Democrats like James and Whitley along with men involved in state politics allowed the farmers to have their Alliance without grumbling too much. They felt that if they pushed back too hard the Democratic Party would splinter, and they wanted to avoid it, but that's exactly what the Alliance leadership including Charles C. Post wanted and began calling for.

They wanted a third party – the Populist Party.

Staunch Democrats would have none of a third party. They had suffered the indignities of having carpetbaggers and scalawags control the state legislature during Reconstruction. They had finally gotten themselves back in control, and weren't going to let a bunch of farmers led by a Yankee create a third party.

During the spring and summer of 1892 things really heated up.

Politicians like John B. Gordon and W.J. Northern looked upon some of the wants an needs of the Alliance with favor, but were adamantly against a third party. Gordon had returned to the Senate and Northern, past president of the State Agricultural Society had been elected governor. Even the President of the Georgia Alliance from 1888 to 1892 – Leonidas F. Livingston would not jump the Democratic Party ship for the Populist Party.

Post and his Alliance cronies continued their fight, however. They crisscrossed the state speaking to groups of farmers at barbecues, in churches and even in fields if need be.

The Atlanta Constitution had a field day with the political fracas reporting every move C.C. Post and the third party men made, but it was clear they favored the Democrats more. On April 1, 1892 *The Atlanta Constitution* wrote concerning the third party…"a new party, gathering strength from men who have had no experience in the management of party politics. It is blundering along in the darkness, bungling things as it goes, and when they get through with the job, a pretty mess they will have."

While most third party gatherings were simple speeches where converts were or were not made before heading off to the next town some of the gatherings were more interesting.

So, what about Douglasville? Did Post ever speak here?

Of course he did.

In April, 1892 a great meeting between the Democrats and the third party men were advertised for Douglasville on the thirteenth, to be exact. Both sides advertised the event heavily. *The Atlanta Constitution* advised, "This is Post's home, and is regarded as the home of third partyism in Georgia. Douglasville will be alive with people to hear the political issues of the day discussed. One of Atlanta's best brass bands will be furnishing the music."

The day after the event *The Atlanta Constitution* published a lively account that was furnished by *The New South* paper from Douglasville, no doubt since it was written with a more Democratic slant.

The article began rather dramatically stating,"Not since the flaming torch was applied to the city of Moscow and Napoleon's army began its disastrous retreat to the…waters of the Beresina in the bitter days of 1812 has such a signal rout been given to men as that which marked the flight of Post and his third party followers today."

See, dramatic, isn't it?

The article continues,"This day's business will go to history."

Unfortunately, it didn't, and I doubt that even a handful of Douglas County residents know about it today.

The article continued, "Its parallel has never been known to Georgia politics. Never ever amid the exciting times of warfare between the old Whig and democratic parties has the instance been known when one party after lining its forces for a battle on the stump gave up the fight and beat a hasty and sudden retreat before a single speech was made or a single orator introduced.Never! And yet this is just what the third party people did here in Douglasville today."

Congressman Livingston was invited to Douglasville to speak on behalf of the Democrats. He returned to Atlanta from Washington D.C. for that very purpose. Committees from each side met on the morning of April 13 and decided how the debate would unfold.

Congressman Livingston would speak followed by Charles C. Post on behalf of the third party. Then a host of others would speak as well from each side. Livingston would respond again at the end of the day.

The stage was set.

The Atlanta Constitution article goes on to say, "Hundreds and hundreds of people [went to Douglasville] – not alone from neighboring regions, but from all parts of Georgia – to participate in the political sensation that was promised. Newspaper correspondents came by the dozen representing all the leading daily journals of the state.

297

The newspaper continued, "The train arrived carrying the speakers, and even though the agenda and rules for the debate had been agreed to earlier in the day, as soon as Post alighted [from the train] and sought his committee on arrangements a sudden change of the program was demanded. Post did not want to allow Livingston to have the final say. He wanted equal time man for man. By this time the crowds had already arrived for the debate and were pressing upon the courthouse in downtown Douglasville. The People's Party Paper advised there were four People's Party men in Douglasville for every one Democrat stating...They left their plows sticking in the furrows and came by scores and by hundreds…They filled the courthouse, they overflowed and filled the town…a great sea of people."

The event changed, however, from the debate the crowds were expecting to see to two separate meetings with each competing for the crowd.

Joseph S. James stood on the courthouse steps and welcomed the throng of visitors who had come to listen to the debate and he assured the people they would witness an orderly and fair minded gathering.

Livingston and E.P. Howell led off the Democratic speeches from the courthouse steps while Post led his supporters away. It is estimated around 500 people had left the courthouse with Post and marched across the pedestrian bridge over the railroad and down Strickland Street.

The paper for the People's Party advised it was County Alliance president J.W. Brown who suggested to the third party followers they should adjourn to the Alliance Warehouse on Strickland Street.

The paper advised someone yelled, "Cross over the railroad bridge so everybody can see," and the surging crowd turned aside at the intersection of the street and crossed the high bridge over the railroad, thus making their numbers apparent to every onlooker.

Two blocks further down the street stood the Alliance Warehouse and when the head of the marching column reached there they looked back and saw the crowds still surging across the high bridge, where every moment fresh squads of twenty, fifty, or one hundred of those who had wanted to hear what the excited and now dismayed Democratic leaders were saying, turned away from the courthouse on the hill with cheers for Watson, Post and the party of the people, joined the marching columns headed to the warehouse.

The Atlanta Constitution article stated:

Many had apparently left the courthouse under the impression that all the speakers were going to the warehouse....[Post] naturally took in hand the direction of affairs, and had half a dozen bales of cotton rolled out in front of the warehouse. The idea was for the ladies to sit on the bales, but they were provided with other seats, and the men mounted the bales...Couriers kept going back and forth between the courthouse and the warehouse to report what was going on at the other meeting...The composition of the crowd at the warehouse kept changing as folks would venture to the courthouse and reinforcements would come down.

The gentle breeze wafted the hearty democratic cheers over to the warehouse and the burst of enthusiasm up there came down like the rattling of distant guns. Now and then there would be a tremendous roar as if from a whole battery. Then there would be the rattle of musketry as volley after volley of applause greeted the telling of the speeches.

The People's Party cheered, too, and in defiance, but their hurrahs, mingling with the odor of the phosphate were mostly borne by the zephyrs over towards Cobb County.

After the meeting a young planter, who had gone from Lithia Springs said, "I had thought there would be a much larger gathering of third party folks. They cannot carry Douglas County," and after their first success they never did.

Chapter 69

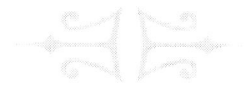

THE POSTS – THE FINAL CHAPTER

So, after you have breezed into a small sleepy little southern town and:

* ingratiated yourself with the town's power brokers
* been named president of one business and invested in others
* become a lecturer for the downtrodden farmer and totally turned every major Democrat in the state of Georgia against you
* supported your wife's belief that she has the ability to heal
* along with your wife began a school of mental science attracting students from all over the world
* persuaded ten of the twelve members of the local Democratic Party leadership to jump ship for a third party
* attracted hundreds and hundreds to town
* have certain town leaders refer to you as an infidel, an anarchist and a "stench in the nostrils of all who love morality, Christianity, virtue and abhor socialism…"

Well?

What do you do next?

You head to Florida where you proceed to build a "City Beautiful", of course.

Yes, in 1892 Charles C. Post and Helen Wilmans Post ended up in Seabreeze, Florida where they purchased several acres of land from C.A. Ballough, and they began to develop a town across the Halifax River from Daytona Beach.

In her book *Search for Freedom* Helen wrote, "At present our town is called Sea Breeze; but after a while we shall give it another name...we will accept the name that even now by a sort of general consent is being bestowed upon it....that of "The City Beautiful."

Streets were wide and beautiful there with tall palm trees and ornamental planters along the way. Helen wrote in *A Search for Freedom*, "The two words 'happiness' and 'beauty' are our beacon lights."

An article from December, 1901 in *The Atlanta Constitution* states, "Beautiful boulevards and streets have been laid out and paved, and thousands of dollars have been expended in improvements and buildings."

The Posts built their own home located on the Boulevard at Valley Street by the river along with the Wilmans Opera House and a department store. A printing office where all of their books and publications were printed was located on the bottom floor of the opera house.

The town of Seabreeze was formerly incorporated on May 24, 1901, and Charles C. Post was the first mayor.

And what would the beach be without hotels? The Posts were partners with C.A. Ballough in building the Colonnades Hotel which had 125 rooms. They also built the Princess Issena which opened in 1908 along Ocean Boulevard. Originally it had 27 rooms and was located in the middle of a five acre park. It was enlarged after the Posts owned it and existed for several years through the 1970s.

Three dollars a day could get you accommodations that included pastries and milk from the hotel's very own Jersey and Holstein cows. Helen willed the ownership of the hotel to her daughter Ada, and when Ada sold it, the new owner granted her the right to live in a cottage on the property for the remainder of her life.

How could the Posts have money to develop a town? By the turn of the century most people were earning $900 to $4,500 per year, yet

Helen's "mental science" efforts were bringing in $25,000 to $50,000 a year during a time when income tax did not exist.

They certainly had the money to develop a town.

My research indicates when Charles C. Post got off the train at Douglasville in April, 1892 to meet the Democrats for all the speechmaking, he had already been forced to move from the town because newspaper accounts mention Douglasville was his "former" home.

The Posts sold their Chicago Avenue home and property to Joseph S. James in 1892, and while they tied up their business here they moved into the Sweetwater Park Hotel for approximately six months.

They were basically run out of town though Helen writes nothing about the town being unwelcoming.

Helen described their exit from Douglasville in her book *A Search for Freedom*,"But finally we wanted to get away. We had always desired to be close to some large body of water…a suppressed longing for Florida…We had seen that whatever place we remained long enough to impregnate our view, that everything seemed charged with a strongly magnetic power to draw others to us."

She also said Douglasville was too small to accommodate her students and growing financial empire.

Helen writes about the move to the Sweetwater Hotel in *A Search for Freedom*, "Just six miles from us on the road leading to Atlanta was the celebrated Sweetwater Park with its large and splendid buildings. It was a summer resort, and my classes were held in winter. But the proprietor of the hotel consented to open his house provided there were enough of us to pay him for the trouble. So we sold our beautiful home and went there with sixty or seventy others, and were there for six months."

She then recounts how she went to Florida, then Boston and back to Atlanta. At some point records indicate the Posts were living at 296 Crew Street in Atlanta, but eventually the Posts ended up in Seabreeze full time.

Of course Helen Post remained busy with publishing, writing and placing ads in various newspapers and journals. Her paper was sent to over 10,000 subscribers. They paid ten cents for a six week subscription. She remained busy with actual "patients", too. In one article she estimated she saw seven to ten thousand patients during the 1890s alone. She perfected her mail-order business and came up with a successful hard sell approach.

Her ad in *Freedom!* stated, "Do you own the *Wilman's Home Course in Mental Science*? If not you surely want it and if you want it you can surely get it now..."

The ad continued, "Have you not heard that through the power of 'right-thinking' you can be healed of every form of disease whether it is physical or mental?....you can be healed in your own homes while the healer is hundreds of mile away...Thought...goes from the brain of the healer to the brain of the patient and corrects the error existing there... It not only cures disease, but strengthens the broken will, and plants hope in the breasts of the despairing, and opens the way to success in every undertaking. For particulars send for the *Mind Cure* circular. Circulars free. Consultations free. State your case and receive an early reply."

She charged three dollars a week or ten dollars a month for the "absent treatments".

The replies to Helen's ads were so enormous she had to hire a team of stenographers to handle them.

But, a storm was brewing.

Not only was the volume of mail overwhelming Helen and her staff, the sheer number of envelopes addressed to her was overwhelming the post office at Daytona, so it was moved to Seabreeze to be closer to the Post home.

Naturally, the move didn't set well with some of the folks in the area, and they began to complain.

They complained enough that certain government officials began to check into Helen's "business".

A government investigation was the last thing Helen Wilmans Post needed.

On October 5, 1901, *The New York Times* reported an order had been issued by the Assistant Attorney General to the Post Office Department to stop Helen Wilman Post's mail by issuing a fraud order. Charles C. Post, Helen and their son-in-law, Charles Burgman were actually arrested in August that same year.

Basically, Mrs. Post was accused of running a scam and using the post office to run it. Part of the language in the affidavit included "Helen Post aka Helen Wilmans, did devise a scheme and artifice to defraud diverse persons..."

The words "false and fraudulent representation" was bandied about the affidavit as well. She was accused of making false and wild claims that her "mental science" could cure and heal "every form of disease and weakness."

Part of the problem with the scheme was Mrs. Post would advise her "patients" to connect with her mentally at certain times during the day. The government stated their investigation showed during some of the times she indicated, Mrs. Post was otherwise engaged. She had been seen fishing, entertaining friends, or absent from the city.

Mr. Post was charged and arrested because he was "in charge of the financial branch of the enterprise, and devote[d] his time to the development of the property and community" The son-in-law, Mr Burgman, was the business manager of the concern with the Affidavit stating, "he had general supervision of the printing, distribution and sale of Mrs. Post's books, etc."

An article published in *The Altanta Constitution* dated February 3, 1904 reported from the ongoing trial that evidence had been produced that Mrs. Post would open her mail to extract the money and then hand the correspondence over to her staff. Of course the evidence was given to show that Mrs. Post was not familiar with her patiets since she didn't correspond with them, so how could she heal them?

A Mr. Bishop had been interviewed. He was in their employ in Douglasville. Bishop published a labor paper and at some point Mrs. Post began to run her "Mental Science" ads in his paper. Later, Bishop advised his hands were tied. He felt he had to run the ad copy she submitted or he would lose his position. Wild claims were made that so many believed and were being helped by Mrs. Post's "Mental Science" that "every morning the yard around the Post residence was filled with carriages, wagons and ox carts filled with people who had come from miles around to take advantage of Mrs. Post's healing powers.

The government asserted this was a gross exaggeration and that "there never were more than three people to see Mrs. Post at any one time…".

Fannie Mae Davis's account of the legal entanglements mentions that Dr. T.R. Whitley was at the center of the allegations against the Posts, and while I never saw his name mentioned in any of the legal reports I don't doubt that he and Joseph S. James who were very well connected far and wide was following the events very closely and got a certain enjoyment from the whole thing.

In March, 1904, *The Atlanta Constitution* was almost gleeful as it reported a guilty verdict against Helen Wilmans Post, "The sentence was that she be confined for one year and one day in the penitentiary at Nashville, Tennessee."

Of course an appeal was filed right away.

Helen said, "You cannot pronounce sentence of guilt against me. The sentence you are going to pronounce will be against the ignorance of the age and this sentence will not only fail to condemn me, but it will exonerate me from all participation in such ignorance.

After a second trial in January, 1906 Helen Wilmans Post was found guilty again. She was ordered to pay a $500 fine and serve 30 days. She was then 75 and appealed again.

One of the last mentions of Helen Wilmans Post published in *The Atlanta Constitution* advised on December 3, 1906, "Helen Wilmans Post, the alleged 'divine healer' joins the …'down and out club' with an admission she is stricken with a disease her own cunning cannon reach."

Yes, Helen was sick, and couldn't seem to heal herself. The stress of having her income flow totally stopped plus the added stress of the arrest and trials took a toll on Helen and on her husband.

He passed in June, 1907. She passed in September, 1907 during the midst of yet another re-trial. Both are buried at Pinewood Cemetery found at the corner of Main Street and Peninsula in Daytona, Florida.

But wait, there IS another Douglas County connection with the Posts.The son-in-law mentioned above, C.F. Burgman, who was married to Helen's daughter, Florence Nightengale Baker. They had a daughter who married a Baggett about the the time Charles C. Post and Helen Post went to Florida. Baggett family history relates William Alfred Baggett was a music teacher at Daniels Mill here in Douglas County during the 1880s. He and his wife, Missouri Ann Dorsett Selman, moved to Seabreeze, Florida at the turn of the century where he began to deal in real estate with none other than Charles C. Post. It seems that Mr. Post was still persuasive regarding getting Douglas County folks to buy into his plans, but in this case it actually paid off.

Later on the Baggett's son, Billie Byington Baggett married the daughter of C.F. and Florence Burgman who was named for her "mental scientist" grandmother, Helen Wilmans Burgman.

Billie went on to be very prominent in local politics serving as mayor of Daytona Beach.

Chapter 70

DOUGLASVILLE WAS IN THE HANDS OF THE NORTHERNERS

That title sounds a little ominous, doesn't it?

Of course, during the summer of 1864 many towns and cities across Georgia found themselves "in the hands of the northerners" over and over as General Sherman's men came through.

Wait a minute though…

Douglas County didn't exist during the Civil War.

Douglasville didn't either.

The above sentence was part of an article dated June 19, 1890 from *The Atlanta Constitution* dealing with the Northern Society of Georgia.

The Northern Society of Georgia was a group of northern born citizens who made Georgia their home and wanted to promote the benefits of living in the state and conducting business here.

Their first convention was held in Douglasville.

C.C. Post, a Yankee from Chicago and a Douglasville resident in the 1890s brought the convention to Douglasville. He was in an investor in the canning plant and the reason why Chicago Avenue received its name. He was a political operative intent on bringing a third party to Georgia.

Eventually, he and his wife were run out of town, but that's another story for another time.

Before things went sour Post was able to persuade people here in Douglasville to go all out to welcome the convention-goers.

The newspaper article advises, "Business was almost wholly suspended and the town turned out in holiday attire...Fifteen hundred southerners took part in the welcome to their northern-born neighbors and fellow citizens. Shortly before ten o'clock, a special train from Atlanta arrived. Several hundred delegates with their friends were on the train, among them many members of the Northern Society of Georgia, recently organized in Atlanta."

As the train pulled into the Douglasville depot a brass band began playing *Yankee Doodle* followed by *Dixie*. Both tunes were met with great applause. The visitors were given silk convention badges and then escorted to James Grove, a beautiful grove of trees that served as a city park. It was located in the area across from Ace Hardware running between Church Street and Broad.

In the Grove, "a large tabernacle formed by pine boughs and supported by posts and stringers, sheltered the convention from the sun. Beneath this leafy bower seats to accommodate fifteen hundred people were arranged, with those in front reserved for the delegates."

After C.C. Post opened the convention several speakers manned the podium followed by the announcement for lunch, an event that had been advertised in the Atlanta paper for days promoting a free barbecue.

Here is where Douglasville really shined as many locals provided the food and much of it was served by former Confederate soldiers "who took particular pride in their part of the day's entertainment."

Before the lunch was served, Captain J.V. James, head of the barbecue committee read:

"Whereas, the Yanks are coming again, and
    Whereas, it behooves us now as in the past to give 'em the best we have and to make it warm for 'em, and

Whereas, they did once on a time eat meat which we had roasted for ourselves; therefore be it

Resolved…That they can't do it again.

Resolved…That we roast some meat especially for 'em

Resolved…That we keep it warm for 'em

Resolved…That four thousand pounds of beef, pork and mutton when roasted be placed with unlimited quantities of bread, hams, chickens, turkeys, pickles and other good things that will be brought by our good housewives upon breastworks of pine boards and the Yankees be requested to charge the same with all the enthusiasm of their natures."

After lunch the convention took up more business and set up a committee called the "immigration committee". The members would have the job of promoting the South to their Yankee friends as great place to live and work. Mr. Post and Dr. J.E. Howland of Lithia Springs both landed spots on the immigration committee.

At that point the first general convention of northerners ever held in the south adjourned, and Douglasville just happened to be the host!

Chapter 71

THE UPSHAW FAMILY

Once I left the classroom I was determined I would never leave my house before ten a.m. ever again, and many of you who know me privately know that I've stuck to my plan, more or less.

It has to be something really important or earthshattering for me to venture out early, but Tuesday morning there I was, hair barely brushed with camera in hand, standing in the middle of Broad Street looking at the shell Town & Country Upholstery had become in just a few short hours due to a fire.

Earthshattering.

My heart goes out to business owner Chris Hedgecock, his family, the employees and customers. The fire has robbed the city of Douglasville of an important business and so much more. The building represented over one hundred years of thriving businesses with interesting histories. The magnificent renovation the building had experienced in the past few years is testimony to how important historic preservation can be.

Kudos, of course, need to be extended to members of the Douglas County Fire Department who tried to save the building and to keep the blaze from spreading to other historic buildings along the block. Town & Country's space was entirely gutted and two businesses on either side experienced water damage, but the fire was contained.

It did my heart good yesterday morning to see the iconic façade with the arched openings still standing, but it may eventually be judged too fragile to remain, and if so, we will all have to accept a total demise.

Perhaps it is time I document a bit of the family history that goes along with this building.

After putting together various bits of research I've gathered regarding the Upshaw family it's very easy to draw a few conclusions. Like any family they had their fair share of trials and tribulations, there was hard work and success as well, but not many families can boast a U.S. Congressman in their line, as well as successful businessmen and a former mayor of Douglasville.

The father of the family was Isaac David Upshaw who was born on February 19, 1834 in Walton County, Georgia. By 1850, his parents had died, and the census that year indicates he was living in Coweta County with an uncle named Adkin Upshaw.

Isaac married Charity Adeline (Addie) Stamps in 1860 – when our nation was on the brink of war. The romantic in me would like to think it was a hurried marriage as many were in those days as the Confederates lined up to face the Union, but I have no knowledge of that, however, I do know that Isaac served in Company G, 47th Alabama Infantry during the war.

A year later the couple's first born entered the world on March 16, 1861. They named him Herschel Mckee Upshaw. Towards the end of the war a second son was born on March 16, 1864 named Lucius C. Upshaw.

Did you notice that both brothers were born on the same date but three years apart?

A third brother, William David would be born in 1866 and a sister named Ada (Addie) Lee Upshaw would be born in 1869. William David would go on to be a Congressman as well as a prolific writer and even make a run for the White House.

Even though Atlanta suffered terribly towards the end of the Civil War people flocked there once peace was declared including the Upshaw family.

Various city directories for Atlanta including *Beasley's* and *Haddocks* indicate Isaac and his growing family were living in Atlanta between 1875 and 1879 where he was a grocer and had rooms for rent at 91 S. Broad. He also kept a residence at 82 S. Forsyth. During this time a second daughter was born named Sarah (Sallie) Blanche Upshaw and another son, Glenn Oglesby Upshaw was born on April 29, 1879. The records indicate these last two children never married. Sadly they both passed at young ages. Sallie was sixteen at her death, and Glenn was just eight years old.

At some point in 1880, Isaac packed the family up and moved close to Wild Horse Creek eight miles southwest of Marietta where he was the postmaster, teacher, blacksmith, and owned a general store.

In one of his books William David Upshaw explained, "My father became afraid that his boys might fall prey to the gilded temptations of city life. Because he loved his boys better than he loved money, he moved away from Atlanta to grow up amid the beauties, glories, and wholesome inspirations of rural life."

Some sources indicate Isaac Upshaw had a hotel of sorts, too. I located notes compiled by Joe Baggett that indicate the business name was I.D. Upshaw & Son. The area took on the name Upshaw since he was the postmaster. Today we refer to the area as Macland.

Sound familiar?

By 1888, Isaac Upshaw was living in Douglasville, Georgia. Apparently he became very involved with the First Baptist Church of Douglasville. Fannie Mae Davis relates a history of the church and advises during the 1890s I.D. Upshaw was an "untiring elderly worker." He passed away in February, 1897 and is buried at Douglasville's City Cemetery.

Lucius and Herschel, the brothers who shared a birthday, also lived in Douglasville and had become very involved citizens by the 1890s.

Recently, one of the buildings along Broad Street has undergone a wonderful restoration which seemed doomed for a time when the second floor collapsed last year. Town and Country Upholstery is a great addition to the overall look of Broad Street in my opinion, but years ago, in the 1890s, two of the Upshaw brothers followed in their father's footsteps and developed a thriving store in that very location known as Upshaw Brothers General Merchandise Groceries and Fertilizer Store.

Lucious C. and Herschel M. Upshaw were the owners. Per research conducted for the City of Douglasville by Stephanie Aylworth, I discovered the business operated between 1891 and 1930. In 1909, their receipts totaled $100,000 second only to the Duncan Brothers who were also Broad Street merchants.

I'm told that the unique arches on the front of the building were once filled in with windows.

I have also been told that particular building was built around 1892 and was constructed by the same contractor who built the building where the Irish Bred Pub is located today. Apparently, there was is a rather large hand dug basement in the rear of the building. During the 1990s a rusted out commercial coal stove for heating the whole building was in the basement complete with a coal shoot and leftover coal.

Originally, the building had a skylight in the center of the roof. On the second floor was a rectangular opening in the floor which had a hand rail all the way around it to keep people from falling to the first floor. The daylight would come in and illuminate the second floor and then part of the light reached down to the first floor.

It sounds pretty fancy for an early 20th century store in Douglasville, doesn't it?

Somewhere along the decades, someone took the skylight out and sealed up the roof.

The Upshaw brothers weren't just businessmen. They were civic minded citizens, too. Lucious C. Upshaw was a member of the city council in 1894, and during the 1902 commencement exercises for Douglasville College, Lucius Upshaw gave an address to the junior class entitled 'Men and Money.' He served the community as a state representative from 1909 to 1912, and also served as Douglasville's 15th mayor from 1913-14.

At this point the brothers had to be making good money because in 1902, Herschel Upshaw bought a large residence on Bowden Street. The home blended American and Victorian architecture and had been built by J.V. Edge, an attorney and former mayor of Douglasville in the 1890s. Today history and genealogy minded folks refer to the residence as the Edge-Upshaw-Bennett-Sherrod residence.

There is an image of the home in *Portraits of Douglasville* compiled by Earl Albertson, and clearly shows the house has been remodeled and rebuilt through the years when you compare it to today's very attractive version. The caption in *Portraits of Douglasville* states the home served as a boarding house for the shirt and sock factory that was located in Douglasville at one time and indicates up to four families lived in the home during those days.

The New South, a paper that existed in Douglasville when the Upshaw brothers lived here published a brand new phone directory for the city on November 8, 1900. Phones were new-fangled devices at that time and less than 30 phones are listed, but the Upshaw brothers had them along with several of the town's most prominent citizens at the time. Lucius Upshaw's phone number was "8" while the Upshaw Brothers store was "13".

Lucius Upshaw built a home at the corner of Rose Avenue and Broad Street. After discussing the home's location with several people in town, I believe the house stood on the same location where Hudson's Hickory House stands today. The home was torn down in the late 20th Century.

Lucius was involved with the beginning of the *Douglas County Sentinel* when the business was incorporated in April, 1905 along with Thomas R. Whitley and James A. Pittman. The paper began with capitol stock that totaled $800 and was located on the second floor of the building at the corner of Bowden and Broad where several attorneys have offices today. At that time James A. Watson owned the building.

Later, the paper moved to the building next door where Jeff Justice & Co. Relators is located today. Prior to the *Sentinel* moving in this building, it was home to a bank at the turn of the century.

At some point following his brother's election to Congress in 1918 Lucius left Douglasville and went to live in Washington D.C. I can only surmise that he took a position with his brother's office, but I have not been able to confirm that to date. We do know Lucius passed away in 1921 while living in our nation's capital. He was brought home to Douglasville's City Cemetery for burial. Herchel Upshaw is also buried in the cemetery along with his family.

Chapter 72

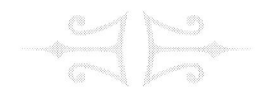

WHO THE HECK IS BILL ARP?

The Bill Arp community can be found five miles south of Douglasville along State Route 5. In fact, a section of the route is named Bill Arp Road. There is a school and a park by the same name.

So the question has to be asked – who the heck is Bill Arp?

Do a little digging and the name Charles Henry Smith keeps popping up. Mr. Smith was one of the South's most famous writers spanning approximately forty years beginning with the Civil War when he wrote popular pieces from the battlefields.

Smith served with the 8th Georgia Voluntary Infantry also known as the Rome Light Guards. The soldiers from Rome saw action at battles such as First and Second Manassas, Gettysburg, and Chickamauga as well as several others.

Smith wrote his first piece as the Rome Light Guards were assembling and preparing to depart for Virginia following the surrender of Ft. Sumter in April, 1861. Literary critics agree there were many writers during Smith's time who were far superior writers, but Smith gained popularity because he spoke to the average person, and his Civil War pieces utilized the Cracker dialect mixed with humor.

His first piece was a satire addressed to President Lincoln titled "Mr. Lincoln, Sir" responding to the President's pleas to Southerners they should just stand down and go home following the events at Ft. Sumter. Smith wrote, "I tried my damd'st yesterday to disperse and retire, but it was a no go."

Smith read the piece aloud to a crowd who had assembled. When he finished he asked them how he should sign the response to Lincoln. A man in the crowd – an everyday simple man- told Smith he agreed completely with everything he had written, and he directed Charles Henry Smith, "Sign my name!"

The common citizen name was Bill Arp, of course!

From that moment, Smith used the name Bill Arp as his pen name.

The people loved it!

Smith's wartime writing numbered at least 30 pieces where he attacked the Union for their policies and served to inspire the Confederates. He brought the war to the people in a way they could understand, feel and respond to.

After the war Smith lived in Cartersville and landed a weekly column with *The Atlanta Constitution*, but he left most of the Cracker dialect behind. His writing still spoke to the average man – focusing on home, rural life, Georgia's average citizens, and youthful memories. Smith gained much notoriety as his writing was printed and republished in papers far and wide including those published in northern cities

He wrote his last column for the *The Atlanta Constitution* on August 9, 1903, a few days before he died.

So, considering that Charles Henry Smith aka Bill Arp was so popular, it's no wonder a group of folks in Douglas County wanted to honor him by naming their community after him.

For years it was just assumed that he had a huge fan base in the area who wanted to honor the writer, but there had been no confirmation that I could find – until now.

Just recently I located a newspaper article from the *Macon Telegraph* dated April 13, 1895 that relates, "Bill Arp, a pretty village in Douglas County has a 'literary circle', and its recitations and declamations and original compositions reflect the humor of the far-famed humorist."

So, now we know.

Chapter 73

A.J. BRYAN – THE MAN WHO BUILT COURTHOUSES

Court House, Douglasville, Ga.

I've been in love with small town courthouses since I was a little girl. I love the similarities and differences in architecture, I love the stories regarding the folks who worked in the building, the records the building holds and the life and death decisions made in them, and I love the attention the building garners just because it's in the middle of town.

Simply put – courthouses make a town

Wilbur W. Caldwell states it best in his book *The Courthouse and the Depot: The Architecture of Hope in an Age of Despair* when he states, "Courthouses, more than any other building of the era [between 1870 and 1910] symbolize the aspirations and the collective self-image of the people of these towns."

Caldwell continues, "Architecture supplies us with a direct conduit to the spirit of the past….These structures sing to us in rhythms of hope and pride and sweat, dirges of ruin and failure and dashed dreams, anthems of triumph, broken waltzes of irony. In short they sing for us the music of history."

Courthouses sing for us the music of history?

Yes!

I certainly believe they do, and while we have a wonderful Douglas County Courthouse on Hospital Drive, and the 1956 Courthouse was preserved as a museum for county history, I still mourn the loss of our 1896 Courthouse.

Yes, I never walked through its hallways, never had any county business to conduct there, I was never even able to drive by the building since it burned in 1956, but I mourn for it. I wish the grand old building still graced our courthouse square in the downtown commercial district, and I often wonder how different things might be had it not burned.

Earlier this week when I was perusing through my pages and pages of notes I have regarding Douglas County history my eyes lingered on one paragraph. I had written, "The arrival of the Georgia Pacific Railroad in 1882 brought the usual clamor regarding a new courthouse. In 1884, the Grand Jury suggested that the old courthouse, which was only a few years old, 'was in bad shape and perhaps dangerous' and recommended that the building be 'bolted and banded without delay.' Local legend holds that the bricks for the building had been improperly fire, some say owing to alcohol induced negligence on the park of the local brick maker…It would be twelve years before Andrew Bryan's new courthouse finally rose."

Andrew Bryan.

I'd never really paid much attention to the name. I wondered to myself who he was.

It's always the little things that grab my attention and send me down the rabbit hole most folks refer to as research. I spent close to twelve hours trying to find everything I could about Mr. Bryan.

I've actually found quite a bit about the man who designed Douglas County's 1896 courthouse including the fact that he is sometimes referred to as Andrew J. Bryan & Co. or Andrew J. Bryan, or even Andrew Jackson Bryan.

Let's just say that Mr. Bryan was a busy architect with offices in Atlanta (344/346 The Equitable Building, 1897) as well as New Orleans (708 Hennen Building, 1906).

Besides designing our 1896 courthouse here in Douglas County, he designed several others around the state as well as buildings all across the South. Unfortunately, like our own 1896 Courthouse, many of the examples of Mr. Bryan's designs succumbed to fire.

Caldwell advises A.J. Bryan designed at least eight courthouses in Georgia proving himself to be a versatile innovator on varied projects. The Douglas County Courthouse was one of his earliest projects in Georgia along with the Stewart County Courthouse in 1895 located in Lumpkin, Georgia. It was destroyed by fire in 1922.

A.J. Bryan also designed the Muscogee County Courthouse in 1895. Per Caldwell, "The up-to-date styling of Bryan's design at Columbus points directly to a remarkably progressive spirit in that city. The architectural style of court buildings of this period were driven more by local hopes and attitudes than it was by the artistic tastes and convictions of the architects who designed them." The building survived until 1972 when the building was demolished.

Apparently Mr. Bryan was applying to design courthouses all over Georgia. *American Architect and Architecture* for October 3, 1896 advised Bryan's company had plans to build a new courthouse in McDonough, Georgia. A month later *The Henry County Weekly* advised Bryan had been employed to inspect the old courthouse, but apparently his designs didn't meet their expectations since another architect by the name of James Golucke got the Henry County nod.

Engineering News-Record in January, 1897 advised Bryan had designed the new courthouse in Randolph County, Alabama located in Wedowee. Sadly that building was destroyed by fire in 1940.

A.J. Bryan was creating a name for himself. He was mentioned in *The Atlanta Constitution*, in 1897. The paper advised Bryan's work was confined almost exclusively to courthouses and other public buildings throughout the southern states, and that the firm had plans for a number of county courthouses throughout Georgia in hand and would deliver them within the next few weeks…as soon as the weather will permit.

The year 1900 saw the courthouse in Coffee County completed, but like the others it no longer survives. It was destroyed by fire in 1938.

The Colquitt County Courthouse at Moultrie followed in 1903, and he also designed the Troup County Courthouse in 1904. Over 600,000 bricks from Trimble Brick Company of Hogansville were used to build Bryan's design in LaGrange.In 1936, the building caught fire. Two women died. Few records were destroyed in the fire, however, because citizens formed a line and passed the documents and docket books from one to the other until most of the papers were removed from the building.

A.J. Bryan also designed the Monroe County Courthouse in Alabama. Many experts state the design is very similar to the Troup County Courthouse. Per the *Encyclopedia of Alabama,* "The courthouse's most significant claim to fame is its inspiration for the fictional courthouse in Harper Lee's novel *To Kill a Mockingbird*…None of the film was shot in the courthouse, but the film set constructed for the courtroom scenes was patterned after the building's unique oval courtroom. Although the cost of the building nearly bankrupted the county, the structure was finished and in use in 1904. "

Summerville, Georgia welcomed Mr. Bryan in 1909 as he designed the Chattooga County courthouse.

Chapter 74

MOONSHINE IN DOUGLAS COUNTY

This week I'm going to shed a little light on moonshine in Douglas County. You might immediately think I'm referring to some point in the 20th century because moonshine was rampant in Douglas County then, but I'm referring back our earliest days.

In fact, Georgians have been making liquor since colonial times. Many farmers made whiskey and brandy with produce they raised. It was a cottage industry that provided extra cash. The distillers were often respected and more importantly they were accepted members of the community.

The first sign of trouble occurred when the Federal government began collecting taxes soon after the Civil War. Many suspended their operations rather than pay the tax, while others hid the fact they were making liquor in order to avoid the tax. This meant they had to go into hiding and some ended up making their spirits at night hence the term "moonshiner". Making the "shine" wasn't illegal, but failure to avoid tax could earn you a trip before a judge.

Gradually, the distillers' accepted place in society began to erode as the battle lines were drawn between people who followed the law and those who didn't. Many moonshiners aligned with members of the Ku Klux Klan and used intimidation against those who might turn them in as non-tax paying distillers.

Finally, during the 1880s the temperance movement succeeded in making the issue a choice each county could make.

Prohibition hit Douglas County early in the movement. While the state as a whole didn't accept Prohibition until 1908, Douglas County was one of the places who led the effort going dry as early as 1885.

The saloons close to the courthouse on Pray and Church Streets shut their doors, but several moonshiners kept on making their liquor including John Crumpton.

Mr. Crumpton knew he was breaking the law. He didn't care. He knew the consequences if caught, but kept on going, and at some point in 1897 he was caught and sentenced to four months in the Douglas County jail along with fines and court costs of $200.

Four months doesn't seem like such a long time, but of course Crumpton didn't like it. He was the only moonshiner among the inmates, and he was lonely. News reports at the time advised, "He longed to get back among the familiar scenes of big copper stills surrounded by congenial friends" so, he decided to make a daring escape from the Douglas County jail.

Apparently, he kicked his way through the ceiling, crawled out on the roof, and jumped to the ground. "He went away leaving everything behind but his address."

He disappeared totally and for several weeks there wasn't even a hint he had ever been in the county.

Then suddenly without any prior notice Crumpton walked into U.S. Court in Atlanta to testify for his son, Thomas Crumpton, who had also been arrested for running a still.

John Crumpton had hoped no one in the big city of Atlanta would remember him. After all, there were hundreds of moonshiners from all over the state who were arrested and sentenced every week.

John intended on testifying for his son in hopes the judge would continue the case using an excuse that Thomas' baby was sick with "the dropsy". The ploy didn't work. The judge heard the case and gave Thomas four months to serve with a fine and court costs totaling $200.

It was at that point the District Attorney told the court that John Crumpton had an unfinished sentence to serve. A very surprised Crumpton was re-arrested on the spot and returned to the Douglas County jail to serve the rest of his sentence alongside his son.

Well, at least he wasn't the only moonshiner at the Douglas County jail anymore, and he certainly had no excuse for being lonely.

Chapter 75

DOUGLAS COUNTY'S SPANISH AMERICAN WAR STORY

There are many ways to define history, but it can be described as a study of how things change over time. Many historians examine the different ways land is used over time, and it is something that I find fascinating.

Take any spot in Douglas County and that spot – that plot of land – has a history. More than likely it was first used by the Creek or Cherokee Nation as a hunting ground, and later by this area's first settlers as farmland. Later sections of the land would become community areas like Dark Corner, Mt. Carmel and even the town of Douglasville itself.

Let's take a plot of land and trace its history a little. The plot in question is near the intersection of Veterans Memorial Parkway (Bankhead Highway) and Baker Drive. The street is east of Lithia Springs Church of God and next to Pro Body Shop. Today the land down Baker Drive is dotted with homes. Hundreds of cars travel through the area daily passing Baker Drive. The occupants of the cars driving through heading to work, to school, to run various errands never consider what might have been going on in the area fifty years ago or even a hundred years ago.

Would you ever consider there was a military camp located there?

There was.

I would imagine that when most people think of Douglas County the last thing that comes to mind is the Spanish-American War, but like any American towns that existed in those few weeks during the Spring and Summer of 1898 the events of the war were first and foremost in everyone's mind, and that patch of land located at Baker Drive was very important to some of the troops who were undergoing training for the conflict with Spain. That plot of land might very well have been the ingredient that saved their life.

The state of Georgia played a very important role in training soldiers. Georgia had more camps than any other state with twenty-five different facilities. Some of the camps were located in Albany, Athens and Augusta to name a few. Camp Thomas was one of the more notorious camps. It was located on the Civil War battlefield at Chickamauga and had a population of 7,000 regular soldiers and more than sixty regiments of state troops. Todd Womack's article at *New Georgia Encyclopedia* correctly advises "overcrowding and poor sanitation led to a serious outbreak of typhoid" during those war months. There were more than 752 deaths at Camp Thomas from typhoid.

Douglas County was important in the war effort as well. Typhoid is the key that brings us to the Douglas County connection. Disease, mainly typhoid, was the number one killer during the Spanish-American War rather than actual warfare. In fact, Vincent J. Girillo advises in his book, *Bullets and Bacilli*, "for every soldier killed during the Spanish-American War, more than seven died from diseases such as typhoid."

Typhoid was nothing new to Douglas County. Fannie Mae Davis' book advises there were constant outbreaks of typhoid every summer in the 1880s and 1890s leaving doctors and citizens baffled because a cause had not been isolated. Folks called it the "putrid fever" or "the sickness," and thought the illness was "brought here from other places."

At one point Douglasville doctors pointed to a constant mud puddle that stood at the intersection of Broad and Campbellton as a possible cause of the sickness. It seems the puddle was such a permanent fixture of foul water in town that citizens had given it a name – "Hog Wallow." It was finally filled in and eradicated, but "the sickness" kept coming back.

Finally, doctors across the world finally began to understand typhoid was caused by poor sanitation and close quarters. They began to understand the role flies played in carrying the disease, as well. While a vaccination had been created in 1897, it wasn't until the 1930s that typhoid would finally be under control.

Getting back to that plot of land near Veterans Memorial and Baker, it seems Fort McPherson created a camp there in 1898 mainly to move soldiers away from an outbreak of typhoid. Fannie Mae Davis, as well as other historical sources, indicates the land was used as a sub-post for Fort McPherson.

Headlines from a *New York Times* article dated Aug. 12, 1898 explain, "Three deaths from typhoid. This makes a total of ten victims in 60 hours at Fort McPherson – Fifty serious cases." The article goes on to state, "The 3,000 recruits remaining at Fort McPherson will be removed to small camps as soon as possible. Eighteen hundred are now at Camp Hobson, near Lithia Springs." Military records suggest soldiers were also removed from Fort McPherson to Camp Waco and Camp Cleary near Newnan. The movement of so many soldiers away from Fort McPherson probably saved more lives.

The poor conditions at Camp Thomas in Chickamauga and at Fort McPherson actually helped medical personnel to learn more about typhoid. Womack's article states, "The use of female military nurses, improved hospital operations and camp-planning techniques, and sanitary hygiene courses for all personnel were just some of the positive outcomes resulting from the miseries that befell Camp Thomas [and other training facilities]."

Camp Hobson was named for Richmond Pearson Hobson, a Spanish-American War hero who sank the *USS Merrimac* in Santiago Harbor.

Chapter 76

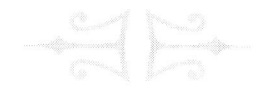

REVISITING CAMP HOBSON

While I strive to get the whole story with each and every column I write I often stumble across additional sources or bits and pieces of information after I've published something. In this case I recently came across a mention of Lithia Springs in Clara Barton's book *The Red Cross in Peace and War.*

Yes! Clara Barton. THAT Clara Barton you remember from your history classes!

Clara Barton was the founder of the American Red Cross in 1881. The website for the Atlanta chapter of the American Red Cross advises, "Miss Barton's most significant act during her closing years as head of the American Red Cross was to take Red Cross supplies and services to Cuba during the Spanish-American War. Miss Barton…went to Cuba with her nursing corps, medical supplies, and food. Aid was given to the American forces, to prisoners of war, and to Cuban refugees. This effort was the first step toward the broad programs of service to the armed forces and to civilians during wartime that have become traditional in the American Red Cross.

The Atlanta chapter of the Red Cross, per Ms. Barton's book, was also involved with providing meals at an emergency camp that was set up in Lithia Springs, Georgia.

Camp Hobson was set up to provide a place for patients to basically escape after typhoid broke out at Fort McPherson early in August, 1898. Camp Hobson was short-lived, but because it existed, it may have saved the lives of the men who were sent there.

In her book, Ms. Barton mentions a report that was sent to her regarding the camp. Ms. Barton states, "At Camp Hobson, Lithia Springs, Georgia, a diet kitchen was also maintained under the direction of Miss Julia McKinley, assisted by the Atlanta Committee of the Red Cross, of which the following account is received: The diet kitchen was opened here on Monday, August 9, and remained in operation three weeks; at the expiration of which time the camp broke up. During the first week after the kitchen was established, when detachments from the Sixth, Seventh, Eighth, and Twenty-Fifth regiments were in camp, 1,176 meals were served."

The next week orders were received for the removal of the Eighth and part of the other regiments to Montauk Point, consequently the number of convalescents was reduced, but during the second and third week 2,066 meals were served, making a total of 3,242 meals served at the table and in the hospital during the time the kitchen was in operation. The meals were furnished to convalescents in the hospital, men relieved from duty but not sick enough to be in the hospital, and to the hospital corps.

The report then went on to describe the various foods served including many of the same things any hospital kitchen serves – breakfast cereals, milk, eggs, toast, bouillons, rice, etc. – before continuing, "The only paid help were two men and one woman, the latter lived near the camp and reported for duty at the first meal call and remained until dining tent and kitchen were in order.

This last sentence confirms something I had wondered when I first researched the subject regarding the citizens of Douglas County – if they helped or volunteered in some way. I certainly would like to know the names of the individuals, but sometimes points of history are lost for all time.

While the Douglas County workers are not named members of the Atlanta Red Cross Society were mentioned in the next portion of the report.

From the report, "The other work in the kitchen was graciously done by Atlanta members of the Red Cross Society assisted by Mrs. Edward H. Barnes, Mrs. Loulie Gordon Roper (niece of General J.B. Gordon), Miss Emmie McDonnell, Miss Estelle Whelen, Mrs. George Boykin Saunders, all of Atlanta, and the ladies from the Sweetwater Park Hotel, who came over daily from the hotel, about half a mile distant from the camp, and assisted in serving table meals, also in carrying delicacies to hospitals and distributed flowers among the patients. It affords us pleasure to acknowledge the uniform courtesy of the army officials, especially the commandant Major Thomas Wilhelm, Chief Surgeon Major E.L. Swift, Assistant Surgeons Street, Baker, and Johnson and Lieutenant Norman, Quartermaster Major Wilhelm had our kitchen built and fly ten for dining hall put up in a few hours after our arrival; detailed men to help wherever needed in kitchen and with finest courtesy assured us of his appreciation of what was done to add to the comfort of his sick and convalescent men. Besides regular kitchen work at Camp Hobson, the Red Cross furnished for a short time to the hospitals one special nurse.... Miss McKinley....and one trained nurse....Miss McLain, who remained until our last patients were sent to Fort McPherson General Hospital and went with them in the hospital train, ministering to their wants until they were transferred to their respective wards there.In this connection we think proper to state that many of our Camp Hobson patients now in Fort McPherson Hospital, one of the best equipped and best managed hospitals in the country, assure us that they can never forget the unfailing kindness of Chief Surgeon Swift and assistants the faithful care of their Red Cross nurses, nor the delicacies furnished by the diet kitchen at Camp Hobson."

Even though I have looked at the pictures and visited with all of the historical documents and accounts through my research, it is still difficult to realize that not only was Lithia Springs home to a magnificent hotel during 1898 but also played host to a military camp with a thousands of soldiers.

But, the hotel WAS there and so were the soldiers.

Chapter 77

SHARED SPACE

In a recent *Douglas County Sentinel* article it was reported the City Council had decided to clear the site of the City of Douglasville-owned Smith Dabbs Building which recently sustained significant damage due to heavy rains and make it part of Plaza East.

Here we are again with a part of our downtown commercial district destroyed – destroyed to the point we can't feasibly repair it, and now the Smith Dabbs building is in the process of being gathered up and thrown in a dumpster.

So, while the city is in the process of dismantling the building and clearing the space I decided to investigate some of the history of the Smith Dabbs building and find out how it fits in to the Douglasville puzzle.

Originally the building had a granite stone façade.

For many years the space housed an appliance and furniture store owned by Thad Smith and his wife Patsy. Back then the space we know as the Smith Dabbs building was larger. It included the space with the green front called Gold n Goodies, too. The store fronts are a little deceptive now since the front of Golden Goodies is painted over, and way back when Thad Smith completed a plaster upgrade to the business and installed storefront picture windows so he could display furniture. I'm told Patsy was a talented interior decorator and she created all the window displays.

As I've asked around about the Smiths I've only heard nice things. In a *Facebook* thread where I inquired about Thad and Patsy several shared their recollections. Jeff Connally advised he still has a refrigerator in his shop that was bought at J. Thad Smith Appliance and Furniture Store. Elaine Banks Wilson told me she and her husband bought their first furniture from the Smiths when they were married in 1955, and Jim Goad thought so much of Thad Smith he named his son after him.

In later years Marie Dabbs worked for the Smiths and eventually bought and took over the operation of the business, and the building became known as the Smith Dabbs building.

During the early days of the business Thad and Patsy lived on Church Street. Today their lot is home to a vacant bank building and a layer of asphalt. I'm told you actually had to peer down the driveway to see their home because the property was so thick with old trees.

While we formally define history as the chronological record of events we can also think of history as the past events relating to a particular thing like a street such as Church Street or a building such as the Smith Dabbs building and how humans share spaces over time.

The lives of Thad and Patsy Smith are a perfect example regarding how we tend to share space over time.

Directly across the street from the Smith home on Church Street sat the Stewart home. In fact, it's still there at 47 Church Street.

Dr. F.M. (Francis Marion) Stewart built the home in the late 1800s, and he and his wife, the former Willie Edna Selman, raised six children there. Dr. and Mrs. Stewart were well known figures in town and involved citizens. Many people referred to them as "Doc and Miss Willie."

Frances Thompson Pritchard, granddaughter of Dr. Stewart has advised folks today would not recognize Church Street if we could go back to the middle of the last century. She also lived in the Stewart home growing up and advises, "The area around Church and Duncan Streets was a wonderful neighborhood to live in. There were big trees that lined the street."

Living in a residence along Church Street isn't the only space the Stewarts and the Smiths shared.

Dr. Stewart and his older brother Rader (Eldorado R.) became visible fixtures in the Douglasville business community before the turn of the century. Dr. Stewart was mason, a member of the Methodist Church and served on the school board. The brothers also owned several farms together, and were investors in the Farmers and Merchants Bank.

The brothers had a mill on Anneewakee Creek known as Stewart's Mill. Of course, we are more familiar with a road by that name, but must remember the mill came first!

My research indicates the mill was in operation before 1900. It was a grist mill, meaning it ground corn or grain into flour. However, the brothers were so busy with other businesses they trusted their employees to run the mill pretty much on their own. I'm told the mill building was torn down in the 1950s.

Dr. Stewart attended the Atlanta Medical College where he studied dentistry. His dental practice was located on the second floor of the building where the Irish Bred Pub stands today.

My research indicates the Stewart brothers were very close. Both brothers had a first in their lives. Dr. Stewart's wife was the daughter of the first sheriff of Douglasville while Rader married Odessa James - daughter of Joseph S. James, the first mayor of Douglasville. Sadly, during the first year of his marriage in 1900 Rader lost his wife. He moved in with F.M. and his wife on Church Street, and he continued to live with them the rest of his life.

The Stewart brothers also ran a store together a few doors east of Dr. Stewart's dental office.

Yes, you guessed it…

The space where the Stewart Brothers operated Stewart Brothers General Grocery Store is the same spot where we refer to as the Smith Dabbs building.

The store didn't just provide groceries for the folks of Douglasville to purchase. It was an important place for folks to gather.

As people come and go they leave behind their story. They leave behind their imprint on their surroundings even though the tangible evidence – the buildings may come and go, but one thing is for sure, we share space not only with those here with us now, we share space with those who came before us, and we will share space with others in the future.

Chapter 78

DYNAMITE IN DOUGLASVILLE

This week my story opens on Saturday, December 7, 1901 at Atlanta's Union Station. It no longer exists, but back then it was located between Pryor Street and Central Avenue.

Two men had arrived in the city earlier that day on a mission. They were looking for a man by the name of Jule Wylie, but as the day wore on all their leads dried up. Frustration had set in because they were going to have to return home empty handed.

Suddenly, as they were getting ready to board their train they spotted Mr. Wylie on the platform.

Jule Wylie, a self-confessed reformed bad boy, worked for the railroad as a freight conductor. He was going about his business when two strangers rushed at him. They seized him and almost carried him onto the train just as it was departing the station. The men didn't let go of Wylie until the train was outside the city limits.

The train's destination was Douglasville and points beyond, and the identification of Jule's kidnappers?

Well, they were police detectives from Douglasville who were investigating a bank robbery that had taken place earlier around 2:30 that morning.

The robbery had not been discovered until the Douglasville Banking Company opened at nine. Most were surprised the robbery wasn't discovered as it was happening since the thieves used dynamite to blast their way into the vault.

It must have made a terrific noise.

Nearly $3,000 in gold, silver and bills were taken.

Fortunately, for the bank something scared the robbers away before they could empty the vault.

The investigation revealed the thieves made their way out of town via a handcar stolen from the railroad depot on East Strickland Street. It was later discovered abandoned in Austell. When the "usual suspects" were questioned, Jule Wylie's name kept coming up hence the trip to Atlanta by the Douglasville policemen.

Another suspect surfaced as well by the name Tom Smith. He went by several aliases and had a criminal record several inches thick. Law enforcement officials had creditable information that Smith had at least $500 of the stolen money with him.

The police had also determined Smith was living with a woman close to the Whitter Mills on the Chattahoochee River about eight miles outside Atlanta.

After spending several hours watching the house in the bitter cold the detectives grew weary and alerted the elderly night watchman at the mill to contact them if Tom Smith made an appearance.

Apparently, the night watchman took his "extra assignment" extremely seriously. The next day the detectives received a call from the watchman who advised, "I have arrested Smith for you and now have him in a room at the mill."

The detectives lost no time in riding out Marietta Road to the mill.

The weather was bitter cold that day with the thermometer registering near zero. The officers had to face the wind in an open wagon, but they knew big game awaited them.

They found a dumbfounded night watchman. "The robber just left," he exclaimed. "He hasn't been gone more than two or three minutes. I never thought of his getting away like he did. He broke through a window and jumped to the ground 22 feet below. It was all done so quickly that I didn't have time to stop him."

So far, in my research I've not been able to determine if Tom Smith, or whatever his real name might have been, was captured and tried for the bank robbery. It's currently one of my open threads of Douglas County history I'm trying to tie up.

And Jule Wylie?

Well, he was found to have an alibi and was released a few weeks after his arrest, but he wasn't really a reformed bad boy. It seems he was arrested, tried and convicted of another theft in January, 1902 and was sentenced to five years in the penitentiary where he was eventually shot and killed by a guard.

Chapter 79

A MARATHON COMMENCEMENT

Douglasville College, Douglasville, Ga.

As I write this my daughter is off to her last official day of high school. It's all downhill from here. The next few days leading up to Friday's commencement ceremony will be filled with graduation practice, but her thirteen years of academic classes including kindergarten are over for her.

For the first time in twenty-two years I will not have to worry with excuse notes, teacher conferences, or deal with report cards. I will never be a room mother again, a PTA officer, or participate in a school fundraiser as a parent.

No more homework wars or the never-ending battle to get someone out the door before the tardy bell sounds. No more agonizing fraction lessons or mad dashes to the drug store for glue or poster board when a forgotten project is suddenly remembered at 9:30 at night.

Fairly soon back to school clothes shopping will be replaced with dorm room shopping, and she will be making that trek for school supplies on her own now.

But in our immediate future is the commencement exercise – the graduation ceremony.

My son's graduation ceremony a few years ago was the first one I had experienced since my own in 1980, and I have to be honest here – the overall atmosphere had changed.

Back in my day – gee, did I really use that phrase?

Well, back in my day I remember my own ceremony being a bit reverent, fairly quiet and you could just sense the importance of the occasion. In fact, all of the graduations I went to as a young girl were rather sedate rites of passage whether they were held in a gymnasium, on a school lawn, or auditorium.

My sister's graduation in 1974 was held at the old Municipal Auditorium in Atlanta where Georgia Championship Wrestling made its home for awhile, however, her ceremony was nothing like a wrestling match. I remember a stern admonishment from my mother regarding talking and fidgeting, so I had to forget thoughts of a takedown or a half Nelson pin.

Nowadays most graduation ceremonies are held on the school's football field because of the large number of graduates and guests. While the atmosphere is still thick with the knowledge that an important milestone has been reached, and there is some seriousness to the occasion, the events are also loud with bullhorns, bells, whistles, cat calls, and sometimes it's a little hard to hear your child's name being called. Parents jostle for the perfect camera angle, people stand in front of the bleachers blocking your view, and if you don't arrive at least three hours early Grandma won't get a seat.

Turn back the dials on my own version of Douglas County's Way Back machine, and we might be attending the graduation exercises for Douglasville College.

Douglasville College was in existence from 1888 to 1914 and was founded at the insistence of Dr. T.R. Whitley, a citizen of Douglasville who wanted to educate his children locally. He was strongly opposed to boarding schools as the only means of providing higher education for youth. Unfortunately, his ideas were slow to catch on as many members of the Town Council were afraid to allocate any money for the school because they feared the idea would be unpopular with citizens. They were wrong, of course, and pretty soon Douglasville College was built and opened where today's National Guard Armory sits along Church Street.

The school included what we consider to be elementary, middle and high school grades today even though it was referred to as a college. Children from other towns were accepted and boarded with local families.

Fannie Mae Davis' history of Douglas County advises the commencement excises at Douglasville College were marathon events. I would have to agree. Commencement exercises often began on Sunday morning and ended the following Wednesday night.

This seems very long and drawn out to us today, but basically what the school did was combine several events for various grade levels into one long event instead of spacing out various award days, chorus performances, and other events over several days with breaks between.

The 1902 commencement for Douglasville College was just as extensive lasting from Sunday to Wednesday. Sunday, of course began and ended with some preaching – two sermons to be exact.

An article from the paper at the time, *The New South*, advised during those few days of commencement, "College Hall was crowded... every nook and corner filled. The old and the young, the children and grandparents, from town and country, from other towns, far and near, the professional men and the plowmen, the stalwart and the paralytic, the preachers and parishioners, crowded into the spacious college hall."

Monday's events included activities for the junior Class. The members of the class read their essays followed by an address from L.C. Upshaw titled "Men and Money". Later members of the class participated in a debate taking sides with issue of Prohibition. W.T. Roberts also addressed the junior class and a four hour banquet followed.

Monday evening included two operettas and a garland drill with many younger members of the student body participating.

On Tuesday the seven graduating seniors read essays they had written, and the featured speaker was B.C. Griggs. The article from *The New South* regarding an earlier ceremony advised "one of the girls seemed to realize the momentousness of the occasion and whispered to those in the rear, and said: 'Pray for me.' The afternoon gave way to entertainment included recitations, essays and music.

Tuesday evening belonged to the school's music department with a brief comedy sketch, and operetta. The evening of music was a ticketed event and apparently $63.25 was taken in at the box office in 1902.

Wednesday morning belonged to the senior class and they provided their literary addresses followed by Sam Small, a well known orator during that time who was a journalist, Methodist evangelist, and prohibitionist. His topic was education focusing how "prior to the Civil War the South had lagged behind in the education of the masses and [Smalls] pointed with pride to the progress made since the war. Education, he said, was not cramming the mind with information, but teaching the mind how to give out things of value."

Wednesday afternoon was dominated by the school's alumni followed by what we consider the traditional graduation ceremony as the final event of the day. The Salutatorian and Valedictorian provided their addresses and the presentation of diplomas rounded out the program and music was provided by a five-piece orchestra from Atlanta.

Can you imagine?

Commencement activity after activity all jammed together in four consecutive days, and here I am wondering how I'm going to get through a reception, graduate recognition at church, Baccalaureate on Sunday, followed five days later with Commencement. At least I have breaks built in even if I will probably have to put up with a noisy bull horn during the actual graduation ceremony, and I will more than likely have to pack a telephoto lens in order to get a decent picture of my daughter as she receives her diploma.

Like many parents throughout Douglasville and Douglas County this week I'm one proud mother, and heartily congratulate my daughter, Rachel, and the rest of the class of 2011.

Well done!!!!

Chapter 80

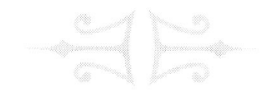

DOUGLAS COUNTY'S CONNECTION TO THE SILK INDUSTRY

Most Georgia history students are taught that due to the colony's warm climate and southern location many felt it was the perfect location for the cultivation of silk. They are also taught that eventually the manufacturing of silk failed and other crops became more important like cotton. Usually, the silk industry in early Georgia is just a blip on the history map, a mention lasting about ten minutes at the most.

Well, there's more to the story.

The silk industry in Georgia began in 1734 with some experimental plantings of mulberry trees in the Trustee's Garden in Savannah. The trees were planted because silk worms live off of the mulberry leaves. In fact, the cultivation of silk was so important all Georgia colonists were required to plant mulberry trees once they took possession of their plot of land.

After a few months the colonist had to admit there were significant issues regarding the silk worms themselves. The whole process was labor intensive.

Eventually the industry could not overcome the ups and downs in the Georgia climate, and cotton proved to be a far easier and more economical crop to produce.

Even so, silk didn't just go by the wayside. It was still around in the 1830s as far inland as Cherokee County. In fact, the state of Georgia historical marker at the square in front of the courthouse in Canton, Cherokee County's county seat states, "Early settlers tried to start silk production, but were not successful, and today there remains no trace of this except Canton, hopefully named for the Chinese silk center."

Douglas County has a silk connection as well. One of the county's earliest newspapers, *The New South* mentioned in May, 1902 that W.O. (William Owen) North of the Bill Arp community had planted an orchard of white mulberry trees for the purpose of manufacturing silk.

Mr. North had visions of erecting a filature (machinery) on the premises for unwinding the cocoons of his own production as well as drawing trade from the other growers around the state.

As early as the 1890s Congress allocated monies for the industry to be explored by creating silk experimentation labs around the country to see what might be viable. George Washington Carver of Tuskegee Institute even got in on the early experimentation by planting 300 trees.

The Georgia Silk Growers Association was organized in December, 1902 representing all areas of the state. This was followed by several articles over the next few years in the Atlanta papers encouraging Georgia farmers by explaining how they could become silk growers. Farmers were told all they needed to get started were a few twigs from white mulberry trees and a willingness to invest some time. Within two years the trees would have leaves, and for just a few dollars silk worm eggs could be purchased.

But it wasn't long before the revival of the attempt to have a silk industry in Georgia failed for a second time, and eventually a cotton field replaced the mulberry trees on W.O. North's farm.

Even with experimentation certain things weren't anticipated. A flood of cheap raw material before manufacturers were actually ready to handle the supply led to a rapid reduction in silk prices. Even with advanced machinery to aid in drawing out silk fibers from the cocoons the process wasn't as easy as people were being told. The entire process proved to be too labor intensive.

There was also the cotton hurdle to overcome. Cotton proved to be detrimental to the silk industry for the second time as it continued to be the dominant cash crop through 1915.

The marketplace simply wouldn't budge and provide a little space.

Still, I have to applaud Mr. North's actions in attempting to do something that on paper looked promising.

W.O. North, Douglas County's connection to the revival of Georgia's silk industry, passed away in 1925 and is buried along with his wife Nancy at Pray's Mill Baptist Church.

Chapter 81

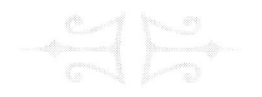

HOW THE ELECTION OF 1902 BECAME THE LAWSUIT OF 1904

"Judge Janes is dead."

So read the headline in the *Cedartown Standard* on March 21, 1912. Judge Charles G. Janes had passed in the very early morning of March 17th after an illness lasting at least ten years.

Janes entered public service after receiving degrees from both the University of Georgia and University of Virginia. He was elected to the state legislature as a representative for Polk County in 1878, five years after he began his law career. In 1888, he was elected Solicitor General of the Rome Judicial Circuit. A few years later when the Tallapoosa Judicial Circuit was created, he was named its first presiding judge.

Judge Janes is connected to Douglas County via his twelve years as a Superior Court Judge.

The Tallapoosa Judicial Circuit included Douglas County then as it does today though the circuit is now known formally as the Seventh Judicial Administrative District.

From his home in Cedartown, Judge Janes regularly traveled to Douglasville to preside over cases within the walls of our 1896 courthouse.

Janes' obituary states he was a man of "incorruptible character and preeminent ability."

Apparently, not everyone in Douglas County had such a high opinion of him as Judge Janes found it necessary to file a $50,000 lawsuit against 27 different defendants in July, 1903.

The lawsuit involved events surrounding the election of 1902 where almost every race in Douglas County was contested. The election season had been hard fought with accusations slinging forth from both sides, so it was no surprise the outcome would be contested as well. As the presiding Judge it was up to Janes to decide the outcome.

It wasn't the first time Judge Janes had to decide a contested election in Douglas County. At the conclusion of another case the tension was so bad the judge "carried his decision with him to the train and handed it out the car window, the presumption being he realized the feeling was so strong that he was afraid to let his decision be known until he got out of town."

The 1902 election outcome was fraught with all types of irregularities including false registrations, manipulating the black vote to offset the votes of whites, and charges of "the old ring" referring to what we would recognize as "the good old boys" holding control in Douglas County.

There were also allegations that Douglas County contained "a combination of a few of the most corrupt and unprincipled politicians that ever infested any community."

My, that's hard to imagine, isn't it?

Things became more heated when Judge Janes decided in favor of every single person contesting the elections.

His decision resulted in public outcry with three to four hundred people showing up to protest the decision at the Douglas County Courthouse followed months later by the Judge filing his own lawsuit.

The Janes lawsuit became THE case to follow as 1903 became 1904. The train between Douglasville and Atlanta was full each day with folks traveling to the state capital to testify or just observe the two James brothers, Joseph S. and W.A., going legal toe to legal toe against each other as they represented opposing sides in the legal battle. With 27 various defendants several other attorneys were involved. Closing arguments alone took nearly three days to complete.

The Atlanta Constitution advised at the outset that "The case is very much mixed up and when all the evidence is in and the lawyers have gotten through arguing the case the jury will have one of the knottiest problems that any jury was ever called to solve in a damage suit."

During May and June, 1904 the crowds of people making their way to the Douglasville train depot on Strickland Street each morning were a little larger than they were in April or July. The extra folks weren't heading to work in the city nor were they simply going into Atlanta to shop. They were attending court at the Fulton County Courthouse for one of the most sensational cases of 1904.

Some of the folks Judge Janes sued were some of Douglas County's most involved citizens including folks with names such as Whitley, Hyatt, Nalley, and Speer. Other names included Price, Upshaw, Bowen, and Daniel.

These men along with others had contested the elections that were held in Douglas County in 1902. Some of the races included J.T. Healey versus W.J. Hembree for the office of county treasurer; M.L. Hathcock verses C.W. McGouirk for the office of sheriff; and J.W. Harding and R.M Smith verses W.P. Tackett for tax receiver.

The issue ended up in Judge Janes' courtroom since he decided most of the contested elections in Douglas County. Later he advised he spent "considerable time and gave the whole cause extended consideration."

Of course, his decision didn't set too well with some. A few days following the decision a mass meeting was held at the Douglas County Courthouse where several speeches against Judge Janes were made. T.R. Whitley along with a few others authored a written document "denouncing Judge Janes and accusing him of falsifying his oath as judicial officer and with having acted corruptly."

They also advised the corrupt politicians had "debauched the negro vote; had bought votes openly; had voted men under assumed names;

used the public funds for corruption purposes, and had "in many instances contested elections, and with the decision of a corrupt judge turned the men elected out of office."

They charged that these actions had resulted in many of the best citizens of Douglas County moving away to other places in disgust and/or had forced a large number to move their businesses outside the county.

The critics of Judge Janes printed the meeting's outcome in at least two local papers.

The Judge felt he had no other recourse, but to file a lawsuit.

Two years later, Judge Janes had his own personal day in court feeling that serious doubt had been cast upon his character.

After hearing more than one hundred witnesses and after large crowds had witnessed some of the most dramatic courtroom antics each day the jury only took seven to eight minutes to deliberate finding in favor of the Defendants.

Judge Janes lost his case. He retired from the bench and went home to Cedartown to a more quiet law practice, but at the time of his death in 1912 he was serving as the County Attorney for Polk County.

And did those who were politically inclined learn their lesson and decide that in the future they would have calm elections based solely on the issues at hand.

Well, I leave it in your hands.

What do you think?

Chapter 82

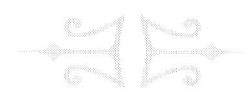

THE ROBERTS-MOZLEY HOUSE

I'm sitting here a little perplexed because I need a focus for this, my weekly column, and I'm just not sure which way to go. My overall topic is the Cultural Arts Center, but there is so much to share!

I could write about the Roberts/Mozley House with its architectural elements and the history of ownership, or I could write about the Cultural Arts Center itself regarding the impact the center has on life here in Douglasville regarding so many aspects of the arts.

351

Wait a minute.

It's MY column, isn't it?

So, I'm forging ahead with a two-pronged attack regarding the Cultural Arts Center.

First of all you can't help but notice the home located on Campbellton Street with its graceful lines, large front porch and wide front windows. From a written history compiled by Judy Verg and published at the Cultural Arts Center website, the story of the home begins with the marriage of Colonel W.T. Roberts and Emma Quillian in 1886. Miss Emma's father was Reverend J.B.C. Quillian, an original settler in the county and owner of the land where the Cultural Arts Center sits today. Work on the home began in 1901 after Miss Emma's father passed away and when Colonel Roberts purchased some land from his mother-in-law.

The New South, the local paper in Douglasville during January, 1902 printed various events and developments in world, national, state, and local news during the previous year. They mentioned the Aswan Dam opening along with the fact the Douglas County had hired a doctor for the new jail, the first typewriter had been purchased for Douglas County government use, and "W.T. Roberts, attorney, erected the beautiful nine-room residence on Campbellton Street in 1901. An Atlanta architect designed and supervised the building of this late semi-colonial structure."

Regarding the impressive home Verg advises, [The Roberts/Mozley Home is] "one of the few structures in Douglasville which embodies the characteristics of a period style…with its air of classic Greek architecture, the low sweeping line of a grand front porch, and an entrance of mahogany doors enriched with the serenity of stained glass…"

I visited the center a little over a week ago to meet Laura Lieberman, executive director of the Cultural Arts Council of Douglasville/Douglas County. She gave me a gracious welcome and allowed me to explore the house at will. I enjoyed discovering all the design elements from the courting bench in the entry hall, the beautiful staircase, the fireplaces inlaid with ceramic tiles, the lovely woodwork and beautiful pocket doors with brass fixtures. The house is on the National Register not so much because of the design of the home itself, but due to Colonel Robert's accomplishments, and I have to agree with Verg who states, "The house reflects the prominent social status of Colonel Roberts" [who was very active in politics and civic activities.]

Per Fannie Mae Davis' book regarding Douglas County history Colonel Roberts was a member of the committee to usher in the city's first water system. During the city's "Glorious Fourth Celebration" of 1886, the very first public celebration in Douglasville, Roberts read the Declaration of Independence aloud to an estimated crowd of three to four thousand people creating "a precedent followed for years afterward on Independence Day." In 1900, *The New South* paper advised Douglas County citizens about the new telephone system and published the twenty-three numbers that had been assigned to date. The Roberts' residence was assigned number 16.

During the seventeenth reunion of the 7th Georgia Regiment held in Douglasville in 1901, Colonel Roberts gave "an address of welcome to the old veterans…on behalf of the people of the county." Forty years before these men had been on the battlefield at Manassas.

This would be a good place to add even though Mr. Roberts was addressed as Colonel I haven't found any reference to any military service, and there's a very good reason for that. W.T.Roberts grew up in Campbellton and at the age of 5 became fatherless when Melville Roberts was killed at Gettysburg. Roberts studied law and soon was a practicing attorney in Douglasville. It is very common for attorneys in the state of Georgia to be addressed as Colonel even when there is no military service evident. Many governors in southern states and in the states of New Mexico and North Dakota have the ability to confer the title of Colonel on certain people. When you delve into the research there are several stories regarding why this practice exists, but most certainly it is covered in Georgia's legal code under section 38-2-111. Roberts partnered with J.R. Hutcheson practicing law and also served as Solicitor General of the Tallapoosa Judicial Circuit until 1914.

During the few years right before and right after the turn of the century Colonel Roberts served as Mayor of Douglasville and he was also elected to the State Senate in 1911.

In 1914, per Fannie Mae Davis, Roberts "accepted a government appointment to the Board of Trade, under the administration of President Woodrow Wilson. He moved to Washington D.C. never to return to his former Douglasville business ties." Verg advises the Washington appointment was with the Bureau of Markets, but either way he landed a job in Washington D.C. and off he went.

The home was sold to the Mozley family who owned it from 1927 to 1971. Look for a future column to focus on the prominence of the Mozley family including the fact they produced two Douglasville mayors in the 1930s and 40s. Walter Turner purchased the house in 1978, and in 1986 he sold it to the Douglasville/Douglas County Cultural Arts Council.

Twenty five years later the Cultural Arts Center is still going strong.

Chapter 83

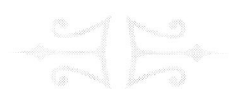

STORAGE WARS – THEN AND NOW

Recently the concept of reality television has hit Douglasville in a big way. The folks at Atlanta's Finest Catering are stars of *Catering Wars* on television. A few days ago we saw members of the sheriff's department in action on *Scared Straight*, and one would be food entrepreneur from Douglasville was featured on *Supermarket Superstar*.

One of the most popular reality shows is *Storage Wars* where folks bid on abandoned storage units and then search through the items to find things they can sell. The goal is to turn a profit on the merchandise.

I think the allure of the show is that anyone can attend these auctions and has the chance of striking it big. Storage unit treasure has included original Picasso drawings, an original signed Abraham Lincoln letter that netted $15,000, and not too long ago gold coins and gold bars were found in a storage unit – honest to goodness treasure!

I was surprised to discover that hunting storage units for treasure is nothing new. In fact, Max Hart, a post office employee from New York City was an avid storage unit treasure hunter in 1904. For five years Max had been attending book and storage auction sales, making some money, especially out of rare books. Rather than bid on whole storage units, Max opted to bid on trunks that had lain unclaimed for years.

Unlike storage units auctioned off today, Max was not able to peer inside the abandoned trunks. It was a gamble. Once he purchased a trunk only to find it full of old rags. Few yielded him anything, but he kept on in the hopes of striking it rich someday.

At one sale in 1904 he bid on a very old trunk covered in cobwebs and dust. Its hinges were rust-bitten, and it wasn't hard to tell how long the trunk had been in undisturbed repose for some time.

Hart bid four dollars and got it without competition. It seems like such a small amount today, but in 1904 Hart's bid could be judged liberal. Hart had the trunk carted to his home and forced the rusted lock.

On top he found ancient newspapers, some worn clothes, and a few books of no special value, but wrapped in a faded bit of brown paper at the very bottom of the grimy trunk Max Hart found what he thought could be – might be – a little treasure.

Hart held in his hands one hundred bonds of a southern electric lighting and water company which at that time held a market value of between $17,500 and $20,000. In today's figures the market value could have been over $500,000.

The southern electric company named on the bonds was Douglasville Electric Lighting and Water Company, a company organized and operating in Georgia.

It was thought the owner of the bonds died and his relatives knew nothing about the securities. Nothing was heard by the warehouse proprietors from the owner of the trunk for years. They had sent frequent notices to an old address and obtaining no reply placed the trunk at auction, as the law allowed them to do.

Hart took the bonds to bankers and brokers to investigate his find. They found that the company that issued the bonds was still doing a successful business, and the bonds were registered with a large trust company in New York.

At first bank officials advised that accrued interest at six percent would more than likely add $10,000 to the value making the find worth as much as $30,000. Several of the large brokerage houses offered him $200 each for the bonds.

Suddenly Max Hart who at 29 years old was only earning $1,000 a year, was faced with managing a fortune. He said, "I have dreamed of this luck for years, and my dream has come true at last."

Sadly, it was not to be.

An inquiry was sent to Douglasville where Max Hart was advised his imagined wealth was worthless as the bonds had never been negotiated.

I just have to wonder about the original owner of the trunk.

Who was that?

Chapter 84

FARMERS AND MERCHANTS BANK

You can't help but notice the building if you get caught by the red light at the intersection of Campbellton and Broad Streets in downtown Douglasville. The tile work showcasing the business name, the little architectural flourishes that make the building so unique, and the exquisite round and fan windows all boasting imported German glass takes you back to another time.

I'm speaking of the beautiful Farmers and Merchants Bank building, of course. The location happens to be the original home to the second bank organized in Douglasville.

As the South moved from Reconstruction into the New South era there was a sudden spike in the number of applications for new national banking charters by business men who had taken over as the new leading class. These men understood the New South philosophy calling for changes in the southern economy in the areas of industrialization and in the textile industry, in particular.

Douglasville Banking Company, our first bank, opened in 1891. The space that bears their name now serves as the welcome center for the City of Douglasville.

The second bank, Farmers and Merchants Bank was opened in 1907 with assets of $25,000. The Farmers and Merchants Bank was established after a visit from W.S. Witham, the founder of the Witham Banking System. Witham Banks were state banks, organized under Georgia laws with individual officers and directors and each had their own individual capital.

The Witham Banking System focused on small rural areas with populations of 1,000 or less. Mr. Witham would meet with local citizens and persuade them they needed a bank. In Douglasville's case he would push the fact that competition was good for the market. My research indicates Witham was a masterful speaker and his position on the State Sunday School Board for the Methodist Church probably didn't hurt either.

By the time the Farmers and Merchants Bank was organized in Douglasville Witham had approximately 80 banks in Georgia and Florida involved in his chain. Each member bank would appoint Witham as fiscal agent, and he would receive a fee from each location.

His company operated with two mottoes that seemed to satisfy his customer base. The first was "Safety First!" which was meant to calm the nerves of any depositor. In fact, Witham was the first banker to institute the practice of guaranteeing deposits before the FDIC, however in the end it did little to help.

His second motto was "Success!" and Witham certainly promoted that. He took all of the executives within his system on retreats to the mountains or some resort as a morale booster. Sometimes as many as 200-500 people went on these trips. Once he reserved an entire train for a trip to New York for one of the "Success!" jaunts.

He also spoke at any convention or for any group he could manage an invite for. His very large mansion along Peachtree Street in Atlanta helped his "success" image, as well.

A 1916 *Douglas County Sentinel* article advises W. Claude Abercrombie served as president of the Farmers and Merchants Bank. His brother Joseph S. Abercrombie was identified as a stockholder. Both men were former mayors of Douglasville as well. Rader Stewart, was also involved with the bank.

I became very interested in the history of the Farmers and Merchants Bank when I noticed a small blurb in Fannie Mae Davis' history of Douglasville and Douglas County that read, "When hard times hit Douglas County in the 1920s, the bank [Farmers and Merchants Bank] failed also and it was taken over by the old Georgia State Bank (not affiliated by a more recent Georgia State Bank)."

Hard times hit the county?

Hard times hit before the actual Depression?

So, I thumbed through Mrs. Davis' book looking for more information regarding the hard times and the bank failure. I was surprised to discover her book covers events during World War I and then basically jumps into the Depression. The 1920s are eluded to but not mentioned in great depth. In her section detailing various banks in the county she only gave the Farmers and Merchant Bank a scant paragraph.

That sent me into heavy research mode to discover what happened to the Witham Banking System, and I found quite a bit.

At some point Witham basically retired from running the chain of banks and his assistant, W.D. Manley, took over. Manley had no previous banking experience and had only served as a cashier when he was first hired. Loyalty to Witham is what seemed to qualify him for the job unfortunately.

Though he worked with Witham, Manley did not adhere to the same conservative course. The chain prospered and grew under his management, but it was a house of cards waiting to fall due to Manley's creative financing.

It was very simple.

Manley would borrow from bank A to buy controlling shares of bank B. Once he owned controlling shares of bank B, it was simple to get a loan from bank B to pay off bank A. The shares of bank B could then be used to purchase control in bank C.

While Witham had his Peachtree Street mansion Manley lived in grand style on Paces Ferry Road in an Italian style mansion complete with a butler, chauffeur, limousine and shopping trips to Europe for his family.

As it became more and more apparent Manley was using the member banks as his own personal cash drawer, state and federal regulators tried to calm depositors by stating the banks were just small country banks operating as independent units, but before the collapse in July, 1926 the Georgia State Bank was one of the state's largest banks, with its branching network of 20 offices throughout the state.

The bank failures shattered the economy in Georgia and Florida.

Many depositors lost their life savings. By the end of 1926, 150 banks in Florida and Georgia were closed and more than $30 million was missing.

The bank failure had to devastate the folks of Douglasville even if the bank was taken over by Georgia State Bank. Fannie Mae Davis advises Farmers and Merchants' stockholders were only paid 0.5 percent of their investment.

THIS is part of the hard times Fannie Mae Davis alludes to in her book.

Manley was tried and was eventually convicted of "fraudulent insolvency." He served seven years.

The bank building eventually became the home of Powell's Groceries and most people my age remember Douglasville Printing Company being in that spot for most of their lives.

For the last few years the spot has been a little sad and vacant. I love the corner location and all the windows. It would be a perfect spot for a little bistro or tea room.

What do you think?

Chapter 85

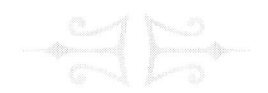

MR. SMITH – THE INVENTOR

Prior to 1908 S.W. (Stephen Wallace) Smith was a well-respected Douglas County farmer known for his progressive stance regarding crop diversification. He didn't put his hopes in just one crop. He planted several different crops including potatoes and melons along with his corn and cotton.

During August, 1887 Mr. Smith did gain some notoriety when he killed a rattlesnake on his property that was six feet, two inches long. The paper advised the snake had "ten rattles and a button", and Mr. Smith had subdued the rattling menace by throwing a noose over its head. The snake's carcass was carried to the Sweetwater Park Hotel where it caused quite a stir and was on display for several days.

Mr. Smith wasn't just progressive in his farming or snake wrangling techniques. He was also interested in ways to improve tasks such as maintaining roads across the county. During his spare time he worked on an invention – a machine that would help ease the poor condition of the roads in Douglas County as well as roads everywhere.

For many years prior to and for many years following the turn of the century folks had to deal with dirt roads. County and town governments tried to maintain them, but most stayed in poor condition. Folks just couldn't keep up with rain and wind that could turn a road into a river of mud within seconds. Though the automobile was a plus in getting folks from point A to point B, roads would soon be filled with potholes and ruts. Road crews waged a constant battle to keep the roads clear as well as to make sure the dirt surfaces were smooth and even. Most of the time drags were fashioned from wood that were pulled over the road surface, but they had to be weighted down for maximum performance, and the wood wore out quickly.

Enter the Good Roads Movement which had its heyday in America from 1880 to 1916. It was a Populist movement dedicated to improving roads across the nation. The Georgia Good Roads Association formed December 9, 1901 with smaller groups springing up in most every county including Douglas.

One of the earliest town ordinances in Douglasville due to the work of organizations like the Good Roads Association had to do with the maintenance of roads. All males between the ages of 16 to 45 had to work on the city streets for 15 days a year or pay $1.75 penalty. Some men were exempt from the road crews including men missing an arm or leg. During the late 1800s men amputees were very commonplace as they were more often than not Civil War veterans. Other men who were exempt from road maintenance were the mayor along with the councilmen and licensed ministers.

S.W. Smith saw a need, and he continued to work on his invention in his spare time. On May 28, 1907, he filed an application for a patent for his road working machine. George T. McLarty and Coleman A. Adcock, fellow Douglas County citizens, witnessed his filing. A patent was issued January 14, 1908, and by October 11th that same year Smith was seeking publicity.

An article dated October 11, 1908 appeared in *The Atlanta Constitution* explaining how an invention would forever revolutionize road work.

The machine was innovative in that it could work on any road and could handle 15-20 miles a day leaving the roads smooth and even. It could be pulled behind a horse or a steam powered engine. One of the best features was the fact that it only took one man to operate it. Soon the ordinances for citizens to work the road would be obsolete.

The paper further advised that the machine would be on exhibition by the Good Roads Association, and Mr. Smith had plans to market his machine.

The story regarding S.W. Smith and his innovative road working machine goes cold in October, 1908. I'm still on the hunt to determine if he sold the machine or if any were ever put into use. I'd love to hear from any Douglas County citizens who might know the rest of the story.

Chapter 86

TALES OF FALLING STARS

In February, 2013 over 1,000 people were injured due to a meteoroid explosion above Chelyabinsk, Russia. The explosion created a sonic boom and damaged hundreds of buildings. Scientists have estimated the object was 50 feet in diameter, and said it was the largest such blast in over a century.

While I have seen a shooting star from time to time, I've never witnessed anything this large or this loud.

I can only imagine.

A shooting star or a falling star simply refers to the visible path a meteoroid –a small particle from a comet or asteroid -- creates as it enters the Earth's atmosphere.

Once a meteoroid enters the Earth's atmosphere it generally burns up, but if it lands on the Earth's surface we refer to it as a meteorite. Objects several meters wide generally explode in the air and can cause severe damage. Most explosions are heard several seconds after they occur. Sometimes people also report hearing crackling, swishing and hissing sounds.

Sightings of falling stars go back to ancient times, and as recently as this past Friday there were reports of meteors all along the east coast of the United States.

With today's technology and "instant" news fueled by social media, we know about falling stars almost immediately. However, for all of our knowledge we only recently were able to track a meteor from space through the Earth's atmosphere. The first tracking occurred in October, 2008 – almost one hundred years to the day that Douglas County citizens heard a meteorite explode. The 2008 meteor exploded above the Nubian Desert in Sudan.

I first came across a mention of a meteorite in relation to Douglas County while researching something else. Similar to the scientists of today I had to "track" the meteorite, but instead of searching through space I had to search through a large volume of newspapers.

Because my access to the Douglas County papers that were published here during the late 1800s and early 1900s is limited, I often count on the Library of Congress and their huge library of newspapers from all across the county to provide me with history trails to follow.

I ran across this "dispatch from Douglasville, Georgia" that was published in the *Keowee Courier* from Pickens Courthouse, South Carolina on October 21, 1908, though the actual event occurred on Friday, October 9, 1908.

It said:

A dispatch from Douglasville, Ga.—People for miles around here … were alarmed by the shock from the fall of a large meteor which struck the ground with enough force to be felt with a radius of fifteen miles. The crash came about 4:30, and within a few minutes afterward telephone messages were received from several places twelve and fifteen miles away asking what was the cause of it.

The dispatch went on to say that before it was determined to be a meteor other possible explanations were given as a large boiler somewhere in town might have erupted, but then citizens began to come forward to express they had seen large streaks of light across the heavens at the same time of the explosion and [there was talk] that it was a large meteor struck the ground.

The talk in Douglasville was correct because on the 10th of October *The Atlanta Constitution* printed a dispatch from Adairsville confirming the noise and confusion in the surrounding area for miles around. The Adairsville dispatch confirmed the date and gave the time of "explosion" as around 4:45 in the afternoon and stated, "The houses shook and the windows rattled, but no flash of light accompanied it. Different themes are advanced as to its cause. The most plausible being a meteor bursting in the upper air. It was rainy and cloudy all day."

Ah, it was rainy and cloudy all day. That would certainly explain why so many folks heard the meteor across northwestern Georgia, but didn't report seeing it.

The Atlanta Constitution finally cleared up any doubt on October 11, 1908 when they printed a dispatch from Kingston, Georgia.

Kingston is located in Bartow County – eleven miles from Cartersville and twelve miles from Rome, Georgia. The small town was a focal point during the Civil War and is remembered as the place where the General was delayed for over an hour which helped to thwart the Great Locomotive Chase in April, 1862. Also, in May, 1864 some three to four thousand Confederate regulars surrendered at Kingston – the last significant Confederate regulars to surrender east of the Mississippi.

Friday afternoon between four and five o'clock a terrific explosion was heard near here, but no one seemed to be able to locate the noise. Some thought it was at Rome; that a magazine or boiler had [busted]. A telephone message was sent to Rockmart, thinking possibly the explosion occurred there.

Today it was learned the noise was produced by the bursting of a meteor.

It is thought that the meteor came to earth somewhere on the Best place, three miles from here as a [person] on the place says he saw the smoke from it, but the noise of the explosion was heard simultaneously in Calhoun, Cartersville, Dalton, Pine Log, Cartersville, and the surrounding county.

A man named Lee was hunting near Saltpeter cave, and when the concussion came gravel fell all around like hail.

J.W. Odom of Cement [a community about a mile and a half north of Kingston] and a [man] named Henry Pritchett say that they saw it burst in the heavens; that it sped through space like an immense red ball of fire in the southwest sky. They saw it break into ten thousand fragments accompanied by the noise that startled everyone.

Apparently, some of those "ten thousand fragments" were quite large. The Douglasville dispatch from October 21st indicated, "the meteor struck the ground three miles south of Kingston and buried deep in the earth leaving a hole as large as a dwelling house and hundreds of people visited the scene Sunday."

I was a little disappointed that the location for the meteor touchdown wasn't Douglasville.

Chapter 87

A POST IN THREE PARTS – A REVERSE S-CURVE, A WAYWARD CABOOSE, AND ANTIQUATED BLUE LAWS

Early yesterday morning – very faintly – I could hear the train moving through downtown Douglasville even though I live a few miles away from the track. The sound wafts down from the ridge at Skint Chestnut and floats across the interstate. It hangs over the Mt. Carmel district for a few seconds as it fades out. It's easy to miss if you are busy doing this and that, so I'm always a little surprised when I hear it, but it always makes me smile remembering my childhood growing up with a train track literally in my front yard.

The sound also got me to thinking about three separate bits of information regarding "our" train, and I decided it was time to share even though each piece of information could stand alone as a separate column, but why should they?

There is an underlying theme, at least.

Part 1: The Reverse S-Curve

I found some still photographs online of trains making their way through Douglas County as well as some videos, too. Apparently there are folks that are real train fanatics – often referred to as railfans – people who actually follow trains and take pictures along the route at various locations.

Many of the entries mentioned Douglasville's "famous Reverse S-curve".

Seriously?

The rails passing through Douglas County curve at some point, and form an "S"? I began to look closely at the pictures and the videos and couldn't deny the fact that we DO have a reverse S-curve west of town at the N. Baggett Road crossing. I even got in the car and headed west on Highway78/Bankhead, and yes, there it was. I have driven by the spot hundreds of times, and it just never registered with me.

So, I had more questions. Why is this reverse S-curve so famous among the railfans, and why was the "S" built into the track? It just seems that straight lines would be safer. Everything I've read about curves mentions the fact that friction and wear on the wheels and rails are problems. The curves also reduce speed, but that wouldn't be such a bad thing as trains approach town, right?

I sent an e-mail to one of the railfans who had been to the Douglasville S-curve, and luckily he answered me.

Nikos stated, "It's not famous really, it's just well known within the Atlanta railroad photography circle, since it's a very nice place to photograph trains. As for why it's built like that, I don't know a specific answer, but I imagine it has to do with the topography of the land and a way to gain elevation, if you ever see a train coming through the S curves it often will not be moving that fast and the locomotive prime movers will be working hard. The stretch of railroad between Atlanta and Birmingham is known for its curves and hills."

A friend of mine and long time Douglasville resident advised, "One thing to keep in mind is the period in which they cleared land and took into consideration the topography of the land. Once you get west of Douglasville, the Appalachian [imprint] of the land rolls and ebbs. I would imagine back then that the railroad surveyors took the least construction impact path to lay a rail bed. They didn't have equipment back then like we do today."

I'd like to get my hands on some of the information regarding the route of the track and how it was decided. I'm thinking a trip to the Norfolk Southern archives is in order, at some point. It's on my long list of things to do.

Part 2: The Missing Caboose

Back in December I visited the Douglas County Public Library on Selman Drive and took a few photographs of their art collection.

One image is titled "The End of the Line" by Jim Perkins. The title makes perfect sense because Mr. Perkins captured the caboose that sat along the railroad tracks between Broad Street and Strickland Street where Campbellton crosses Broad and the tracks. The library's guidebook to the art collection advised me "the caboose was acquired by the City of Douglasville."

I remember seeing the caboose there. Several people I've asked remember seeing the caboose there, so at least I know I wasn't seeing things, but it has disappeared.

I thought it might have been moved to Hunter Park, a caboose is on display there, but was told it was a different one.

What on earth happened to it?

I have inquired with various people to no avail. I'm still waiting on some answers, but so far…..nothing.

Part 3: Antiquated Blue Laws

Hearing the train whistle yesterday morning also got me thinking about another tidbit of train related history I've been hanging onto, and it connects to antiquated laws we still have today. The situation involves a piece of litigation originally filed in the Superior Court here in Douglas County before reaching the Georgia Court of Appeals in 1908. The case involved one of Georgia's blue laws.

In case you are unaware a blue law refers to a law that is passed based on religious standards. The origin of the term "blue law" is unknown, but the concept dates back to the Puritans in the 17th Century when they passed laws requiring church attendance on Sunday.

Blue laws abounded back when I was a little girl. Whether you went to a Christian church or not there were certain things you simply did not do on a Sunday including shopping and apparently at the turn of the last century it was against the law for a train to blow its horn on Sundays and disturb the Sabbath.

Yes, not only were stores closed across the state in 1908 it was also against the law for trains to disturb the Sunday quiet. The Defendant in the matter was A.H. Westfall, the superintendent of transportation for the Southern Railway Company. The complaint advised:

> *...on the 14th day of April, 1907, said day being the Sabbath day, [the Defendant] unlawfully run and cause to be run in and through Douglas County, over said railroad six freight trains of the Southern Railway Company, all going east pulling a train of freight cars, all of said freight trains arriving and departing from the city of Douglasville during the afternoon of said date.*
>
> *...The six freight trains in question ran through Douglas County after eight o'clock a.m. on the Sunday charged in the indictment, arriving at their destination, Atlanta, at different hours in the afternoon and evening of that Sunday.*
>
> *...These trains were all prevented from making their trips in schedule time, and were delayed at Waco, by the fact that there was no water in the tank at that place to supply the engines; and the tank was not supplied with water at Waco until about noon on Sunday.*
>
> *...The failure to keep water at Waco prevented the freight train from complying with their regular schedule, and caused them to be delayed more than 12 hours; and when they left Waco on Sunday about noon, they were ordered to make the run to Atlanta on what was known as an "extra schedule."*

Eventually the Court of Appeals did not uphold the original verdict against Mr. Westfall for several complex legal reasons I won't bore you with here, but the case was dismissed.

Today this case seems a little silly, doesn't it?

How could we have a law preventing a train from blowing its horn? Even without the sort of automobile traffic we have today it would seem folks would need to know when a train was bearing down on them, but the blue laws prevailed.

Over the years one by one the blue laws have been repealed. I can remember finally having the ease and convenience of entering a store, any store, on a Sunday to shop. Today, the thought of not being able to is just ludicrous, and far be it from me to judge anyone, but I would imagine the same folks who attend church venture into those stores for a little shopping, order their favorite dish at a restaurant, or even buy a movie ticket on the once stark and quiet Sabbath.

However, one blue law remains.

In November, 2011 *The New York Times* advised, "Religiously motivated blue laws were once common across the Bible belt, but over the decades, they have been struck down as anachronistic or unfriendly to business. Georgia was the last Southern bastion of a statewide all-day ban on Sunday alcohol sales in package or grocery stories.

After years of debating whether to do away with a century-old law that banned selling alcohol on Sundays, Georgia politicians decided to let the people vote, city by city and county by county, on what they preferred in their communities. The results were resounding. Out of the 127 communities voting, 105 communities voted to chose to end the Sunday restriction, often by huge margins.

It is a compromise that both sides agree is probably best for an issue where views differ so starkly. "It's hard to argue with people who just want to vote, even when you disagree with what they want to vote for," said Jerry Luquire, president of the Georgia Christian Coalition. "

So, I can hear the train in Douglasville now, I can go to a movie, a restaurant and do some shopping, but can I buy that same bottle of wine on a Sunday that I can pick up the day before or the day after?

No.

I can't, and unlike so many Georgia communities that have held elections, I haven't been given the right to exercise my right to vote concerning the issue.

Richard Segal, the administrator of the Facebook page called "Douglasville & Douglas County for Sunday alcohol sales," advises, "What could be the last of the blue laws in Georgia fell last year when the Georgia General Assembly passed, and Governor Deal signed, SB-10 which permits cities and counties to place a question on the ballot to allow the retail sale of alcohol beverages. The Douglasville and Douglas County governments have not acted on this, but the two cities that are partially in Douglas County have. Villa Rica voters approved Sunday retail sales in November, and Austell voters get to decide on March 6. Even with these changes, alcohol sales on Sunday are still treated differently than on other days of the week – no sales before 12:30 p.m. are allowed."

It really doesn't matter to me how the vote turns out. What matters to me is that our citizens here in Douglas County and the City of Douglasville should be able to speak out on the matter by getting to exercise one of the most important rights and responsibilities we have – the right to vote.

I certainly hope our elected officials wouldn't have the audacity to deny citizens their right to vote since so many communities in our state have already had their say.

Section Eight

BOOM AND BUST

Chapter 88

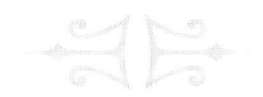

THE CIVIC LEAGUE

"Where there is no vision, the people perish…." This was the motto for the Georgia State Federation of Women's Clubs, a division of a national federation formed in 1890. The Federation is responsible for seventy-five percent of the public libraries, developing kindergartens in public schools, and food and drug regulation during the 20th century nationwide. Areas of outreach included, but were not limited to, education, home life, international outreach, and legislation. Members strived to improve the social, cultural, and physical needs in their city or town. By 1895, Atlanta boasted a Civic League, so it should be no surprise that the ladies of Douglasville eventually organized their own league in January, 1914.

The CivicLeague began with eight members but within six months over fifty women had joined the club. By 1920, membership hovered close to seventy. Mrs. D.W. Peace served as president from 1914 through 1921. Other members included ladies from families with names such as Selman, McKoy, Baggett, Abercrombie, Huffine, and Vansant.

The club undertook all sorts of projects and regularly petitioned the city council regarding a growing list of needs including improvements for James Park (a grove of trees just east of the building where Hartley, Rowe & Fowler is located today), new ordinances involving parking wagons and cars, a wish for the city to have a sewage system, and at one point the ladies campaigned for cleaner streets including the alleyways behind the businesses.

Douglasville's Civic League did simple things such as improving the performance stage at Douglasville College by replacing the curtain and adding a little wallpaper. They also took up the fight demanding the city of Douglasville provide electricity during the daytime. The city had provided electricity for a few years during the night hours, but it took Mrs. F.M. Stewart and Mrs. Ralph Morris to make the case for the city to allow the current to flow at least half the day for newfangled machines such as electric irons.

Another major project had to do with a city swimming pool. It was built along Campbellton Street on the same side of the road as the post office. The pool opened in July, 1917 with specific days for ladies to swim. Skinny dipping was never allowed and smoking was also a no-no.

Of course, the women mobilized during World War I sending care packages to the soldiers, selling Liberty Bonds, and sponsored a dinner for returning soldiers.

The largest undertaking of the Civic League had to do with what they called the pavilion at the cemetery along Church Street and Rose Avenue. The structure still stands today. It was finished in the fall of 1920 with many local businesses contributing to the construction.

One project that never got off the ground was plans for a public library. For some reason there was resistance, and Douglasville did not see a public library until the 1950s.

Of course the heyday of the Civic League here in Douglasville was a time when women's rights were suppressed, so the state chapters and in turn the groups like the one in Douglasville were the lifelines for grassroots efforts to begin lobbying for the right to vote. The groups provided opportunities for women to educate themselves and to develop a voice to take a stand in their communities.

While it was no substitute for the right to vote, the clubs served as the best opportunity for women to have a voice prior to the vote, and Douglasville's women of the Civic League were right on the front line.

Chapter 89

A KOZY THEATER FOR DOUGLASVILLE

Spend any time on the *Facebook* pages involving reminiscing about Douglas County history, and you will soon understand the love folks had for the Lithia Springs Drive-In and the Alpha Theater. In fact, the drive-in has a page of its own. While it's true both places existed for many years and provided access to the newest offerings from Hollywood, neither place was the first movie theater in these parts.

The award for first movie theater would fall to the Kozytorium.

Yes, I agree. The name is interesting right down to the intentional misspelling of the root-word "cozy". Advertising experts advise intentional misspellings for business names such as "La-Z-boy" and "Tastee Freeze" are ploys to get people talking, they set the business apart, and help with recall."

Of course, a movie theater is a bit cozy. Even though you are sitting in a dark building, you are able to dive in the plot of the movie and lose yourself in the story. Hopefully, you sit in that theater with someone you really care about. It is "kozy", right?

On June 26, 1914 the headline in the *Sentinel* read, "Smith has Faith in Douglasville Dirt".

The story advises how Mr. V.R. (Vander) Smith "closed a deal with J.T. Duncan for the two lots adjoining the Douglasville Banking Company." Yes, that would be the general area along Broad Street where Fabiano's Pizza is located today.

The article states, "…within the next few days [Smith] will proceed to break dirt for a modern pressed brick structure that will be second to none in Douglasville."

By November, another heading appeared in the *Sentinel* stating "Opening of New Opera House Tuesday Night."

The article advises Smith considered no expense in building his theater stating, "The new building is a real up-to-date modern picture show in every respect; everything betrays comfort and convenience…The front of the building will be of marble whiteness with an attractive ticket booth, beautifully ornamented, and a spacious lobby in which posters will be displayed for advertising the shows…The woodwork will be of mahogany finish and the walls a brilliant color adorned with rare tapestries. A commodious [or spacious] stage has been erected in order that vaudeville may be put on at some time."

Vaudeville! Right here in sleepy little Douglasville!

Vander R. Smith first entered the business community in Douglasville in 1896 when he bought the inventory of Theo and Charles O. Dorsett. I've seen several entries in farming journals published at the turn of the century where Smith's name was connected to selling fertilizer, and he was a cotton buyer. Smith and his wife Carrie lived on Strickland Street, but I'm still trying to determine exactly where. He served on the city council in1908 and possibly again during the 1920s, and by 1918 he was leading the city as Douglasville's mayor.

I don't have an exact date for the closing of the Kozytorium, but a theater owner's journal described as "Film Year Book" for 1927 advised the Kozytorium in Douglasville, Georgia served a town population of 2,100 and had the capacity for seating 200 theatergoers.

Just as today growing businesses were important to Douglasville and Douglas County as a whole back then, and it appears that the paper was in full support stating, "To say that Mr. Smith has faith in his town and county goes without question. He is enterprising and progressive, not a knocker, but a builder. Faith without works, availeth nothing. Give us more Smiths."

Times really don't change, do they?

Where are our "Smiths" today?

Give us more Smiths!

Chapter 90

CHANGING PERSPECTIVE

We change our clothes, we change the television, but how often do we change our perspective – the way we interpret or see things? Not very often, I suspect.

Just log into any social media site and you see plenty regarding how your friends feel on one particular issue or another.

I could launch off from this point and discuss viewpoints regarding tax increases, stadium moves, taking a "selfie" at a funeral, or even immigration reform, but being the history person I happen to be I'm going to use local history to make a point.

Some of what I do involves using images taken around Douglas County at different time periods to spark conversation. I'm looking for information, identifications, thoughts and feelings, and most importantly memories.

Perspective and memory are closely tied yet they are unique to each and every individual. We may experience the same event, but remember it differently. The same thing applies to various locations as well.

Take the Hutcheson Building in downtown Douglasville where Gumbeaux's Cajun Cafe is located. The building was erected by J.R. Hutcheson in 1915, and just so we wouldn't forget it over the years, Judge Hutcheson put his name on the building.

Each one of us has a different memory or impression of the building based on our perspective – a perspective that is generally linked to our age.

Folks like me who are immersed in the history of a place often associate a building with the builder or first tenant while others associate a place with a strong memory they had growing up as they interacted with the building on and off.

J.R. Hutcheson built the structure with his law offices in mind for the second floor while the first floor was leased to the U.S. Post Office. It was the first time in Douglasville's history that the post office was housed in a space that was entirely given over to mail service. Prior to that Douglasville's post office might have been inside a store, but it shared a corner of the location with the store's inventory.

There are folks around today who would associate the Hutcheson Building with Hoke Bearden's store since it took up the first floor for a few years.

Later on R.L. Smith teamed up with J.T. Arnold and Economy Auto in that space, while Quillian Bonds had his photography studio upstairs.

Of course, for those of us who have a more recent perspective of the Hutcheson Building, we automatically default to Gumbeaux's Cajun Café, right?

All of us know the building, yet we have different perspectives based on our unique interaction with the space.

Our different impressions of the building take nothing away from the site itself. We understand different viewpoints don't change the historical significance or importance to the downtown area one bit. We understand why someone who is 60 might have a different view point of the building than someone who is 40 or even 20.

Getting back to issues other than impressions and memories of historic buildings, wouldn't it be refreshing if we could come together as a city, a county, a state, and as a nation to view things with new eyes – to see a different perspective?

We tend to become so fixed in our perspective, and this results in rigid judgment on issues of all types.

I'm certainly not talking about someone going against their principles, but I am calling for folks to stop, take a step back, and consider another viewpoint with fresh eyes.

It might be what's needed to move our little piece of the world along without so much gridlock.

Chapter 91

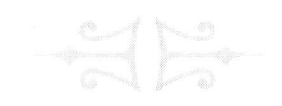

FIVE LITTLE BOYS – FIVE GROWN MEN

I have a Word document where I store bits and pieces of the Douglas County story as I find them – bits and pieces where I feel I need more details or I need to verify facts. I currently have a 68 page document full of bits and pieces.

Yes, 68 pages!

I need to whittle it down a bit, so I decided I would hold my nose and go ahead and dive in with the story of the five little boys.

Many, many months ago a few lines I read in Fannie Mae Davis's book concerning Douglas County history caught my eye.

She said, "Five little boys born in Douglas County played ball, hunted, fished, swam in the same creek together, attended the same schools, played tricks and jokes on each other."

Now that one line isn't very special other than I'm the mother of a former little boy, and I can testify he did all of those things. In fact, now that he's a handsome grown man, he still does those same things.

Most men do, right?

Fannie Mae Davis continues, "Only one remained in Douglas County once grown. All prospered and became leading citizens. In 1915, their counties sent them to the state legislature where they had a reunion for the first time since they were boys."

Ah, there's the interesting turn of history that I like.

Even though they all went their separate ways, they ended up as productive citizens and served in the Georgia General Assembly.

The five little boys who served in the General Assembly were: W.I. Dorris representing Douglas County; W.H. Dorris, representing Crisp County; L.Z. Dorsett representing Carroll County; John Edwards representing Haralson County; and J.B. Baggett representing Paulding County.

So, for a three year period beginning in 1915 the five served in the General Assembly.

Historically speaking, let's set the context of the time when these five men were creating laws that effected citizens across the state of Georgia.

The year was 1915, the year Leo Frank was hung by a mob of citizens for the murder of Mary Phagan, and Gutzon Borglum met with members of the United Daughters of the Confederacy regarding a proposed carving on Stone Mountain. Frank's hanging would lead to a resurgence of the Ku Klux Klan atop Stone Mountain when a rally was held in 1915.

The men would have known about an earthquake that struck just 30 miles southeast of Atlanta in 1916, and in 1917, with the United States entry into World War I eminent, the battleship *Georgia* was commissioned again to serve as an escort and troop transport ship. The five men would have been in shock over the Great Atlanta Fire when 300 acres of homes and businesses were destroyed.

Now that our perspective has been sharpened a bit regarding the time period lets see what exists "out there" about the five men.

I found the least amount of information for John S. Edwards (1867-1941). The representative from Haralson County was married to Margaret M. Head and prior to being a member of the General Assembly he was the Mayor of Buchanan, Georgia in 1907.

W.I. Dorris – William Irvine Dorris (1867-1940) was married to Sarah Elizabeth Tayor. He served as the representative from Douglas County from 1913 to 1917. *The Atlanta Constitution* dated June 26, 1915 advised

Dorris introduced a bill to provide for a method of changing county lines for redistricting. Later on that summer he introduced other legislation to amend an existing act regulating elections.

L.Z. Dorsett – Leander "Lee" Z. Dorsett (1864-1948) was the son of Joseph Smith Dorsett (1811-1895), a pioneer of Campbell County who originally came from Laurens, South Carolina. His half-brother, Samuel N.P. Dorsett was Douglas County's first Superior Court Clerk. Dorsett attended Holly Springs Academy at Chapel Hill. His political life included serving as Douglasville's mayor in 1901 and 1907, Recorder from 1902 to 1905 and represented Carroll County in the General Assembly.

Dorsett was involved with a bill against concealed weapons and in August, 1916 another bill he sponsored dubbed the Dorsett Bill was killed in the Ways and Means committee of the Georgia House. It was a bill that provided for the levying and collecting of state income tax.

Gee, is HE the one we need to blame?

No, not by a long shot since Georgia's tax laws had been revised by passage of the Lipcomb-Anderson-Miller Bill in 1913 (the bill that called for the appointment of a state tax commissioner). 1913 was also the same year the Sixteenth Amendment was passed giving the federal government the right to rifle through your pockets, so, Dorsett is free from total blame.

Dorsett returned to Douglas County in 1935 and served as mayor from 1938 to 1939. During his term as mayor he made the first dialed call from the city on July 7, 1939. Operator assisted calls had been in existence since 1899.

Finally, Dorsett returned to the state house again from 1943 to 1945 representing Douglas County.

W.H. Dorris – William Herschell Dorris (1870-1937) was the son of William C. Dorris, a Confederate veteran and grew up on a farm near Douglasville where he eventually attended Douglasville College. He studied law under Judge A.L. Bartlett of Brownsville, was admitted to the bar in 1896 and was a public spirited person from what I can see. He was Mayor of Cordele in 1910. One of his accomplishments there was getting a Carnegie Library for Cordele.

In an August 13, 1915 *The Atlanta Constitution* article mentions Dorris is involved with the leadership of the "radicals" in the General Assembly that year. The radicals were folks who were favoring Prohibition. The paper went on to mention the radicals had a job ahead of them to sway folks to their way of thinking. Apparently they were successful because in March, 1917 *The Atlanta Constitution* reported the "Bone Dry" bill was signed by Governor Nat Harris and Dorris gave him his own ink pen to sign the legislation into law.

Dorris was a state senator for Crisp County into the 1920s.

J.B. Baggett - Joseph Brown Baggett – was born in 1859 to Allan Jacob Baggett. He was a large landowner, farmer, merchant, saw miller, cotton ginner, notary, postmaster, and justice of the peace. Baggett was married to Capitola Beall, daughter of Noble N. Beall, a judge who had at one time been a state representative for Paulding.

While it has not been verified via deed records, family sources state he owned several hundred acres in the Hay Community of Paulding County where he is listed as the postmaster.

Around 1908 the Paris Telephone Company had reached Paulding County and they located their switchboard in Baggett's home. Whichever family member happened to be free at the time worked the board for the community.

When not being the consummate businessman and farm Baggett served as a state representative for Paulding County

So, there you have it!

Everything I have so far on the five little boys Fannie Mae Davis wrote about so briefly. As things tend to go with my research regarding Douglas County history something will plop into my lap next week or a puzzle piece will fall into place a few months from now making more connections and drawing me back into the story, and I have to be really honest here, that's what keeps me going, the delightful chase!

Chapter 92

JOSEPH C. MCCARLEY – MAKE YOUR MARK!

It's rare to find someone content with passing through life quietly. Most people want to leave behind a legacy – some sort of proof they were here and their life mattered. The character Brooks in Stephen King's

Shawshank Redemption comes to mind. After serving more than forty years in prison an elderly Brooks is paroled, but can't seem to make it in the real world. He takes his own life, but before doing so he feels he must make his mark on the world by scrawling "Brooks was here" on the wall.

Yes, making our mark seems to be so very important to humans.

Today it seems we have many different ways to make our mark just to say, "Hey! I'm here." These are ways that can be argued as being negative or positive depending on your point of view. We have vanity plates for our cars; people earn a particular status for what they do or say, and for what they wear. People become notable just for being on a reality show, we can have a blog, a website, and it's not totally lost on me that we make our mark by having a *Facebook* profile. We can even make our mark anonymously by donating to charity, working behind the scenes for a needy family, or even invent a screen name to post anonymously on a message board.

Making a mark on the world could simply involve raising your children to be contributing members of society to carry on the family name, leaving behind a business that continues to grow and prosper, voting, or perhaps you simply make your mark by showing you owned something.

Claiming things seems to be very important to humans no matter what type of person, place, thing, or idea we want to focus on.

I remember one of the rituals of the new school year was watching my mom place my name prominently on all of my school things, and when I was old enough to be trusted with the household permanent marker I wrote my own name.

Making your mark to show ownership is nothing new. The practice dates back to ancient times. Hieroglyphic inscriptions tell us which Egyptian pharaoh commissioned each and every pyramid and obelisk. Darius I, a Persian king living between 550 and 486 B.C., prominently placed an inscription on his royal palace of Susa stating, "I built this palace." The Romans took the practice of marking buildings to an all new high. The Pantheon, home of the world's largest unreinforced concrete dome has an inscription that states, *M.AGRIPPA.L.F.COS.TERTIUM.*

FECIT, meaning "Marcus Agrippa, son of Lucius, having been consul three times, built it."

Perhaps it just boils down to human ego. Think about the big letters that spell out TRUMP in New York City advertising Trump Tower. Yet Donald Trump's monument to himself and his empire isn't unique. Most cities and towns in the United States have buildings that bear the name of the owner showing that the ancient practice continues today.

Perhaps not as notable as Mr. Trump but very important to the Douglasville story is Joseph C. McCarley.

Fannie Mae Davis indicates in her section titled "Small Town Gossip, 1915", that McCarley was a native of [Douglasville] and highly esteemed.

She further advises McCarley started his business, a dime store, housed in a small wooden building on a Broad Street lot, [and] after a few successful years, he cleared the lot and erected, [in 1909], a large, brick building, then opened McCarley's, a well-stocked novelty store. When McCarley vacated the building and it was torn down approximately in 1914, the spot became Douglasville's first moving picture theater and was called the Kozytorium.

Today the spot known as McCarley Store Number 1 is where Fabiano's Italian Deli enjoys our patronage today.

Apparently the five and dime business was booming in Douglasville during the early 1900s because Joseph McCarley was able to go up the street just a bit in 1915 and build an even more handsome location where he really made his mark by incorporating his name directly into the brickwork of the building. His name is prominently seen as you drive past on Broad Street. A 1919 *Douglas County Sentinel* ad advertises a Brownie #6 Kodak camera that McCarley sold for $2.00. Today, the location is home to Magnolia One Realty.

Joseph C. McCarley also stands out in Douglasville history since he built the city's first brick residence. My research indicates the construction process was very interesting to the folks in town. They would gather in the front yard to watch the brick laying process.

Imagine that!

There was a time in our past when brick-laying was an oddity!

In more recent times Seth Godin, an American entrepreneur, author and public speaker used the phrase "Put your name on it!" referring to improving quality and responsiveness. In my opinion this phrase implies so much more than making your mark in the business world.

Perhaps you and I will never have our names emblazoned across a building that will endure one hundred plus years, but we can still make our mark on society. It would be a sad legacy to live a life like the character Brooks and feel like the only thing you can do at the end is leave bit of hasty graffiti on a wall to indicate you were here.

Live each day to the fullest and be the best person you can be. Find your passion and pursue it with all your heart. Get involved with your community. Don't be satisfied with allowing others to make choices that impact you. You have a voice. Use it. End each day knowing you did everything you could to make your part of the world a better place through your work and your comments to others.

Go ahead.

I dare you.

It's YOUR life.

Put your name on it!

Chapter 93

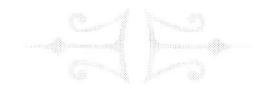

LIVING ALONG THE DOG RIVER IN THE EARLY 1900S

A few weeks ago a good friend handed me a history of the Vansant family compiled by Sarah Elizabeth Woods Carter.

I finally got around to looking at it.

Mrs. Carter did a great job researching her family and presenting the information in her book. Her introduction really grabbed my attention mainly because it's a well written and an informative narrative.

After thinking about it for a bit, I decided Mrs. Carter's narrative is very important to the Douglas County story not only because of the contributions she and her husband, Glenmore Carter, made to the region during the 1960s to the mid-1980s, but because the narrative paints a portrait regarding how many citizens of Douglas County lived their lives during the early days of the Twentieth Century – from 1900 to the early 1920s as well as they made their mark later in the century.

Think of it as "Little House on the Prairie" meets the turbulent 1970s.

Mrs. Carter's time here in the county is a great case study of how Douglas County changed from an extreme agricultural and rural community to a suburb and part of the Atlanta Metropolitan region.

Her words are italicized. My comments appear in regular print.

It will not be a long story telling you about the life I have lived. These seventy-seven years have flown by so quickly. On October 28, 1909 I arrived on Clifton Boulevard in Atlanta, Georgia. When in my fourth year a little baby brother, John David, arrived. In my fifth year my parents decided the six of us needed to be on a farm, two older brothers, Curtis and Ottis, and two older sisters, Fannie Lou and Orella. The half dozen needed more exercise than city life could give.

Mrs. Carter first published the book in 1976. The residence she speaks of on Clifton Boulevard is actually Clifton Road that cuts through Atlanta from Ponce de Leon over to Briarcliff. Per Mrs. Carter's obituary the property was located along Clifton where we find Emory University today. Eventually both of Mrs. Carter's sons would earn degrees on the land where their mother was born.

The narrative continues:

In a covered wagon I rode with my father on a cold day in November the forty miles to our country home on Dog River in Douglas County. I kept warm underneath a quilt with a lighted lantern. The only thrill I had for the day was crossing over the bridge on Dog River. We were going to a farm on which my father lived as a youth. The house was there – trees had grown up through the porch. But even though we arrived after dark, my father picked up limbs from the trees that had fallen and in no time the huge fireplace was crackling with fire and we were perfectly warm. The straw ticks for mattresses and springs were filled with pine straw. No need for more, we slept through it all.

Mrs. Carter's father was Edgar Woods who married Carrie Vansant in 1874. Carrie's father was Young Vansant who is well known in the history community of Douglas County because he donated the original 40 acres that would become the city of Douglasville.

Turning the Woods family property back into a working farm took hard work by all of the family members at a time when folk's didn't have the machines we have today.

Trees had to be cut and hand piled to burn in clearing the land for planting crops the spring following. I was there and came in at night with the rest, black from carrying burnt brush into piles ready for burning. I was greeted by the rolling stream from the kettle of hot water and into the tin tub I went and was soon like new. Soon we were proud of the four hundred acre farm. A dairy was started. Orella, my sister two years older, was my pal. We made a game out of all we did and raced on every task.

We were given the calves to care for. A barn on a rented place near our home was given us, a place to call our own in which to care for our calves. We fed them and cared for the cleaning of the barn. If a grown person came around it scared our calves.

At the ages of ten and eight we milked cows, ran the big old barrel churn, cleaned the "De Laval" cream separator, and walked two miles to school, getting there on time and back home for chores again. My first administrative task was at the age of eight managing my dozen calves. They followed me and minded me like my pet dog.

The cream separator Mrs. Carter mentions was basically a centrifugal device that separated milk into cream and skimmed milk. Most of the time the skimmed milk would be used for the family and some used to feed farm animals. The cream would be used for churning butter and the excess was sold.

We never thought of keeping busy as work. It was real life. And never a day passed but we found time for a game or foot race, or hurried to the piano to see which one reached it first. That mother of ours taught us music. And not only that, but at the age of six I had finished every word in the old blue back speller.

The blue back speller dates back to 1783 and was created by Noah Webster – author, political writer, and textbook pioneer. He's the Webster in Webster's Dictionary. Over five generations of Americans used the book to learn how to spell and read in the days when standardization wasn't a bad word.

How often I have thanked heaven for that mother of mine. The Vansant blood that ran through her veins never failed to circulate. She managed the seven of us. (I had a little baby sister, Claudie Mae, arrived on the "ole Dog River" place.) The lessons I learned on mother's knee saved me many a woe in life. I can never forget the day, sitting on her lap at five years old, and the admonition she gave me. She said, "There is a God in heaven and he expects me to guide you till you get old enough to know right from wrong. No matter where you are He sees you and will help you. Every day learn to do something new, and do something you know you should do but don't like to do, and do it with a smile. I have a Bible text for everything I teach you."

Yes, I understand that not every parent uses the Bible to teach their child right from wrong, and I understand it's every parent's choice, but more and more I see parents who choose to be a friend to their child instead of a parent. I see parents who treat their child more as an accessory than a responsibility. Mrs. Carter's statement, "The lessons I learned on my mother's knee saved me many a woe in life" is very true.

It was a regular custom at our house to get up at 3 a.m. One morning it came to my mind as I came bouncing down the stairs at 3 a.m. I thought, I'll bet she doesn't have a text to prove we have to get up at 3 a.m. each morning. Yes, I found her already in the kitchen, up and making those good biscuits that would be piping hot for breakfast. I said, "I bet you haven't got a text to prove we have to get up at 3 a.m" I can see her yet as she turned her head from me to laugh to herself. But instantly she came back with the answer – "a little more sleep, a little more slumber, the way of the sluggard." went on to the barn to milk the cows with the rest of the family and never questioned her integrity again.

Three in the morning! Okay, I give. That's a little extreme.

So in case you are wondering about Sarah's mother's response…"a little more sleep, a little more slumber, the way of the sluggard"…you can find it in the Bible at Proverbs 24:33…meaning a little procrastination, any procrastinations can ruin men's souls.

I do understand the point. Procrastination is my nemesis.

I caught up with Orella in school work. In fact, we raced in everything we did. Many tasks were given us, chopping cotton, picking cotton, helping the men folk bailing hay, and any odd jobs were ours. If I could ride the horse or mule to the house from the field, or sit on top of the load of hay as it was hauled in, was pay enough for the day.

I'm thinking about most of the children I know between the ages nine and late teens and trying to visualize them chopping cotton, picking cotton, bailing hay, etc. Broadening my thinking a little I don't know many adults who could do this sort of work these days.

The day came when we were told we were moving to Texas in 1922. I still feel the heartache when, as the cars were loaded and we were on our way, we passed a calf of mine in a neighbor's pasture. I choked up and hoped that Mary, my calf, didn't see me. I didn't want her to think I gave her away.

As to the results of our move to Jefferson, Texas, to make the story short, five of us married Texans. The stay in Texas was not too long and all came back to Georgia.

At seventeen I went back to Jefferson to attend school and took several classes under a young teacher, Glenmore Carter. After two years we were married at what is now Andrews University in Berrien Springs, Michigan, and we continued our education together.

Andrews University is a Seventh Day Adventist sponsored college dating back to 1874. The school's motto, which the Carters seemed to take to heart is, "Seek knowledge. Affirm faith. Change the world."

Glenmore and Sarah Carter were an amazing couple. They returned to Douglas County eventually, and built a hospital.

That's not exactly something most people set out to do in their retirement years.

Maybe you remember the hospital. It was the round building at Thornton Road and Interstate 20 – Parkway Regional Hospital, but that's a story for another time.

Chapter 94

THE LOG CABIN LIBRARY AT LITHIA SPRINGS

I've written about how the Douglas County/Douglasville library came to be, but the efforts at Lithia Springs were entirely separate in the beginning, and those efforts in Lithia Springs beat the folks in Douglasville by thirty-seven years.

The Lithia Springs project was spearheaded by women in the community. The library would be housed in a log cabin that sat north of the railroad tracks. They decided to fund the library by holding a box supper and invited the general public. A *Douglas County Sentinel* article from the time reported the event was well attended, especially by the men in the area. They enthusiastically bid on the dinners and bought chances to win quilts that the ladies displayed.

The *Sentinel* articles goes on to say, "The ladies of Lithia Springs are eternally grateful to the Boosters for the nice donation of $25 to build a chimney to their beloved Log Cabin Library which was in danger of being left in the cold, as Lithia Springs is building a new school house and now feeling a might poor. Some of these days they will return the favor when Douglasville and her boosters turn their attention to such institutions in their town."

The Boosters the *Sentinel* spoke of were a large group of businessmen in Douglasville who were headed at the time by Dr. Tom Whitley.

The Lithia Springs Log Cabin library was governed by the Lithia Springs Library Association with Miss Lily Reynolds, a school teacher and outspoken promoter of the project at the helm.

Volunteers made up the library staff and in those early days the library was open to the public from 2 to 4 o'clock on Monday, Wednesday, Friday, and Saturday afternoons.

The book collection was described as "marvelous" and circulation and membership seemed quite good. A fine of one cent per day was charged for books kept over 14 days.

In 1917, Mrs. George Bass and Captain J.C. Joyner laid a brick walk from the porch to the sidewalk. The library was used at this time for various meetings of the women. It also served as Town Hall for Town Council Meetings.

At some point around 1918, Miss Reynolds left the area and interest in the library began to decline. Sadly, the building burned down in the late 1940s. However, one book, a Bible, survived the fire, and is a treasured relic at the Lithia Springs branch of the Douglas County Library System.

I've looked through several collections of old photos taken in and around Douglas County. I've yet to see a picture of the old log cabin, but would be greatly interested and seeing and sharing one.

The efforts to maintain a public library at Lithia Springs took off again when Mrs. Annette Winn, principal of what was then Lithia Springs Elementary School wanted her students to have more access to reference materials than just what the board of education could provide. Fannie Mae Davis advises in her book, *From Indian Trail to I-20*, that Mrs. Winn was never one to leave a stone unturned, if it concerned a benefit for her beloved adopted Douglas County and her own community of Lithia Springs.

At last there was a reason for hope with West Ga. Regional Library, Carrollton, Ga. was founded. After the library's bookmobile served was inaugurated, Annette Winn contacted the director, Miss Edith Foster, the State department of Library services and our county officials, whereby permission was granted for the bookmobile to come to the Annette Winn Elementary School once a month. The children knew the schedule and eagerly awaited the monthly visits. A library was needed. Mrs. Winn and Miss Foster talked with parents, civic groups and clubs to get their interest.

It was decided that the little courthouse located in Lithia Springs near the fire department would be the perfect location.

The front room of the little building was made available and volunteers from the local Ruritan Club built bookshelves. Mrs. Betty Hagler took over as the librarian on a volunteer basis.

Fannie Mae Davis continues, "In May, 1963, East Douglas County Library opened. The first library board was comprised of Mrs. Annette Winn, chairman; Mrs. A.B. Craven, Mr. George P. Argo; Mrs. Agnes Green, Mrs Ethelyn Cooper and Mr. Louie Wood, Miss Edith Foster, West Ga. Regional director was advisor. Mrs. Hagler contined as librarian, but on a salary. The library was now open longer hours."

Mrs. Davis' book further advises, "Before Miss Foster retired from the regional library all plans had been made for the new Lithia Springs Library. And finally on a cold December Sunday, groundbreaking ceremonies took place. The following is a section taken from the *Douglas County Sentinel* on December 5, 1977. In this article Mrs. Winn gave a brief history of the library services in Lithia Springs.

The article related:

"Greetings to you from the LS library board. This is a great day for our community. We indeed are grateful.

Benjamin Franklin established our first library in the United States in Philadelphia in 1731. This library still exists today. He also started the "friends of the Library" which exists as a tax deductible organization today. There will always be library needs that are not met by our government."

This occasion brings us to the long awaited realization of our fondest dreams, a public library in Lithia Springs. When I came to Lithia Springs in 1926, there was an interesting, deserted log cabin which had housed a collection of books donated by local citizens. I learned that Miss Lillie Reynolds had organized the library and had served as librarian on a volunteer basis for many years..."

They registered 200 people in the first week alone. Of course it didn't take long for the small front room of the Lithia Springs little courthouse to overflow with books and library patrons. A larger space was needed and the library that you and I know as the Lithia Springs branch of the West Georgia Regional Library was opened.

Chapter 95

FROM MILITARY ROAD TO BANKHEAD HIGHWAY

The year is 1917 and you are heading up Bankhead Highway heading west. Try to follow these directions:

Once you reach Lithia Springs go straight through by taking the right fork and crossing the rail road. Cross the rail road again. Take a left and go straight ahead.

Yes, that's right. You crossed the railroad track twice.

Once you reach Douglasville follow the road by crossing the rail road track not once but twice. At the fork take the right side not once, not twice, but three different times.

Yes! There were three forks in the road.

Then as you approach Winston turn left around the post office. Do NOT go down the hill to the station, but DO go down a rough steep grade and take a right under the rail road. Cross the rail road tracks and take the right fork.

Yes, there used to be a post office stop in Winston.

At Villa Rica go two blocks from the station and take a left…then the right fork…and here's where the trip takes a fun turn…ford the creek. It's a good size and has a smooth sand bottom…deep to the left. Cross the wood bridge. Then cross the rail road and take the left fork (the right side takes you to Cartersville).

Head down the long steep grade and manage the very rough dangerous curve. Cross a wood bridge at the bottom. Go under the rail road track and take the left fork. Make sure it's the left because if you take the right you head out towards Cedartown and you might not realize it until you have traveled the entire 26 mile route."

I find the numerous forks in the road to be interesting, and the fact that you could go "under" the railroad in so many places very fascinating.

This route would not have been titled Bankhead Highway, however, not in 1917, but it would have been referred to as the Military Road, and the road would have been dirt as it was not paved until the 1930s.

During the summer of 1917 the Studebaker Corporation gave the folks at *The Atlanta Constitution* a car which became known as the "Dixie Rover". The car along with her driver Ned M'Intosh completed a series of eleven road tours in Georgia, Alabama and Tennessee in the interest of better roads and better motoring conditions. M'Intosh was staff correspondent for the paper and was secretary for the Georgia State Automobile Association. He traveled over some of the best roads and some of the worst roads in the south. Some of the roads had never even had a car on them.

M'Intosh also road the proposed routes for the proposed Bankhead Highway, and the above directions were published in an article he wrote concerning the route.

In June, 1917 M'Intosh advises the importance of Bankhead Highway by writing, "Certainly it is a prize worth fighting for, because it is to be a great trunk highway, not only between Atlanta and Birmingham, but between the west coast and the Atlantic with the rapidly increasing use of motor vehicles, the development of such a highway is inevitable. It is not difficult to foresee the day when passenger traffic between Atlanta and Birmingham will be carried on almost solely by automobile. The advantages of a town being located on the main highway now will therefore grow most appreciably in the immediate future, and there is apparently no limit to the possible development of automobile traffic."

When word was handed down that Congress was going to appropriate money to building a national highway from coast to coast, routes were proposed and groups were set up to boost or support the road. In November, 1916 *The Atlanta Constitution* reported a group of highway boosters would held a meeting in Douglasville. At that time five counties – Douglas Fulton, Cobb, Haralson, and Cobb – were planning on having the new Bankhead Highway pass through their borders, but the legislation wasn't a done deal.

Douglasville's own Dr. T.R. Whitley was a delegate to the Bankhead Highway Association and along with other delegates was responsible for the final route the road would take. In fact, it can probably be argued rather successfully that Dr. Whitley's position as a delegate helped Douglas County greatly. The purpose of the meeting was to discuss methods for delegates and supporters to building even more support for the road to be routed through their particular area.

By February, 1917 more meetings were being held.

Dr. Whitley was interviewed for *The Atlanta Constitution* article dated May 11, 1917 which discussed how the labor was to be performed on road. At the time World War I was still underway and many German prisoners were in the state including at Fort McPherson. Dr. Whitley referred to these prisoners in his remarks and discussed how he thought it would be good idea for the prisoners to work on the new road.

By May, 1917, Dr. Whitley advises the road had already been surveyed and the section from Fort McPherson to the Chattahoochee River was in good shape, and some of the road on the other side of the river was complete "with the exception of some eight miles that would have to be built." The eight miles was later identified in the article as the stretch between the river and Lithia Springs. The work was needed in order to correct several bad grades.

Regarding German prisoners working on the eight mile stretch that needed work Dr. Whitley, advised, "The Germans must be worked somewhere, and there will be no additional expense in working them on the roads and the government has mules enough now doing nothing to work the roads."

In June, 1917 M'Intosh drove the proposed routes and reported their condition to *Atlanta Constitituion* readers. There was the route we are familiar with today out to Birmingham, but there was also a route where the road would have been built through Cave Springs and Rome, and per M'Intosh it was the most preferable even though it was longer.

M'Intosh gave reports concerning all sections of the proposed roadway saying, "The present condition of this road, in the stretches which have been allowed thus to wear out and run down, is but one degree removed from the unimproved dirt road…Such a road condition is hardly a criterion of the people who have made such cities as Birmingham and Gadsden."

He also wasn't impressed with the proposed route through Cobb County saying, "As has been said before a very considerable amount of work is needed. The strange part about this Cobb County road is that perhaps the worst part of the road lies between Marietta and the Chattahoochee River Bridge, a stretch of road which is more traveled perhaps than any other stretch of the same length in Georgia."

Regarding the road from western Cobb County line to Douglasville M'Intosh reported the road was in pretty good condition but from Douglasville to Villa Rica the drag is again badly needed.

A drag?

Basically it's a device that can be pulled after a team of mules to help even out the road.

Of course, once he crossed the Alabama line the road conditions worsened per M'Intosh…"after one crosses the state line into Alabama, the road is unspeakably rought and it winds back and forth all over the face of the earth and goes up and down small knolls without the remotest semblance of grading with such frequency that it all but makes one sea sick.

Not only did M'Intosh call for the drag to be used more often he also called for installing sign posts at every cross roads and every fork of main roads and street corners in towns.

Think about that for a minute. He was calling for road signs, something we take for granted.

It took M'Intosh ten hours to travel from Atlanta to Birmingham.

Yes, ten hours. M'Intosh reports he left Atlanta at six in the morning and didn't reach Birmingham until close to four in the afternoon.

I don't think I would have wanted to reach Birmingham that much to endure a ten hour trip.

Chapter 96

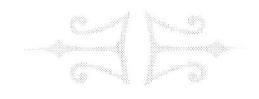

DOUGLASVILLE DURING WORLD WAR I

World War I is known as "the war to end all wars" for good reason. At one point more than 70 million people were wearing uniforms and involved in the war in some way. It was the first war to be fought on three continents, the first use of the word "trillion" in estimating war costs, and the first war where art was used for propaganda purposes.

World War I was also the first industrialized conflict with the use of airplanes, flame throwers, chlorine and mustard gases as well as the first tank battles.

If you peruse the Georgia teaching standards for history you see that they leave no war unturned. From the American Revolution to the most recent military actions in Afghanistan and Iraq each conflict is covered. Students learn about the causes of each war, the various events including battles, important people, dates, treaties, and one important standard includes an examination regarding how each war affected our county.In other words—while our men were off fighting what was happening here at home?

Even though World War I began in 1914, the United States managed to stay out of the war until the last seven and half months. Don't let the short time period fool you. During those few months our nation, our state and our little town of Douglasville was affected.

Beginning in 1914, events of the war were reported here in the states, but for most people at first it was just static in the background. Daily life took precedence and those European names and places just didn't have much meaning to folks who walked behind a plow or worked at the cotton mill in Douglasville. As the conflict advanced ripples were felt here in the states. The British had blockaded many European ports meaning many American farmers and businessmen couldn't get their crops and products to many markets.

Once the United States declared war in 1917, the Selective Services Act was enacted and quotas went out to every state from the Federal government for the large numbers of men that would be needed.

Registration dates were set up and the word was sent out. The date for registration here in Douglasville was first set for July 5, 1917.

Every man between the ages of 21 and 31 had to register. It didn't matter if they were married or what type of job they had. Names would be selected from those who registered.

Young ladies showed up wearing their Red Cross uniforms and pinned badges of honor on the chests of each man who stepped up and received the call of his country.

Douglas County had an issue or two meeting their quota as did other counties across our state and nation. In fact, there were three different registration dates set up before the process was over.

Please don't read too much into this. The men from Douglasville were just as brave and willing to serve their county as any other location in the United States; however, our country had gone from a nation totally against the war to one that declared war on Germany and her allies in April, 1917. Daylight and dark would be an apt description regarding the reversal the United States took regarding their official stance.

Prior to World War I the United States had become a peace-loving nation. Very few folks wanted to enter a foreign war, and many had to be persuaded to accept the declaration of war against Germany since they had not invaded our borders. Many Georgians objected to the Selective Services Act including our elected representatives like Thomas Hardwick, Rebecca Latimer Felton, and Thomas E. Watson who challenged the legality of the Selective Services Act in court.

President Woodrow Wilson had been re-elected in 1916 on the promise he would keep the United States out of the war in Europe. But by 1917 things had changed.

The *Lusitania*, a British liner, was torpedoed and sunk on May 7, 1915 by a German U-boat. 128 innocent Americans were killed. President Wilson called for the Germans to stop attacking passenger ships, and for a time they did stop, but by January 1917, Germany began attacking any ships they had in their sights and had begun negotiating secretly with Mexico for an alliance. Germany wanted the United States to enter the conflict. If Mexico became their ally they would be awarded their lost territories of Texas, New Mexico, and Arizona once the United States was defeated. President Wilson made the plan public and most people understood at that point war should be declared. The last straw was the sinking of seven additional merchant ships.

Overnight the media went from being against the war to embracing the conflict. Various slogans were used across the nation to gather support for the war such as "Make the world safe for democracy," "a war for freedom," and "the war to end all wars."

The majority of the recruits from Douglas County were sent to Camp Gordon which was located in Chamblee on the spot where Peachtree-Dekalb Airport is now. The human war eagle posted here is from Camp Gordon. It makes sense that a few of the men in the photo were from Douglas County given the time it was taken. There are approximately 12, 500 men in the formation.

Here at home people did their part for the war in any way they could mainly through participating in rationing. Food items such as flour, salt, and coffee were diverted to the military.

There were Fueless Days–five to be exact–where folks in Douglasville did nothing. The days were strictly observed by the largest employers –the cotton and hosiery mills. Nothing was sold on Fueless Days except food and drugs. At one point J.T. Duncan, the Douglas County Food Administrator asked citizens to cut back on their use of flour and recommended they prepare biscuits with a combination of flour and cornmeal.

Liberty Bonds were sold. They were war bonds issued by the United States. Purchasing the bonds was just one way for the folks on the home front to show their support of the war effort. For many people in small town America it was the first time they were introduced to financial securities, and spurred by patriotic fever they snapped them up.

While I have no direct reports at this time regarding Douglasville per se across the state there were calls to be on the lookout for German spies once war was declared. The actions of others were often analyzed for their patriotism. Farmers draped their plows with the American flag and schools stopped teaching German history for fear it would seem sympathetic to the enemy.

Soldiers from Douglas County sent countless letters home to their families and friends. A few of these letters were published in the *Douglas County Sentinel*.

Corporal Frank P. Dorris was the first soldier from Douglas County to give his life during World War I. Today our American Legion post–Number 145–is named in his honor. Also, Corporal Dorris' unusual tombstone can be found at the Douglasville City Cemetery at the corner of Rose Avenue and Church Street. His marker includes a bust of Dorris in his uniform including his campaign hat.

Today we know Nov. 11 to be Veterans Day, but in 1918 Nov. 11 was Armistice Day–the day peace was agreed to and hostilities during World War I ceased. The *Douglas County Sentinel* wrote, "Douglasville people were aroused from their morning slumber by the ringing of bells…"

Peace didn't mean the war was forgotten by the citizens of Douglas County. Many soldiers especially those from South Georgia were sent to Douglas County to muster out of the army in 1918. They were sent to Camp Douglas, a tent garrison located in Lithia Springs. Actually, Camp

Douglas was on the same grounds as Camp Hobson and was used during the Spanish American War in 1898.

Just as it happened in 1898, sickness came to the camp. In fact, the sickness wasn't just confined to the camp here in Douglas County nor was it just confined to Georgia or even the United States. The sickness was a terrible flu epidemic, and it swept over the world beginning around June, 1918, and continued in various locations across the world until 1920 killing millions of people–many of them at Camp Douglas and across Douglas County.

Fannie Mae Davis quotes someone who experienced the flu epidemic and stated the soldiers at Camp Douglas "died like flies." She also states dozens of bodies were crated and sent home.

Can you imagine? Your loved one survived the war, but then died from the flu.

The citizens of Douglas County numbered about 10,000, and at that time Fannie Mae Davis states over three-fourths of the population were affected with the flu. During the height of the sickness all public functions stopped–no school and no church. She states it was a "life and death struggle" with the flu that would come on suddenly. One minute someone would seem fine, and the next the entire family would be down with it. Davis states, "Town and country doctors were nothing short of heroic as they labored night and day with little rest."

Cemeteries all over the county had fresh graves and many funerals were put on hold until after the sickness had passed.

While Douglas County citizens were glad the Great War was over, they didn't really have time to celebrate as the flu hit and ravaged the county.

Chapter 97

THE JAMES BOYS AND WORLD WAR I

On this Memorial Day for 2013 I'm thinking of the thousands of soldiers through the years our nation has been in existence who have fought, who have been injured, and those who have died defending our rights to be free and live in the greatest nation ever conceived.

Many of us can look through our family trees and identify family members who served in the armed forces during each conflict that involved the United States.

One such family here in Douglas County is the James family.

From time to time I run across old newspaper articles that are just too good not to share, and I have to share them in their entirety because it would be a shame to leave out one little detail.

The article in question comes from *The Atlanta Constitution* dated July 14, 1918 and is titled "The James Lieutenants Uphold Record of Fighting Forebears".

The article states:

Linton Steven James and Royal Percy James, two Douglasville boys, born and reared, are now wearing the uniforms of the United States army, the first as a first lieutenant now in France, while the second, working under a second lieutenant's commission, is at present stationed near Waco, Texas, drilling and preparing selectmen for service overseas.

The lieutenants James are the sons of W.A. James, well known lawyer of Atlanta and Douglasville, and as privates both saw service on the Mexican border as members of the old Fifth Georgia and both came home with excellent records.

They came from old fighting stock, their forefathers having taken faithful having taken faithful parts in the Mexican war in the later War Between the States.

After the United States entered the war Linton Stephen James, still with the old Fifth, then at Camp Wheeler, Macon, secured admission to the second officers' training camp and was sent to Oglethorpe, near Chattanooga. Then he was put through the paces by English, French and American officers, and in a class of 700 faced an examination board seeking a commission.

In the grading by that board he was rated seventh, of the six men ahead of him two came from Florida, two from South Carolina and two from Pennsylvania. The latter part of November, 1917, he was assigned to the Eleventh Regiment, U.S. Army, then stationed at Camp Oglethorpe where it remained until about two months ago, when it was sent across and is now presumed to be on or near the fighting line in France.

First Lieutenant James is 24 years old, is six feet one inch tall and weighs 210 pounds. He is married and his wife is now in Douglasville.

Royal Percival James was yet in the service at Camp Wheeler when a third training camp for officers opened. He stood an excellent entrance examination and, when the finals came, won out with a commission as Second Lieutenant, standing second in his rating in a platoon of 63 men. When handed his commission he was ordered to report to Camp Stanley, at Leon Springs near San Antonio, Texas.

That was the first of January last, and there he remained until a month ago when he was transferred to Camp Pike in Arkansas where he remained but a short time, a second transfer sending him to Waco, where is his now whipping new selectmen or raw material into finished fighters for the western front "over there" and for a final spurt into old Berlin herself.

Second Lieutenant Roy James – that's the name he prefers – is just past 21 years old and while he is a full-blooded James, he is not quite as large as his big brother.

However, I'm as big as dad," he is want to say when a comparison is made between him and his elder brother.

And now he thinks five feet and ten inches combined with 150 pounds of bone and muscle is enough for any Boche he may encounter when he gets across.

He is yet single and he's been the baby at the James home in Douglasville ever since he tossed aside his rattles for the old family shotgun, how discarded for Uncle Sam's shooting irons. Just the same, he is large enough to have graduatedwell up in his class from Atlanta Tech High school before he essayed to invade Mexico with the old Fifth.

That these boys came from good fighting stock is certain, for their ancestors have had part in every war in which the United States has participated. Six generations back the James name was on General Washington's muster rolls. Again the same name and the same branch took part in the war of 1812. In the war with Mexico Georgia sent the James name into Monterey and the city of Mexico. And in the War Between the States the father of these two boys and two of his brothers took part. G.W. James went to Virginia with the old Seventh Georgia and served under Stonewall Jackson, while another uncle, John M. James, enlisted in the Twenty-First Georgia and was also with Stonewall Jackson. G.W. James never came home. He died at Port Royal in the Shenandoah Valley, while John M. James left one leg at Kelly's Ford on the Rappahannock in the Old Dominion.

After the war John M. James become prominent in state politics and represented his district in the senate. Their father, W.A. James, because of his age, had only two years of service during that struggle, but that those two years were busy years, about the busiest of his life, is attested by the fact that he served under General Joe Wheeler and that the surrendered with General Joe Johnston in North Carolina on April 26, 1865.

Also the maternal side of these Lieutenants James boys has a war record of which anyone might be proud. The maternal grandmother had two uncles William Danforth and John W. Danforth, both of Campbell County, Georgia and killed in Virginia while serving under Stonewall Jackson. She also had three brothers in the Confederate Army, William, John and George Powell, all of Cobb County.

And still the Jameses are not satisfied with their war record for on the last day of June, Sunday June 30, a son was born to First Lieutenant Stephen James at the family home in Douglasville, and as if to bequeath him a soldier's career, his mother named him Linton Stephen James, Jr. So the cablegram sent the next day to the father somewhere in France informed him.

"I told my boys when they went into the army," said W.A. James, the father, "to stand by their country to the last. That they are fighting for the greatest principles man ever battled for and that they are being led in the greatest conflict of all time by the greatest leader of this or any other age of the world – President Woodrow Wilson."

I know that L.S. James went on to practice law like his father, but it was noted in a small note in the Atlanta paper for October 18, 1918 that Lt. Linton S. James of Douglasville had been "gassed in the St. Milhiel drive. He was identified as an adjutant to Major Mahin."

Lt. Linton S. James draft card indicates he was only slightly wounded and discharged in February, 1919. Thankfully, both of the James brothers made it home and lived long and productive lives.

Chapter 98

RADIO DAYS

The year 1922 saw the first Reader's Digest published, Babe Ruth signed a contract with the New York Yankees for $52,000, the Lincoln Memorial was dedicated in our nation's capital and in Douglasville, Georgia folks were crazy over some newfangled gadget called "the radio".

Various sources state that there were about 1,000 homemade radio receivers in the Atlanta area in 1922 even though there were no radio stations in the city, but what many didn't realize was the two major newspapers in town, *The Atlanta Constitution* and *The Atlanta Journal* (both separate entities back then) were in a neck-in-neck race to see which media outlet could get the first radio station on air.

The Atlanta Journal won by mere days and WSB was on the air in March, 1922 followed by the *The Atlanta Constitution's* station WGM.

WGM's broadcast was transmitted through the radio plant of the Georgia Railway & Power Company, and the paper devoted an entire page of the paper titled "The Atlanta Constitution Radio Department" where various people and shows that were offered every day on WGM were discussed. Telegrams and letters the station received were printed to share what listeners were enjoying. There were also articles from time to time regarding the perils of become addicted to the radio.

If only those people could see us today glued to our smart phones.

Folks began to gather around the radio and often parties would be given in homes where the main entertainment was to listen to a particular radio show.

WGM presented a radio show each week showcasing the musical students of one man, Sigor E. Volpi who was described as "Atlanta's noted coach of opera and teacher of voice".

On the night of January 14, 1923 Volpi's program included Miss Charlotte Crumbley and Jimmy Finley who were both singers who were known to national radio audiences.

The program also included dramatic readings performed by Miss Louise Shamblin who hailed from Rome, Georgia but at that time was employed as a teacher of dramatic fine art and expression at Douglas County High School.

Also, *The Atlanta Constitution* for January 15, 1923 reported, "Last night's program was arranged for the particular pleasure of Miss Catherine Geer and radio party of Douglasville, Georgia. The party was arranged through the courtesy of Mrs. Floyd House whose radio apparatus received each of the numbers clearly. The appreciation of the party was expressed by long distance messages and in the following telegram received just as the program ended:

> *We are enjoying the program immensely, thanks!*
> *Catherine Geer and party"*

It should not escape our notice that Atlanta was a long distance call and a telegram was sent – something no longer needed today.

Catherine Geer was the daughter of M.E. Geer, an executive with the cotton mill who lived on the northeast corner of Colquitt and Strickland Streets.

The Atlanta Constitution advised, "Miss Shamlin's debut to radio fans was a distinct triumph and no more talented or accomplished reader has appeared at this station."

At the helm of WGM's operations was Clark Howell, Sr. *The Atlanta Constitution's* owner. By March of 1923, Mr. Howell had allowed the broadcast license for WGM to expire, and the equipment including the transmitting tower was donated to Georgia Tech where Mr. Howell was a Trustee. The station continued as WBBF. By 1925, the call letters had changed to WGST.

Chapter 99

HUGH WATSON – SOARING THROUGH LIFE

My Papa Blanton loved his family and friends, loved his Bible, and loved to tell stories concerning his youth. After begging him to tell me about the "olden" days, he would launch into tales regarding growing up at the turn of the century telling me about courting young ladies at ice cream socials and explaining the proper way to prepare a turtle stew for a gathering of men. He seemed to enjoy watching my nose crinkle up in disgust regarding the details concerning de-shelling that poor sweet turtle. Then one afternoon he told me a new tale about seeing his very first airplane as it flew low over his father's fields and eventually landed.

I was mesmerized by the story.

Can you imagine a time when a plane was an oddity –a cause for excitement?

After the Wright Brothers completed their flight in 1903, towns and cities all across the United States experienced their first airplane sighting including Douglasville. Since there were no flight plans or rules and procedures in those days I'd like to think the pilot flew in and circled Douglasville's downtown commercial district a few times waggling his wings a bit to say hello to the folks on the ground before landing on a grassy field at a nearby farm. Finding a spot to land wouldn't have been difficult since there were plenty of fields brimming with crops and cotton or dotted with grazing livestock on the edge of town in every direction and as far as the eye could see.

It's very probably the pilot of the first plane to land in Douglasville was Hugh Watson – a barnstormer, which means he flew from town to town performing stunts and providing rides in his flying machine for anyone who had $10 and was brave enough to climb aboard.

Hugh Watson wouldn't have been just any barnstorming pilot who happened to land in Douglasville. He would have been coming home to visit family and friends since he was born and bred here, and I'm sure he would have wanted to show off his aviation skills. Fannie Mae Davis writes that when Major Watson landed in Douglasville it was the first time many citizens had seen an airplane.

Born in Douglasville in 1894, Watson, like many young men during the early years of the twentieth century became completely entranced by the Wright Brothers and other early stories of aviation. Watson knew by the time he was 15 he wanted to be an aviator, and he knew in order to follow his chosen path he would have to leave home.

During World War I he served in the U.S. Army Air Service, forerunner of the U.S. Air Force, where he earned the title of aviator and made many cross-country flights. Several sources confirm Watson was an instructor and at the end of the war he had achieved the rank of lieutenant.

After the war like many military pilots Watson returned to barnstorming and flew from town to town doing stunts and giving people rides. He helped Cecil B. DeMille, the famous Hollywood director, with some aerial stunts and participated in a flying circus that traveled all the way to Japan and China.

In 1921, along with his brother, Parks, Hugh Watson established Grisard Field in Cincinnati, Ohio named for Lt. John K. Grisard, the only Cincinnati pilot killed during World War I. The brothers purchased war surplus aircraft and used the field to provide pilot training for Army aerial reservist and local citizens, deliver mail, and ferry passengers. They also sold aircraft, and from time to time Watson took assignments to cover major events with aerial footage for newsreel companies. The April, 1927 edition of *Popular Mechanics* contains an ad placed by Major Watson where he indicates he taught a new method of aviation and advises he was a flying instructor during the war and had been "a leading commercial aviator for the past ten years."

Several sources indicate the field also became a very popular place on the weekends for spectators to watch the planes and interact with the pilots. It wasn't long before the field was referred to as Watson Field.

By 1925 Watson had become involved with surveying air routes for commercial air lines and helped to pioneer air mail service between many U.S. cities.

Fannie Mae Davis indicates Hugh Watson was the first pilot to land at the old Municipal Airport in Atlanta – a spot that had previously been known as Candler Field Race Track, and today is known as Hartsfield-Jackson Atlanta International Airport. While she doesn't give any information beyond that one detail, I checked into the Atlanta airport's history a bit and discovered the very first plane to land at Candler Field was in fact a mail plane on September 15, 1926, belonging to Florida Airways, an airline owned by Eddie Rickenbacker who was a World War I flying hero and contemporary of Watson's.

Yes, the pilot of that mail plane could indeed have been Hugh Watson!

Apparently, a crowd of 15,000 people showed up to see the mail delivered that day.

Apparently Watson also taught aviation from Candler Field for a time as well because Mrs. Davis indicates he spent a year in the hospital suffering from numerous injuries after the plane crash landed in Atlanta with a student pilot at the controls.

A scholarly paper published online by Stephen G. Craft explains how Watson formed Grisard Field Company with T. Higby Embry and John Paul Riddle. Embry had the money to buy planes, but he had no knowledge of flying. Riddle taught him how to fly. Hugh Watson later remembered Embry 'took to the air just like a duck goes to the nearest pond'. Embry and Riddle eventually formed what is today Embry-Riddle Aeronautical University. An article from *The Enquirer* dated September, 1928 states, "Credit for starting the commercial flying era in Cincinnati must be given to [Watson, Embry, and Riddle]."

Following World War II, Cincinnati officials bought Watson Airport from Hugh and Parker Watson reportedly for $2 million dollars. They renamed the field Blue Ash Airport. Today it serves as a base for charter, corporate and general aviation much like Charlie Brown Field east of Douglasville.

Major Hugh Watson was one of only three Georgians who received their wings prior to 1916 giving them the right to belong to the Early Birds Organization, a group dedicated to the history of early pilots of gliders, gas balloons, or airplanes prior to December 17, 1916. Major Watson was also a member of the Day Line Pilots which includes aviators who received their wings prior to 1918.

American Legion Post 530 in Ohio is named for Major Watson. Their website indicates his widow provided financial assistance and support for the post.

The United States Congress elevated Hugh Watson's military rank to Major in 1936 for his pioneer work in aviation.

Major Hugh Watson returned to Georgia after he sold the airfield, but soon after suffered a heart attack and died January 22, 1955. He was buried with full military honors in the Douglasville City Cemetery.

While we could mourn the fact that Major Watson died soon after he retired – a time when folks think they have finally reached the point when they can do as they wish and finally have the money to pursue their dreams – Hugh Watson had already lived his dreams along the way.

His life sends an important message.

Don't wait for tomorrow. Do what it takes to live your dreams now.

Chapter 100

REVISITING HUGH WATSON

I watched a man fall to earth last week – on purpose.
You may have watched it as well. The man's name was Felix Baumgartner. I watched as he was carried aloft in a capsule hanging from a helium balloon to the very edge of space where he and I (thanks to technology) could actually see the curve of the earth and the edge of space. The only things he had to protect him were his space suit, a helmet and a parachute.

When Baumgartner reached the right height and after going through an exhaustive check-list he opened the hatch, stood on the platform and stepped off free falling for several thousand feet.

Baumgartner wanted to be the first person to break the sound barrier without the protection of a vehicle, and he did it! News sources report that at one point Baumgartner hit Mach 1.24, and tumbled at times to earth from a height of 128,000 feet or over 24 miles. In case you are wondering Mach 1.24 is somewhere around 833 miles per hour.

It took him two hours to get to the appropriate height, and it only took him four minutes and twenty seconds to complete the fall. Most of that time I was holding my breath and more than likely so was the other 8 million or so others watching on television, YouTube and other sources around the world.

Baumgartner broke two other records, including the highest exit from a platform at 128,000 feet and the highest free-fall without a drogue parachute. One record Baumgartner did not break was the longest elapsed freefall record. Joe Kittinger, Baumgartner's mentor and voice in his ear as he fell to earth, still holds the record he set in 1960.

So, the whole event gave me pause to think about how far we've come since 1960 with technology and how the data gathered during Baumgartner's fall will be used to advance flight technology even further.

Then my mind settled on a piece I wrote several months ago regarding Hugh Watson, an early aviator from Douglasville.

Recently, I found a couple of articles from *The Atlanta Constitution* involving Mr. Watson in his younger days when he first started flying.

I've printed the newspaper articles in italics and my comments in regular type.

The first article dated December 8, 1918 and carried the headline "100 Miles an Hour Made by Aviators".

The article reads:

At the average rate of 100 mph three aviators – Lieutenants Wilson, Weaver, and Moncrief – yesterday came from Taylor Field at Montgomery to Atlanta where they landed on the speedway at Hapeville. They only stop made en route was at Columbus.

All three aviators are stopping at the Ansley. On Sunday afternoon Lieutenant Watson will fly to his home in Douglasville for a visit.

The Ansley refers to the Ansley Hotel built in 1913 by Edwin P. Ansley who is best known for developing the neighborhood still known as Ansley Park which is just east of Midtown and west of Piedmont Park. The Ansley Hotel was located on the 100 block of Forsyth Street. Later it was known as the Dinkler Plaza Hotel before being demolished in 1973.

Just a couple of days later another article appeared on December 10, 1918 with the following headline…"Aviators Crash to Earth Monday at the Speedway".

The article states:

Lieutenants Hugh Watson, of Douglasville, Georgia and Lincoln Weaver of Wilkinsburg, Pennsylvania, both fliers from Taylor Field, Montgomery, Alabama are in the base hospital at Fort McPherson in a serious condition as a result of an attempted tailspin executed yesterday morning at 11 o'clock while the plane in which they were flying was at a height of about 300 to 350 feet and moving at a rate of speed too low to maintain its balance during the movement.

It would appear that Watson was making several cross-country trips at this point. Douglas County historian Fannie Mae Davis mentions the fact that Watson was a flight instructor in Alabama.

Taylor Field was Montgomery's first military flying installation established November, 1917. Approximately 139 pilots completed eight weeks of training there.

As a result of the attempted difficult air "stunt", instead of righting the plane after it had plunged downward for some distance, the two airmen lost control of the machine and it crashed to earth on the old Atlanta automobile race track about 3 ½ miles beyond Fort McPherson.

The track the article refers to is Atlanta Speedway or Atlanta Motordome built by Asa Candler in 1909. He wanted to build a racetrack that would rival the newly built track in Indianapolis, so he bought 287 acres bordering Virginia Avenue south of the city and got busy. The track was only open for two seasons, and if you haven't already guessed the property today is part of Hartsfield-Jackson Atlanta International Airport. Watson had the right idea at the time when he attempted to land there and/or crash landed at the speedway. It would later be the "right" spot.

Atlantans in an automobile happened to witness the accident and rushed to the badly damaged plane and pulled the lieutenants from underneath the wreckage. They immediately rushed the injured airmen to the base hospital at Fort McPherson where they were given medical attention.

Officials of the medial department at Fort McPherson last night stated that Lieutenant Watson suffered innumerable cuts, bruises and sprains, and although in a critical condition physicians at the fort believe that they can save his life.

My earlier column regarding Hugh Watson referred to this accident, but at the time I didn't have all of the details. It took Watson over a year to recover from his injuries and my research indicates the officer in charge at Taylor Field put the word out he didn't want any more "stunts" taking place with his planes.

......The accident occurred as the two lieutenants were flying to Atlanta Monday morning on a cross-country practice trip from Taylor Field. Experiencing some trouble enroute, they made a successful landing on the old Atlanta Automobile Speedway and worked on the engines. After this was done they made ascension and after rising some 300 to 350 feet into the air fell into a tailspin that caused the accident. Lieutenant Watson is reported to have told medical officers at Fort McPherson Monday night that he could have righted the plane from the spin, but he misjudged the height at which they were flying and was too near the ground.

Information that the steel helmets worn by the Lieutenants probably saved their lives was also supplied by officials at Fort McPherson who were told by those who pulled the two unconscious men from under the plane that heavy parts of the machine were resting on their heads when they were removed from the wreckage and that the steel helmets probably kept their skulls from being crushed in.

Lieutenant Watson, who was formerly an automobile racing driver for the Sunbeam Company, is the son of M.B. Watson, prominent citizen of Douglasville...

The fact that Hugh Watson drove race cars for the Sunbeam Motor Company is a brand new fact for me.

The accident Monday was the second Lieutenant Watson has had in Atlanta while in a cross-country run from Taylor Field to his home in

Douglasville to spend the day with his parents there, his machine crashed into a rough piece of ground just outside the city limits of Atlanta on Sunday, December 1st. Lieutenant Watson escaped from the accident with a few slight bruises and small damage to his plane.

It's interesting to note that both crashes were within days of each other.

Accompanying him on this trip was Lieutenant E.T. Dennis, also of Taylor Field, who Lieutenant Watson had invited to visit his home with him for the day. He also had to make a forced landing in his plane due to gasoline trouble, but he was able to pick out a smooth piece of ground in east Atlanta and escaped practically uninjured.

They resumed their trip the next morning and spent the day in Douglasville after which they returned to their planes at Taylor Field.

Crash after crash, yet early aviators kept getting back up in the air. They kept flying. They kept forging ahead making new advances and laying the ground for men in the 1960s like Kittridge and then later in the 21st century astounding feats like Baumgartner's plummet to earth could become a reality.

Chapter 101

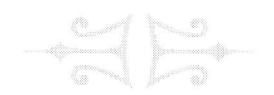

VERIFYING THE RAILWAY BRIDGE

At the end of this column each week is the web address for my blog *Every Now and Then* where I publish my research and thoughts concerning Douglas County history.

The blog has a Facebook page also under the name *Every Now and Then* you can follow. Every evening during the week I post a few pictures taken in and around Douglasville through the years. The community of folks following the page continues to grow.

I'd love to have you join in!

I consider this a win-win for the folks here in the county that are interested in locating, verifying and documenting our history mainly because I'm able to communicate stories I'm currently researching, and I'm able to advise areas where there are gaping holes in my research.

I'm always in need of pictures. My missing puzzle pieces might be found in your old family photos. Perhaps a building, a portion of a street, or a long lost home that no longer stands could be identified in the background of a photo in your possession.

Douglas County resident Mike Garrett is a member of the community that follows my blog on Facebook. Wednesday morning I logged on to find a picture I've been searching for in a message from Mike. My birthday was Monday, so I told Mike he had given me a fantastic present. The old wooden bridge that used to cross the tracks in downtown Douglasville has long been an interest of mine. It has not been easy to verify through the historical record. In fact, I had been told by a few people the bridge never existed, but I kept seeing references to it.

Earl Albertson had a few pictures showing the steps leading to the bridge, but I wanted a full shot of it.

The picture belonged to Mike's grandmother who was a member of the Baggett family. The picture is looking east on Broad Street in downtown Douglasville. We aren't quite sure yet on the date of the picture, but I'm thinking anywhere between 1900 and 1920.

An article from *The Atlanta Constitution* regarding Douglasville dated May 5, 1888 mentions the wooden bridge stating "….near the center of this town, a bridge arched like a rainbow, spans the railroad. From the top of the bridge one gets a good view of the city and the surrounding country."

Initially when I located the newspaper article and then looked at the Albertson images, I thought the bridge's location might have been on the west side of the old courthouse since the newspaper uses the words "center of town". It seemed to me the center of town would be close to the spot where the old skint chestnut tree was located, which has been documented as being just west of the old courthouse square.

Based on the picture Mike gave me I was able to verify the railway bridge was located opposite Bowden Street, and we have Mike Garrett's Granny Baggett to thank for taking the picture!

This former educator wants to give you a little homework. Go through those old family photos you inherited from Aunt Gert or Jimmy Sue, and let's get them scanned and online.

No picture is too old or too recent.

Your picture might be another one of those missing puzzle pieces in the Douglas County story!

Chapter 102

A LITTLE LIGHT FOR DOUGLAS COUNTY

Your life is moving along smoothly and suddenly the power goes out. It's like everything comes to a screeching halt. Instantly you feel as if you have been transported back in time to an alien environment where none of our modern conveniences work, or least they don't once the charge wears off.

For all of our technology and supposed "smarts", we can be quite wimpy when faced with day-to-day life that excludes hair dryers, refrigeration, and air conditioning.

There was a time when folks weren't so wimpy. They had no concept of enjoying electricity because it wasn't used for homes and businesses.

In 1909, under the leadership of Mayor J.R. Hutcheson and a few other "forward thinking" councilmen the lights came on in the city of Douglasville. Well, the lights came on for just a few families at first and then only at night.

Douglasville built its first electric plant on Parker Street and power began surging through the lines on October 15, 1909, but it wasn't just a matter of flipping a switch.

The Douglasville Argus explained, "The start-up was not easy. First, the packing blew out the boiler, and it was repaired the fifth time before the system surged with electricity. The linemen were busy all day...making connections with the feed wires in order to give customers electricity by that night. Now, watch Douglasville grow!"

Growth for the city's power company was a little slow. By the next year the initial 43 customers had expanded to 103. Many were scared of electricity. Others were waiting until they could get daytime service, too.

In the beginning the Douglasville Power Company would allow the power to travel through the lines each evening until five minutes before 10 p.m. Then they would flicker the lights three times signaling an end to everyone's "electrified" evening. You had five minutes to wrap things up.

Daytime power was finally begun five months after the Douglasville Power Company began operating. It seems the ladies had been complaining. Many had bought the new-fangled electrified irons and wanted to use them during the day when they were completing the laundry.

In 1926, the city's power plant was serving nearly 700 customers when it was bought by Georgia Power Company. They continued to service the city of Douglasville as a franchise and gave a portion of the proceeds back to the city each month.

It took a bit longer for the rural part of Douglas County to begin to have electricity.

Folks outside the city had to wait until the late 1930s, and money had a lot to do with it. Georgia Power estimated that the cost for constructing power lines throughout rural Georgia would cost $1,500 per mile. Most of those miles only had three paying customers where the Atlanta area had 70 folks per mile. It just wasn't profitable for areas like Douglas County, they said.

Then along came President Roosevelt and his REA, or Rural Electrification Administration. Their goal was to help rural areas become electrified.

In August, 1936 seven men met at the Douglas County courthouse to get the ball rolling – J.H. Abercrombie, J.S. Bomer, W.G. Johnson, N. P.

Barker, H.V. Branan, R.O. Boatright, and A.A. Fowler. The new venture would be called the Farmers Electrical Membership Association with attorney Astor Merritt giving legal guidance.

While the five dollar membership fee was more than some could afford other folks who lived in rural Douglas County were afraid they might lose their farm if they joined the co-op and then the concern failed. Others argued the venture would fail because the roads were so bad throughout the county. Still, the organizers pressed on to gain members because the REA required 3 homes per mile to sign up before they would approve the loan.

Finally, in September, 1936 the REA provided a loan of $83,000 and the J.B. McCrary Engineering Corporation began the process to string 83 miles of lines that would bring electricity to 320 members in and around Douglas County.

By 1940, the electric membership corporation we now know as Greystone had over 1,000 members and continued to grow steadily.

Chapter 103

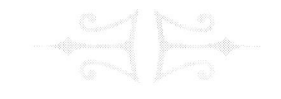

MAC ABERCROMBIE – DOUGLASVILLE'S OWN MULE WHISPERER

The Sheriff's Department page at *CelebrateDouglas.com* has a wonderful listing of every sheriff who has served the county with a small amount of biographical information compiled by the late Joe Baggett.

With regards to Sheriff Mac Claude Abercrombie, Sr., the site states he served as sheriff from 1933-1952 defeating Seawright Baggett in the 1932 election by 24 votes. Abercrombie started business in 1923 with a grocery store on Broad Street, later moving to Church Street near his father's barn and blacksmith shop. At the time of his election, he operated a dairy on Fairburn Road on Dura Lee Lane.

Abercrombie retired to operate a stable at the corner of Church Street and Club Drive, now the county jail parking lot, and later owned Timber Ridge Stables.

Early on in his life Mr. Mac, as many around Douglas County remember him, worked with his father trading mules. In 1918, his family moved to Phoenix, Arizona where they remained for three years trading mules and delivering them all over the area when Mr. Mac's father had a contract with the Harvey Company.

Now the Harvey Company – or the Fred Harvey Company to be exact – had been granted the concession contract with the Grand Canyon in 1922. The Harvey Company had started operating many of the restaurants found along the rail lines throughout the western section of the United States. They were basically the first restaurant chain established in this country, and early in the 20th century they saw an opportunity with the Grand Canyon.

Mules had been used since the 1840s to carry men and materials down into the canyon when prospectors were thinking there was treasure to be found, but early on folks realized the real gold mine at the Grand Canyon wasn't from prospecting but from tourism. When Theodore Roosevelt rode down into the canyon in 1913 he made the trails even more appealing to tourists.

In order to fulfill the contract with the Harvey Company, Mr. Mac's father had to travel to Texas and bought 30 mules. The animals were then broken and trained before delivering them to the Grand Canyon.

Mr. Mac has been captured on video telling about staying on at the canyon with the mules stating they were a bit short-handed. My research indicates that in 1920 the Phantom Ranch was being built at the bottom of the canyon, so more than likely the mules the Abercrombie family delivered to the canyon were, for a time, involved with transporting the building materials down to the bottom of the canyon, as well as tourists.

There are also videos where Mr. Mac mentions the decline of the mule business as gradually more and more farmers stopped depending on them to pull the plows and began using tractors. As a result he began to get more and more involved with horses at that point during the 1950s.

Today, there are dozens of folks who remember hanging around Mr. Mac's barn and helped him through the years. He referred to as "barn rats", and they called him "Mr. Mac." He would give the kids a quarter back when times were simpler and you could actually go to a movie and get some form of refreshment for such a small amount.

Of course, I haven't even begun to touch Mr. Mac's long career as our sheriff which was filled with interesting events as well including a few stills that were tracked down and destroyed.

Mr. Mac passed away at the age of 90 in 1994. An article published in the *Douglas County Sentinel* states, "At 'the barn' one could find an honest horse trader, gifted storyteller, and a real man of integrity in Mr. Mac."

An even nicer tribute can be found at the website, *www.mrmacsbarn.com*, which was put together and is maintained by some of Mr. Mac's dear "barn rats".

Chapter 104

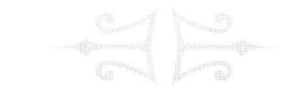

TAKE A BRIDGE TO THE PAST

If you have ever ventured outside of Douglas County at some point you have crossed one of the bridges over the Chattahoochee River connecting Douglas County to Fulton County.

"If I had a nickel"–is the phrase that come to mind, right?

We use our roads and bridges so often that we begin to take them for granted, and only when they are taken away from us do we begin to realize their importance in our daily lives. During the floods of 2009 we all got a taste of what it would be like to be cut off from the rest of the world when all of the bridges across the river were closed and Interstate 20 and numerous state routes were closed as well.

Douglasville was an island, and it was a bit unsettling, wasn't it?

Even experiencing the aftermath of the floods it is still hard to imagine having no bridges at all across the Chattahoochee River, but there was time prior to 1937 when there WERE no bridges.

If you wanted to cross the river you had to depend on the ferry and luckily there were a few men who ran ferries in the area. Claiborne Gorman has the distinction of running one of the first ferries as early as 1837. He had a large plantation along the river where the Dick Lane Bridge crosses the Chattahoochee River today along Campbellton Road/Highway 166. In fact, by the time the Civil War occurred he had amassed

1,250 acres of farmland. Claiborn's son, James M. Gorman, took possession of the plantation and ferry in 1869.

This is the point where the Atlanta National Bank and Alfred Austell, Sr. come into the picture. You might be wondering if Austell has anything to do with the city of Austell in Cobb County, and you would be right. Alfred Austell, Sr. was very involved with business affairs in Atlanta including Southern Railway. When the rail officials needed a name for the place where two of their lines converged near Salt Springs–the line to Birmingham and the line to Chattanooga–they decided to honor Alfred Austell, Sr. by naming the city of Austell for him.

The year was 1873–a year having some distinction with historians since they named a time of economic difficulty after it–the Panic of 1873. Effects from the Civil War were still being felt and the railroad boom resulted in too much capital involved in projects offering no immediate or early returns per Oberholtzer's *A History of the United States since the Civil War*. A total of 18,000 businesses failed between 1873 and 1875. Unemployment in the United States reached 14 percent, and real estate values fell. Men who depended on farming to make their living were hit very hard. James Gorman borrowed money from the Atlanta National Bank to pay off some debt, but his financial woes continued through 1873 when Alfred Austell, Sr. took the land and plantation home off Gorman's hands for a sum of $12,000.

Austell continued to live in Atlanta but used the plantation house as a country home and made many improvements to the property. At this point the place took on the title of "Austell Farms." He kept the farm and ferry operational over the years as the land was sub-divided and sold.

The story becomes even more interesting once Alfred Austell, Sr. passed away and left the plantation and ferry to his son, Alfred Austell, Jr. who graduated from Yale University in 1902. Alfred, Jr. decided he would return to Atlanta and live in the plantation home his father had left him. He created quite a stir as many believe he has the distinction of being the first resident of Douglas County to cross the ferry with a motor car. He left New Haven Connecticut after graduation in July, 1902 and continued

South in a 1902 Winton Touring Car. Fannie Mae Davis identifies the car as a "Locomobile," but since the Winton car was red in color her mention of the nickname "The Red Devil" is probably correct.

Today we could make the trip in just a few hours, but it took Austell and his Swedish chauffeur, Charles Swenson, three months arriving at the ferry on Sept. 8. Roads back then were not like they are today. Most were unpaved and in poor condition. Jeff Champion who is well versed concerning the history of the Gorman-Austell plantation advises, "Only two breakdowns were reported, a burned out induction coil at Staunton, Virginia, and a broken brake just before Atlanta was reached."

Alfred Austell, Jr. was the quintessential rich boy of the early 1900s. He was a member of the Capital City, the Piedmont Driving, and Atlanta Athletic Clubs. He had money, and he spent it on his hobbies—cars and horse racing. Jeff Champion's research indicates Alfred, Jr. wrote to the Yale alumni magazine, "My time has been spent mostly in Atlanta and a country house located about twenty miles from town. My time seems mostly spent automobiling." In fact, Alfred, Jr. participated in the Good Roads Tour of 1909 from New York City to Atlanta. Champion advises, "He drove an Apperson Automobile valued between $3,000 and $4,000. After the event he was named the Apperson Agent in Atlanta, and planned to open an Apperson dealership on Auburn Avenue later that year."

Alfred, Jr. wasn't into running the farm, and fortunately he had Miss Mamie Wier for that. Miss Mamie Wier lived on the plantation with Alfred Austell, Jr. She has been described as his house keeper, property manager, consort, and lifelong partner. She took over the daily operations of the farm and ferry leaving Alfred, Jr. to dabble with his automobiles. Fannie Mae Davis advises Miss Mamie oversaw the home's entertainments as well. Rumor has it there were some fine times on the plantation when parties were held. Fannie Mae Davis states, "Gossip in the area told of their all night dances."

Sadly, Alfred, Jr. passed away in 1922 and left Miss Mamie the proceeds of a $20,000 savings bond he had from the railroad, a car, and appointed her as dower of the estate until a time where she married or passed away. She continued to oversee the work on the plantation and also the parties continued at the home.

Besides running the farm and entertaining friends Miss Mamie ran the ferry. Jeff Champion advises, "She ran the ferry until the winter of 1935 when an ice slide took out the flat. Knowing the state would soon be building a bridge she didn't replace the ferry."

Chapter 105

DOUGLASVILLE'S PRESIDENTIAL CANDIDATE – WILLIAM D. UPSHAW

I'm continually amazed regarding how things I run across end up connecting to other things later on. Bits and pieces of history tend to connect in the most fascinating ways if I just wait long enough.

One day about six years ago I was sitting in the Douglas County Public Library on Selman Drive looking through various books dealing with Georgia history. I was trying to find some interesting bits of history I could bring to my readers at my Georgia history blog, *Georgia on My Mind*. One of the images that intrigued me was of a man who was reclining in a wheel chair type-contraption. The caption told me the man's name was William D. "Earnest Willie" Upshaw and he was a Congressman from Georgia.

I added Earnest Willie to a list of items titled "further research" and then I promptly forgot him until just recently.

As I research the early days of our county the same names keep coming up – Vansant, James, Selman, Upshaw – and many others.

Some of our streets are named for the people including Upshaw.

Recently, I discovered the man in the wheelchair had family that lived in Douglasville. He may have even lived here for a time, and not only was he a U.S. Congressman for the Fifth District, he ran for President in 1932.

Yes, he was a U.S. presidential candidate.

William D. Upshaw (pronounced "Upsure") was born in Coweta County in 1861. During the 1870s his father, Isaac D. Upshaw ran a grocery business and also had some sort of hotel in Atlanta At some point he decided to move his family out to the county in Cobb County, Georgia. "My father," Upshaw once said, "became afraid that his boys might fall prey to the gilded temptations of city life. Because he loved his boys better than he loved money, he moved us away from Atlanta to grow up amid the beauties, glories, and wholesome inspirations of rural life."

The family lived on a plot of land close to where the Macland community is today near Powder Springs, but while the Upshaw family lived there the community was known as Upshaw since Isaac was the postmaster as well as a store owner, blacksmith, teacher and farmer.

In 1884, William D. Upshaw's life changed tragically when he was injured during a farming accident. He slipped and fell across a wagon crosspiece fracturing his spine. The accident left him paralyzed. His injury meant he had to endure a body cast, brace, a wheelchair and crutches for all but the last few months of his life.

445

For the next six to seven years he was immobile, but William kept himself busy. The picture I saw way back when in the library had a note on the back in Upshaw's own hand stating, "Yours Earnestly, William Upshaw. September 13, 1891. Sunday afternoon. My heart's motto: Looking unto Jesus, Hebrews 12:2, My heart's message: Remember, without a new heart in Christ all else is vain."

The "Yours Earnestly" is important. During his confinement William began to write. He contributed poems and inspirational letters to Cobb County's weekly newspaper and an Atlanta paper called *The Sunny South*. He signed his writing and letters "Yours in Earnest" resulting in the nickname "Earnest Willie". His writings became very popular, and he began to lecture. He also wrote a book titled *Earnest Willie, or, Echoes from a Recluse* where he stated, "I do believe in being deeply in earnest. It is the very passion of my soul. Earnestness is the secret of nearly every man's success, and it is the lever that persistently pushes to completion nearly every movement for reform, whether it be great or small…"

The book was so popular it went into eleven editions.

Eventually, Upshaw managed to substitute a steel jacket for his body cast, and he moved from his bed into a wheelchair. An apparatus was devised which allowed him to ride in carriages, and he began traveling about, lecturing. The money he earned eventually gave him enough money to enroll at Mercer University in 1895.

By the turn of the last century Upshaw was vice-president of Georgia's Anti-Saloon League where he fought hard for Prohibition by lobbying for the passage of the Volstead Act. He lectured for the Women's Christian Temperance Union and made many speeches at Bessie Tift College in Tifton, Georgia. You have probably passed the campus on your way to Florida along Interstate 75. Eventually, Upshaw succeeded in getting a building on the campus named for his mother. Completed in 1904, the building was named Addie Upshaw Hall.

In 1906, Upshaw founded the magazine *The Golden Age*, a weekly forum for his writings regarding his call for Prohibition as well as other issues such as the Atlanta Race Riots, a condemnation of lynching and the creation of vigilante organizations.

Upshaw was encouraged to run for Congress. In 1918 he won the seat for Georgia's Fifth District defeating six seasoned political veterans in the process. He ran again in 1922 receiving 95% of the vote, and in 1924, he was unopposed. He ended up serving four terms.

While in Washington D.C. Upshaw became known as the "driest dry" in Congress. One resource states he startled folks by holding evangelistic meetings, in addition to fulfilling his duties as a Congressman, because as he said, "all the laws made on Capitol Hill will fall like chaff to the ground unless they are planted in character."

Another website advises, "His first important vote was for the 19th Amendment, providing for national women's suffrage; he was the only member of the Georgia delegation to support suffrage. He espoused a "square deal" for both capital and labor, but he clearly favored "the man in overalls and the man behind the plow." He supported a constitutional amendment to restrict child labor. He helped defeat the anti-strike clause in the Railroad Transportation Act. He urged Congress to provide pensions for Confederate veterans, as well as for Union veterans. He wished to provide Jewish chaplains in the Armed Forces, as well as Christian chaplains."

Colliers Magazine said of him, in 1924, "In a materialistic age, given over to thought and discussion of gross profits, net income, public debts, and taxation, Upshaw is an incurable romantic. He is a sentimentalist, an idealist, a dreamer, an exhorter, an evangelist, but with all these impractical qualities and attributes, he has ¬ and this is our final test ¬ the ability to put his stuff across; to do things. Upshaw would be intolerable if he were not so absolutely sincere and genuine. He has had an amazing career, because he believes in all the copy book maxims. He is one of the old Sunday school storybooks come to life.

During the 1932 presidential election William D. Upshaw ran against Franklin D. Roosevelt for the Prohibition Party. A vigorous campaign across 20 states was held.

Upshaw received almost 82,000 votes nationwide and for the remainder of his life, he fought an increasingly lonely battle to revive the Prohibition Cause. He tried again in 1942 running on the Democratic ticket, and was unsuccessful and another stab to return to Congress. The Prohibition cause was dead at that point.

Following his election defeats Upshaw returned to lecturing. Later, he moved to California and joined the faculty of Linda Vista Bible College in San Diego. He also became an ordained minister at the age of 72 and traveled across the United States for the National Christian Citizenship Foundation preaching against liquor and Communism.

On May 2, 1951 William D. Upshaw walked!

He was healed by a Christian minister by the name of William Branham who was purported to be a Christian healer.

Upshaw stood and walked at the meeting and walked every day afterward for the rest of his life.

William D. Upshaw passed away November 21, 1952 and is buried in California at Forest Lawn in Glendale.

I find it to be a bit ironic that the 1932 election had two handicapped inviduals running for president. Upshaw was very honest regarding his disability while Franklin D. Roosevelt hid the severity of his issues.

Section Nine

THE WAR YEARS

Chapter 106

THE SELECT FEW

This week we are going to travel back in time 73 years to October-November, 1940 when young men in Douglas County between the ages of 21 and 36 were registering with the local Selective Service Board.

In fact, Douglasville's mayor at the time – Astor Merritt – proclaimed Wednesday, October 16, 1940 a holiday in accordance with national and state proclamations in order to get everyone registered. Mayor Merritt urged business owners to give their employees time off to register that day.

During 1940, the United States was at peace. No war had been declared, but earlier in the summer, Germany had moved against France. As a result many in the United States called for some sort of military preparedness.

A national survey published in *Life* magazine in July, 1940 indicated 67% of those polled felt that a German-Italian victory put the United States in danger. Also, 71% of those who took part in the survey believed there should be some sort of military training in place for all young American men.

Congress answered the call by passing the Burke-Wadsworth Act better remembered as the Selective Training and Service Act which President Roosevelt signed into law on September 16, 1940. It was the first peacetime conscription in United States history.

The registration board in Douglas County was made up of Mac Abercrombie, F.M. Winn, R.H. Hutcheson, Robert O'Kelly, and Mrs. Mack Winn. Superintendent of schools, J.W. Shadix was the director of registration.

On October 16, 1940 every male between the ages of 21 and 36 in Douglas County was directed to report to the local school in their area to register. Every teacher or other deputized persons would be available at the schools to handle the process.

The *Sentinel* listed every school that would be available to registrants that day. In 1940 schools were segregated, so the list was divided into two categories: Black and White.

The white schools listed were Beulah, Bill Arp, Chapel Hill, Douglasville Grammar, Douglas County High School, Ebenezer, Fair Play, Lithia Springs, Mt. Carmel, Mt. Zion, Union Hill, Winston and Yeager. Black schools holding registration included Chapel Hill, Douglasville, Fairfield, Winston and Will Love.

Once registered, men would be selected for military service through the lottery system. Initially they were to serve for a twelve month period, but just a few months into the program President Roosevelt asked Congress to increase the term of service. The move wasn't very popular with the men or even Congress. The extension passed by a slim margin, and many men who had been drafted in October, 1940 painted the letters O...H...I...O on the walls of their barracks. It was an acronym meaning "Over the hill in October" which meant they intended to desert once their twelve months was up. Some did, but the desertions weren't widespread, and there is no information that anyone from Douglas County deserted in protest.

Within fourteen months the United States would no longer be conducting a peacetime draft due to the attack on Pearl Harbor on December 7, 1941. Any thoughts of deserting evaporated as thousands volunteered for service and others continued to be selected via the lottery.

It's not totally lost on me that tomorrow we celebrate all of those men and women who have served their country through military service no matter if they volunteered or were drafted to service, and no matter if they served during World War II, any other war, or even during peacetime.

We have so much to remember, and I'm glad we have a holiday to thank them.

Happy Veteran's Day to all of our men and women who have proudly served our nation!

Chapter 107

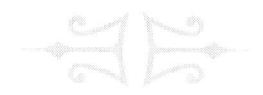

BIRTHIN' BABIES – A LITTLE HISTORY BEHIND DOUGLAS GENERAL HOSPITAL

Last week a particular news story gave me pause. The story deals with the death of a mom who lobbied heavily for home birth in Australia, and then died following her own home birth.

This story provides more information including reader comments. One thing the articles don't provide is more information regarding the cause of death. While it's very easy to say her choice to give birth at home killed her that just isn't necessarily so. We have no knowledge regarding her health condition leading up to the birth or many other variables that can come into play in any situation.

One reader commented that even though the majority of women give birth in hospital settings these days, we still have women that die in the hospital.

True.

Every birth has a unique set of variables where many things can happen no matter where the mother gives birth.

This story does hit home with me.

Our second child – our dear daughter – was born at home in 1993.

Yes, it was on purpose.

Yes, it was planned.

Yes, I had assistance, and yes, I'm all for women having a choice regarding where and how they give birth. I didn't choose to have a home birth lightly. I gave it a lot of consideration.

I actually had three certified midwives who assisted me. They didn't just show up when the time came. I spent the entire nine months doing what many pregnant women do – I took vitamins, I had ultrasounds, I saw medical professionals, and I met with my midwife regularly. If it had been my first birth or if I had had complications during previous births I wouldn't have even been considered for a home birth.

Home birth worked for me. In 1993, hospitals were just beginning to relax some of the constrictions that had been in existence for years for women giving birth. I experienced the prevalent clinical atmosphere with the birth of my son in 1985 and didn't want to repeat it. Midwives take a major role in birthing centers now, having family around the birth mother are prevalent now, and getting the mother home as soon as possible are the norm. In 1993, when I gave birth to my daughter things were still in transition regarding birthing options, and I wanted a different experience.

One area where mothers who give birth at home have absolutely no wiggle room, or at least I didn't, was pain management. I wasn't even able to take an aspirin, but my recovery time afterward, my ability to get right back to caring for my family was much quicker than my first birth.

Within an hour after the birth I was in the shower, dressed and walked under my own power into the Emergency Room at Douglas General Hospital where a doctor did conduct a follow up exam to make sure everything was as it should be, and of course, I was closely monitored for the next few days, as well as my daughter.

Georgia's midwives, those that work in hospitals and those who don't, are all well trained.

I'm just glad women have a choice.

There was a time here in Douglas County when women didn't have a choice. All babies were born at home during a time when medical care during the entire nine months wasn't given like it is now. Many babies were lost during pregnancy and during birth because we just didn't know the things we are privy to today.

In fact, Douglas County history tells us that it was the death of yet another mother giving birth that finally – finally spurred the community to build a local hospital.

The year was 1946. Medical care in Douglas County existed. We had doctors in private practice. Many surgeries were conducted on dining room tables, and all babies were born at home. One night in 1946 yet another mother died because there just wasn't time to get her to the closest hospital in Atlanta.

The book, *Douglas County, Georgia: From Indian Trail to Interstate 20* written by Fannie Mae Davis advises Mrs. Clyde (Alma C.) Gable can be credited for founding Douglas Memorial Hospital. This happened after she had spent the night aiding the local physician in delivering a baby where the young mother died because a trip to the Atlanta hospital could not be made in time.

The next day Mrs. Alma stood before the Douglas County Board of Commissioners in tears and pleaded with the commissioners to provide residents with a hospital. Thankfully, the men agreed with Mrs. Alma, and felt it was time as well. On May 9, 1946 the Douglas County Hospital Authority was formed with the following members – Dr. W.S. O'Neal, Guy Baggett, William Chatham, R.H. Hutcheson, A.H. Stockmar, W.D. Palmer, E.M. Huffine, J. Cowan Whitley, and A.A. Fowler, Sr.

Frank P. Dorris was instrumental in providing a location for the hospital via the American Legion. They donated the old Clover Mills School building located on 3 ½ acres of land on Fairburn Road. In the more recent past the United Way was located in the building.

The public donated money and labor to get the building ready to house a hospital. The cost for outfitting the building with the necessary wiring and plumbing was $22,716.66.

Most certainly a bargain considering today's costs.

Douglas County Memorial Hospital opened its doors on April 1, 1948 with up to fifteen beds for immediately use, and just in time, too!

Their first patient was five-year-old Richard Laird. He had a tonsillectomy.

By April, 1949 the hospital had added five more beds and boasted 207 babies had been born within its walls. They had treated a total of 800 patients.

In 1950, the hospital had a new addition and the beds numbered 35… by 1965, the beds numbered 51.

In January, 1971 the hospital moved to its present location beginning as a 98 bed facility and costing $3,675,000. There would be enough space for 15 doctors on staff and 25 nurses. A medical complex consisting of four building was also built adjacent to the hospital. Construction was completed on the new hospital in 1974.

During 1985, Douglas Memorial Hospital treated 4,700 patients and the Emergency Room saw 15,000 people pass through their doors!

During the 1980s Katherine Gunnell was appointed to serve as Chairwomen of the Douglas County Hospital Authority. Her goal was to provide quality healthcare for the entire community. Mrs. Gunnell's obituary published in the *Douglas County Sentinel* advises: [Mrs. Gunnell's] goal was nearly thwarted in 1992 when Douglas General Hospital suffered from financial problems…An informal discussion in [a] church parking [lot] with Mr. Jim Fowler, a Cobb Hospital Board member, led to a key role in laying the foundation for the WellStar Healthcare System.

This discussion led to meetings with Mr. Tom Hill, Cobb Hospital Administrator, who supported some kind of union between the hospitals and pitched it to his board. In a little over a month the two hospitals merged to form a buying cooperative. This successful effort led to the 1994 formation of the Promina Health Systems that included Douglas, Cobb, Kennestone hospitals, and others joined later.

In 1999, WellStar Healthcare System was formed from some of the hospitals in Promina. Today, WellStar, over 11,000 strong, meets the needs of many communities by utilizing state of the art equipment and nationally recognized physicians and staff. WellStar now serves over 600,000 people.

Chapter 108

DOUGLASVILLE, 1948 – A GLIMPSE

I spent a large majority of my time this past week finalizing things for the pictorial history of the city of Douglasville I'm putting together. It should be on store shelves in July per the last word I had from Arcadia Publishing.

Since October I've viewed hundreds of images from various sources depicting Douglasville, and one thing has really hit home. Through the decades since 1875, this has been very interesting and pleasant place to live, but right now I want to focus on one year in particular – 1948.

Having thumbed through every *Douglas County Sentinel* issue for that year I found an interesting reoccurring feature in the paper titled "Piktup 'Round Town" which was basically anonymous sightings from "around town". I find the snippets very interesting because while 1948 Douglasville was very different than 2014 Douglasville, the basics of life and humanity are the same.

See what you think?

*Seen late Friday afternoon – young new father gathering three-cornered baby apparel from clothesline and neatly folding them before taking them into the house.

I guess the thought that fathers only helped during recent times can go out the window.

Two local doctors having the time of their lives at a banquet last Friday night playing with miniature Chevrolet cars, lining them up and racing them across the banquet table.

Boys will be boys no matter the age, right?

Seen early Sunday morning, preacher sitting on front lawn washing his feet.

I have to wonder if he was practicing for a church service later that day.

Two cars dashing up street Wednesday afternoon come to stop in front of post office. Out steps local tailor and preacher. Tailor proceeds to get coat from his car and fit it on preacher in full view of passing traffic and pedestrians.

I can only assume the pastor was in a rush to a funeral or wedding.

A certain young man walking into the post office and seeing a young lady standing reading a letter, thinking it was someone he knew, grabbing the letter and whirling her around, finds to his chagrin that she is a perfect stranger.

Who hasn't had an oops moment, right?

Young lady receives a letter from out of town glances up at return address and finds Bethany Home, a home for old ladies. Guess they wanted to make her reservation early to avoid the rush.

I can relate. I've been receiving AARP forms since I was 38.

Overheard in drugstore man saying to lady clerk, "I want a Toni refill. Do you know what that is? I don't."

Just goes to show that even nearly 70 years ago husbands went to the store for their wives, and for those of you who are unaware a Toni refill was a permanent wave product ladies could use at home.

Night policeman chagrined as he discovers what he thought was a marauder in a local store and drawing his gun demands said thief to "Come out with your hands up" to be a huge pair of overalls with a paste board head.

Now this next one seems a bit "fishy" to me.

A fresh fish placed in the deep freeze around noon still alive when taken out late that evening, according to local fisherman.

Small girl dressing boy kitten up in a doll dress and calling him, "Linda".

I'm sure the kitten was more distressed at being in the dress than being called "Linda".

Seen last Sunday at a filling station on Bankhead Highway, man filling radiator of car with water being carted in a dripping Journal mailbox.

Hey, never let it be said that folks in Douglasville are resourceful, and at least it wasn't a *Douglas County Sentinel* box.

Chapter 109

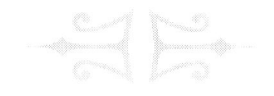

A SUBMARINE FOR DOUGLAS

I've been researching and writing about Douglas County history for a couple of years now, and I'm always amazed regarding what I discover. Folks ask me how I come up with the things I write about, and my answer is always the same.

Douglas County was and is an amazing place!

Most of the time my subject matter simply falls in my lap. Something I read spurs me to write, something someone says, something a reader sends me, and sometimes my writing begins with just a photograph.

The other day I came across a picture of a captured Japanese submarine on the back of a truck being carried through the middle of Villa Rica. I realized that if the submarine was being driven through Villa Rica the chances of it being driven through Douglasville were very high.

I was intrigued, and I decided to dig a little deeper.

I knew the time period for the picture was 1943, so I wanted to pour over the *Sentinel* issues archived at the library. Unfortunately, the microfilm copies for 1940-1943 are missing, so I turned to the Internet for the rest of the story.

During the early morning of December 7, 1941 it wasn't just Japanese aircraft bearing down on Pearl Harbor. Five midget submarines were also launched from the Japanese fleet as well.

The submarine that eventually made its way through Villa Rica and Douglasville was 78 feet long and carried the designation HA-19. There was just enough room for two men – Ensign Kazuo Sakamaki and Chief Warrant Officer Hiyoshi Inagaki.

There were problems with the submarine as soon as it hit the water. At one point it nearly sank. When the men were finally forced to surface, the submarine was spotted by a U.S. patrol, and our men began tracking it.

Sakamaki and Inagaki finally decided to scuttle the submarine and make for shore. Explosives were rigged to destroy the craft in case the men had to abandon it, but when there was no explosion Sakamaki swam down underneath the submarine to determine the problem. He became unconscious from the lack of oxygen and washed ashore near Waimanalo Beach, Oahu.

When Sakamaki finally awoke he found himself the "guest" of the United States. In fact, he is recorded as the very first prisoner of war captured by the United States during World War II.

The submarine was salvaged by Navy and Army personnel, and for the remainder of the war it toured the country as part of a war bond drive. That's how it ended up being carried through Villa Rica and Douglasville.

The submarine served as a symbol – a reminder regarding how the United States entered the war and of our loss. The submarine ended up raising millions of dollars for the war effort.

Sakamaki's name was stricken from Japanese records as if he never existed. He begged his U.S. captors to allow him to commit suicide, but of course, his request wasn't granted. He spent the entire war on the U.S. mainland as prisoner of war, number one.

At the war's end Sakamaki was released and returned to Japan where he refused to discuss the war. He eventually became an executive with the Toyota Motor Corporation and served as the president of its Brazilian subsidiary during the 1970s.

Sakamaki eventually wrote a memoir entitled *I Attacked Pearl Harbor*. He was reunited with his submarine in 1991 when he traveled to Texas for a historical conference regarding the war.

He reportedly cried.

Chapter 110

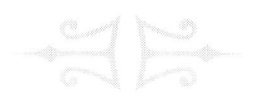

LITHIA SPRINGS, FIRST BAPTIST – A DREAM COME TRUE

When I first wrote this column the country was focused on the 2012 presidential election. The political season was wearing on me, and I made the observation judging by the comments I was hearing and reading it seemed the election was wearing on most people.

They were tired of the spin, the attacks, the gotchas, the convoluted issues, the negativity when we have serious problems, and we are in need of real solutions if not bona fide action-plans.

Several months later I still am weary of the political and social climate in our county.

It shouldn't be about who got us into the mess or who might want the credit for getting us out of the morass. It should be about fixing things. Just give me your plan with no static or spin. Don't tell me about the other guy. Give me your plan, and I'll decide which one I like and press my guy in Congress to do their part.

It seems simple, right?

You'd think so, but politicians get sidetracked with ego and power and just wanting to be "the one."

I would like to think that most people want to do something worthy with their life. They want to have purpose and leave behind something meaningful, and if they get the chance to leave behind something tangible, something that can be seen, used, and enjoyed by others, that it would be even better.

I don't usually find those types of people deep in the confines of politics. People who want to have real purpose and meaning hang out in everyday life quietly going about their work, their plans, and living life.

They tend to dream.

They tend to work on projects of their own and with others.

They have goals.

Those people – the everyday normal you - and - me types of people amaze me because more often than not they don't see their dream the first time around. Their projects go awry and goals have to be restructured.

Yet, they keep going even when everything they work for is suddenly taken away from them.

It's easy to give up, but the human spirit can be a remarkable thing when it meets up with adversity. Sometimes the right group of people come together and make something happen not once, but twice.

Take a group of citizens from Lithia Springs in the year 1946. A committee was appointed by Union Grove Baptist Church to look into the possibility of moving the church to the business area of Lithia Springs.

Members of the committee included Tom Gore, Ed Ralls, Loy T. Chandler, and I.C. Williams.

The committee discovered the John James family had given the land for the church only on condition that it be used as a church. If the church was moved or disbanded, the land would revert back to the James family. The committee's report was presented to the church, and the suggestion to move to downtown Lithia Springs was not approved.

However, a small group of twelve people still believed God was leading them to establish a church at Lithia Springs. One member of the group in particular, Loy T. Chandler had a dream one Sunday afternoon after church where he later advised God had given him a vision of a church in downtown Lithia Springs.

At one time Glen Florence owned several lots of land along Bankhead Highway in Lithia Springs. He was also involved in various business concerns and later was a member of the Georgia General Assembly for the 39th District. Ed Ralls contacted Mr. Florence on behalf of the group.

Mr. Florence responded to Mr. Ralls by letter on March 1, 1946 and a copy is stored within the historical archives of First Baptist Church, Lithia Springs. Mr. Florence wrote, "I will be glad to donate a church site....Have you looked at the place next to the school house, as you could utilize part of the school grounds for large Sunday crowds? ...You might want to get Mr. Watt Mozeley to show you the places and write me the amount of frontage needed and the depth of the place, and I am sure we can get together. Thank you for the chance to do something."

The church was organized on April 7, 1946 in the auditorium of the present Annette Winn Elementary School then known as Lithia Elementary School. Finances were discussed and a budget plan approved. The group pledged to tithe their income, and it was unanimously voted to have services every Sunday.

The group continued to meet in the school building until the basement of the church was complete. At the conclusion of the first year the basement was completed and services were held there.

The church members completed much of the building themselves. Men would head to the church site after work and complete another shift until late at night. Every Saturday was spent seeing to the construction at the church as well with the women providing picnic lunches when necessary.

On October 23, 1949 the LIthia Springs First Baptist building was dedicated to the glory of God. The dedication theme was "A Dream Come True", and it was. It is said the building was just as Mr. Chandler had envisioned.

A regular Sunday schedule was held using all of the new equipment and all of the spaces that were available. Following the morning service a basket lunch was enjoyed and during the afternoon a congregational singing was held and a message of dedication was given by Pastor Pat Johnson from the Douglasville First Baptist Church.

The dedication was followed by a week-long revival, but on that Friday night, October 28, 1949 to be exact, tragedy struck.

As the congregation gathered for the evening services the building caught fire. Instead of gathering to sing hymns and listen to the pastor's message the congregation watched their many hours of labor and the result of many months of financial sacrifice burn to the ground. Later the cause was determined to be a faulty gas heating system.

In those days Lithia Springs didn't have regular fire service. In fact, it would be the 1960s before Douglas County would have regular fire service. Firefighting equipment was called from Austell and Douglasville, and a bucket brigade was formed to no avail due to the town's lack of a water system.

All equipment including a new grand piano, new white pine pews, carpeting, four pianos in the Sunday school departments, all chairs, heaters, and much more were destroyed. Written histories filed within the church archives state, "It was well the church had a firm foundation because it went from a mountain-top experience of exaltation to the valley of despair in five short days. It was in the testing time that the real church emerged to build again an even larger, stronger organization, with more facilities to proclaim God's love in the community."

Three days after the fire a meeting was held where the congregation met to discuss plans for the future. A plan was put in place to raise the funds and go forward with building another "new" church. Surrounding churches offered their buildings, plus a store building, the Scout Hut, and private homes were used on a temporary basis. Later meetings were held in the school until a new sanctuary was completed in August, 1951. The building still stands on the church campus today as a testament to faith, dreams, and sticking to a goal.

Section Ten

THE FABULOUS FIFTIES

Chapter 111

LOUISE SUGGS – LESSONS FROM THE FATHER

I'm sure that many fathers are taking a few minutes today to think over the moment they first became a daddy since this is Father's Day.

What a life changing moment, right?

Two important things happened the night Johnny Suggs became a father. His beautiful daughter Louise was born, and Ponce de Leon Ball Park burned down.

While both events were significant it's a safe bet that the fire at the ball park received more notice since it was the home of the very popular Atlanta Crackers. The fire and the birth of a daughter are also a little intertwined since Johnny Suggs happened to run the ball field for his father-in-law, Rell Spiller, who also owned the Atlanta Crackers.

The ball field was rebuilt and the team went on to play for years, but Johnny Suggs took on a new role in Rell Spiller's business empire. The former left-handed pitcher for the New York Yankees decided to try his hand building a 9-hole golf course in Lithia Springs.

Rell Spiller already owned the plot of land where hundreds of thousands had flocked years before for the lithia water. There are some who have told me he actually had a small motel there close to the corner of Thornton Road and Bankhead Highway. At some point the motel was torn down. Spiller and Suggs decided to cash in on the resort history of the area and began designing the 9-hole course using a mule team and pad of paper to map out the course.

By 1932, the Lithia Springs Golf Club was in full operation with Johnny Suggs at the helm.

The first tee was actually behind where the water company office stands today, and the course was laid out in a circle with one of the holes on the other side of Bankhead Highway. Nine holes cost 25 cents, and if you wanted a full 18 you could pay another quarter, but on the weekends 18 holes would cost a whopping 75 cents.

Suggs built a home adjacent to the course and settled in to a comfortable life raising his family and running the course. Louise Suggs, the daughter that was born the night Ponce de Leon Ball Park burned down, went on to learn the game of golf from her father and become one of the greatest female golfers of all time.

Over the years Miss Suggs has repeatedly told the story regarding the one home run her father hit during his baseball career and how that led to her interest in golf. In fact, looking at that home run on a broader scale, it would seem that it also led to the Lithia Springs Golf Club.

When Johnny Suggs was a baseball player, the A.G. Spalding Co. would award any player a set of golf clubs when he hit a home run. Once the family moved to Lithia Springs and built the course, the story goes that the wooden clubs were cut down so that Louise could use them as she followed her father around on the course.

A *Time* article from 1947 advises, "Many days playing in the late afternoons when the course was ready to close, Louise and her father would take one club each and play until dark," following the numbered holes across Bankhead Highway and up the hill to their home.

Louise Suggs won her first major tournament at 17. In 1947, she won the U.S. Amateur Golf Association Championship, and she turned professional in 1948. She is one of the founding members of the LPGA, and she was the first woman inducted into the Georgia Sports Hall of Fame in 1966. She is also a member of the Douglas County Hall of Fame.

The last round of golf at the Lithia Springs Golf Club was played in 1975. Today, the property is part of a 50-acre recreation park known as the Louise Suggs Memorial Community Recreation Area.

It's hard to imagine what the course would have looked like back then, but from now on when I'm heading down that stretch of Bankhead Highway towards Austell, I'll never think of the area in the same way again. I'll picture a perfect father-child moment–Louise Suggs and her father each holding a golf club making their way across the highway and up the hill toward the ninth hol

++++e and home.

Chapter 112

CITIZEN O'NEAL – THE MAN BEHIND THE PLAZA

Over the last few weeks as I have been researching this week's topic I would throw the name W.S. O'Neal out to various Douglasville citizens.

Over and over again I was met with the same response.

"Oh, what a nice man."

"A great man."

"He was always nice to me when I was a kid."

"He's well thought of."

The reactions were so positive from long time residents I am very sorry I never got the chance to meet him, however, we remember him even if we didn't actually know Doctor O'Neal simply because his imprint is all over Douglasville in so many different areas.

O'Neal came to Douglasville from Haralson County and Standing Rock, Alabama where he was born, and in his youth he attended Bowden College and the Georgia School of Pharmacy in Atlanta.

Originally Dr. Selman ran a pharmacy where the Irish Bred Pub is today in downtown Douglasville, and beginning in 1919 his son Paul took over before selling the business to Mr. O'Neal. Eventually O'Neal struck a partnership with another pharmacist named Fred Morris making O'Neal Drug Company a heavy presence on Broad Street until they both retired in 1962.

As a pharmacist, O'Neal made house calls and assisted local doctors with surgeries. Fannie Mae Davis states in her history of Douglas County, "He mixed his medicines from bulk shipments of simple compounds: sulphur, castor oil, turpentine. In those days ingredients like that arrived at the drugstore in barrels and left in medicine bottles…"

Doc O'Neal, as he was is often referred to by those who knew him also provided space for the Douglasville Telephone Exchange when operators were needed to place phone calls. When dial phones hit Douglasville in 1948, Mr. O'Neal enlarged the space on the second floor to give the new system the room that was needed.

From 1948 to 1968 Doc O'Neal was chairman of the Douglas County Hospital Authority and oversaw the establishment of the first hospital in Douglasville.

In the early 1950s, O'Neal took on another role. He became the mayor of Douglasville and served two terms. Fannie Mae Davis states he guided the city during "a time of unprecedented growth in Douglasville and the county." He was the mayor when public housing first reached Douglasville and in October, 1952 the Lithia Springs Drive-In was opened.

In July, 1953 Mayor O'Neal published a list of accomplishments for citizens to review. It's quite interesting to read since there are many hints in the list regarding what Douglasville citizens in the 1950s considered to be new and innovative. In some instances we have to remember the context of the times and realize how different Douglasville was then. Certain words and phrases would be used that would be considered inappropriate now.

Mayor O'Neal listed the following:

1. The Douglasville Clinic is modern in every respect – made possible by county officials.
2. City Hall with a new jail – which merits the pride of our citizens.

3. New police car, one of the latest models, geared for high speed, when high speed is necessary.
4. New modern jail, erected by county officials.
5. Bus station in new location, which relieves congestion of traffic.
6. Paving the following streets: Strickland, Duncan, Fairview Drive, Katherine, Upshaw Lane, Hollis, Wedge Alley, Rose Circle and the extension of Church Street to Rose Avenue. Also the drive around Douglas County Memorial Hospital, Price Avenue and Campbellton Streets has been resurfaced.
7. Telephone service has been extended into more rural communities and our system has been placed into the Atlanta division.
8. The City Council has arranged to have a man on duty at all times to answer fire alarms.
9. Last, but most important of all is the new annex to be added to our present hospital building. This will include rooms and facilities for the colored people. Plans are underway to improve the present hospital building.

Mr. O'Neal also served as a founding director of The Commercial Bank, now known as Regions Bank, in Douglasville from 1928 to 1977. Having lost money in two different banks as a young man O'Neal vowed he would never put his money in a bank again where he wasn't a director. Fannie Mae Davis writes Doc O'Neal helped to guide the bank with his experience as "a conservative investor and [as] as student of the stock market." He also served on the loan committee.

In 1979 he was the longest surviving founding director of the bank. To recognize his contribution the bank named their new community room to honor him – the W.S. O'Neal Community Room. The room was established for the board of directors to meet, and to have room for civic groups to meet and to have exhibit space.

In his personal life Mr. O'Neal was married and had three sons. Tragically his oldest son was killed in a plane crash in 1949. The family was very involved with the First United Methodist Church of Douglas to the point that Doc. O'Neal was chairperson of the building committee for the church in the 1940s.

O'Neal was granted the title Director Emeritus of the Commercial Bank and continued to attend meetings until his death on June 6, 1979.

O'Neal Plaza, named to honor W.S. "Doc" O'Neal, is located at the end of Price Avenue in the heart of the historic district in downtown Douglasville. The plaza is adjacent to the commercial space where Mr. O'Neal ran his pharmacy for so many years, and his sons also had a clothing store for several years where the city government offices are located today. O'Neal Plaza has become a favorite place for prom pictures, sunrise Easter services, festivals such as the upcoming Taste of Douglasville, and the stage area is perfect for outdoor concerts and other entertainments.

It is the perfect space to honor a man who gave his time and devotion to our city.

Fannie Mae Davis said it best – "In business, politics, and community work, Doc O'Neal helped develop Douglas County through a half century of dramatic growth and changes."

Douglasville is already a great place to live but what if each and every citizen aspired to be the sort of involved citizen like Doc. O'Neal?

I think we would be very amazed regarding what we could accomplish.

Chapter 113

TURKEYS AWAY!

Ah, Thanksgiving.
That time of year when visions of cranberry sauce, giblet gravy and dressing cross our minds. It's that time of year when we all become turkey experts of some sort – either knowing the perfect way to cook it, carve it, or handle the leftovers. It's also that time of year when the newsfeed on *Facebook* is filled with that now classic scene dating back to 1978 from the Emmy award winning *WKRP in Cincinnati* where Mr. Carlson, the bumbling station manager declares, "As God is my witness, I thought turkeys could fly!"

The folks at the radio station had decided to get some much needed publicity by creating a stunt with a Thanksgiving tie-in. They decided to throw live turkeys out of the station's news helicopter. Of course, the result was several minutes of hilarity as Les Nessman, the bow-tied fastidious WKRP newsman reported the event a la the Hindenburg disaster exclaiming at one point, "Oh, the humanity!" as the turkeys were hurled from the helicopter and plummeted to the waiting crowd below.

Many of the situations portrayed on the show, including the Thanksgiving episode were based on real situations surrounding Atlanta's WQXI radio station. Bill Dial, one of the WKRP writers actually worked at WQXI in 1968 along with DJ "Skinny" Bobby Harper who was Dial's inspiration for the character Dr. Johnny Fever. The Thanksgiving episode was inspired by a WQXI promotion where an 18-wheeler was leased, and several dozen turkeys were tossed from the roof of the trailer.

So, I have to wonder if the folks at WQXI had heard of our own J.Thad Smith here in Douglasville. Smith, along with the Downtown Retail Merchants Association planned a "turkey fly" in 1957 to promote downtown businesses as Thanksgiving approached.

I have a *Facebook* page titled "Every Now and Then" where I post pictures relating to the history of Douglas County.

A few months ago Willard Bowen, a friend and reader, asked me if I had pictures of the turkey drop in Douglasville. Intrigued I chased down a few pictures and the story.

I found an ad in the *Sentinel* dated November 12, 1957 stating "If you can run – if you can walk – come to Douglasville this Saturday, November 23…for the most fun you've seen in years!" The rest of the ad advised that "27 live turkeys would be turned loose, one by one from the top of a building on Broad Street…This turkey fly should be the funniest thing you've seen in years – big, full grown, live turkeys flapping through the main streets of Douglasville, and if you catch one of them, he's yours to keep."

From the pictures it appears the crowd was large.

Philip Shadix commented on my *Facebook* page that the "turkey fly" was a big deal and that his family came to town all the way from Bill Arp to see people chase turkeys. Willard Bowen remembers standing in the middle of the road waiting expectantly for a turkey to come his way. He remembers the ensuing confusion as each turkey was thrown as great fun.

So, how did the "turkey fly" turn out?

Let's just say that I checked the *Sentinel* for several days after the event and never saw a follow up post.

Ed Landers commented on the pictures I posted at *Facebook* and summed it up this way, "Can you imagine a 20 pounder coming off a 30-foot building and landing on or hitting you?"

No, I can't, and that might be why no one else has tried to throw live turkeys off a Broad Street building.

I hope each one of you has a blessed holiday.

Happy Thanksgiving!

Chapter 114

THE VILLA RICA EXPLOSION

Every teacher worthy of carrying a grade book realizes lessons plans cannot be written in stone – not if we truly want to meet our students where they are and truly design a prescribed course of study to help students reach various goals. Of course, teachers do have lesson plans they use over and over. I certainly did, but I never taught them the same way twice. They were always tweaked and fine-tuned or tailored to fit the needs of each new group of students I encountered.

One lesson that I wrote while I was in the classroom stayed the same year to year with little change. It was a lesson I used during the first week of school when I was attempting to introduce my fourth graders to their first encounter with a full-range American History course that would span the entire year. The lesson was my attempt to show students how history is all around us if we begin to closely observe our surroundings.

Villa Rica Elementary School –the school where I spent several years – is separated into four different buildings that form a large square. In the center is a large grassy area with a great shade tree. During the first week of school in August I would gather up my students, and we would have class in the grassy area underneath the tree.

Once everyone had settled in I would ask students to look around and notice where they were. I asked them to look at the tree, the grass, and the spots where there wasn't any grass. I would ask, "Is the ground completely flat or do you notice it rising and falling in certain areas?"

I told students their job description in my class would be to act as historians, and they would need to be aware of the lay of the land. They would need to be able to make observations for anything that could be used as a frame of reference or a landmark of sorts when exploring a historical site. Anything can be a clue regarding how the land was once used or who lived there.

I show students a picture of a pile of rocks and ask, "What could this be trying to tell us?"

I get all sorts of crazy answers. I also get a few plausible one such that the rocks could be covering a grave. We discuss all of the answers, and then I would tell students, "Sometimes it just takes a different viewpoint to really identify something.

I then show students a picture of a pile of rocks taken from the air.

Generally, at this point I would hear several ohs and ahs, and I would tell students the picture is Georgia's Rock Eagle, of course. Rock Eagle is a Native American rock formation located in Eatonton, Georgia.

The second picture I showed students is a deep gully. I would pass it around and allow students to observe it up close. We discussed possible causes for the gully – erosion, earthquake, Mother Nature, God…

As I showed students the next image I would ask, "How about man? Could this gully be caused by hundreds of wagons over a fifty year period?"

The gully image I share with students is actually part of the Natchez Trace running between Nashville, Tennessee and Natchez, Mississippi, and thousands of settlers traveled the Trace making their way to new lands.

Finally, I show students a picture of a trench. Generally, when I asked students how the trench was formed they reacted predictably and guessed incorrectly the trench was caused by wagons. Some usually thought it was an early picture of the Grand Canyon.

We discussed the possible causes at length, and then I showed them the last image where it is obvious the trench was manmade.

The first trench image hints it was man-made because rocks and wood placed on the sides of the trench. I usually followed this with a very quick explanation regarding trench warfare that took place during World War I.

I ended our discussion by telling students history is everywhere around them if they would take the time to examine, to wonder, to question what they see.

I guess the same thing could be said of adults as well, right?

A pile of rocks could be just that, but if you know a little history you might guess the pile of rocks might be a burial spot, if I just happen to know Native Americans in my area were doing that hundreds of years ago. If I knew a little history I might realize a pile of rocks could be part of a much larger design that could be seen from the air.

It's at this point of the lesson I could predict several wiggle worms, so I would change our location. We would walk down to the recess field where I would gather everyone in a group and impress upon students that historians never know what they are standing on unless they truly observe their surroundings.

I would have students verify we were standing on the recess field before asking, "Is that all we are standing on?"

Then I would remind them that sometimes you have to change your viewpoint. I take students to the edge of the playground and down some steps towards an area that had been set up as our outdoor classroom for nature walks and science experiments. From this vantage point it was very easy to see the playground wasn't what it seemed. From the outdoor classroom the recess field was hidden at the top of a very large hill. Sticking out of the side of the hill in various places were all sorts of debris. Rocks, long pieces of rebar, broken signs, glass, wires, bricks, and assorted hunks of concrete litter the hillside.

I would point out the debris and ask students to come up with ideas about what happened.

Finally, I would tell them the story.

Many loads of dirt were hauled in to build up the playground at Villa Rica Elementary, but before the dirt was dumped the town of Villa Rica brought in remnants of a section of town. Much of the debris from the Villa Rica Explosion is underneath the playground. Usually, I would have a student or two who would nod their heads and confirm they had heard about the tragedy from their grandparents or parents. Generally, most students had not heard about it, and were amazed.

The fateful day was Thursday, December 5, 1957. People were going about their normal business on a weekday. They were going to the store, keeping appointments, seeing to some early Christmas shopping, and some folks were simply out to cast their ballot in municipal elections going on at the time, but shortly after 11 a.m., a natural gas explosion took the lives of 12 people and injured at least 20 others.

In an instant the lives of so many changed.

In 1997, the 50th anniversary of the explosion, *The Douglas County Sentinel* published an article recounting that fateful day. Many folks remembered the sound of the explosion – a loud whoomp, that was more like a clap than a bang, and others said that the town suddenly looked as if it had been hit by an atom bomb.

Ethyleen Tyson said that an announcer came on WSB-Radio shortly after the noise and reported that a bad explosion had occurred in Villa Rica. Authorities asked that people stay away from downtown since only emergency vehicles were being allowed into the area and a search was under way for bodies.

Reporters from as far away as Atlanta swarmed the scene. Eyewitnesses told them that right after the explosion the air was filled with clothing, papers, wood, bricks, and other falling debris.

Buildings several hundred yards away were damaged. Four cars were completely smashed.

Fortunately, rescuers found them to be empty.

Newspaper accounts from the day reported that Berry's Pharmacy was believed to have been ground zero for the blast. For several days prior to the explosion, employees at several downtown buildings had complained of smelling gas, especially at the drugstore.

Ralph Fuller is one of the few who can claim he was inside the drugstore that morning and lived to tell the tale. "I was in the drugstore, and I was sitting with a girl in the back having something to eat," the Villa Rica barber remembered. "We were sitting by the jukebox, and I thought the jukebox had blown up. I thought I would smother once I realized what had happened, what with all the debris on top of me," he continued. Fuller received severe burns in the blast and was hospitalized. Although Fuller said that does not remember how long he had to stay in the hospital, he did remember the reaction of family members who visited him there. "My own sister didn't recognize me from the burns I had," said Fuller.

James Harrison, [a longtime pharmacist] was downtown when the blast occurred. He had been out making house calls with a doctor friend, and had returned to town just before 11 a.m. His friend had dropped him off in front of Berry's Pharmacy, and Harrison had started inside to have a soft drink and relax. [He remembered,] "As I opened the door and began to walk inside, I remembered that it was Election Day, so I decided to go vote…Just as I reached it, the explosion took place."

The following persons perished in the December 5, 1957 natural gas blast in downtown Villa Rica:

Mrs. Ann Pope Smith, age 23
Mrs. Margaret Berry
Bobby Roberts, age 13
Miss Carolyn Davis, age 22
Oscar Hixon, age 34
O.T. Dyer, age 60
Johnny Dyer, age 30
Rob Broom, age 54
Dr. Jack Burnham, a dentist
Kenneth Hendrix
Carl Vinter
Rozella Johnson

In 2010, Douglas County historian and author, Elaine Bailey published a book titled, *Explosion in Villa Rica* in an effort to make sure the history regarding the tragedy would not be forgotten.

Mrs. Bailey recounts in her book how members of Douglasville's National Guard were among the first rescuers on the scene. In an interview with the *Times Georgian* Mrs. Bailey recalls, "One of my most interesting interviews was with an 85-year-old man, who was head of the National Guard in Douglasville at the time. He was on the scene 30 minutes after the explosion and stayed for three days. After the story hit the news, National Guardsmen put on their uniforms and took off for Villa Rica."

Bailey further advised the Guard troops provided security to prevent looters from stealing from the damaged stores, including a jewelry store whose merchandise was scattered all over the street. She said, "Many years later, people were bringing back jewelry, because they felt guilty about taking it."

While downtown Villa Rica is actually in Carroll County the explosion remains one of the most catastrophic events in area history in terms of injury and loss of life.

Chapter 115

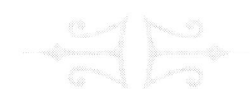

JANUARY, 1955 – DOUGLASVILLE GRAMMAR SCHOOL BURNS

Think about Church Street for a minute.

What are the main focal points as you mentally go from one end of the street to the other?

You might mention the large Regions Bank building, City Hall, the new conference center and parking deck or even the former First Baptist Church building.

The Douglasville City Cemetery might be your focal point or the recently vacated jail or even the armory building.

All of these are worthy focal points, but why don't we zero in on the space between the church and the armory building.

Today we know a fire station sits there, but between 1918 and 1955 the space was home to Douglasville Grammar School, a three-story brick and wooden structure housing 25 classrooms and anywhere between 600 to 800 students.

From the pictures I've located it was a lovely building. Even though it wouldn't meet today's education needs, it would be a nice structure to connect with our past for offices, meeting rooms or even a boutique hotel of some sort.

Sadly, we lost the building forever on January 27, 1955 when a slow moving fire took it from us.

The fateful day was a Thursday. Students and staff had already gone home when Jimmy Gable, a high school student at the time, noticed smoke billowing from the building as he traveled down Church Street around 5 p.m.

A newspaper article a few days later advised several surrounding communities helped with fighting the fire including Austell, Marietta, Villa Rica and even Atlanta, but the fire was too far out of control.

Even though the building was a total loss, a few of the high school boys and men on the scene were able to remove some of the desks from the basement classrooms and, most of the school's lunchroom equipment was saved.

There had been some initial speculation that water-pressure had been an issue in fighting the fire, but it was ruled out. The cause of the fire was thought to have started in the school's boiler room.

The school's principal, Mrs. H.N. Kemp and Board of Education Superintendent, J.E. Walton scrambled to provide a place for the students to finish out their school year. Double sessions began at the high school with the older students attending class from 8 a.m. to 1 p.m., and the grammar school students were in class from 1 p.m. until 4:30 p.m.

A new grammar school that had already been planned was quickly built, and as you already realize – Douglasville Grammar School did not rise again along Church Street.

The school became a memory for the hundreds of students and teachers who called it their educational home for 37 years.

Chapter 116

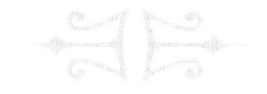

MY LOVE AFFAIR WITH O'NEAL PLAZA

In 1969, William H. Whyte was helping the City of New York with urban planning by studying human behavior in urban settings. Over a span of 16 years he conducted the Street Life Project to understand how people use city spaces. As unobtrusively as possible, he watched people and used time-lapse photography to chart the meanderings of pedestrians. What emerged through his intuitive analysis is an extremely human, often amusing view of what is staggeringly obvious about people's behavior in public spaces, but seemingly invisible to the inobservant.

Regarding his observations Whyte said, "If there's a lesson in street watching it is that people do like basics – and as environments go, a street that is open to the sky and filled with people and life is a splendid place to be." Whyte began to advocate for a new way to design public spaces that focused more on answering questions involving how the space would be used rather than the attitude, "Here it is. Use it."

Whyte advised in order for humans to actually use an urban setting the space has to provide for civic engagement and community interaction. I'd like to add another "C" word – charm. Therefore, the space should be easy to get to, easy to use, attract all types of citizens and drip with charm.

Douglasville is fortunate to have a space like that – O'Neal Plaza.

Yes, O'Neal Plaza is a street open to the sky. It is people friendly, often filled with life, and it is a splendid place to be. O'Neal Plaza is located in the middle of the historic commercial district, has plenty of space for movement, blends with the architecture of the existing buildings, and has interesting features such as the fountain and a unique stage area – my most favorite area of the plaza.

Years ago Baggett's Pool Hall filled the area where the award winning stage area is today alongside Dr. T.B. Taylor's medical office.

I love the character of the space.

The cut-outs where windows used to be, the uneven brickwork, the spots where crossbeams for the buildings used to rest in the brick walls, and other hints that something used to be there. I love where the moss and other vegetation is actually growing out of the wall. It just draws me in, and of course the canopy over the stage is exceptional.

Without the canopy the stage area would be just a small brick area fading into an even larger brick area, but the canopy's unique design sets the space apart, creates the space and makes it unique to Douglasville.

The stage area is exactly what its designer, Terry Miller of Miller and Associates wanted it to be – an icon for downtown Douglasville – a spot where everyone will want to have their picture taken.

If you think the canopy resembles train tracks then you have a great eye. That's exactly what Terry Miller had mind since the location of the railroad was important to the growth of our town.

The railroad design pays homage to our past while it leads us to into the future.

According to a recent *Douglas County Sentinel* article O'Neal Plaza will experience some construction in the next few months as work has begun to complete O'Neal Plaza East which will create a pedestrian alley between the buildings that front Broad and Church Street in essence making the East side of the Plaza match the West side.

While I'm glad the project will finally be completed, I was a little alarmed to learn that the tree that hangs over the back area of the stage might be cut down and the patio area of the Irish Bred Pub might have a different look once the construction is completed.

I do love that tree. It's one of those things that give the Plaza its charm.

The D.H. Gurley grocery ad featuring Snowdrift Shortening is another aspect of the Plaza's charm. The ad takes us back to the turn of the century and our earliest roots as well.

O'Neal Plaza is versatile since it attracts so many different people for so many different activities including festivals like Taste of Douglasville, weddings, the recent Chili Cook Off, and the weekly Farmer's Market.

We haven't been very fortunate over the last few weeks as rain has rolled in each and every Thursday afternoon, but the vendors keep showing up and so does my longtime friend Jeff Pike to provide live music.

Through his work with observing people and how they use city spaces, William H. Whyte also said, "The street is the river of life of the city, the place where we come together, the pathway to the center."

I firmly believe that O'Neal Plaza is the City of Douglasville's river of life – the place where we come together – the pathway to our collective center.

Chapter 117

SO LONG, TEX

This week I'm going to take us back to a time when country and western music was really country and really western. A time when it was heard in living rooms all across the country via radio waves and performances were not watched on television, a cell phone, or even a computer screen.

The one thing in common between then and now is that young people hearing the music were instantly smitten and wanted to become music stars as well.

One such young person was Ortho Woodrow Forman who took on the name Tex.

From an early age Tex was learning the harmonica and singing harmonies, and in the late 1920s when most young boys were eyeing baseball gloves or a fishing rod, he had his heart set on a Bradley Kincaid "Houn' Dog" guitar from the Sears-Roebuck catalog. Tex regularly heard Bradley Kincaid, a popular folk and country singer, on the radio, and dreamed of performing himself. Eventually, Tex went into debt for the guitar borrowing the necessary three dollars from a cousin.

After traveling around performing with Chief Black Hawk's Medicine Show and other groups where Tex added comedy to his list of accomplishments he landed a job with Pop Eckler where he performed with the

"Happy Days" show airing over NBC radio. Eventually the group moved to Atlanta to be regulars on WSB's "Cross Roads Follies". Forman's role was chief comedian and all-around cut-up.

By the late 1930s the group was performing a regular Saturday night show called the "Radio Jamboree" at the Atlanta Burlesque Theater that would air live. He also played the guitar and even won a yodeling contest in 1936 held at the Atlanta Municipal Auditorium.

During his career Tex performed at the Grand Ole Opry and could boast of singing alongside Ernest Tubb, Hank Williams, and Chet Atkins. In an August, 2012 *Sentinel* article to mark Tex's 97th birthday, Haisten Willis correctly notes," [Tex] has outlived most of them, and their music is remembered today only by a select few."

Forman moved back to Ohio in 1946 and worked as a brick mason and builder, but twenty years later he made Douglasville his home where he and his wife Marjorie raised two children. Foreman continued to work as a brick mason and builder until his retirement. One of the many jobs he oversaw was the Westin Peachtree Plaza where he was the lead brick mason. He also hosted live country shows on WDGL, Douglasville's own radio station at the time.

Current WSB radio personality and one of Douglas County's favorite citizens, Captain Herb Emory, recently heard about Tex's passing and said, "[Tex] was a great teacher of the art of entertainment to those of us lucky enough to have spent some time around him. He had the power to summon musicians to a little radio station and the magic to transform a bland little room on Hospital Drive into what some of his fans loved just as much as the Grand Ole Opry. Thanks for the lessons and memories, Tex…"

Tex was inducted into the Georgia Western Music Hall of Fame in 1989 and received an award from the Atlanta Society of Entertainers in 2001.

Foreman was also honored by Jeff Champion with a *Facebook* page titled "Tex Forman – Fan Page". Champion states, "I've been a thankful friend and fan of Tex since the mid-1970s. He and my father, Jerry

Champion built an addition to our home and clock shop." Videos and pictures are included on the *Facebook* page along with memorabilia from his career.

The citizens of Douglas County lost a true country and western star a few days ago after a long and full life.

So long, Tex

Chapter 118

GROOVER'S LAKE

I was driving down Vulcan Drive yesterday and began to think about the great weather we have been having. Then my mind naturally turned to Groover's Lake as I crossed Beaver Run Creek.

Back in the late 1930s continuing for twenty years or so Groover's Lake was THE place to be for summer fun.

Now you can barely get to the lake even though a few subdivision houses back up to the water's edge. I doubt those homeowners realize they are sitting on what used to be a summer resort.

I'm not sure of the exact date but at some point John Freeman Groover decided to dam Beaver Run Creek running through his property and created a large lake that many came to enjoy.

Groover's Lake was advertised as a summer resort complete with 16 cabins that could be rented, a large boathouse for fishing and speed boats, and a store with a dancehall on the second floor.

Local historical fiction author Steven D. Ayers discusses the lake in his book *We Danced until Dawn* stating, "It was pretty exciting to make your way down to Groover's Lake and traverse the iron and wooden bridge which went over the spillway and big gorge on Beaver Run Creek. It was one lane with side railings and very high. You were very careful to keep your Model A on the runner boards of the bridge. As you pulled across the gorge, you entered into a sort of magical pine forest, as you drove over to the big parking lot and beach. Yes, I said beach, a big nice white sandy beach for swimmers and sun bathers."

Looking through some old newspapers I found notices of speedboat races sponsored by the Atlanta Motor Boat Club going back to 1938. Ralph Cutter, a southern motor boat racing champion often defended his title at Groover's Lake and even the women raced, including Mr. Groover's wife, Katie. Some of the more popular speed boats had names such as *Dixie Dew* and *Water Flasher*.

The May,1942 issue of *The Technique*, a Georgia Tech newspaper discussed how the school's Co-Op Club would be visiting Groover's Lake to honor new members. The festivities included swimming and softball followed by an evening dance.

Apparently the windows along the second floor dance hall could be "folded up and suspended for a full view of the lake making dances an open-air affair" per Ayers' book. When live bands weren't available there was a jukebox belting out the musical hits of the day.

The Atlanta Fly and Bait Casting Club also had championship fishing contests at the lake, too. A 1939 article bemoans the fact that no fishing tales could be told with embellishment after a certain championship because all the important fishermen would be in one place that weekend – Groover's Lake, and they would already know the truth!

By 1940, Groover's Lake was also the home of the "Miss Neptune" beauty contest and advertised afternoon and evenings filled with fireworks, barbecues, swimming, boating, and the famous drill maneuvers of the Georgia Rainbow Drill Team. Swimmers enjoyed a high jumping tower and a cable where you could ride across the water and drop off when you were ready.

There was boxing, too! High up on what was described as "Boxing Hill" was a real regulation boxing ring featuring amateur and professional matches that attracted hundreds of spectators. One particular Atlanta boxer, Ben Brown made Groover's Lake his training facility. He was a middleweight boxer who in 1938 was ranked in the world's top ten boxers in the 160 pound weight class. Brown had been a sports star at Hoke Smith High School where he was the football quarterback, the center for the basketball team and was the catcher for the baseball team. In 1939, Brown had to box Teddy Yarosz for the championship and by 1940 he was defending his title against Ken Overlin.

I understand progress, but part of me wishes we had a local place like Groover's Lake to enjoy again.

Chapter 119

RUTH BLAIR'S HISTORIC FIND

I'd have to say with some certainty that the one woman in Douglas County who devoted her entire life to history research and preservation has to be Ruth Blair.

She was director of the Georgia Department of Archives and History and carried the title "State Historian" for many years back when the archives were housed at Rhodes Hall.

During the 1920s, Miss Blair had the distinction of discovering an original signature of Button Gwinnett, one of the three men from Georgia who signed the Declaration of Independence. Not only did her discovery make the Atlanta papers, but the find made the news across the nation due to the rarity of Gwinnett's signature.

Today, we know of at least 51 original Button Gwinnett signatures. There aren't as many as some signers because Button Gwinnett didn't have a lengthy business career, and he died soon after the Declaration of Independence was signed.

The signatures are a prized possession for those who desire a complete collection of all 56 men who signed the Declaration of Independence. The signatures are a bit pricey, too. In 2012, a Button Gwinnett signature was expected to sell at auction for close to $800,000.

Ruth Blair found the signature in a seven hundred page manuscript volume which contained information regarding land grants from 1758 to 1772. As most great finds go it was done quite by accident and might not have ever been found due to the way it was indexed.

Button Gwinnett had signed for another man who had received a land grant by the name of John Barber. The signature reads, "Button Gwinnett for John Barber". The date attached to the signature is 1767, and since the item was indexed under Barber's name Gwinnett's signature had been overlooked for decades. Finally, it could be authenticated.

Miss Blair was the daughter of Hiram Columbus Blair (1836-1901) who lived along Sweetwater Creek in Lithia Springs. The Confederate veteran had also served as a state representative for Douglas County in 1895. Miss Blair attended Austell High and later attended Cox College in College Park.

Miss Blair was also instrumental with the formation of the Atlanta Historical Society. By 1953, she had built up the society's collection of photographs to several thousand items which are now digitized and accessed by hundreds of people each day for research purposes as well as for those who simply like to explore Georgia history via photographs.

Through the years she served as the official state historian Miss Blair received many honors including an honorary degree from Oglethorpe University in 1935 and a Woman of the Year award in 1956.

Due to Miss Blair's efforts millions of pieces of state historical items from photographs to letters and other printed materials are made available each day for Georgia citizens to view and research.

Miss Blair understood something very important. We can't expect people to enjoy history, to learn from history, and to appreciate history if we don't make it accessible not just for viewing but for research as well.

Section Eleven

SUBURBIA, SHOPPING CENTERS, AND THE SUPERHIGHWAY

Chapter 120

LIVING YOUR DREAM

My Sunday began very normally for me. I began to pour over the pages and pages of Douglas history notes I've accumulated over the last several months waiting for a topic to raise its hand and speak to me. I keep scrolling through page after page, but the notes were very still and quiet.

I got bored and clicked over to *Facebook* and complained that nothing was speaking to me, and as my friends often do…someone inspired me. Susan, a friend who shares the benefit of growing up in Red Oak, Georgia with me asked, "Got any Olympic athletes from Douglas County? That might be interesting, if there are."

Hmmm…well, it might be interesting especially since Douglas County can claim an Olympian.

I'm sure it wouldn't be a surprise to anyone who reads my posts here that I'm not athletically inclined.

It just wasn't my thing growing up.

Recess during my elementary school days consisted of a few tense moments when teams were chosen for daily kickball games where I was usually one of the last ones picked, or periods of paralyzing fear that my teacher would make me climb the various obstacle course stations that involved climbing up and over a ladder or tower.

If sports weren't my thing then climbing and heights were certainly my downfall.

It just wasn't going to happen.

Life became a bit simpler when I discovered a well written note from my mom could excuse me from those hard to deal with areas of the obstacle course and friends were always willing to step in and kick the ball for me or more importantly RUN for me when we broke off into teams.

However, I do admire athletes and love to watch sporting events from time to time.

For the next two weeks I'll get my fill with the 2012 Olympic Games in London watching everything from Archery to Soccer to Wrestling and let's not forget those very interesting swim meets.

Watching the Olympic Games makes it even more enjoyable when we realize we have our own Olympian who hails from Douglas County.

When you think of an Olympian from Douglas County you think of someone who might have competed in any number of areas such as swimming, track and field, gymnastics, etc. but Elana Meyers is an American Bobsledder.

Yes, you read that right…bobsledder as in ice and snow.

Meyers was one of the less experienced athletes on the U.S. Bobsled team during the 2010 Olympics in Vancouver, with barely three years of experience, but that didn't stop her from winning her first World Cup Bronze medal in 2008 as a brake woman for driver Shauna Rohbock and then topped the previous performance with a Gold medal at the World Cup in Whistler, Canada and Silver at the 2009 World Championships also with Rhobock.

A *Douglas Sentinel* article advises, "Meyers grew up playing softball, and was a standout at Lithia Springs High School before moving on to Georgia Washington University where she was a standout shortstop and finished with a .356 batting average. She actually recorded the first hit, run and win in George Washington softball history."

Growing up and playing on the Olympic softball team was always a dream, Meyers said. "I was fortunate enough to tryout, but didn't make it. So when I realized that dream might not happen I looked around and saw that they were looking for bobsled athletes. So, I checked it out and came to Lake Placid and just never left."

She walked away from the 2010 Olympics with a Bronze medal.

I love how Elana Meyers hit a wall. Her dream wasn't going to happen, so she changed her dream and moved forward.

I wish team USA much success in London, and send out a loud shout out to Elana Meyers as she continues to train for the Winter Olympics in 2014.

While it was very easy to find news stories, videos, websites, etc. regarding Meyers it was a little more difficult to find information, at first, regarding a second Douglas County athlete I wanted to share with you.

Have you ever heard of Oliver Clinton Hill?

What about Johnny Hill?

In a way he's Douglasville's answer to Moonlight Graham whose career was used as a focus in the movie "Field of Dreams."

If you were growing up in Douglasville during the 50s, 60s I'm told that you might have known Mr. Hill. From what I'm told most people called him Johnny, and many considered him a real sports icon because he had a professional sports career before returning here to Douglasville to lead a quiet life.

Mr. Hill was born Oliver Clinton Hill in 1909 in Powder Springs, Georgia. I'm not sure at what point he became known as "Johnny" or why, but I do know the Winn Family genealogy indicates a Johnny Hill who played for the Atlanta Crackers married Verda Smith, but does not give the year.

I began searching through the Atlanta Cracker rosters from 1916 forward looking for the last name Hill. Finally, I hit the name Oliver Hill around 1938 and discovered an Oliver Hill playing for the Crackers had been born in Powder Springs. I felt I was getting closer, but once I mentioned something on *Facebook* a dear reader mentioned a *Find a Grave* site for Oliver Clinton Hill. At that point I had to admit there were too many coincidences NOT to think Oliver Clinton Hill and Johnny Hill were one and the same.

Mr. Hill's baseball career certainly appears to be one where he didn't know what give-up meant. During his eleven seasons playing professional ball he spent the most time with the Atlanta Crackers helping them win the league, play-off titles as well as the Dixie Series.

He was sold to the Boston Bees in September, 1938, and made his debut with them in April the next year. As the site states he only lasted three or four days with the Bees before he was sold again to the Milwaukee Brewers. He had worked his way up to the big leagues, and spent less than a week there.

There several American League teams after that prior to a three year stint in the Army during World War II followed by twelve years as a player-manager for various minor league teams.

He left the game for good in 1948 and moved to Douglasville. I've been told he worked for Thad and Patsy Smith at their furniture store loading and delivering furniture for a few years.

Hill passed away from cancer in 1970.

My Sunday may have started off normally, but I ended up getting to examine two very different athletes during two different time periods, but each had goals and dreams and pursued them.

I think the most important thing is doing something you love. That's the important thing. Elana didn't get to represent her county playing softball. She ended up in a very different place but didn't give up satisfying her desire to compete. Johnny Hill didn't give up either when season after season he kept plugging away doing something he loved. He didn't exactly get to spend a lot of time playing in the big leagues, but he got there. He saw the course through to his goal, and sometimes that's all that matters.

Chapter 121

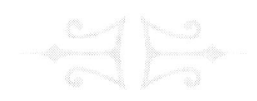

THE GOOD, THE BAD, AND THE UGLY REGARDING CRACKER

It often astounds me when I receive an e-mail from readers. While I do hope that people will find my efforts here worth the time to take a few minutes to read, I'm still amazed that people do read...let alone take the time to make a comment or send me message.

Any type of communication is dearly appreciated.

The other day I received an e-mail from a reader named Susan. She wrote, "I'm from southern California and moved to Douglasville in 1998. Between Burnt Hickory and Fairburn Road on Highway 78 alongside the railroad tracks (on the south side) there used to be a little sign posted near the rail that said "CRACKER." It was green and looked like it was a sign posted by either the railroad or the county. I always wondered what it meant. One day it was gone. Was it a racial thing?"

Great question, Susan!!!

I knew the very sign she was referring to and had wondered myself. I instantly did a little research and asked around and was able to get back with Susan fairly quick. I decided to share the information here.

The word cracker has many meanings including a racial reference to rural poor Whites, but the sign along the railroad tracks was not racially motivated. The sign was placed there by the railroad to alert the engineer they were coming up on a particular area where railroad cars might need to be left or picked up. The sign served as a marker and until just the last few years it was still there along the tracks.

The name "Cracker" referred to a company that stood along the tracks named Cracker Asphalt Company owned by Dr. Young, a chemist, who moved to Douglasville sometime in the mid-1950s.

Cracker Asphalt was an asphalt and petroleum refining company.

Today we are taken a little aback regarding what was going on at the site, but we do need to remember from the 1950s through mid-1970s there were no regulations regarding businesses like Cracker Asphalt. The site covered over 40 acres and most of the waste was buried on the back part of the property.

Everyone knew there were issues with the property. Several longtime residents have told me that if the weather was just right all of Douglasville smelled like roofing tar. It got into your house. The smoke stacks were too close to the ground. Later after citizen complaints the government told Dr. Young to raise the stacks and the problem did get better, but there were still issues.

Later the EPA did get involved and labeled the property as a hazardous area.

Let's get back to the word "Cracker". Why would Dr. Young use the word in the name of his company?

Was he making reference to Georgia Crackers? "Cracker" can be a slur against rural white people as I stated above. In fact, Georgians who lived in the extreme southern part of the state were often referred to as Georgia Crackers by their Florida neighbors. The term came about as the Georgians would drive their cattle across the state line during the late 19th century and early 20th century looking for better grassland during the winter months. They drove their cattle with bullwhips that made cracking sounds earning them the nickname "Crackers".

I've heard Dr. Young was actually from Alabama, so I don't think he named his business after cattlemen from South Georgia.

There were the Atlanta Crackers – a minor league baseball team that called Atlanta home from 1901 to 1965. The team was very popular, but somehow I don't thing Dr. Young was thinking baseball when he named his asphalt company.

Maybe we should focus on the business of Cracker Asphalt which was refining petroleum. A report I found online prepared by the Environmental Protection Agency stated "it is believed Cracker Asphalt disposed of waste sludge by on-site land application." The report goes on to say that from 1955 to 1971 the site where Cracker Asphalt was located was used for various activities but most are undocumented mainly because prior to the 1970s the refining industry was largely unregulated across the United States.

If we connect the word "cracker" to petroleum geology and chemistry the choice of name makes perfect sense. "Cracking" can occur during the refining process basically when long-chain hydrocarbons are converted to short chains. Yes, I know. It sounds very involved scientifically, and it is. Perhaps it might be best if we know that "cracking" is a process that occurs in refining, so it makes sense Dr. Young would use the word as a name for his business.

At some point during the early 1970s Dr. Young put his own name on the business changing it from Cracker Asphalt to Young Refining Company. The EPA report I read stated that, "beginning in 1971, refining asphaltic crude; the facility also refined waste oil and produced JP-4 jet fuel."

Around 1976, the EPA became involved when residents in the area made complaints. The report advises they were concerned about possible leaking tanks, piles of scrap metal and debris all over the site, possible waste buried on or behind the site; including drums containing toxic and radiological wastes, and potential excess cancers and respiratory illness in the area."

Since 2004, the business covering 40 acres along Huey Road and bordered the tracks along Bankhead has changed hands two or three times, but has always retained the Young name.

Chapter 122

MY INTERVIEW WITH HARRIS DALTON

Historically speaking the years from the mid to late 1960s were a tumultuous period in United States history, and while Douglas County weathered those years far calmer than most places across the country, it wasn't exactly quiet.

Various stories speak loudly as you skim through the microfilmed copies of the *Douglas County Sentinel* from 1964 to 1968. Drag racing was rampant across the county in 1964 including races down Campbellton Street in downtown Douglasville.

When the police weren't dealing with drag racers there were moonshiners to contend with. As late as the 1960s, moonshining stills were being located and busted up across the county on a regular basis.

Interstate 20 was brand new and causing people to question the impact the superhighway would have on the county. One article mentioned there were new model cars and new model highways, but old model drivers. Could Douglas County folks who were used to country roads keep up with the fast speeds?

Of course, Douglas County was impacted by some of the more serious stories of the day. Events in Vietnam were taking some of our best and brightest while the folks at home were holding their breath as school integration became the law of the land, and on the night of April 4, 1968 folks from all racial backgrounds wondered what the assassination of Dr. Martin Luther King, Jr. would bring.

Later that summer Douglasville became the focus of the nation for twenty-four hours as the Poor People's Campaign and their Mule Train would be detained here for having the audacity to utilize Interstate 20 on their way to Atlanta.

During those years, W. Harris Dalton, Jr. was at the helm of the *Douglas County Sentinel* keeping folks informed with the news of the day.

A few weeks ago I had the honor of meeting Mr. Dalton face-to-face to discuss his time in Douglas County as well as his new book titled *Excitement!! In War and Peace* which his publisher describes as a "humorous and amazing potpourri of fascinating reading."

I have to agree.

The memoir follows Mr. Dalton's journey through a stint in the Navy serving as a radar man on the aircraft carrier *USS Sicily* during the Korean War, editing six different newspapers as well as an oil and gas magazine that was distributed around the world.

While many Americans are aware of the Korean War very few actually understand the events leading up to U.S. involvement or various events during the war. I found Mr. Dalton's recollections a great starting place to learn more including his interactions with members of the famous World War II group, the Black Sheep Squadron who were stationed on the *USS Sicily*.

While Mr. Dalton's book is not entirely about his time in Douglasville he mentions certain situations throughout the book.

In a chapter recalling the continued battle with moonshiners across the state Dalton recalls how Douglas County Sheriff Mac Abercrombie told about "whiskey runners who carried logs on the backs of their cars and would push them off and drag them with a chain when being pursued over winding dirt roads".

Mr. Dalton was also a close personal friend of Red Palmer, Douglas County's famous pioneer developer of the tranquilizer gun who gained fame with his "bring 'em back alive" exploits. Mr. Dalton describes Red Palmer as "friendly, loquacious and strangely unpredictable." The book contains a vivid recall of the wild animal menagerie Mr. Palmer kept on his "600-acre compound of lions, tigers, elephants, hyenas, cougars, cheetahs, llamas, guanaco, elk, monkeys, alpaca and other animals", but I'll let you get the book and read about that yourself.

During Mr. Dalton's time at the *Douglas County Sentinel* the paper received a Georgia Press Association General Excellence Award for best weekly paper, and Mr. Dalton received a nod for best feature story. Truly, the paper was living up to its motto as "the best paper in the world for Douglas Countians!"

Chapter 123

DEPUTY TOMMY AND THE BEAR

Doing a quick survey over my life I think I've seen a black bear once. It was during a trip through Cades Cove in Gatlinburg, Tennessee with a couple of friends. We happened upon a crowd of folks surrounding a scrawny little oak sapling about thirty feet high. As we got closer we could see the little tree was swaying back and forth, and the cause happened to be a small black bear cub clinging to the tree's trunk in an attempt to escape the human gawkers. The bear cub should have been expected since we had entered its habitat, but perhaps even more surprising would be if we happened upon a black bear in our yard here in Douglasville.

That actually happened to Claude Pope in June of 1967 at his home along Midway Road. For two nights Mr. Pope had heard some commotion outside before finally catching sight of the bear chasing his mule. Mr. Pope attempted to pump some buckshot into the bear, but it scurried up a tree in an effort to hide.

So, what does one do in Douglas County in 1967 when a rather large bear of at least 300 pounds is hanging on for dear life in one of your trees?

Mr. Pope called Palmer Chemical Company owned by the renowned Red Palmer of tranquilizer gun fame. Not only was Mr. Palmer's business located here in Douglas County, he was also a resident and known to many.

Soon Herschel Bomar and Robert Cook arrived on the scene with a tranquilizer gun. The plan was to put the bear to sleep, allow it to slip from the tree, and add the bear to Red Palmer's collection of interesting animals on his property.

Even though a spotlight was shining on the tree, the first shot went over the bear's head, but the second shot hit the target, and soon the bear was snoozing away. Unfortunately, the animal didn't fall. The bear's arm had become caught in the Y of a limb.

So, what do you do in Douglas County when you have a 300 pound bear knocked out and hanging from your tree?

Apparently, that's when you call the Douglas County Sheriff's office.

Deputy Tommy Nicholson went to the rescue around 2 a.m.

The first plan was to shoot the limb out from underneath the bear's arm, but one shot from Deputy Nicholson determined the limb was very sturdy and wouldn't budge.

There was only thing left for Deputy Nicholson to do.

He climbed up the tree with the hope that he could slip a rope around the bear's foot and disengage the 300 pound wild and sleeping bear from its snagged position. The hope was to ease the bear down to the ground.

Unfortunately, before the bear could be guided to the ground it toppled to the dirt. Mr. Pope's wife who had been standing at a distance watching the whole event unfold stated to the *Sentinel* later, "[The bear] hit with a thud like a bale of cotton."

The bear was quickly loaded up and taken to Palmer's Zoo. Unfortunately, the bear had received some injuries in the fall and died soon after. UGA's school of medicine determined two things. The bear was not rabid and they also determined the fall had killed the bear. It was not an overdose of tranquilizer.

Deputy Tommy Nicholson, a man I remember as Carol's husband, Debbie's father, and Nicole's grandfather has a title that I would guess won't be toppled anytime soon.

He was the only man as far as the local historical record reads to shake a bear out of a tree in Douglas County.

Chapter 124

THE RIGORS AND REWARDS OF GROWING UP IN BILL ARP

One of the perks of researching and writing about Douglas County history is the fact that I constantly get to meet interesting people. A couple of weeks ago I met up with Neal Beard and his lovely wife Charlotte over lunch.

Neal is known to many in Douglas County as the author of a column that appeared in *Chapel Hill News and Views* called "Local Lore". Many more know him as pastor currently leading the flock at Douglasville Baptist Temple.

Neal Beard is also the author of a book titled *Buttermilk and Boxer Shorts* which detail his experiences as he grew up in the Bill Arp community of Douglas County during the 1940s and 50s.

Neal explains he "writes stories plucked from [his] past…My southern roots drink deeply from a fast fading culture…There are few left who remember the rigors and rewards of being raised in the country – in the south – in Bill Arp."

These types of first-person biographical accounts are vital to the historical record of a community, and I applaud Neal for his book. Plus, I found it a very entertaining read. More often than not I found myself laughing out loud.

Neal's book begins with the Beard family's move to Douglas County in October, 1945. Throughout the book Neal discusses various aspects of living in Bill Arp mentioning he survived "the bloodiest and best seven years" of his life at Bill Arp grammar school. He recalls, "Serious disciplinary problems among us first and second graders were handled in a long skinny room in the back called the cloak room…In this wretched retreat [Miss Floy] lectured longer than it took the *Titanic* to sink – with no hope of a lifeboat. She then applied the board of education to the seat of learning."

Neal fondly remembers swimming in Bear Creek and speaks of Kings Highway and Big A Road during a time when asphalt was far into the future.

Describing his home Neal states, "Some homes in Bill Arp had five rooms and a bath. Ours had five rooms and a path." Neal also introduces us to concepts long forgotten such as the party line and hog killing time which had to be done on a cold day.

Throughout Neal's story we are introduced to various folks who resided In Bill Arp including Herbert Fouts who had a water powered mill on Bear Creek where Neal worked for a time.

Neal also fondly remembers the hub of Bill Arp's community – Bart Duke's Store by introducing us to a cast of true life characters stating, "Over half a century ago Bill Arp was home to some distinguished visionaries, philosophers and profound thinkers. The Supreme Court of the United States with its pomp, pageantry and professionalism wasn't as impressive to me as were these country sages…Their seats of higher learning were empty upturned Coke and R.C. Cola cases. They smoked cigarettes rolled from Bull Durham, Prince Albert or Country Gentlemen while they deliberated current concerns."

Among the many stories in his book Neal admits to being "the only male who ever held membership in the WMU at Prays Mill Baptist

Church…If you need to know anything about WMU work in the late 40s I'm the authority."

You'll have to buy the book for the rest of the story.

I salute Neal on his efforts to memorialize his experiences growing up in Bill Arp. We need this type of historical record to remember times gone by, and to salute folks in our past.

Chapter 125

PARKWAY REGIONAL HOSPITAL – A HISTORY

Glenmore and Sarah Carter spent thirty-eight years in the ministry of the Seventh Day Adventist Church. They lived along with their two sons, Lee Edwin and Glenn Thomas, in places such as India.

Sometimes their assignments were in dangerous and near-dangerous situations.

The *Southwestern Union Record*, a Seventh Day Adventist newsletter, dated September 4, 1935 mentions the Carters. The article states, "A letter just received by Mr. and Mrs. L.N. Carter from their son Glenmore brings the news that because of the Suez situation being so serious word was received from Washington for them not to sail from New York via Europe. It also advised that the missionaries in Addis Ababa have been ordered to leave. This without doubt bespeaks of the seriousness of things in the east Mediterranean. Glenmore Carter and family will now sail from Seattle, Washington September 13, 1935."

In her book titled The *Vansant Family Tree: Branch of Sarah Elizabeth (Vansant-Woods) Carter Ancestors and Descendants*, Mrs. Carter advises, "There came a time when these sons reached college and their bills were more than our salaries, so I did special duty nursing and we always had the bills paid at the end of the school year. One dollar per hour was the pay for the special duty nursing in those days."

An issue of *The Record*, a Seventh Day Adventist newsletter from 1956 indicates Glenmore Carter was the pastor of Houston Central Church and the announcement was being made regarding the purchase of property for a new church and school facility. The church – with a membership of 600 – had outgrown its building.

By 1963, the Carters were in Little Rock, Arkansas where Glenmore had become a regular on local television appearing on various religious shows.

Mrs Carter advises, "After retirement I thought it was my turn to suggest where we would live. That ended with our going back to the county where the old Dog River flowed. But retirement was not for us."

In the 1960s along with 42 other Adventist the Carters bought the old church used by the Methodist in the center of Douglasville – at the corner of Price and Church Streets (where the city parking lot stands today) – with the handsome stained-glass memorial windows and organized a new Adventist church there.

In March, 1964 they named it Lou Vansant Memorial Seventh Day Adventist Church in honor of Sarah's grandmother who is listed as the first practicing Seventh Day Adventist in Douglas County. The property was sold to the City of Douglasville in 1970 and the church moved to the Bright Star property where it's located today.

Mrs. Carter advises, "We saw the need for medical and hospital work in that county on the edge of booming Atlanta. We saw the plans for the big new freeway, Interstate 20, to be built right by us, so invested in 500 acres of land and this paid off. We used the gain to put up a lovely nursing home, The Georgian Villa, on a beautiful lake. Then we built a school, and last of all a 400 bed ultra modern hospital, Atlanta West Hospital, just twelve miles west of Atlanta, right on I-20. It was a dream come true when I had the privilege of planning a modern hospital with every nook and corner designed for the best in nursing care."

In 1973, projections to build the 11-story cylindrical nursing tower with an attached rectangular medical building stood at 17million dollars, however later editions of the Seventh Day Adventist newsletter advised the final cost was closer to 27 million dollars.

The hospital was funded through bonds.

Mrs. Carter advises in her book constructon was very successful, and the hospital opened on time, but "the administration we had chosen failed us and quickly wasted over a million dollars in opening reserve."

Fannie Mae Davis remembers the early days of the hospital in this way, "The advanced architectural design was matched by a far-sighted approach to equipment inside the hospital. Unfortunately, low utilization of the facility resulted in financial problems."

Mrs. Davis continues,"The hospital operated efficiently, but lack of operating funds forced the founders deep in debt and finally, the hospital faced bankruptcy. In 1976, a class action suit was filed against Atlanta West, its corporation and officers, the bond trustee bank, the bonding company [The First Dayton Corporation, Dayton, Ohio], and others. The case hung in Court for six years, but finally came to trial in federal court in Ohio in December, 1981. The Carters relinquished legal responsibility three and half months before the bonds went into default, but never hesitated to enter the court and acting as their own attorney, defended every charge. After a lengthy trial, the federal court jury gave a clear verdict on every point, favoring the Carters and the hospital corporation. Their defense was complete and decisive, and it was said to have helped save millions for the bond holders, who ultimately received their full original investment and considerable interest."

The Hospital Corporation of America ended up purchasing the hospital, and eventually it was one of the best operated hospitals in America.

My research indicates they purchased the hospital for 22 million dollars.

An article from the *Douglas County Sentinel* notes "real stability happened in 1980 when the Hospital Corporation of America bought the hospital and changed its name to Parkway Regional." The Georgian Villa nursing home was also part of the purchase and its name was changed to Garden Terrace. One important first for the original Georgia Villa was it was the first facility of its kind in the nation to receive a Medicare check for nursing home care.

Parkway Regional eventually met its demise due to the swing of a wrecking ball in 2004. I'm told the recyclable steel was sold and shipped to China for their building boom. Today a Home Depot store sits on the spot where the hospital once served as a unique landmark along the expressway.

In 2008, the nursing home changed names again to Douglasville Nursing and Rehabilitation.

The Carters finally took that retirement…

Mrs. Carter advises, "There comes a day when retirement becomes a reality. We thought it would be wonderful to be up in the mountains of Tenneessee near the Smokies and figured that was the answer. It was beautiful and relaxing, looking out over the hills and mountains. But one thing we did not take into consideration, the legs that had been faithful for over seventy years now did not desire to carry up the hills. On icy winter days we did not always go in the right direction. So in 1981 we moved to Texas, level and plenty of heat to care for arthritis. After six years back home in the college town of Keene, where Glenmore grew up, we are doing grand. At present, (1986) we travel for our hobby and thoroughly enjoy taking life a bit easier.

Glenmore passed away in 1996 while Sarah reached the age of 98 before passing away in 2007.

Chapter 126

DRAGRACING – THE TRAFFIC TIPPING POINT

Think back to a time when Douglas County was on the verge of change. There was no mall, Interstate 20 was just open from Atlanta to Highway 5, and there was still a heavy agricultural presence in the county.

Former sheriff Tommy Waldrop was still with the Georgia State Patrol, Douglas County Commission Chairperson Tom Worthan's father was serving as Douglasville's Mayor Pro Tem, J.C. Hicks was the assistant police chief and Robert S. Alexander was serving on the Douglasville city council.

The number one problem during the summer of 1967 had to do with drag racing, and I'm not just referring to the less desolate roads or even folks trying out the new stretch of Interstate 20. While it wouldn't be hard to find a person in Douglas County today who would admit to doing a little racing along the expressway or even down one of the straight stretches along a country road, I'm referring to drag racing in downtown Douglasville.

To be more exact, I'm referring to drag racers using Campbellton Street as their raceway of choice. In 1967, Campbellton Street contained a very sharp curve with a blind spot in front of Dr. Claude Vansant's home. Even so, that didn't seem to stop the drag racers.

One Sunday evening two racers caused a head on collision at the sharp curve. The car in the wrong lane struck a third vehicle head-on and flew up into a thicket of pine trees in Dr. Vansant's yard. The impact ripped the car in two, and there was one fatality. Both drivers who were racing were charged with involuntary manslaughter.

More than one family was changed for life.

For some time open highways in the county and summer weather had been blamed for the racing fever. Many were hesitant to crack down and felt it was just a matter of "boys being boys", but the racers covered many age groups – not just boys. Folks had to admit once the racers began using city streets as their venue something had to be done.

A delegation of Campbellton Street residents appeared at a city council meeting to make their case for action.

Councilman Alexander told Assistant Police Chief Hicks, "We don't want a speed trap, but we do want to catch speeders." Mayor Pro-Tem Worthan chimed in that the speeders needed to be caught no matter who they were. All agreed the police would need the backing of the community when giving tickets for speeding and racing.

Many at the meeting voiced wanting to solve the problem of the curve on Campbellton which had been an issue even before the drag racing had begun. Many knew that it would take the county and city working together to make that happen, and apparently they did from the look of Campbellton Street today.

While the issue on Campbellton was solved, other traffic problems remain all over the county, and they don't necessarily involve the physical characteristics of the road. Over the last few weeks I've seen folks too impatient to wait turning dangerously in front of oncoming traffic, creeping along until almost at a standstill looking down at their phones, and changing lanes erratically sometimes two or three at a time with absolutely no thought to their surroundings.

I don't believe the issue can be solved with more police presence. At some point personal choice and responsibility have to be put into play, and we all just seem to be too busy in our hurry to get where we are going to care.

A head-on fatality wreck was the tipping point in 1967.

What will be our tipping point today?

Chapter 127

A QUILT FOR DOUGLAS COUNTY

When my Nanny Blanton passed away in 1962 due to a massive heart attack my family was in shock. Nanny hadn't been sick. In fact, as she entered her sixth decade Nanny remained just as busy as she always had taking care of her home and family. She was an expert seamstress having worked in Canton's cotton mill for years and making clothing for family as well as paying customers when the opportunity appeared.

One of the projects Nanny had been working on was a rather large quilt. It was several years before my mother could look at the quilt long enough to hand it over to an aunt to finish up – mainly because she missed her mother so, and because the quilt held so many memories.

The quilt was made from scrap pieces of fabric, but each held meaning for our family. Everyone could look at the quilt and point out fabric that had been used to make a shirt, a dress, a skirt, a jacket, or even a tablecloth.

The quilt held all sorts of memories – the first day of school, a honeymoon outfit, a flannel shirt that kept my father warm and even a baby dress for me.

Even though it was just scraps of fabric the whole quilt is a touchstone that provides the spark that triggers memories for my family.

In 2002, the Douglas County Art Guild did something similar for you, for me and all of the other citizens of Douglas County.

The Douglas County Art Guild was founded in 1973. It is a satellite of the Cultural Arts Council of Douglasville & Douglas County and exists to allow local artists to share common art interests and goals.

Using money received from a grant awarded by the Georgia Council for the Arts along with money raised from local sponsors, members of the Art Guild created a very unusual quilt fashioned entirely out of paper. The grant money was used to pay Mona Waterhouse to "facilitate, teach and direct the creation of the quilt."

Waterhouse is a nationally acclaimed artist living in Peachtree City. Many of her works are owned by individual collectors and corporations from Hartsfield-Jackson International Airport to Kimberly Clarke's corporate office. Just recently, Mona Waterhouse was included in the book, *500 Paper Objects: New Directions in Paper Art*.

Upon viewing the quilt on permanent display at the Douglas County Courthouse, Waterhouse's talents are evident as well as her ability to successfully assist the Art Guild members with their creation.

The quilt tells the history of Douglas County one square at a time in a very lovely and unique way.

So many events and places are included. Street scenes from Douglasville's history, well known businesses such as the Alpha Theater and Mr. Mac's mule barn, the courthouse, the Carnes cabin, the skint chestnut tree and many more elements of our history are included.

The hope was the quilt would "revive a community spirit in the midst of a county experiencing tremendous growth. Its purpose [would] be to teach people and demonstrate Douglas County is a great place to live."

The quilt is on permanent display at the Douglas County Courthouse on Hospital Drive. You can find it on the second floor. A book placed on the table below the quilt provides more information concerning the project including the various squares.

Stop by and take a look!

Chapter 128

LOCAL HISTORY IS A BIG DEAL

I had someone the other day ask me why I waste my time writing about Douglas County history since nothing of any value ever happened here.

I smiled and allowed the person to continue with their statements. They actually made a few decent points arguing that on the whole Douglasville and Douglas County has made a pretty good practice of allowing local history to be demolished, thrown away, neglected, and forgotten, but then he spouted some more fighting words stating state and local history was irrelevant since most folks grow up and move away.

Why teach it? We don't use it.

You never really need local history later in life, right?

Look–I get it.

There are people who could care less what happened on any given street corner in the 1870s or even the 1970s for that matter.

I understand.

I don't exactly get the warm fuzzies over the steps to bleed the brakes in a car or the intricacies involved with building a skyscraper, but I know those things hold value to certain members of society, and they benefit me as well.

I've taken on the job to champion history and history education. I try to get naysayers to understand why it's so important to know a little about it, or at least admit I make a good argument for knowing some local history and the purpose behind saving it.

Local history IS a big deal!

Obviously the past has value to society. Thousands of people throughout history have gone to great lengths to record history through newspapers, diaries, journals, saved letters, family Bibles, and oral traditions.

Here in Douglas County the descendants of Alston Arnold hold on to a precious millstone.

During the 1880s a terrible drought lasting six months hit north Georgia including Douglas County. Many of the small mills dotting the countryside could no longer grind grain and corn because the water powering the millstones had dried up. However, due to its position at the mouth of Anneewakee Creek, Arnold Mill was able to put precious corn meal into the hands of hungry settlers.

History is our narrative. It provides answers to how people lived as well as provides for us the roots to certain ideas concerning laws, customs, political ideas and local symbols.

Our history provides the explanation why a tree is at the center of the city seal. A tall skint chestnut stood at the highest point on the ridge close to where the Old Courthouse Museum stands today. It served as a directional marker at the intersection of two important Indian trails, and of course, became the original seat of our local government.

The repetition of history is important. It teaches the value of certain social changes and governmental policies. Today we see our elected officials at every level struggle to make choices for the rest of us amid a climate of partisan politics, but it's really nothing new. There have always been struggles where government is concerned. In fact, the location for the county seat for Douglas County was finally settled out of a lawsuit that drug on during the early 1870s.

History when presented properly lends itself to critical analysis. Local history brings a sense of realism to state, national, and even world events.

Most of us are familiar with the period of Prohibition in the United States lasting from 1920 to 1933, but few of us realize alcohol was prohibited in Georgia as early as the late 1800s.

Examining how our local forefathers handled this issue in the late 1800s with comparisons and contrasts can help us examine why Prohibition didn't work then or during the 1920s, and lends to the argument regarding Sunday sales today regardless of which side you fell on during the last election.

It is my firm belief that a study of local history might actually encourage preservation by helping to point out how certain places are linked to the past. We have let too many of our important places disappear or have forgotten their importance.

We should be about the business of celebrating the history we have saved and fight to save more of it for future generations.

Chapter 129

THE MULE TRAIN

There are five historical markers scattered around Douglasville. Two markers identify the Blue Star Memorial Highway – one at the west end of town on Highway 78 and the other on Douglas Boulevard in front of Arbor Place Mall. The remaining markers can be found on the grounds of the old courthouse on Broad Street. The formation of Douglas County is the subject of one marker, another commemorates how Young Vansant gave the county forty acres to be used for the county seat, and the third marker honors our veterans.

I'm wondering why we don't have a marker along Highway 92 in front of Stewart Middle School or in front of the National Guard Armory on Church Street, because for one brief sliver of time Douglas County was thrust into the national limelight stuck in the middle of a game of tug of war between Governor Lester Maddox and leaders of the Civil Rights movement.

On May 13, 1968 a group of horse drawn wagons set out from Marks, Mississippi with over one hundred participants ranging in age from 88 to six months old. The mule train's destination was Washington D.C. Their target date of arrival was June 19th to commemorate Juneteenth, the day that news of the Emancipation Proclamation reached many slaves in the Deep South. There would be several caravans converging on Washington

D.C. to take part in Dr. King's Poor People's Campaign. The fact that Dr. King has been assassinated just weeks prior made everyone in the group more resolved in their purpose.

Thirty-one days later on Friday, June 14, 1968 the mule train slowly made its way east on Highway 78 and entered Douglasville without incident. The wagons made their way to R.L. Cousins School where they stopped to camp overnight on the playground in front of the school. Today, the school is known as John W. Stewart Middle School.

As the mule train participants watered and fed their mules, many curious Douglas County residents drove by the location while others lined the banks surrounding the playground. Several persons took photographs of the marchers as cameramen from at least one national network took background footage for a documentary being compiled for showing later that summer.

Governor Maddox and the Georgia State Patrol were adamant that the mule train would continue into Atlanta down Highway 78 using the Georgia law that prohibits operation of non-motorized vehicles on interstate highways to back up their edict, but mule train leader Willie Bolden, a Southern Christian Leadership Conference official wanted to take advantage of the new stretch of Interstate 20. Bolden argued the mule train had used the interstates in Mississippi and Alabama without incident and the route would save time.

Once they were underway again the mule train did attempt to use the Interstate. Police formed a human wall across the highway and told the marchers they were under arrest. The marchers fell to their knees alongside the route praying and singing as law enforcement transported them to the National Guard Armory.

Members of the news media descended upon Douglasville including print and television journalists.

Douglas County Sheriff Claude Abercrombie told the leaders that all charges would be dropped if they would agree to use Highway 78 rather than Interstate 20.

When that didn't work Governor Maddox offered to provide flatbed trucks to pick up the mules and wagons and transport them to Atlanta.

The offer was also refused.

It looked like the standoff wasn't going to be solved soon. Sheriff Abercrombie made arrangements for one of the restaurants in town to feed the mule train participants.

As the hours ticked by marchers sat on blankets and quilts on the armory's concrete floor, some singing and praying while others played cards at a table in the rear of the building.

At some point the Atlanta Humane Society showed up and attempted to buy five of the mules after pronouncing them too exhausted to continue on the trek. The marchers refused to sell.

Finally after many phone calls back and forth to Atlanta and Washington D.C. by both sides, Governor Maddox blinked. He finally agreed that if the mule train would leave Douglasville at 3:45 a.m. and if they could make it into Atlanta by 7:00 a.m., they could use Interstate 20.

Sheriff Abercrombie then agreed to drop all charges.

The Mule Train along with their Georgia State Patrol escorts left Douglasville at 3:45 a.m. traveling along Interstate 20. They reached Atlanta one hour and 15 minutes past the deadline set by Governor Maddox, but it was quietly overlooked.

For days afterward folks in Douglas County breathed a sigh of relief that their one moment on the national civil rights stage ended as peacefully and as quietly as it did.

Chapter 130

REMEMBERING THOSE WHO SERVE

Tragic things happen, but over time we realize life somehow does go on. A new normal is created. Most people can go on with their normal routines, but some events have such an impact and leave such an imprint they become pivotal moments whether we are directly involved or not.

Days later I'm still lingering over the procession for Lance Corporal Scott Harper. I'm still feeling the effects of the awesome turnout by folks all along the procession route from Brown Field in Fulton County through Austell, Lithia Springs, along Veterans Memorial Highway and all along Church Street in downtown Douglasville.

Many moments during the procession have become embedded in my mind including:

* Observing a fellow school teacher as she lined her students up along the sidewalk to pay their respects.
* Seeing young teenage boys walking along Church Street carrying small U.S. flags as they looked intently for their place to stand. A couple of the boys had the flags casually put in their back pockets.
* Noticing an obvious veteran standing near me wearing his veteran's cap laden with medals and pins. The Marine emblem was

emblazoned across the back of his jacket. At some point a young man approached him, shook his hand and said a few words to him. I can only assume he was thanking the veteran for his service. He shook the older man's hand and then handed him a flag.

* I was touched by the young children – many of whom would later have no recollection they attended a historic occasion, and make no mistake this was a historic occasion for our city.

Yes, the procession for Scott Harper was sad. It was most certainly tragic, but it was also historic. I firmly believe anytime our community comes together we witness a historic occasion. It was most certainly an outpouring of collective mourning and praise that our society still produces young men like Lance Corporal Scott Harper.

As long as there have been wars, the folks on the home front have recognized the fallen soldier and his or her sacrifice with parades, with statues, and with the written word. While especially poignant last week's procession wasn't the first such recognition the City of Douglasville has experienced.

We have recognized other fallen soldiers.

One in particular stands out.

Tragically, Robert G. "Jerry" Hunter was Douglasville's first son to be lost during the Vietnam War. Hunter Park is named for him. He was the only son of Robert and Zelma Hunter, and was a graduate of Douglas County High School where he received many honors for his artistic and leadership abilities. He was voted Most Talented, was editor of the yearbook and starred in the senior play.

For years his goal had been to attend The Citadel in Charleston, South Carolina. In a 1988 article from *Looking Good Douglas County* Vicki Harshbarger advises, "[Hunter's] dream of wanting to be a pilot began with an essay written on how Lindbergh's flight across the Atlantic would affect the future of aviation."

After graduating from The Citadel with honors Hunter went to Moody Air Force base in Valdosta, Georgia to undergo pilot training, and was soon flying bombing missions over Laos to disrupt the enemy's supply lines. Harshbarger states, "His parents had suggested their son choose a line of work in keeping with his Citadel degree in business administration, but he would not settle for less than his dreams."

Harshbarger's article continues, "He didn't want us to worry," Mrs. Hunter says lovingly of her son. "I'd ask him on the telephone if he'd been shot at, wanting him to say no. He'd say, "Yes, but they missed. Don't worry about it, Mom, sometimes it is fun."

Hunter flew the F-105D, a supersonic fighter-bomber used by the United States Air Force during the early years of the Vietnam War. The aircraft on display at Hunter Park is a F-105 or a Thunderchief, and is representative of the plane Hunter flew over Laos.

The plane was capable of exceeding the speed of sound at sea level and Mach 2 at high altitudes even though it weighs 50,000 pounds. The earliest versions of the F-105 had only one seat. Hunter completed all of his missions alone.

Laos allowed North Vietnam to use its land as a supply route for its war against the South. In return the U.S. regularly bombed those routes and supported regular and irregular Communist forces on the ground there. U.S. bombers dropped more ordinance on Laos between 1964 and 1973 than was dropped during the whole of World War II.

Hunter was 25 years old when he boarded his jet on May 25, 1966 for his 34th and last mission. He had been overseas for just two months, and had been busy during that time bombing supply lines throughout Laos. His last mission involved attacking what one source describes as a truck park in a heavily wooded area near Ban Ban in Laos.

Hunter released his bomb and as he was turning up and away from the target he was hit by enemy fire. He bailed from the jet. Other pilots in his group saw his parachute open and watched him until he disappeared below the tree line. They could hear the beeps from his locator signal. A rescue was attempted, but enemy fire was coming from the area where Hunter's beeper signal was coming from. When a second plane was hit the team was forced to return to base.

It took two agonizing months before Hunter's fate was fully known.

Once the area become safe enough a team was sent in to investigate. People who lived in the area advised the recovery team Hunter had indeed died. They showed the team where he had been buried.

Funeral services for Robert G. "Jerry" Hunter were held on July 22, 1966 at the First Baptist Church of Douglasville. The church was overflowing. One long-time resident of Douglasville tells me the mood of the town during this time was reverent, respectful and somber.

During the days leading up to the funeral members of the Jaycees visited over one hundred Douglasville businesses and left U.S. flags to be displayed. The day of the funeral many of the town's businesses closed out of respect.

A four man fly over took place during the burial at Rosehaven Memorial Park. Harshbarger advises, "Four planes flew across the horizon in unison, three planes returned."

Hunter was the very first Vietnam casualty Douglasville endured during the long war. Also killed in Vietnam was SP4 Gene Thomas Bailey, GMG1 Hubert Eugene Belcher, 1LT Leon G. Holton, PFC Brian Edward Jay, PFC Melvin Johnson, Sgt. Thurlo McClure, PFC Nathan Bedford Simmons, 1 LT Robert Paul Tidwell, and 1 LT David Beavers Wood.

Hunter was also the 11th victim during the war from The Citadel.

Hunter's name can be found on Panel 07E, Row 109 on the Vietnam Veterans Memorial in Washington D.C.

During my research I reconnected with a longtime blogging friend of mine named Eddie Hunter, Jerry Hunter's cousin. He continues to remember his cousin and his military service to our country often at his blog, *Chicken Fat*. Eddie advises, "The Hunter family continued to take interest in veteran's affairs and ceremonies in memory of their only child [up until their own deaths]."

General George S. Patton advised, "It is foolish and wrong to mourn the men who died. Rather we should thank God that such men lived."

I agree. I'm very thankful for the men who serve.

Chapter 131

A LITTLE REGARDING SHERIFF EARL D. LEE

If you have read any of my meager offerings regarding Douglas County history you know I'm not originally from here. I grew up during the 1960s and 1970s in the South Fulton area, so I didn't exactly know the daily news in Douglasville, but one person I did know about was Sheriff Earl D. Lee. Most people from this part of the state know who he was.

Some people take on a persona – they become a larger than life character – a person who ends up with so many stories swirling around regarding their accomplishments and exploits that it's hard to know where the truth ends and the myths begin.

Sheriff Lee is such a person, and as far as most are concerned regarding him the delineation between fact and myth doesn't matter.

Sheriff Earl D. Lee was a giant of a man and most certainly deserves the recognition of having a street named for him. Today the street leading to the new Douglas County Jail will officially become Earl D. Lee Boulevard in a dedication ceremony scheduled for 1:30 p.m. The ceremony will take place at the intersection of S. Cherokee Boulevard and Fairburn Road.

Sheriff Lee was a native to Douglas County born here in January 1931 to Eva Inez Couch Lee and Grover Clinton Lee, a Douglas County commissioner. Sheriff Lee attended schools in Douglas County including Winston Elementary, Mt. Carmel Elementary, and graduated from Douglas County High School in 1948.

Before becoming involved with law enforcement Sheriff Lee worked for Firestone Tire and Rubber Company, and in 1953 he began working for his father-in-law, Wade Belcher who owned a feed and grocery business in Austell, Georgia. Sheriff Lee had married Mr. Belcher's daughter, Betty in 1950. Eventually they would have three daughters.

By 1964, the political bug had bitten Sheriff Lee, and he ran for Deputy Sheriff at the time Claude Abercrombie was running for Sheriff. While it seems a little strange to us today there was a time when deputies ran for office just as the candidates for sheriff.

Claude Abercrombie was elected, and he and Deputy Sheriff Lee began their term on January 1, 1965. At that time the Douglas County Sheriff's Office was located within the Sheriff's residence which was provided by the county. It was located at 6730 Church Street.

Sheriff Lee resigned his position in April, 1972 in order to run for the office of sheriff. Approximately 800 votes separated Lee and Abercrombie but the newly elected Sheriff Lee began his reign as sheriff on January 1, 1973.

During the next several years the Douglas County Sheriff's Office expanded greatly with Lee at the helm. He began in 1973 with eleven deputies, and one of his first moves was to do away with the sheriff's county provided residence. He used the residence by converting it to offices for the Sheriff's Department.

While he served as sheriff, Lee attended workshops, seminars, and schools honing his skills as a lawman both at the state and national level. He attended the FBI National Academy in Washington D.C. and the Management School for newly elected sheriffs in Los Angeles, California. The training and education wasn't just for the Sheriff though. Sheriff Lee also sent his staff to the FBI Academy and the National Police Institute.

Apparently Sheriff Lee was doing something right because the citizens of Douglas County elected him for another four-year term in August, 1976 followed by two more four-year terms in August, 1980 and August, 1984, and he was named Douglas County Citizen of the Year in 1973.

Several new divisions were set up during Sheriff Lee's time in office including a Patrol, Communications, Detective, Warrant and Narcotic Divisions. A detective who handled the schools was also hired, and in 1976 the first female deputy to become a certified peace officer worked for the Sheriff's Department.

1980 saw the first drug dog, Lt. Bandit, serving the citizens of Douglas County. At one point due to the efforts of Lt. Bandit and the department approximately $365,000 in drug related money was confiscated.

In 1983 the Sheriff's Department moved into the facility they are moving out of currently. At that time the new facility was replacing a 30-year-old jail that was overcrowded and inadequate.

While in office Sheriff Lee assisted state legislators to update Georgia laws regarding standards and requirements for sheriffs around the state, and was the first sheriff appointed by the Governor to investigate another sheriff.

Current Douglas County Sheriff Phil Miller stated in a *Douglasville Patch* article, "[Sheriff Lee] was a law man's law man…I heard many FBI agents, many GBI agents and many law enforcement agents say, 'If anything ever happens to me, I want Earl Lee to investigate it.'"

In an article written for the website *Officer.com*, Randy Rider remembered Sheriff Lee, "…as one of the finest investigators that I ever met. He would run 72 hours and look behind him to see who was hanging in there. He would fall on the couch in his office take a few and off we went again. The man loved the chase and when it was over he would find a new one. Several times there were strings of crimes in neighboring counties and we knew he prayed for one to step over the line. "Stay out of Douglas County" meant something then."

Sheriff Lee took part in several high profile investigations including the Missing and Murdered Children in Atlanta, and a 2008 *Douglas Sentinel* article details a few of the others:

Paul John Knowles, a serial killer whose 18 known victims included a Florida highway trooper. On December 18, 1974, Lee and GBI agent Ron Angel was transporting Knowles to a site where the killer claimed he disposed of the weapon used to kill the trooper. Knowles used a paper clip to free himself of his handcuffs and tried to take Lee's gun. He was shot dead by Angel.

Billy Sunday Birt, mass murderer and reputed member of the "Dixie Mafia." Birt reportedly once had a death contract on Lee and planned to kill Lee as the sheriff left church. Fortunately, Birt went to the wrong church that Sunday. Lee later befriended the imprisoned Birt and played Santa Claus for Birt's children.

Louis Poetter, founder of the former Anneewakee Treatment Center, who pleaded guilty in 1988 to several counts of sodomy against boys in his care.

Byron Ashley Parker convicted of the 1984 kidnapping and murder of Christy Ann Griffith in Douglas County. Parker was executed December 11, 2001.

George Dungee, one of the accused killers of the Alday family in Seminole County, while being held in the Douglas County jail confessed his role in the killings to Lee.

Timothy McCorquodale was arrested in 1973 for the torture and murder of an Atlanta girl after Lee received a tip of his whereabouts. McCorquodale was later executed for the crime.

Sheriff Lee was also involved with the arrest of two suspects involved in the death of Judy Smail, killed in 1990 when a rock was pushed off an Interstate 20 overpass and crashed through the windshield of Smail's automobile.

I could go on, but I think I've made my point about Sheriff Earl D. Lee being larger than life and more than deserving of any and every honor the folks in Douglas County should want to bestow on him.

Chapter 132

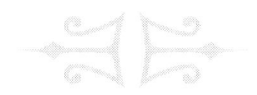

MEMORIES OF THE STORM OF 1973

As I begin to write this piece the weather service is predicting the Atlanta area including Douglasville will not have any significant thawing until Friday.

It looks like the ice is here to stay and stay and stay.

We haven't been off our property since Saturday. We anticipated the snow and ice with lots of excitement tempered with a modicum of skepticism. After all, the weather folks tend to make their predictions. We make the mad dash to load up on supplies, and then we are rewarded with enough milk, bread and eggs to feed a small army a substantial breakfast of French toast, but usually the snow and ice barely make an appearance.

This time was different. The official Hartsfield-Jackson Atlanta International Airport measure for snow and ice we have received is 3.7 inches though my official porch measurement here at Cooper central is more like 5.5 inches, but I won't argue. As a result tomorrow we will be facing our third day of closures and our third day in the house together as a family.

It has been – an experience.

We are not yet at each other's throats, but each one of us is getting a bit restless in our own way. We have plenty of food, we have heat, and we have our power for lap tops, televisions, and we can charge those precious cell phones. It is a great time to watch a movie together, begin a project, or just read a good book.

So far I've heard this recent weather event referred to as Snowmageddon and Snowpocalypse; however those names were used for storms in 2010. Since our current storm has included snow and ice I've seen where it was referred to as SNICE, 2011 – a word combination using "snow" and "ice". Then again, the nickname the Storm of 2011 is a great identifier as well.

Storms are nothing new to Douglasville citizens. Using a nickname for them helps us to remember the details and keep them straight much like we tend to give political treaties and agreements formal names.

Storms similar to what we are enduring now most certainly leave an indelible mark on our psyches. Many of today's 40 and 50-somethings were young children and teens in 1973. Ask any of them why they dash off to the store at the hint of snow or ice and they will recount how that particular storm affected them. They remember the fun of being children and camping out for a time in their living rooms, but they also look back as adults and realize what could happen if you are caught unaware.

The Storm of 1973 began early in the afternoon of January 7, 1973 with a heavy dousing of freezing rain and sleet across the metro area including Douglasville. Weather resources advise between 7 and 9 p.m. that night a liquid equivalent of 2.25 inches of freezing rain and sleet had fallen. By the time the ice stopped on January 8th the Atlanta metro area had received 1 to 4 inches of ice.

As a young girl of 11 I remember how the pine trees bowed low to the ground because they were so heavily laden with ice. It was beautiful, but by nightfall the beauty was marred by terrifying sounds.

Bob Smith of Douglasville remembers hearing what sounded like gun fire until he realized the sound was limbs snapping off the pine trees in his parent's yard. The trees simply could not withstand the weight of the ice, and the pop, snap, crash sounds continued all night long and into the following days. Smith states some of the trees lost limbs while others broke in half. He advises there is a tree in his backyard that still has growth scar damage from the storm. Calvin Quinn was living in Lithia Springs, and states he can still remember the sickening sound a pine tree makes when it breaks and hits the side of a house. It is terrifying to hear that sound over and over again throughout the dark cold night.

The danger of trees falling on homes or other property wasn't the only danger from the Storm of 1973. More difficulty came during the next 96 hours when temperatures never rose above freezing. Everything was frozen solid for days.

Around the third day of the storm I remember the hushed tones of my parents discussing food. My mom told my dad we might have enough to last us through the week if she was careful with it. By the end of the week the milk was gone and so were the eggs. Some of my friends report their fathers eventually walked out of their neighborhoods on foot to get to a corner store, but back in 1973 stores weren't on every corner like they are now.

Just as the trees could not withstand the heavy coating of ice neither could the power lines, and they began to go as well as the transformers. When the transformers blew they gave off illuminating light shows for a quick minute before turning a street totally dark.

Whole sections of Atlanta including Douglasville were dark for several days. There we all were. We couldn't travel, we had no power and there was no heat for many.

Several families got by with gas heaters and fireplaces. A lucky few had generators. Many of my friends remember playing in the snow and ice by day and huddling by a fireplace at night playing board games, talking or putting together jigsaw puzzles. You couldn't talk with friends on the phone because phone lines had snapped along with power lines. Cell phones didn't exist.

Some groups of neighbors ended up at the house that had the most firewood. Sometimes four or five families stayed together in crowded conditions. If the only source of heat was the fireplace all the rooms in the house were closed off to keep the precious heat from escaping.

Bob Smith remembers his father solved their heat and power issue by checking the family into the Holiday Inn on Fulton Industrial Drive as soon as they could manage to get there safely.

Deanna Morris Dickinson remembers her family getting by with a fire in their fireplace. Her mom even used the fire to cook their meals until the family could travel down the road to her grandmother's house where gas heat and a gas stove awaited them.

Calvin Quinn's father worked for the railroad and spent the Storm of '73 away from the family. Calvin's mother prepared eggs over the fireplace for them to eat.

I don't foresee our current ice event to turn into the inconvenience and hardship the Storm of 1973 became, but recalling those events helps to explain why so many of us run around collecting gallons of milk, fill up our car gas tanks, hit the ATM, and collect sticks of firewood.

We know firsthand how a storm can hit and hit hard.

Chapter 133

SWEETWATER CREEK STATE PARK – THIRTEEN THINGS

I have to wonder how many of us living in Douglas County have actually ventured onto the grounds of Sweetwater Creek State Park.

I'm ashamed to admit I have never sat at a picnic table, never hiked a trail, never visited the Manchester Mill ruins or attended a festival there or any other type of event.

Twenty years ago I did visit the park a few times with my son to feed the ducks, and we were on the lake a couple of times in my husband's bass boat, but other than those three occasions my participation with Sweetwater Creek State Park has been close to nil.

I visited the park Friday, and hope to return very soon.

If you are like me and have basically ignored one of Douglas County's most important resources for history, recreation, and tourism here are 13 reasons why we should visit the park:

1. The State of Georgia controls 48 state parks and 15 historic sites, and one of those – Sweetwater Creek State Park – is right here minutes from our homes. Douglas County is in an exclusive club, and as citizens we can brag we have a state park.

2. It's amazing to me that minutes from downtown Atlanta, close to I-20, and seconds from most of our homes Sweetwater Creek State Park provides over approximately 2,500 acres of peaceful wilderness including wooded hiking trails, rocky bluffs, a 215-acre lake, ambling streams, rapids to navigate, forests full of all types of flora and fauna, and historic ruins. Fannie Mae Davis describes the park as an extensive wilderness setting within 15 minutes of downtown Atlanta, and further mentions the park's extensive size allows it to support a diversity of native fauna.

3. Sweetwater Creek runs through the park, feeds the George H. Sparks reservoir, and runs south over the Brevard Fault to the Chattahoochee River. Yes, a geological fault – where pieces of the Earth's crust move against each other. I don't think we need to be too worried, though. The Brevard Fault is ancient, and geologists tell us it hasn't experienced any movement for 185 million years.

4. Every day thousands of people – many of them residents of Douglas County – travel I-20 east into Atlanta. When you pass Thornton Road and reach the top of Douglas Hill looking out towards the Atlanta skyline you are on the very western edge of the Brevard Fault with the Chattahoochee River positioned at its lowest point. Approximately five miles away the eastern edge of the fault is located at I-285 where you see rock cliffs. *The Riverkeeper's Guide to the Chattahoochee River* by Fred and Sherri M. Smith states, "Seen from a globe-circling, picture-snapping satellite high above the Earth's surface, the Brevard Fault looks like a monstrous incision across the torso of Georgia made by the Great Physician operating under battlefield conditions." It's a fairly long incision travelling across the state of Georgia from South Carolina and into Alabama for a total of 160 miles. It is the unofficial dividing line between the Appalachian Mountains and the Piedmont Plateau, and forms a channel for the Chattahoochee River for approximately 100 miles of is 540-mile course.

5. The Brevard Fault is the reason why the Sweetwater Creek area gives us a feeling of being in the mountains. It is why we see such steep grades, rolling hills, and why the water flows so fast in certain sections like a mountain stream. In fact, the Smiths state, "....Sweetwater Creek, for example drops 120 feet from Austell to the Chattahoochee River; it drops 80 feet within the boundaries of Sweetwater Creek State Park alone. North-facing coves on [the creek] harbor trees, shrubs [like Mountain Laurel], herbs and wildflowers usually associated with the Appalachian Mountains to the north. The Fault also made it possible for the historic mills – New Manchester, Ferguson and Alexander's Mill – to be located along the creek since they needed the water power.

6. The park borders the 215-acre George Sparks Reservoir which is supported by a bait shop, and during the summer months, the park rents fishing boats, canoes, and pedal boats. I don't think I've ever traveled down Mt. Vernon Road and not seen someone fishing the waters even during the drought a couple of years ago. Key species include largemouth bass, bluegill, sunfish, and channel catfish. Picnic tables dot the shores of the lake and the ducks are great to watch and feed.

7. The lake is used for recreation, but it was originally constructed as a water supply for the City of East Point. The city continues to draw water for its needs. Back in 1960 the City of East Point purchased what was known as the "McCreary Property" from a private owner. They created Beaver Dam Reservoir which was renamed George H. Sparks Reservoir to honor the Public Utilities Director of East Point who served from 1936 to 1963.

8. Though the park was acquired by the state in 1974, they lacked a Visitor's Center or as it is officially referred – the Interprctive Center. Thanks to the efforts of The Friends of Sweetwater Creek State Park, a viable Interpretive Center was finally built and opened in 2006. Stating its mission was to conserve the environment the park opted for a center that uses the most cutting

edge methods to create an environmentally responsible building including bioretention ponds, solar panels, green roofs, and a composting toilet.

9. The center has been described as one of the most environmentally responsible buildings in the United States, and has received the Leadership in Energy and Environmental Design (LEED) Platinum Certification from the United States Green Building Council. In 2007, there were only 20 such buildings at the platinum level across the world and only one in the Southeast – the Sweetwater Creek State Park Interpretive Center.

What a wonderful distinction, and the Interpretive Center certainly deserves it. The building is built into a hillside to minimize the physical and visual disturbance to the land. The building has a green roof. A 2007 online article from *Architecture Week* advises "Thirty-eight percent of the building's total roof area, or 4000 square feet (370 square meters), is used for rainwater collection." And according to a handout at the Interpretive Center approximately 35% of the building's roofs are vegetated with native plant species.

10. *Architecture Week* also goes on to state, "The Center incorporates a composting toilet system, greywater irrigation, and a rainwater harvesting system. In fact, a 77% reduction of potable water use was achieved by use of a composting toilet system and rainwater harvesting, and the system allows the Visitor Center to forgo a septic system and save about 82,000 gallons of potable water each year."

Most importantly, while the Interpretive Center is mainly there to help people get the most out of their visit to the park with printed guides, snacks to take along on the trail, and some of the best interactive exhibits I've seen, they also have exhibits to educate visitors regarding the various green components of the building.

11. The Interpretive Center isn't just about being green. The center has a gift shop, various educational exhibits, wildlife displays, and

a window-lined meeting room can be rented for small gatherings. The Center is the gathering spot for the hikes organized by the park.

The Native American exhibit at the Interpretive Center has pottery and numerous arrowheads found within the park. One of the most interesting displays is the petroglyph found in 1909 by William Harvey (W.H.) Roberts in what today is the Jacks Hill section of the park where a Native American burial ground can be found.

An article by Richard Thornton regarding the petroglyph advises the location where it was found would suggest it was a religious shrine or marker. The boundary separating the Cherokee and Creek Nations was close by and the petro glyph could have served as a marker. To date no definitive explanation has been determined, and I'm not sure if there ever will be.

Many of the exhibits focus on the town of New Manchester and the mill that was burned by Union forces in 1864. Part of the exhibit includes information regarding Synthia Stewart and her family's experience during that time. I was thrilled to see more pictures of her at the Interpretive Center and actually hear her voice. Other exhibits cover daily life during the mid-1800s and examine the cotton industry while some exhibits showcase the rich biodiversity and geology of the park.

12. For those that enjoy a tad of popular culture one of the founders of Sweetwater Brewery, a micro brewing company begun in the 1990s, spent some of his down time when the business was taking shape by kayaking down Sweetwater Creek since their first brewery was located off Fulton Industrial Boulevard. The company website states, "The name of the brewery became obvious and the motto "Don't Float the Mainstream" became [their] guide."

13. As I stated above I plan to return to the park to enjoy the solitude that can be found in such natural setting and to listen to the history that whispers from the land.

There are more stories to be told regarding the land Sweetwater Creek State Park encompasses, and I want to discover them.

One story in particular has been thrown out to me by a couple of people regarding the fact the lake covers a community that used to exist by the name of Ralph in the early part of the 20th century. One longtime resident of Douglas County, Bob Smith, has advised me he visited the site when the lake was being constructed in the 1960s and can remember walking down an old road that is now covered with water.

They also advise the roadbed showed up again during the drought a few years ago and part of an iron frame for a bridge could be seen as well. There are even rumors of a big moonshine operation next to the creek bank in the 20s and 30s. Since there is information that documents a speakeasy in the area during Prohibition this is more than plausible.

Chapter 134

A TRAGEDY AT NEW HOPE

I grew up about three miles from the runways of Hartsfield, so it's rather an understatement for me to say that the airplanes flew low over my childhood home. We lived under a major landing pattern. The planes flew so low that the engine noise would drown out my favorite cartoons. My mother would joke the pilots could get a glimpse of her through the window in her "gown-tail" washing the breakfast dishes at the sink.

Yes, the planes flew close – and they were loud – and from time to time I played the "what if" game.

What if a plane got into some trouble and crashed into our house? It could happen – it was a possibility, and after the events of Monday, April 4, 1977 it was even more of a real possibility.

That Spring I had other things on my mind. I had recently transferred to a new school and suddenly found myself covered with several hours of homework each afternoon.

Another concern was the weather. It had been a busy storm season, and Monday, April 4, 1977 was no different.

You know the drill – wave after wave of winds, rain, lightning and hail. In fact, during the last week of March, 1977 Douglas County had had so much rain the folks here experienced severe flooding.

The afternoon of Monday, April 4, 1977 started off fairly normal. I had arrived home around 4 p.m. lugging several thick textbooks and bulging notebooks, and had just settled down to my afternoon of assignments when a "special report" broke into the television show I was watching.

It was 4:20 p.m. – and while my afternoon was about to be taken up with something much more dramatic than homework, there were folks forty-five minutes from me experiencing life and death. For those who survived or witnessed the events and the aftermath in Paulding and Douglas Counties their lives would be forever altered.

One of my worst fears had come true – not for me, but for them.

Earlier that afternoon a Southern Airways flight – Number 242 – originating from Muscle Shoals, Alabama stopped in Huntsville to take on more passengers. They were prevented to take off on time, however. Bad weather was passing through. Flight 242 finally headed for Atlanta fifteen to twenty minutes late.

Bobby Bruce, a city of Dallas maintenance worker was busy on a hillside at Dallas Cemetery just after 4 p.m. He looked up and noticed a DC-9 flying way too low and even more alarmingly the plane was silent. There was no engine noise. Mr. Bruce got on his city radio and reported the plane and mentioned that it was heading towards the community of New Hope, a small farming area four miles northeast of Dallas, Georgia.

The pilots of the plane had already been in touch with the controllers at the Atlanta tower and reported they were experiencing windshield issues and one engine had lost power. The plane had experienced bad weather that once again had dumped rain and hail over West Georgia.

Several folks heard Mr. Bruce's call on the City of Dallas radio concerning the plane. The folks at Martin's Funeral Home dispatched an ambulance to head towards New Hope, the Dallas Police sent a car out to the area, and Steve Wills, a deputy with the Paulding County Sheriff's office also headed in the direction of New Hope – just in case.

By this time the second engine had gone, and the plane was floating with no power whatsoever. The pilots were talking to the tower in Atlanta. They knew the plane wouldn't remain aloft for long. There was some discussion regarding gliding into Dobbins, but it was fifteen miles away – too far to glide. The nearest airport was in Cartersville – also too far away.

The pilots were left with one alternative – an attempt at landing on the highway – State Highway 92 to be exact.

An article from the April 5th issue of the *Douglas County Sentinel* recounts the events this way.

"Witnesses said the plane was coming straight in on the road when its wings began to clip trees and a utility pole. The plane reportedly touched down at least once, but the aircraft veered to the right, striking cars and gas pumps at Newman's store. The plane then skidded out of control about one hundred more yards before if left the road exploding among several trees between two houses."

Deputy Steve Wills picks up the story from his vantage point from the book *The Heritage of Paulding County:*

> "As we came into the community, the smoke cloud was already huge and there was an explosion. There were treetops and power lines down."

He and the Dallas police officer hurriedly parked their cars and ran the rest of the way toward the scene.

Deputy Wills continued, "Just past the store the plane was in view. The plane had broken apart and scattered into pieces in the Poole's yard."

He described the scene as fire everywhere, so much smoke it choked, and the smell was unforgettable. Some rescuers described it as "the smell of death."

Bruce explains the first-responders worked together and worked quickly to get the injured to the hospital stating that when there were no more ambulances a school bus was used to transport victims.

Douglas County's Civil Defense Unit received the call at 4:20 p.m. Jimmy Ball advised in a *Sentinel* article he reached the scene twenty minutes later along with Dick Lovvins and Michael Richardson. The men were among the first to arrive from Douglas County along with an ambulance dispatched from Douglas General Hospital. Several members of the Douglas County Fire Department and law enforcement crossed the county line to help as needed.

Jimmy Ball told the *Sentinel* at the time, "It was a mess – it was one of the worst disasters I've ever been to…I've been in rescue work for seventeen years, and the crash was the worst."

Dennis Chandler told the *Sentinel* he arrived about thirty minutes after the crash. He mentioned at that time the store was still burning, and he witnessed a truck had been backed up to the fuselage of the plane where workers were removing bodies. Chandler described getting sick and said it was the worst thing he had seen.

Working the radio that day for Douglas County Civil Defense was Bob Smith who says the men who went to the scene that day were forever changed. For some reason authorities at the crash scene were unable to hear the messages being sent to them from the Civil Defense offices in Atlanta, but they could communicate with the office in Douglasville. Bob Smith has told me the Douglas County office served as a middleman relaying messages back and forth.

By the time Ball and the others from Douglas County had arrived the first responders had already rounded up the injured and removed them from the scene. Ball, Lovvins and Richardson joined in with the others completing the grim task of removing the bodies.

One of those on the ground – Mrs. Bertie Corlis – had been standing in her yard when she was struck and killed by flying debris. An entire family of seven was killed when their car was struck and caught in the fire that engulfed Newman's store.

One of the plane's landing gears had ended up in the yard of the volunteer fire department's chief, John Clayton.

Bodies were found up to 70 yards away from the actual crash site. The plane itself was in hundreds of pieces. The tail section of the plane was the part that was recognizable.

Initially the remains of the dead were wrapped in linen or plastic and lined up along the roadway, but at some point a morgue was set up in a nearby barn.

The crash of Flight 242 at New Hope was the first crash in Georgia involving a scheduled airline flight since 1941 and had the most fatalities regarding a crash within the state's boundaries.

There is no possible way the true scope and magnitude of the tragedy can be told in a written piece like this, but it is a piece of history that should be documented. Personally, my heart goes out to each and every person who lost a family member or who was on the scene that day.

It truly is a sad day to remember.

Chapter 135

THE DOUGLAS COUNTY COURTHOUSE – CRASH COURSE IN LOCAL HISTORY

Okay, I'll admit the weather over the weekend was not the best, but haven't we had some lovely days over the past couple of weeks? It has been nice to get out in the car and ride around town with the sunroof open and meet various friends for lunch. The weather has made running my weekly errands a little more enjoyable as well.

Thursday was especially bright and sunny as I headed down Hospital Drive. Suddenly I found myself turning into the parking lot of the Douglas County Courthouse. Most people only visit their local courthouse when they have some sort of business to conduct – a deed to record, taxes to pay, or jury duty.

I'm a little different. Courthouses are a real draw for me for many different reasons. During my college years I spent a few months working as a junior clerk for the Superior Court of Cherokee County recording deeds and other documents. I followed that with an eighteen year career as a paralegal and eventually owned my own legal research business. Let's just say I'm one of those people who get excited over a record room piled high with old docket books, and I've been in many of the Atlanta area's courthouses.

There are other reasons why courthouses attract me. The architecture of the buildings old and new draws me in. I love walking through the building and knowing the business of government is taking place within the courthouse walls. I love the history behind the buildings, and a great courthouse will provide a little history for visitors to see as well.

My personal opinion may not mean much, but Douglas County has a great courthouse.

Take a few minutes the next time you are driving by and stop in at the courthouse. There are all sorts of things to see beginning with the marvelous entrance with the grand columns. Notice the years carved into the front of the building – 1870, 1896, 1956, and 1998. The first three represent the years past courthouses served our citizens in the downtown business district with 1998 representing the current courthouse along Hospital Drive.

The side entrances on each side of the building are magnificent leading to the lower floors, and the creative designs in the terrazzo floor are interesting. The most magnificent feature of the building is the interior dome area. It towers over the main staircase and fills the area with light.

Make sure you stroll along the bottom floor corridor beginning at one door, cross under the dome, and then continue down the other corridor to the opposite exit. Along the way you will see several panels depicting Douglas County's history – our history.

There are nine panels in all, and I'm told by Wes Tallon, Director, Douglas County Department of Communications and Community Relations, they were developed under the direction of former Commissioner Claude Abercrombie during the design of the Courthouse in 1996-97. There are panels that detail important people over the years regarding county politics and history as well as panels covering the area's natural resources and early industry. The history of the courthouse covering each of the buildings is the focus of one panel while another explains how important the railroad was to Douglasville from the very beginning.

Mr. and Mrs. Black, their trading post, and the significance of a certain skint chestnut tree I've mentioned before are discussed as well. In fact, you can see an image of the very tree on one of the panels! There are other panels discussing the importance of cotton to the economy of early Douglas County and the factory ruins at New Manchester. The cornerstone to the original 1896 courthouse can also be found at one of the lower exits.

Don't forget to take a walk around the outside of the building where three important memorials can be found. Along the front you will see the Eternal Flame - saluting all of our veterans from various wars. The Douglas County Pathway of Service is the highest accolade Douglas County citizens can bestow on a citizen who has spent his/her life in service to others and the Walk of Honor recognizing acts of heroism and great service such as Christopher Queen, a nine year old who rescued his three year old cousin who had fallen into a swimming pool are both located along the front drive.

Out on the north corner of the property you will see the Confederate memorial given to the county by the Douglas County Chapter of the United Daughters of the Confederacy in 1914.

Yes, Douglas County's current courthouse does an excellent job showing off our history.

Take some time to stop by the next time you are in the area.

Chapter 136

DOUGLAS COUNTY'S LITTLE COURTHOUSES

Though the phrase "government by the people" was included in the Constitution in 1787 it took many years, numerous struggles and a few amendments to ring true, but it still doesn't ring clear, unfortunately.

Citizens of the United States have many rights, but we have responsibilities as well, and some overlap. For example, we have the right to vote, but voting is also a responsibility.

Yes, if you choose to stay home, and you fail to vote, YOU are part of the problem.

You keep us from having "government by the people," and it might just be my little old opinion, but I think it's one of the major problems we experience as a nation.

Imagine how our national, state, and local elections would be impacted if every citizen chose to be responsible and exercised their right to vote.

In the beginning "government by the people" didn't ring true because large segments of the population were left off voting rolls and out of the process.

For the first sixty years or so our nation only allowed white males who owned property the vote. This meant only a very small percentage of the population had a voice in the government. Gradually, states dropped the property requirement and voter rolls included all white men.

Later, in 1870 the 15th Amendment passed allowing males who had been slaves to vote as well, followed in 1920 by the 19th Amendment, which finally gave the vote to all women. In 1924, American Indians were given the right to vote by granting them U.S. citizenship.

Finally, "government by the people"–all of the people–was possible.

Still, people don't seem to take their right/responsibility to vote very seriously. Over the last fifty years–from 1960 to 2010–the percentage of the voting age population who actually voted in national elections only rose above 60 percent once–just once–and that was back in 1964. In 2010, the percentage was a dismal 37.8 percent.

This past Tuesday citizens across the nation were asked to turn out to vote again for mid-term elections. Here in Douglas County several seats were up for grabs including key seats on the school board, the District Attorney and Solicitor-General. Several state offices, as well as positions for our representatives under the gold dome in Atlanta were on the ballot, too.

When I inquired, Laurie Fulton, Douglas County's Elections Supervisor advised 38,087 total votes were cast. But when you look at the total number of registered voters in the county you have to wonder what keeps people away from the polls. We have 83,031 people registered to vote in Douglas County, but only 38,087 exercised their right – their responsibility.

What's up with that?

Most certainly we have a severe problem with voter apathy.

So, what should be done?

Survey after survey indicates one of the reasons for voter apathy has to do with the inconvenience of voting.

Before automobiles were available farmers needed three days to vote. They needed a day to travel, a day to vote and conduct other business, and a day to travel home. Monday through Wednesday worked and didn't interfere with days of worship.

Three days to vote? Knowing this I'm actually ashamed I've ever fussed about the few minutes it has taken me to vote in the past.

However, today we live in a much more urban atmosphere, and we have been groomed to expect convenience in our everyday life, so of course we expect convenience with voting.

Thankfully, we now have early voting for several days leading up to the elections with hardly a wait either at your regular polling place or the courthouse.

I voted at the courthouse with no wait whatsoever. It took all of ten minutes.

However, making voting more convenient for Douglas County citizens is nothing new.

Many years ago, several little courthouses were built across the county—one in each polling district—to serve as polling places, meeting locations and to help citizens conduct business with the county without having to make the trip to "town."

However, in the late 1990s the remaining little one-room courthouses were under attack from groups of people who wanted them demolished. In her book concerning Douglas County history, Fannie Mae Davis advises the remaining little courthouses were about to become relics of the past.

As new schools and fire departments were built across the county the need for the little courthouses diminished, and over time the buildings had been neglected and fallen into disrepair even though they most certainly had a historic past.

Wes Tallon, Douglas County's Communications & Community Relations Director tells me the little courthouse in Lithia Springs was located on South Sweetwater Road next to the former fire department that was torn down a few years ago. Not only was the Lithia Springs little courthouse a former polling place, it had also been the location at one time for the public library in Lithia Springs, as well.

The Mt. Carmel little courthouse was located on Pope Road next to what many remember as the potato barn.

Bob Smith tells me when his father, R.L. Smith, was Chairman of the Douglas County Board of Commissioners during the early 1960s he held town hall meetings in the little courthouses and tried to keep up with the painting and repairs.

In her book, Davis refers to the little courthouses in Fairplay and Chapel Hill in particular stating during the late 1990s citizens in those areas felt the time had come to remove the historic buildings.

At the time C.L. Dodson was the Chairperson of the Douglas County Board of Commissioners. He acknowledged the buildings had suffered deterioration but wanted to move slowly before making a decision. He wanted to check with the Justices of the Peace in those areas and the Probate Judge to analyze the situation and explore their options. It seems very prudent since the Fairplay courthouse had been used for elections as recently as the early 1990s.

In the end it was finally decided the little courthouse at Fairplay would be moved to the campus of South Douglas Elementary where it serves as a storage shed according to Mrs. Davis' book.

The little courthouse at Chapel Hill and another building referred to as Middle Courthouse located on Post Road was saved repaired and are still around to be seen. Both little courthouses bear plaques from the Douglas County Tourism and Historic Commission who helped to identify their historic significance and advised the Douglas County Board of Commissioners who ultimately has control of the buildings.

Jeff Champion reminded me a couple of years ago about the now long-gone little courthouse at Chestnut Log. It sat at Flowers Drive and Fairburn Road. Originally, it had been built of chestnut tree logs which gave the district its name. The building burned in the 1970s. I have to wonder if someone out there has a picture of it.

I'm hopeful that Douglas County teachers include the story of the little courthouses in any teaching unit that addresses election history, government, and how our nation strives to "govern by the people."

I believe the little buildings that remain and our collective memories of the buildings that no long exist are just that important.

Chapter 137

STREETS, ROADS, AND PLACE NAMES

Today we tend to refer to areas of our community in terms of subdivision names. I might tell a friend, "Oh, you know—out there by Bear Creek Estates" or "Just down the road from Sweetwater Bluffs" or "Close to Midway Estates." But if we had been living in Douglas County in her earliest days we would have made far different references to communities that existed at that time—places like Red Hill, Morristown, Yeager, Maroney and Dark Corner would be landmarks.

Yeager and Maroney are somewhat familiar to me in that there are roads named for both, but Dark Corner?

It sounds very ominous.

When I located that name in some old records I instantly thought of a shady dark spot in the road perhaps where thieves might overtake an uninformed traveler.

I was wrong.

Dark Corner was located between Winston and Douglasville. Historical sources state the area was named for a Cherokee leader known simply as The Dark. His claim to fame included developing the first toll road into Cherokee lands. That's all I know—so for now I'll keep digging.

Salt Springs still exists as a community but is no longer known by that name. The name Salt Springs was given by Native Americans who regularly witnessed deer at the site licking the salt from rocks along the creek. Later the place became known as Bowden Springs where a hotel flourished, and the waters were advertised as having curative powers. In 1918, the name of this place was changed formally to Lithia Springs.

Sound familiar?

Names of communities aren't the only identifiers on the maps that have changed over time. Various roads have morphed as well for many reasons.

Rose Avenue was originally referred to as Cemetery Street. When you think about it the name made sense since the road bisected the downtown cemetery, but a few ladies in town thought Rose Avenue was a nicer sounding name, so the town fathers not wanting to upset the ladies put the change into effect.

Old tax maps indicate Fairburn Road was also referred to as Sawtell Road or Austell Ferry Road in days gone by. General Alfred Austell, the founder of Atlanta National Bank, took over the Austell Ferry that crossed between Douglas and South Fulton County that had previously been known as Gorman's Ferry.

One of the oldest roads in Douglas County, Five-Notch Road, dates back to early frontier days. Early settlers used an axe to make five cuts in trees at even distances. This was a method of marking trails and early roads copied from Native Americans.

Now Chicago Avenue has always been a mystery to me. Here in the Deep South why a road would would be named after a city in the far north? More than one historical source indicates the road was named in 1887 because two Chicago transplants, C.C. Post and his wife, moved to town and took up residence on the street we know as Chicago Avenue today.

Simple, right?

Prior to 1950, Douglas County residents used Wedge Alley to move between Price and Club streets. The East-West alleyway was so narrow that in the early days wagons would lock wheels as they tried to pass each other hence the name Wedge Alley.

In the earliest days of Douglasville, Church Street was known as Factory Street. A mill was located where the law firm Hartley, Rowe and Fowler is located today. Unfortunately, it burned one week after opening, and suddenly it seemed a little strange to continue to call the street Factory Street. You guessed it—the location of the First Baptist Church of Douglasville at that time prompted the name change.

And what of Campbellton Street? Well, that was just a way for the city fathers to honor our "mother county"—Campbell County and their original county seat, Campbellton.

Chapter 138

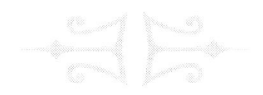

VISIT EIGHT HISTORIC SITES WITHOUT LEAVING THE COUNTY

If I asked you to name three or four historic places right off the top of your head I'm certain you could do it. Even the least historically minded of us are familiar with history hot spots like Mt. Vernon, the U.S Capitol, and Independence Hall in Philadelphia.

Historic places often add a little excitement and variety to a vacation. Who hasn't visited a lighthouse while at the beach or toured a museum or two when away from home?

What we often forget, however, are the historic locations in our own backyard.

How many of us head off to Atlanta or some other nearby location when we want to "SEE" something?

What about the historic locations right here in Douglas County?

We have eight different history hot spots of our own that are worthy of being "SEEN" and all have been added to the National Register of Historic Places.

This week I thought I'd share a few details about each location.

Basket Creek Cemetery is on the property belonging to Basket Creek Baptist Church on Capps Ferry Road not too far from the Chattahoochee

River. The first burial was in 1886, and it's still in use today with approximately 110 burials to date.

At the turn of the century the Capps Ferry Road area was a thriving African American community including single-family houses, saw mills, tenant farms and churches.

The Basket Creek Cemetery is a prime example of the West African custom involving grave mounding to honor deceased family members and friends. Poorly maintained mounds are seen as insults to the dead and are poor reflections on the community as a whole. When you visit the cemetery you quickly notice each grave is represented with a mound of earth, and the entire yard appears to be swept. Twice a year for the last 123 years the congregation at Basket Creek have maintained the graves and continue to pass along the skills to the next generation.

The Douglas County Courthouse built in 1956 and located at 6754 Broad Street is also on the National Register. In April, I wrote - Since 2002, the Old Courthouse building has been listed on the National Register of Historic Places. The building passed muster to be added to the prestigious list because it was built in the International Style of architecture, a style that emerged in the 1920s and 30s and matured following World War II. Today, the 1956 courthouse houses the Douglas County Museum of History and Art which exhibits a wealth of artifacts and information regarding the settlement of Douglas County and the growth of Douglasville.

Beulah Grove Lodge No. 372, Free and Accepted York Masons-Pleasant Grove School is one of the newer additions to the National Register. The building is owned by Pleasant Grove Baptist Church. A *Times Georgian* article states, "Pleasant Grove was a rural community where most of the residents were sharecroppers. Members of the church's Board of Deacons were trustees for the lodge, and Jack Smith — who donated the land — was believed to be a Mason. Smith was a freed slave, born in 1832, who purchased 50 acres of land in 1868 and another 50 acres in 1889, giving two acres of land to the church, school and cemetery." The building had a dual purpose in that it served as a lodge building and school beginning about 1910. Currently there are plans to restore the building.

The John Thomas Carnes Family Log House can be found at Clinton Nature Preserve and is one of the best maintained log cabins in the Atlanta area. The approximate date for its construction is 1828. Members of the Carnes family actually lived in the home through the 1950s. In the 1980s the family donated 200 acres to Douglas County with the provision that the land is to remain in its natural state as much as possible. The National Register actually gives two homes the distinction of National Register status, but the second structure was built much later. The Douglas County Museum of History and Art on Broad Street has an excellent collection of items that belonged to the Carnes family on display.

The William T. Roberts House was added to the National Register in 1989, and today it serves as the headquarters for Douglas County's Cultural Arts Center. In a past column I quote a source stating the Roberts home is "one of the few structures in Douglasville which embodies the characteristics of a period style …with its air of classic Greek architecture, the low sweeping line of a grand front porch and an entrance of mahogany doors enriched with the serenity of stained glass…"

The Sweetwater Manufacturing site has been on the National Register since 1977, and its historical significance dates from before the Civil War. The Sweetwater Manufacturing site is also known as the New Manchester Mill. It was built along Sweetwater Creek in 1849. The building was five stories tall and was powered by a water wheel.

Towards the end of the Civil War Union soldiers were ordered to shut the mill down and arrest the employees who were then shipped north. Today all that remains of the mill are the brick walls and millrace that led to the factory's waterwheel.

Douglasville Commercial Historic District has been on the National Register since July, 1989. While some are very quick to dismiss the commercial area of downtown Douglasville as just another railroad town, it is one of the best examples we have in the state of Georgia. Most of the buildings in the district are original and exhibit various styles of architecture including Victorian, Queen Anne, Craftsman, Colonial Revival, Romanesque, Italianate, Beaux Arts Classicism and Tudor Revival.

When you delve into the history of the downtown area and the backgrounds regarding a large majority of the men who were featured so prominently in its development it cannot be denied that Douglasville was a "New South" town following Henry Grady's call for the development of industrial capitalism to replace the plantation system.

The Pine Mountain Gold Mine Museum is located on Stockmar Road in Villa Rica, Georgia. While most students of Georgia history learn about the gold discovered in Dahlonega they are told that it is considered to be the beginning of Georgia's gold rush. It was actually Villa Rica that led the way with gold being discovered in 1826, four years earlier than Dahlonega.

The miners who discovered the gold in Villa Rica elected to be a bit quiet regarding their find since Georgia had a law at the time declaring any discovery of minerals including gold would have to be handed over to the state. Once the law was repealed in 1829 the mining operations went public. The mine was active until 1936. The discovery of gold in Villa Rica was significant historically because the knowledge helped to speed up the settlement of the lands previously controlled by Creek Indians.

So, the next time you are in the mood for a little history think about exploring Douglas County first.

You never know what you might find!

Chapter 139

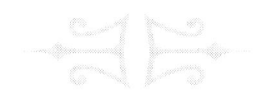

FAMILY HISTORY – REAL FACTS OR WILD EXAGGERATIONS

I'm sure your family has stories that have been handed down over the years concerning those who came before you - stories regarding how your family came to this country, stories involving how your great grandfather made a living, maybe a story regarding how your mom and dad met or how your dad proposed to your mom.

Many of my uncles had stories regarding World War I and II while some families were only left jackets with patches, pictures and medals to decipher.

Most families in Georgia have stories involving how folks hid valuables when Sherman's men came through during the Civil War, or other families have tales concerning the realization they were finally free from slavery and what they did with their freedom.

Did they stay?

Did they go north?

Families have stories, and those stories are all part of the collective tale involving Douglas County history, Georgia history and of course, American History.

Family stories are valuable.

Family stories make history interesting, and negate that tired old excuse that history is just a bunch of dates and a litany of treaties written by a bunch of old dead white guys.

Family stories motivate folks to find out more, to take that trip to the courthouse or the State Archives, to pay that fee to Ancestry.com, or dig just a little deeper through the cardboard box of old papers and pictures in the attic.

Family stories make history worth learning about. They help people, young and old, connect to the bigger picture.

You realize you ARE an American and an important piece of the puzzle when you find out a relative picked up a musket and stood up to the British along with Washington, Jefferson and Adams.

It's much easier to learn about the battles of Vietnam when you know someone in your family was there.

When you find out your great-grandmother was a Suffragette fighting for the right to vote for women or an uncle marched alongside Dr. Martin Luther King, Jr., you are spurred to learn more.

There are problems with family history, however, and recently, I have been admonished concerning my use of family stories in connection to Douglas County history because more often than not there is no proof for family stories, and over the course of many years stories can become embellished or exaggerated to make them more interesting.

There are historians and those who deal with genealogy on a daily basis who are of the notion that family stories without proper documentation should be dismissed and never used.

While I do believe family history should be identified as such, I don't agree that family history has NO place when discussing a historical topic.

It's too important, and there might be a grain of truth to it.

There is a very large oak tree on my father's place in Canton, Georgia. It used to belong to his father and his father before him. My great-grandparents had a home across the road from this tree.

My sister, cousins and I have great affection for this tree. It's right alongside the country lane where my great-grandmother's house used to sit. On one side of the tree there was a large rectangular rock that jutted out from the tree. It was flat on the exposed side making a seat that was just right back then for my fanny to perch on.

I assure you I couldn't sit there today even if the rock was still there, but back during the "olden days" I had to walk across the road, run my hands over that rock, and sit there for just a minute every time I was at my grandfather's place.

My older cousins called the rock the "Love Seat", and to this day I have no idea if my great uncles and aunts used the rock for courting or if my cousins were just "romancing the stone", but it was a landmark on my Grandfather's place that I loved.

The tree isn't there anymore. The rock was misplaced or destroyed, but the story remains.

There is no mention of the "Love Seat" in a law suit at the courthouse.

There is no mention of the "Love Seat" as a boundary marker in any deed.

There are no pictures of the "Love Seat" as far I know.

Does this mean that the rectangular rock jutting out from the old tree didn't exist because there is no tangible proof today?

Well, of course I'm here to testify that it was there. I did sit on the rock. I did play around that tree when I was young, and I've typed it here for all to see.

But a hundred years from now I won't be here. My children won't be here. My cousins won't be here.

Does this mean that the "Love Seat" can't be included if a history of the family property is written since we aren't physically here to testify, and there is no tangible proof?

Will I be accused in some far off future of embellishing the story of a tree that might have been on the property, but no proof was left behind?

I can hear it now, "That Granny Cooper. She was a real nut case!"

A hundred years from now someone may take my mention of the "Love Seat" and dismiss it totally, and I can't do anything about it, but it does make me give pause to other types of family history when we can't document the situation fully.

Did it happen?

Is the story some wild embellishment?

Sometimes, we just don't know for sure, and for that very reason I like to give SOME information the benefit of the doubt.

I certainly don't mind meeting my critics in the middle of the road by trying to advise as much as possible when there isn't any proof concerning my research and writing, but will I totally dismiss family history from the Douglas County story?

No, I won't.

It will never happen.

All history has value.

Chapter 140

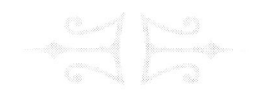

HISTORY IS ALIVE AND WELL IN DOUGLAS COUNTY

At some point over the last three years I was at a meeting of history minded folks when someone – a particular someone who is in a position to know better – said, "Douglasville has nothing to offer historically. Why would anyone want to learn about history here? Douglasville just isn't a historical destination."

If you know me personally or even if you just know me through reading my historical offerings each week then you know "them's fightin' words" as far as I'm concerned.

While I understand Douglas County isn't on the same playing field as Savannah, we do have our history, and it's every bit as integral to the Georgia story as any other town or city.

We offer quite a bit when you think about it, and even though I can't cover it all in just 600 or so words, here are a few things to think about.

The Chattahoochee River serves as a geographical marker for our boundary with Fulton County, but most don't realize that up until the 1950s there were no bridges to cross. Folks had to use the ferry to make the crossing into Douglas County. Ponder that for a bit. It wasn't that many years ago. We've come a long way since then regarding infrastructure.

We have Civil War history. The river area of the county saw action during the war as Union troops moved through. The New Manchester mill was burned by the boys in blue and the Irwin-Bomar-Rice-Austin-Bullard-Henley-Sprayberry home, built in 1835 still stands on Highway 92 as a testament to the many families who dealt with enemy soldiers crossing their land and taking anything that wasn't nailed down.

The story of how Douglas County came to be is interesting. The time was 1870. Reconstruction was in full force in Georgia, yet a committee of determined ex-Confederate soldiers pushed through legislation that carved Douglas County out of Campbell County. They resorted to lying when they had to concerning the true nature of who the county would be named for. I'm not condoning lying by any means, but the situation is historical evidence regarding the political climate during Reconstruction.

During the late 1890s there was a huge political split in the Democratic Party when it was the domineering party state-wide. One of the largest political rallies for the Farmer's Alliance was held here in Douglasville resulting in a few hand to hand fights right out in the streets of town since many staunch Douglas County Democrats would have none of a third party.

Every time you visit the Cultural Arts Center located on Campbellton Street you are walking into a very well preserved grand home from the turn of the century that was not only built by a prominent attorney who later took a Washington appointment in President Wilson's administration, but you are entering the home of three different mayors of Douglasville. The first was the first owner. The next two happened to be father and son. The son, Harold Mozley, was said to be the youngest mayor in the United States at that time being 28 years of age. Later, it was discovered he wasn't the youngest, but one of the youngest.

Many don't know Douglas County led the state of Georgia in becoming a dry county when Prohibition was approved in 1885, a full 35 years before the United States as a whole.

And finally – because I could go on forever – there are plenty of people "doing" history each and every week here in Douglas County.

Just last night I attended the monthly meeting of the Douglas County Genealogical Society and heard published author Sid Brown give a short presentation regarding the long gone town of Campbellton just across the river. Mr. Brown's research in partnership with local historian Jeff Champion is ongoing.

Local authors John and Elaine Bailey will soon be publishing a book on Douglas County's Dark Corner area. Their research has uncovered several unknown before now facts. Another local historian, Steve Lawler, is currently transcribing a huge collection of letters written between a husband and wife during the Civil War that promises to be very interesting as well.

The Douglas County Historical Society meets eight months out the year at the Cultural Arts Center with an interesting speaker to fill out the program, and last but certainly not least we have the Douglas County Museum of Art and History located in the old Douglas County Courthouse on Broad Street full of interesting artifacts from Douglas County's long history indicating the desire of many to preserve our history.

Yes, history is alive and well in Douglas

BIBLIOGRAPHY

Albertson, Earl, *Portraits of Douglasville*

American Architect and Architecture, October 3, 1896

Ancestry.com…….Harold Glover

Architecture Week, April 18, 2007, Retrieved December 9, 2014 *http://www.architectureweek.com/2007/0418/environment_1-1.html*

Ayers, Edward L., *The Promise of the New South: Life after Reconstruction*

Ayers, Stephen D., *We Danced Until Dawn*

Aylworth, Stephanie (2010). A Multifaceted Approach to Historic District Interpretation in Georgia. *The Public Historian*, 32(4), 42-50.

Baggett, Joe, *Who's Who in Douglas County*

Bailey, John. The Douglas County Mint, *Looking Good Douglas County*

Barker, John. Douglasville Names Street for former Sheriff Earl Lee on Friday. *Douglasville Patch*. Retrieved online December 9, 2014 http://patch.com/georgia/douglasville/earl-lee-street-dedication-on-friday

Brown, F. and Smith, Sherri M.L. (2007). *The River Keeper's Guide to the Chattahoochee River*. Atlanta: CI Publishing.

Caldwell, Wilbur W. (2001). *The Courthouse and the Depot: The Architecture of Hope in an Age of Despair*. Atlanta: Mercer University Press.

Carter, Sarah Elizabeth Woods (1976). *The Vansant Family Tree: Branch of Sarah Elizabeth (Vansant-Woods) Carter Ancestors and Descendants.* Douglasville: Carter

Cedartown Standard, March 21, 1912

Cleary, Ben Stonewall's Bounty August 26, 2012 *The New York Times* retrieved from: http://opinionator.blogs.nytimes.com/2012/08/26/stonewalls-bounty/?_r=0

Collier's Magazine, 1924

Confederate Veteran, 1928

Cooper, Lisa. Is History Important? *History Is Elementary.* Retrieved: http://historyiselementary.blogspot.com/2006/01/is-history-important.html

Cornerstone Books, "Helen Wilmans" retrieved from http://helenwilmans.wwwhubs.com/

Craft, Stephen G. *Embry-Riddle and American Aviation* retrieved online from http://www.erau.edu/assets/pdf/erauandeaf.pdf

Dalton, Harris. (2014). *Excitement!!! In War and Peace.* Canton, Georgia: Weatherby Harris Dalton, Jr.

Davis, Oscar King. (2010). *The Life of William McKinley.* Kessinger Publishing LLC

Davis, Fannie Mae. (1997). *Douglas County, Georgia: From Indian Trail to Interstate 20.* Wolfe Publishing.

Eddy, Sherwood. (1969) *Pathfinders of the World Mission Crusade.* Books for Libraries Press.

Edgefield Advisor, September 15, 1892

Engineering News-Record, January, 1894

Finkelman, P. (2009). *African American Encyclopedia of History.* Oxford University Press.

Fox, John J. (2006). *Red Clay to Richmond*. Angle Valley Press.

Georgia Gazeteer, 1879

Georgia Gazeeteer, 1881

Georgia Gazeteer, 1886

Garrett, Franklin. (2011). *Atlanta and Environs.* Athens: University of Georgia Press.

Girillo, Vincent J. (2003). *Bullets and Bacilli: The Spanish-American War and Military Medicine.* University Press.

Goff, John H., Frances Lee Utley and Marion R. Hemperley. (2007). *Placenames of Georgia*. Athens: University of Georgia Press.

Hickman Courier, March 25, 1887

Harrington, Hugh T. (2005). *Civil War Milledgeville: Tales from the Confederate Capital of Georgia*. The History Press.

Harshbarger, Vicki. *Looking Good Douglas County*, 1988.

Hazen, Theodore R. *The Art of Millstones, How They Work*. Retrieved from: http://www.angelfire.com/journal/millrestoration/millstones.html

Kaemmerlen, Cathy. (2006). *General Sherman and the Georgia Belles: Tales from the Women Left Behind*. The History Press.

Kennett, Lee B. (2001). *Marching Through Georgia: The Story of Soldiers and Civilians during Sherman's Campaign*. Harper Perennial.

Keowee Courier, October 21, 1908.

Krakow, Kenneth. (1994). *Georgia Place Names*. Winship Press.

Life, July, 1940

Macon Telegraph, April 13, 1895

Marijay. "Elizabeth (Lizzie) Susan Camp Glover." *Find-A-Grave*. Retrieved from: http://www.findagrave.com/cgi-bin/fg.cgi?page=gr&GRid=6698494

Mastrovita, Mandy, "Canned Goods for the Greater Good in Georgia", *Digital Library of Georgia*, September 28, 2011. Retrieved from http://blog.dlg.galileo.usg.edu/?p=2663

Macon Telegraph, April 13, 1895

Marietta Daily Leader, Ohio, April, 1896

Martin, Thomas A. (1902). *Atlanta and Its Builders: A Comprehensive History of the Gate City*. Atlanta: Century Memorial Publishers Company.

Memoirs of Georgia. (1895). Atlanta: The Southern Historical Association.

Memphis Daily Appeal, August 25, 1873.

Mohr, Clarence L. (2001). *On the Threshhold of Freedom: Masters and Slaves in Civil War Georgia*. LSU Press.

Nixon, Raymond B. (1943). *Henry W. Grady: Spokesman of the New South*. A.A. Knopf.

Oberholtzer, Ellis Paxon. (2012). *A History of the United States since the Civil War*. Forgotten Books.

Rider, Randy. *Be a Leader for Goodness Sake*. Officer.com. Retrieved from: http://www.officer.com/article/10301176/be-a-leader-for-goodness-sake

Perdue, Theda. (2011). *Race and the Atlanta Cotton States Exposition*. University of Georgia Press.

Popular Mechanics, April, 1927

Pound, Merritt B. (1951). *Benjamin Hawkins: Indian Agent*. University of Georgia Press.

Post, Helen Wilmans. (1921). *A Homecourse in Mental Science*. Retrieved from http://www.tigerseyedowsing.com/ds/home_study_courses/home_course_in_mental_science_1921/mental_course.html

Post, Helen Wilmans. (2011). *The Search for Freedom*. Nabu Press.

Potete, Deborah. (2010*). "The Women Will Howl": The Union Army Capture of Roswell and New Manchester, Georgia and the Forced Relocation of Mill Workers*. McFarland.

Priest, John M. (1990). *Antietam: A Soldier's Battle.* White Mane Publishing.

Rothert, Otto Arthur, (2011). *The Story of Madison Cawein: His Intimate Life as Revealed by His Letters.* Ulan Press.

Satter, Beryl. (1999). *Each Mind a Kingdom: American Women, Sexual Purity, and New Thought.* University of California Press.

Smith, Clifford L. (1933). *History of Troup County.* Atlanta: Foote and Davis.

Smith, Steve and Sherri, (2007). *The Riverkeeper's Guide to the Chattahoochee River.* Chattahoochee Riverkeeper.

Southwestern Union Record, September 4, 1935

Stansberry, Richard B. (2008). *So Sings the Chattahoochee.* AuthorHouse

The Atlanta Constitution, September 10, 1882

The Atlanta Constitution, May 10, 1882

The Atlanta Constitution, December, 1883

The Atlanta Constitution, October 1, 1884

The Atlanta Constitution, December 5, 1884

The Atlanta Constitution, April 15, 1885

The Atlanta Constitution, August 14, 1887

The Atlanta Constitution, May 5, 1888

The Atlanta Constitution, June 19, 1890

The Atlanta Constitution, April 1, 1892

The Atlanta Constitution, December, 1901

The Atlanta Constitution, August 9, 1903

The Atlanta Constitition, February 3, 1904

The Atlanta Constitution, March, 1904

The Atlanta Constitition, December 3, 1906

The Atlanta Constitution, October 10, 1908

The Atlanta Constitution, October 11, 1908

The Atlanta Constitution, June 26, 1915

The Atlanta Constitution, August 13, 1915

The Atlanta Constitution November 1916

The Atlanta Consitution, March, 1917

The Atlanta Constitution May 11, 1917

The Atlanta Constitution, June 1917

The Atlanta Constitution, "A Douglasville Outrage", June 16, 1882

The Atlanta Constitution, "A Wheat and Corn Mill", April 10, 1883

The Atlanta Constitution, "Aviators Crash to Earth Monday at the Speedway", Dec 10, 1918

The Atlanta Constitution, "Douglasville's New Council", Feb. 10, 1887

The Atlanta Constitution, "Fairburn Facts" June 13, 1882

The Atlanta Constitution, "Farmers Day Alliance", September 28, 1887

The Atlanta Constitution, "Gartrell at Douglasville", September 21, 1882

The Atlanta Constitution, "Improvements in Douglasville" April 18, 1885

The Atlanta Constitution, "Newspaper Change", December 6, 1883

The Atlanta Constitution, "Newspoint from Douglasville", June 15, 1884

The Atlanta Constitution, "One Hundred m.p.h. made by Aviators", December 8, 1918

The Atlanta Constitution, "Sweetwater Scenes", May 4, 1882

The Atlanta Constitution, "The Italian Peddler", April 18, 1883

The Atlanta Constitution, "The James Lieutenants Uphold Record of Fighting Forebears", July 14, 1918

The Austin Weekly Statement, May 10, 1883

The Campbell News, July 19, 1916

The Douglas County Sentinel, April 22, 1909

The Douglas County Sentinel, November 12, 1957

The Douglasville Argus, 1909

The Enquirer, September, 1928

The Henry County Weekly, Novermber, 1896

The Morning Call, San Francisco, June 20, 1891

The New South, June, 1883

The New South, 1900

The New South, 1902

The New South, January, 1902

The New South, May, 1902

The New York Times, April 12, 1898

The New York Times, October 5, 1901.

The New York Times, November, 2011.

The Newnan and Coweta County Historical Society. (1988). *The History of Coweta County, Georgia* (Roswell, Ga.: Newnan and Coweta County Historical Society.

The Pendleton Messenger, February 23, 1849.

The Record, (1956).

The Technique, 21, No. 31 (May, 1942).

The Weekly Star, August 23, 1881

The Weekly Star, January, 1883

The Weekly Star, 1886

The Worthington Advance, August 1, 1889

Thomas, Henry Walter. (1903). *History of the Doles Cook Brigade.* Atlanta: Franklin Printing and Publishing.

Thornton, Richard. *(2011, April 5). The Sweetwater Creek and Nicka jack Creek Petroglyphs.* Examiner.com. Retrieved from: http://www.examiner.com/article/the-sweetwater-creek-and-nickajack-creek-petroglyphs

Verg, Judy. *History of the Roberts-Mozley House.* Cultural Arts Council of Douglasville/Douglas County. Retrieved from: http://www.artsdouglas.org/aboutUs/aboutUs.htm

White, George. (1855). *Historical Collections of Georgia: Containing the Most Interesting Facts, Traditions, Biographical Sketches, Etc., Relating to Its History and Antiquities, From Its First Settlement to Present Time.* New York: Pudney & Russell Publishers.

Williams, Arden. *New Encyclopedia of Georgia* (10-29-2015). "Textile Industry". Retrieved from: http://www.georgiaencyclopedia.org/articles/business-economy/textile-industry

Womack, Todd. *New Encyclopedia of Georgia* (8-12-2005). "The Spanish American War in Georgia" Retrieved from http://www.georgiaencyclopedia.org/articles/history-archaeology/spanish-american-war-georgia

INDEX

7th Georgia Regiment, Chapter 82
21st Georgia Regiment, Chapters 6, 7, 8
30th Georgia Regiment, Company F, Chapter 45
35th Georgia Regiment, Chapter 11
Abercrombie, Claude, Chapters 129, 131, 135
Abercrombie, J.H., Chapter 102
Abercrombie, J.M., Chapter 48
Abercrombie, J.S., Chapter 84
Abercrombie, Mac, Chapter 106
Abercrombie, Mac Claude, Sr., Chapters 103, 122
Abercrombie, W. Claude, Chapter 84
Abercrombie, W.J., Chapter 63
Accommodation, Chapter 30
Ace Hardware, Chapter 70
Adcock, Coleman A., Chapter 85
Aderhold's Ferry, Chapters 9, 42
African American History, Chapters 37, 39, 53, and 81
Agricultural Clubs, Chapter 38
Agriculture, Chapter 85
Albertson, Earl, Chapter 101
Alcoholic Beverages, Chapter 87

Alexander's Mill, Chapters 4, 9, 133
Alliance Warehouse, Chapter 68
Alms House, Chapter 62
Alpha Theater, Chapters 89, 127
AmaKanasta, Chapters 3, 48
American Legion Post 145, Chapter 46
American Red Cross, Chapter 76
Angel, Ron, Chapter 131
Anneewakee Creek, Chapters 12, 20, 22, 128
Annette Winn Elementary School, Chapter 110
Ansley Hotel, Chapter 100
Anti-Saloon League, Chapter 105
Argo, George P. (Mrs.), Chapter 94
Armistead, Dr. W.S., Chapter 65
Arnold, Alston, Chapters 22, 128
Arnold, J.T., Chapter 90
Arnold Mill, Chapters 22, 128
Arp, Bill, Chapter 72
Atlanta & West Rail Road, Chapter 5
Atlanta Crackers, Chapters 111, 120
Atlanta Historical Society, Chapter 119
Atlanta History Center, Chapter 10
Atlanta Humane Society, Chapter 129
Atlanta Medical College, Chapter 35
Atlanta Municipal Auditorium, Chapter 117
Atlanta National Bank, Chapters 104, 137
Atlanta Preservation Center, Chapter 58
Atlanta West Hospital, Chapter 125
Austell, Alfred, Sr., Chapters 104, 137
Austell, Alfred, Jr., Chapter 104
Austell, Earl Lee, Chapters 104, 130
Austell Bridge, Chapter 30
Austell Farms, Chapter 104

Austell Ferry Road, Chapter 137
Austell-Gorman Ferry, Chapters 104, 137
Austell High School, Chapter 21
Automobiles, Chapter 104
Ayers, Stephen D., Chapter 118
Ayleworth, Stephanie, Chapters 27, 29, 61, 71
Baggett, Allen Jacob, Chapter 91
Baggett, Billie Byington, Chapter 69
Baggett, Capitola (Beall), Chapter 91
Baggett, Guy, Chapter 107
Baggett, H.L., Chapter 63
Baggett, Joe, Chapter 33, 103
Baggett, Joseph Brown, Chapter 91
Baggett, William Alfred, Chapter 69
Baggett's Pool Hall, Chapter 116
Bailey, Gene Thomas, Chapter 130
Bailey, John, Chapter 40
Baker Drive, Chapters 75, 76
Baker, Absolum, Chapter 42
Baker, John Caldwell (Doctor), Chapter 66
Baker's Ferry, Chapter 42
Ball, Jimmy, Chapter 134
Ballough, C.A., Chapter 69
Bandit, Chapter 131
Bankhead Highway Association, Chapter 95
Bankhead Highway, Chapters 42, 52, 55, 58, 87, 95, 110, 111
Banks, Chapters 78, 84
Barker, N.P., Chapter 102
Barn Rats, Chapter 103
Barnett, Marion, Chapter 40
Barron, Joe, Chapter 14
Bart Duke's Store, Chapter 124
Bartlett, A.L. (Judge), Chapter 91

Bartlett, J.T., Chapter 14
Barton, Clara, Chapter 76
Baseball, Chapters 46, 111, 120
Basket Creek Baptist Church, Chapters 14, 138
Basket Creek Cemetery, Chapter 138
Bass, George (Mrs.), Chapter 94
Beall, Noble N., Chapter 91
Bear Creek, Chapters 17, 18, 26, 124
Beard, Charlotte, Chapter 124
Beard, Neal, Chapter 124
Bearden, Allen, Chapter 33
Bearden, Hoke, Chapters 34, 90
Beaver Dam Resevoir, Chapter 133
Beaver Lois Cotton Mill, Chapters 56, 61
Beaver Run Creek, Chapter 118
Beavers, Robert O., Chapter 5
Belcher, Hubert Eugene, Chapter 130
Belcher, Wade, Chapter 131
Beulah Community, Chapter 44
Beulah Elementary, Chapter 21, 106
Beulah Grove Lodge, No. 372, Chapter 138
Big A Road, Chapter 124
Bill Arp Community, Chapters 72, 80, 124
Bill Arp Elementary, Chapter 106
Bill Arp Road, Chapter 72
Billings, John B., Chapter 50
Birmingham, Chapter 29
Birt, Billy Sunday, Chapter 131
Black History, Chapters 129, 138
Black, Eugene R., Chapter 54
Black, James, Chapter 5
Blacksmith, Chapter 103
Blair, Daniel Webster, Chapter 42

Blair, Hiram Columbus, Chapter 42, 119
Blair, Ruth, Chapter 42, 119
Blue Laws, Chapter 87
Blue Star Memorial Highway, Chapter 129
Boarding House, Chapter 33, 71,
Boatright, R.O., Chapter 102
Bolden, Willie, Chapter 129
Boll Weevil, Chapter 37
Bomar, Armistead R., Chapter 20, 38
Bomar, Herschel, Chapter 123
Bomer, J.S., Chapter 102
Bonds, Quillian, Chapter 90
Bookmobile, Chapter 94
Bowden Street, Chapters 14, 34, 71, 101, 137
Bowden, John C., Chapter 21, 25, 26, 42
Bowden, Mary Rosa Summerlin, Chapter 21
Bowden, Willie, Chapter 21
Bowden-Mozley Cemetery, Chapter 21
Bowen, Caleb Perry, Chapter 45, 48
Bowen, Nany (Yarbrough), Chapter 45
Bowen, Thomas J., Chapter 45
Bowen, Willard, Chapter 113
Boyd, David, Chapter 10
Branan, H.V., Chapter 102
Brass Band, Chapter 70
Breckenridge, W.A., Chapter 38
Brevard Fault, Brevard, Chapter 133
Bright Star Road, Chapter 26, 93
Broad Street, Chapters 22, 25, 29, 33, 34, 46, 55, 70, 71, 76, 84, 87, 89, 92, 103, 112 116,138
Brockman, Fletcher Sims, Chapter 64
Brockman, Francis, Chapter 64
Brockman, Whitfield, Chapter 64

Brockman, Willis Allen, Chapter 9, 64
Brown Field, Chapter 130
Brow, Ben, Chapter 118
Brown, Isham M., Chapter 14
Brown, J.W., Chapter 62, 68
Brownfield, Chapter 59
Bryan, Andrew Jackson, Chapter 73
Buchanan, Chapter 91
Bullard, Susan (Miller), Chapter 9
Bullard-Henley Home, Chapter 9, 64
Burgman, Charles, Chapter 69
Burnett, G.W., Chapter 14
Burnett, George W., Chapter 14
Burnett, V.P., Chapter 14
Burnett, W.K., Chapter 14
Burney, Michael, Chapter 63
Burnt Hickory Road, Chapter 36
Buzzard's Roost Island, Chapters 2, 20
Caboose, Chapter 87
Caldwell, Barbara, Chapter 37
Camp Douglas, Chapter 96
Camp Gordon, Chapter 96
Camp Hobson, Chapters 75, 76, 96
Camp, Benjamin, Chapter 7
Camp, C.P., Chapter 63
Camp, Charlie, Chapter 22
Camp, E.H., Chapters 34, 38
Camp, Joseph G., Chapters 7, 38
Camp, Julie Arnold, Chapter 22
Camp, Rebecca, Chapter 22
Camp, W.J., Chapter 38
Camp, Winifred (Arnold), Chapter 7
Campbell County, Chapters 5, 6, 7, 8, 9, 11, 12, 18, 27, 64, 137, 140

Campbell Sharpshooters, Chapter 45
Campbell Volunteers, Chapter 11
Campbell, Duncan G., Chapter 5
Campbell, Henley, Chapter 9
Campbellton Blues, Chapters 6, 7, 8, 9
Campbellton Ferry, Chapter 9
Campbellton Lodge, Chapter 5
Campbellton Road, Chapter 104
Campbellton Street, Chapters 29, 31, 33, 34, 76, 82, 84, 87, 88, 126, 137, 140
Campbellton United Methodist Church, Chapter 5
Campbellton, Chapters 3, 5, 6, 7, 8, 11, 17, 20, 25, 82, 137
Candler Field Race Track, Chapter 99
Candler Field, Chapter 99
Candler, Asa, Chapter 100
Canning Plant, Chapters 45, 70
Capps Ferry Road, Chapter 138
Carnes, John Thomas, Chapter 138
Carnes Cabin, Chapter 127
Carroll County, Chapter 17
Carswell, Dr. E.R., Jr., Chapter 65
Carter, Glenn Thomas, Chapter 125
Carter, Glenmore, Chapters 93, 125
Carter, Lee Edwin, Chapter 125
Carter, Sarah Elizabeth Woods, Chapters 93, 125
Cascade Road, Chapters 2, 12
Cash, S.M., Chapter 38
Cawein, Madison, Chapter 55
Cedar Mountain Road, Chapters 19, 62
Celebrate Douglas, Chapter 25
Cemetery Street, Chapter 137
Champion, Jeff, Chapter 117, 136, 140
Champion, Jerry, Chapters 104, 117

Chandler, Dennis, Chapter 134
Chandler, Loy T., Chapter 110
Chapel Hill Community, Chapters 26, 28, 91
Chapel Hill Little Courthouse, Chapter 136
Chapel Hill News & Views, Chapter 124
Chapel Hill School (Segregated), Chapter 106
Chapel Hill School, Chapter 106
Charlie's Market, Chapter 5
Chatham, William, Chapter 107
Chattahoochee River, Chapters 2, 3, 4, 5, 9, 20, 22, 64, 95, 104, 133, 138, 140
Cherokee Nation, Chapters 2, 3, 20, 133, 137
Chestnut Log Little Courthouse, Chapter 136
Chicago Avenue, Chapters 32, 44, 48, 62, 67, 68, 69, 70, 137
Chili Cook Off, Chapter 116
Church Street, Chapters 34, 38, 41, 46, 65, 70, 74, 77, 79, 88, 103, 115, 116, 129, 130, 131
City Ordinances, Chapter 31
Civic League, Chapters 46, 88
Civic Park, Chapter 46
Civil Defense, Chapter 134
Civil Rights, Chapters 122, 137
Civil War, Chapters 6, 7, 8, 9, 10, 11, 12, 13, 15, 18, 22, 29, 64, 70, 72, 104, 133, 138
Cleveland, Grover, Chapter 27, 34
Clinton Nature Preserve, Chapter 138
Clinton, James, Chapter 35
Clover Mills School, Chapter 107
Club Drive, Chapter 103, 137
Cochran, Cheadle, Chapter 14
Colonel (title), Chapter 82
Colquitt Street, Chapter 57
Colquitt, Walter T., Chapter 5

Commercial Bank, Chapter 112
Common School Act, Chapter 32
Confederate Reunions, Chapters 7, 8
Connally, Jeff, Chapter 77
Cook, James F., Chapter 36
Cook, Robert, Chapters 5, 123
Cooper, Ethlyn, Chapter 94
Corlis, Bertie, Chapter 134
Cotton Mill, Chapters 41, 56, 58, 60, 61
Cotton warehouse, Chapters 33, 56
Cotton, Chapters 47, 53
Cotton, Fred (Doctor), Chapter 36
Counterfeit Money, Chapter 40
County seat, Chapter 26
Cox College, Chapter 119
Cracker Asphalt Company, Chapter 121
Cracker, Chapter 121
Craven, A.B. (Mrs.), Chapter 94
Creek Nation, Chapters 2, 3, 5, 17, 20, 133
Crumbies Mill, Chapter 18
Crumpton, John, Chapter 74
Crumpton, Thomas, Chapter 74
Cultural Arts Center, Chapter 82
Cultural Arts Council of Douglasville & Douglas County, Chapters 82, 127, 140
Cutter, Ralph, Chapter 118
Dalton, W. Harris, Chapter 122
Danforth, John W., Chapter 97
Danforth, William, Chapter 97
Daniel, J.B., Chapter 62
Daniell's Mill, Chapter 69
Dark Corner, Chapters 9, 19, 137
Davenport, W.L., Chapter 14

Denmeade and Johnstone, Chapter 42
Dennis, E.T., Chapter 100
Depot, Chapter 70
Desoto Cotton Mill, Chapter 56, 61
Dick Lane Bridge, Chapter 104
Dickinson, Deanna (Morris), Chapter 132
Dinkler Plaza Hotel, Chapter 100
Dirt Roads, Chapter 85
Dixie Rover, Chapter 95
Dobbs, Marie, Chapter 77
Doctors, Chapters 8, 11, 16, 24, 107
Dodson, C.L., Chapter 136
Dog River, Chapters 17, 26, 93
Dorris, Frank P., Chapter 96, 107
Dorris, Sarah Elizabeth (Taylor), Chapter 91
Dorris, William C., Chapter 91
Dorris, William Herschell, Chapter 91
Dorris, William Irvine, Chapter 91
Dorsett Drug Company, Chapter 34
Dorsett, Charles O., Chapter 89
Dorsett, Joseph Smith, Chapter 91
Dorsett, Leander (Lee) Z, Chapter 91
Dorsett, Samuel N., Chapter 33, 38, 42, 63, 91
Dorsett, Theo, Chapter 89
Douglas Boulevard, Chapter 129
Douglas County –act that created, Chapter 26
Douglas County Armory, Chapter 38
Douglas County Art Guild, Chapter 127
Douglas County Board of Commissioners, Chapters 26, 87, 107, 136
Douglas County Board of Education, Chapters 11, 14, 32, 115
Douglas County Cemetery Commission, Chapter 39
Douglas County Citizen of the Year, Chapter 131
Douglas County Courthouse, Chapters 25, 26, 43, 68, 73, 127, 135, 138,

Douglas County Commissioners, Chapter 25, 126
Douglas County Democrats, Chapter 45
Douglas County Democratic Executive Committee, Chapter 68
Douglas County Fire Department, Chapters 71, 134
Douglas County Food Administrator, Chapter 96
Douglas County High School, Chapters 21, 130, 131
Douglas County Historical Society, Chapter 140
Douglas County Hospital Authority, Chapter 107
Douglas County Jail, Chapter 59, 131
Douglas County Little Courthouses, Chapter 14
Douglas County Marshall, Chapter 38
Douglas County Museum of Art and History, Chapters 138, 140
Douglas County Pathway of Service, Chapter 135
Douglas County Public Library, anatomy, Chapters 87, 94
Douglas County Recorder, Chapter 91
Douglas County School Board, Chapters 35, 77
Douglas County Sentinel, Chapters 27, 71, 108, 122
Douglas County Sheriff, Chapter 62
Douglas County Sheriff's Office, Chapters 77, 123, 131
Douglas County Sports Hall of Fame, Chapter 111
Douglas County State Representative, Chapters 27, 42, 45, 71
Douglas County Superior Court Clerk, Chapters 38, 91
Douglas County Tax Receiver, Chapter 81
Douglas County Tourism and History Commission, Chapter 136
Douglas County Treasurer, Chapters 38, 45, 81
Douglas County Water Works, Chapter 38
Douglas General Hospital, Chapters 107, 134
Douglas Hill, Chapters 4, 133
Douglas Memorial Hospital, Chapter 107
Douglas, Stephen, Chapter 25
Douglass, Frederick, Chapter 25
Douglasville Attorney, Chapter 38
Douglasville Banking Company, Chapters 27, 62, 78, 84, 89

Douglasville Baptist Temple, Chapter 124
Douglasville Café, Chapter 34
Douglasville Canning and Preservation Company, Chapter 48, 67
Douglasville City Cemetery, Chapters 19, 27, 71, 88, 96, 99
Douglasville City Council, Chapters 33, 38, 56, 58, 60, 71, 79, 89, 126
Douglasville College, Chapters 38, 65, 71, 79, 88, 91
Douglasville Commercial Historic District, Chapter 138
Douglasville Convention and Visitors Bureau, Chapter 49
Douglasville Electric Lighting and Water Company, Chapters 83, 88
Douglasville First Baptist Church, Chapters 90, 110
Douglasville Grammar School, Chapters 106, 115,
Douglasville Historic Preservation Commission, Chapters 56, 58, 60
Douglasville Hotel, Chapters 27, 67
Douglasville Masonic Lodge No. 289 F & AM, Chapters 27, 34
Douglasville Mayor, Chapters 23, 27, 31, 33, 56, 57, 71, 77, 82, 84, 89, 91,106, 112, 140
Douglasville Mayor Pro Tem, Chapter 38
Douglasville Methodist Church, Chapter 77
Douglasville National Guard, Explosion, Chapter 114
Douglasville Nursing and Rehabilitation, Chapter 125
Douglasville Police, Chapters 56, 78, 126
Douglasville Post Office, Chapter 90
Douglasville Postmaster, Chapters 33, 38, 42, 43, 45,
Douglasville Power Company, Chapter 102
Douglasville Printing Company, Chapter 84
Douglasville School (Segregated), Chapter 106
Douglasville Spinners, Chapters 56, 61
Douglasville Swimming Pool, Chapter 88
Downtown Retail Merchants Association, Chapter 113
Drag, Chapters 85, 95
Dragracing, Chapter 122
Duke, Bart, Chapter 124
Duke, Thomas A. Drug Company, Chapter 34

Duncan Street, Chapter 77
Duncan, J.T., Chapters 48, 68, 89, 96
Duncan Brothers Store, Chapter 71
Dungee, George, Chapter 131
Dura Lee Lane, Chapter 103
Earl D. Lee Boulevard, Chapter 131
Easly Cotton Mill, Chapter 57
East Douglas County Library, Chapter 94
East Point, Chapter 133
Ebenezer School, Chapter 106
Economy Auto, Chapter 90
Eden Cotton Mill, Chapter 41
Edge, J.K., Chapter 48
Edge, John V., Chapter 63, 71
Edge, John M., Chapter 28
Edge Property, Chapter 9
Education, Chapter 32
Edward, John, Chapter 91
Edwards, R.E., Chapter 46
Edwards, Margaret M. (Head), Chapter 91
Edwards, Tom, Chapter 38
Elections, Chapters 26, 45, 81, 91, 103
Electricity, Chapter 102
Emancipation Day, Chapter 19
Emory, Herb, Chapter 117
Empire Mill, Chapter 18
Ephesus Baptist Church, Chapter 19
Ernest Willie, Chapter 105
Fabiano's Pizza, Chapters 89, 92
Factory Street, Chapter 41, 137
Fairburn, Chapter 5
Fairburn Road, Chapters 103, 107, 136, 137
Fairfield School (Segregated), Chapter 106

Fairfield Methodist, Chapter 14
Fairplay Little Courthouse, Chapter 136
Fairplay School, Chapter 106
Fallen Soldiers, Chapter 130
Falling Stars, Chapter 86
Family history, Chapter 139
Farmer, Kenneth, Chapter 58
Farmer, Jeri, Chapter 24
Farmers Electrical Membership Association, Chapter 102
Farmers and Merchants Bank, Chapter 22, 84
Farmer's Alliance, Chapters 68, 140
Fellowship Christian Center, Inc., Chapter 58
Ferguson, Angus, Chapter 42
Ferguson Mill, Chapters 4, 133
First bale, Chapter 38
First Baptist Church of Douglasville, Chapters 65, 71, 130, 137
First Dialed Telephone Call, Chapter 91
First United Methodist Church, Chapters 46, 112
Fitsquese, Chapter 14
Five Notch Road, Chapter 137
Flint Hill Academy, Chapter 14
Flint Hill High School, Chapter 14
Flint Hill Methodist Church, Chapter 9, 14
Floods of 2009, Chapter 104
Florence, Glen, Chapter 110
Flowers Drive, Chapter 136
Forman, Ortho, Chapter 117
Forman, Tex, Chapter 117
Fort McPherson, Chapter 76, 95, 100
Foster, Edith, Chapter 94
Fourth of July, Chapter 27
Fouts, Herbert, Chapter 124
Fout's Mill, Chapter 17, 18

Fowler, A.A., Chapter 102
Fowler, A.A., Sr., Chapter 107
Frails, Mary, Chapter 22
Freely, John I., Chapter 63
Friddell, W.L., Chapter 14
Friends of Sweetwater Creek State Park, Chapter 10
Fulton, Laurie, Chapter 136
Gable, Alma C., Chapter 107
Gable, Jimmy, Chapter 115
Gainesville, Chapter 22
Garden Terrace Nursing Home, Chapter 125
Garrett, Alexander Stephens, Chapter 11
Garrett, Christopher Columbus, Chapters 11, 16, 35
Garrett, Franklin, Chapter 54
Garrett, Lemuel, Chapter 11
Garrett, Luke, Jr., Chapter 11
Garrett, Luke, Sr., Chapter 11
Garrett, Martha Cash, Chapter 11
Garrett, Mike, Chapter 101
Gartrell, Lucious, Chapter 43
Gaston, Dan, Chapter 14
Gaston, James, Chapter 14
Geer, Catherine, Chapter 98
Geer, John M., Chapter 57
Geer, Major Ernest, Chapter 57
Geiger, Robert W., Chapter 55
George H. Sparks Reservoir, Chapter 133
Georgia 166, Chapter 9
Georgia 92, Chapter 9
Georgia General Assembly, Chapter 91
Georgia Good Roads Association, Chapter 85
Georgia Pacific Railroad, Chapter 27, 28, 29, 30, 38, 42, 49, 54
Georgia Power Company, Chapter 102

Georgia State Federation of Women's Clubs, Chapter 88
Georgia State Representative, Chapter 91
Georgia State Senate, Chapter 82
Georgia Western Cotton Mill, Chapters 56, 58, 61
Georgia Western Railroad, Chapters 26, 28, 29
Georgian Villa, Chapter 125
Giles, G.T., Chapter 14
Glendale Mills, Chapters 56, 61
Glennwood Plantation, Chapters 9, 64
Glover, John F., Chapter 28
Glover, Lizzie (Camp), Chapters 6, 7, 8
Glover, Thomas Coke (Doctor), Chapters 6, 7, 8
Goad, Jim, Chapter 77
Gold n Goodies, Chapter 77
Golf, Chapter 111
Good Roads Movement, Chapter 85
Good Roads Tour of 1909, Chapter 104
Gordon, John B., Chapter 29, 68
Gore, Tom, Chapter 110
Gorman, A.S., Chapters 26, 28
Gorman, Claiborne, Chapter 104
Gorman, James M., Chapter 104
Gorman-Austell Ferry, Chapter 9
Gorman-Austell Plantation, Chapter 104
Gosline, A.L., Chapter 62
Grady, Henry W., Chapters 30, 42, 43, 52, 53, 54, 138
Grand Jury Presentments, Chapter 62
Grant, Lemuel, Chapter 28
Great Migration, Chapter 37
Green, Agnes, Chapter 94
Green, Henry Martyn, Chapter 22
Green, Mary Stiles, Chapter 12, 22
Green, Robert Edgar, Chapter 22

Green, William Ely, Chapter 12, 22
Greystone Power Company, Chapter 102
Griffin, S.A., Chapter 14
Griffith, Christy Ann, Chapter 131
Griffith, Lizzie, Chapter 14
Griggs, B.C., Chapter 79
Grist Mill, Chapters 42, 77
Groover, John Freeman, Chapter 118
Groover, Katie, Chapter 118
Groover's Lake, Chapter 118
Gumbeaux's Cajun Café, Chapter 90
Gunnell, Katherine, Chapter 107
Gurley, D.H., Chapter 47
Gurley, Hiram, Chapter 34
Gurley Road, Chapter 34
Gwinnett, Button, Chapter 119
Hagler, Betty, Chapter 94
Haines, John M., Chapter 62
Hamilton, Ralph (Doctor), Chapter 34
Hannah, Chapter 14
Hanson, J.E., Chapter 63
Hanson, M.D., Chapter 63
Harding, J.W., Chapter 81
Harper, Herman, Chapter 64
Harper, Scott, Chapter 130
Harper, Terry, Chapter 37
Harris, Evelyn, Chapter 55
Harris, Jesse, Chapter 5
Harris, Joel Chandler, Chapter 52, 55
Hartley, Rowe & Fowler, Chapters 46, 88
Hartsfield-Jackson Atlanta International Airport, Chapters 99, 100, 132, 134
Haverty, J.J., Chapter 12

Hathcock, M.L., Chapter 81
Hawkins, Benjamin, Chapter 1
Hawkins, John, Chapter 62
Haynes, J.J., Chapter 38
Healey, J.T., Chapter 81
Hedgecock, Chris, Chapter 71
Heflin Hustler, Chapter 30
Hembree, W.J., Chapter 81
Henley, Tallulah Florence (Bullard), Chapter 9
Hetzner, Edwin Arthur, Chapter 21
Hetzner, Lois, Chapter 21
Hicks, J.C., Chapter 126
High Museum of Art, Chapter 12
High, Hattie Wilson, Chapter 12
High, J.M., Chapter 12
Highway 92, Chapter 5, 64, 129, 134, 140
Highway 78/Bankhead Highway, Chapter 87
Highway 166, Chapter 104
Hill, D. Pike, Chapter 43
Hill, Johnny, Chapter 120
Hill, Oliver Clinton, Chapter 120
Hill, Verda Smith, Chapter 120
Hindmon, William W, Chapter 26
Hines, Joseph, Chapter 14
Hines, Ott, Chapter 14
Hodnett, W.C. Chapter 48
Hog Wallow, Chapters 31, 75, 76
Holly Springs Academy, Chapter 91
Holton, Leon G., Chapter 130
Hopping, Ephraim Stiles, Chapter 22
Hornebuckle, Robert, Chapter 40
Hospital Drive, Chapter 135
Houseworth, Delvous, Chapter 14

Howell, E.P., Chapter 68
Howell, Humphrey Posey, Chapter 42
Howell, Lula, Chapter 42
Howland, J.E. (Doctor), Chapter 70
Hudson-Dobbs Cemetery, Chapter 39
Hudson, Amanda, Chapter 39
Hudson, Charles, Chapter 39
Hudson, Fed, Chapter 39
Hudson, Susanne, Chapter 24
Hudson's Hickory House, Chapters 34, 71
Huey Road, The Good the bad, Chapter 121
Huffine, E.M., Chapters 24, 107
Hurricane Creek, Chapter 1
Hunter, Eddie, Chapter 130
Hunter Park, Chapters 34, 46, 87, 130
Hunter, Robert, Chapter 130
Hunter, Robert G. ("Jerry"), Chapter 130
Hunter, Zelma, Chapter 130
Hurt, Joel, Chapter 51
Hutcheson Building, Chapter 90
Hutcheson, J.R., Chapters 82, 90, 102
Hutcheson, R.H., Chapter 106, 107
Ice Storms, Chapter 132
Immigrants, Chapter 63
Inferior Court, Chapter 21
Influenza, Chapter 96
Inman, Hugh T., Chapters 21, 51
Inman, John H., Chapter 51
Inman, S.M., Chapters 42, 51
Inman, Samuel M., Chapters 50, 51
Inman Park Properties, Chapters 56, 58, 60
Interstate 20, Chapters 3, 104, 122, 129
Inventors, Chapter 85

Irish Bred Pub, Chapters 22, 71, 77, 112, 116
Irwin, Francis, Chapter 5
Irwin-Bomar-Rice-Austin-Bullard-Henley-Sprayberry House, Chapters 41, 63, 140
J. Thad Smith Appliance and Furniture Store, Chapter 77
J.F. Stifel Company, Chapter 56
Jacks Hill, Chapters 30, 133
James Grove, Chapter 46
James, Eunice, Chapter 27
James Grove, Chapters 27, 31, 70, 88
James, G.W., Chapter 97
James, J.V., Chapter 70
James, John, Chapter 110
James, John M., Chapter 26, 97
James, Joseph S., Chapters 16, 23, 27, 46, 48, 56, 61, 63, 65, 67, 68, 69, 81, 102
James, Linton Steven, Chapter 97
James, Martha Shipley, Chapter 23
James, Odessa, Chapter 77
James, Stephen, Chapters 23, 97
James, R.E., Chapter 34
James, Royal Percy (Roy), Chapter 97
James, W.A., Chapters 81, 97
Janes, Charles G., Chapter 81
Jail Breaks, Chapter 74
Jay, Brian Edward, Chapter 130
Jeff Justice & Co. Realtors, Chapter 71
John W. Stewart Middle School, Chapter 129
Johnson, Melvin, Chapter 130
Johnson, Pat, Chapter 110
Johnson, Thomas L., Chapter 45
Johnson, W.G., Chapter 102
Jones, James, Chapter 40

Joyner, J.C., Chapter 94
Judges, Chapter 81
Juneteenth, Chapter 129
Justice of the Peace, Chapter 27, 57, 91
Keller, Samuel, Chapter 5
Kemp, Mrs. H.N., Chapter 115
Kimbrell, J.J., Chapter 14
King, Martin Luther (Dr.), Chapter 122, 129
Kings Highway, Chapter 124
Kiser, Marion C., Chapter 54
Knowles, Paul John, Chapter 131
Kozytorium, Chapters 89, 92
Ku Klux Klan, Chapters 37, 74
La Dell, Dr. M.F., Chapter 24
Labor Day, Chapter 34
Laird, Richard, Chapter 107
Land Family, Chapters 39, 56, 99
Landers, Ed, Chapter 113
Latham, Thomas W., Chapter 26
Lee, Betty Belcher, Chapter 131
Lee, Eva Inez Couch, Chapter 131
Lee, Grover Clinton, Chapter 131
Lee, Earl D., Chapter 131
Liberty Bonds, Chapter 96
Lithia Springs, Chapters 53, 95, 137
Lithia Springs Elementary School, Chapter 110
Lithia Springs School, Chapter 106
Lithia Springs First Baptist, Chapter 110
Lithia Springs High School, Chapter 120
Lois Cotton Mill, Chapters 27, 56
Library, Chapters 88, 94
Lieberman, Laura, Chapter 82
Lindley, W.T., Chapter 63

Lithia Springs, Chapters 3, 21, 35, 37, 52, 76, 111, 130, 132
Lithia Springs City Council, Chapters 42, 76, 94
Lithia Springs Drive-In, Chapter 89
Lithia Springs Elementary School, Chapter 94
Lithia Springs Golf Club, Chapter 111
Lithia Springs Library, Chapter 94
Lithia Springs Library Association, Chapter 94
Lithia Springs Little Courthouse, Chapter 136
Lithia Springs Mayor, Chapters 42, 54
Lithia Springs Water Company, Chapter 11
Little Courthouses, Chapter 94, 136
Livingston, Leonidas F., Chapter 68
Loeb, Moses, Chapter 8
Lone Fishermen, Chapter 68
Looking Good Douglas County, Chapter 40
Lois Cotton Mill, Chapter 59, 61
Love, Charles B., Chapter 42
Love, David Kolb, Chapter 42
Love, Mary Catherine (Baker), Chapter 42
Love Seat, Chapter 139
Lumpkin, William, Chapter 2
McLarty, A.W., Chapter 38
McLarty, George T., Chapter 85
McLarty, George Washington, Chapter 38
McLarty, J.H., Chapter 68
McCarley, Joseph C., Chapter 92
McCorquodale, Timothy, Chapter 131
McClure, Thurlo, Chapter 130
McCrary, J.B., Chapter 102
McDonald, Charles J., Chapter 42
McElreath, Glen, Chapter 33
McElreath, Samuel, Chapters 3, 38
McElreath, Sara Emma, Chapter 33

McElreath, William, Chapter 38
McGouirk, C.W., Chapter 81
McGouirk, W.N., Chapter 26
McIntosh Treaty of 1825, Chapter 17
McIntosh, A.C., Chapter 42
McKinley, Julie, Chapter 76
McKinley, William, Chapter 52, 53
McKoy, James R. (Dr.), Chapter 34
McLarty, A.W., Chapters 48, 63
McLarty, G.W., Chapter 28
McWhorter, Chapter 14
McWhorter, E.H., Chapter 14
McWhorter, Elijah, Chapter 14
McWhorter, M.R., Chapter 14
McWhorter, Matthew, Chapter 14
Maddox, Lester, Chapter 129
Magnolia One Realty, Chapter 92
Mahaffey, Joe, Chapter 36
Mallory, W.H., Chapter 63
Manley, W.D., Chapter 84
Manning, Allen, Chapter 14
Maroney, Chapter 137
Maroney, Alfred, Chapter 44
Maroney, Benjamin, Chapter 44
Maroney Mill Road, Chapter 44
Marsh, E.W., Chapter 21, 42
Marsh, Edwin W., Chapters 50, 51
Martel Mills, Chapters 56, 61
Masons, Chapter 77
Massey, Louise, Chapter 33
Massey, R.A. (Judge), Chapters 33, 41, 43
Massey, Robert Alexander, Chapter 16
Massey, Robert Jehu, Chapter 16

Massey, Sarah Elizabeth (Copeland), Chapter 16
Mayor Pro-Tem, Chapter 126
Merritt, Astor, Chapters 102, 106
Meteorite, Chapter 86
Methodist Episcopal Church South, Chapter 65
Meyers, Elena, Chapter 120
Middle District Little Courthouse, Chapter 136
Midway Road, Chapter 123
Military Road, Chapters 56, 61
Miles, Ed, Chapter 40
Mill Village, Chapter 61
Mills, Roger Q., Chapter 54
Miller, Phil, Chapter 131
Miller, Terry, Chapter 116
Miller & Associates, Chapter 116
Millstones, Chapters 22, 44, 140
Mitchell, William H., Chapter 36
Moonshine, Chapters, 74, 122, 133
Morgan, Richard Geer, Chapter 57
Morris, E.A., Chapter 48
Morris, Fred, Chapter 112
Morris, John, Chapter 33
Morris, John McLarty, Chapter 33
Morris, Ralph (Mrs.), Chapter 88
Morris, Will, Chapter 62
Morristown, Chapter 137
Moore, Thomas, Chapter 5
Moss, J.S., Chapter 14
Mt. Carmel School, Chapters 106, 131
Movie Theater, Chapters, 89, 92
Mozley, Walt, Chapter 110
Mt. Carmel Community, Chapter 87
Mt. Carmel Little Courthouse, Chapter 136

Mt. Vernon Road, Chapter 134
Mt. Zion School, Chapters 14, 106
Mud Creek, Chapter 44
Mule barn, Chapters 103, 127
Mule Train, Chapters 122, 129
Mynatt, P.L., Chapter 46
National Register, Chapters 58, 82, 138
Native Americans, Chapters, 1, 2, 3, 17, 133, 137
National Guard Armory, Chapters 79, 129
National Register, Chapters 61, 82
New Century Cotton Mill, Chapters 27, 56, 61
New Manchester, Chapters 9, 10, 133
New Manchester Manufacturing Company, Chapter 4, 9, 10, 21, 42, 55, 133, 80, 140
New Hope, Chapter 134
New South, Chapters 27, 29, 54, 82, 84, 138
Nicholson, Tommy, Chapter 123
No-Man's Land, Chapter 3
North Baggett Road, Chapter 87
North, William Owen, Chapter 80
Northern Society of Georgia, Chapter 70
Northern, W.J., Chapters 16, 68
Notrica, Jeff, Chapter 58
Nottingham, Curtis Bell, Chapter 36
Nottingham, Warren D., Chapter 36
Nottingham, William, Chapter 36
O'Kelly, Robert, Chapter 106
O'Neal Drug Company, Chapter 112
O'Neal Plaza, Chapters 22, 29, 47, 112, 116
O'Neal, W.S., Chapter 107, 112, 116
Oddfellows, Chapters 27, 34
Order of the Eastern Star, Chapter 34
Owl, Abraham, Chapter 17, 18

Owl, Elijah, Chapter 17, 18
Owl, Ezekiel, Chapter 17, 18
Outdoor Advertisements, Chapter 47
Oxford, J.I., Chapter 90
Page, Thomas Nelson, Chapters 52, 54
Palmer, Red, Chapters 122, 123
Palmer, W.D., Chapter 107
Palmer Chemical Company, Chapter 123
Palmetto, Chapters 5, 11
Panic of 1873, Chapter 104
Parker Street, Chapter 102
Parkway Regional, Chapter 125
Pate, Samuel, Chapter 14
Paulding County, Chapter 134
Pavilion, Chapter 88
Peace, D.W. (Mrs.), Chapter 88
Peavey, Charles O., Chapter 42
Pedestrian Bridge, Chapter 101
Peeples, Greg, Chapter 33
Perkins, Jim, Chapter 87
Peters, Richard, Chapter 28
Phillips, Joe, Chapter 18
Piedmont Chautauqua, Chapters 27, 52, 53, 54, 55
Piedmont Chautauqua Association, Chapters 21, 38, 53
Pilgrim, Bud, Chapter 40
Pitman, James A., Chapters 34, 63, 71
Plaza East, Chapters 77, 116
Pleasant Grove School, Chapter 138
Pleasant Hill Cemetery, Chapter 36
Polk, Catherine (McLarty), Chapter 19
Polk, Charles Selby, Chapter 19
Polk, Eleanor, Chapter 19
Polk, Ezekiel, Chapters 19, 28

Polk, Jack, Chapter 19
Polk, Melissa Jane "Jenny" (Weddington), Chapter 19
Ponce de Leon Ball Park, Chapter 111
Poole, Marcella (Vansant), Chapter 24
Poole, Rueben H., Chapter 24
Poole, Thomas J., Chapter 24
Poole, W.H, (William Haynes), Chapters 24, 28, 36
Poor Farm, Chapter 62
Poor House, Chapter 62
Poor Peoples Campaign, Chapter 122, 129
Pope, Claude, Chapter 123
Pope Road, Chapter 136
Populist Party, Chapter 68
Posey, Humphrey, Chapters 17, 18
Post, Charles C., Chapters 48, 66, 67, 68, 69, 70, 137
Post, Helen Wilmans, Chapters 66, 67, 68, 69
Post Office, Chapter 90
Post Road, Chapters 14, 136
Powell's Grocery, Chapter 84
Powder Springs, Chapter 120
Praray, Charles, Chapters 56, 61
Pray, Ephraim, Chapters 17, 18, 25, 26, 41, 45
Pray, Mary Ann Little, Chapter 17
Pray Street, Chapters 17, 74
Pray's Mill Baptist Church, Chapters 17, 18, 26, 80, 124
Prestley Mill Road, Chapter 65
Price and McElreath Drygoods and Groceries, Chapter 33
Price Avenue, Chapters 33, 34, 125, 137
Price, David W., Chapter 33
Price and Duncan, Chapter 30
Princess Anneewakee, Chapter 3
Pritchard, Frances (Thompson), Chapter 77
Prohibition, Chapters 74, 79, 91, 105, 128, 133, 140

Prohibitionist, Chapter 79
Pullman strike, Chapter 34
Pumpkintown, Chapter 5
Quillian, Emma, Chapter 82
Quillian, J.B.C. (Rev.), Chapter 82
Quinn, Calvin, Chapter 132
REA, Chapter 102
R.L. Cousins School, Chapter 129
Railway Bridge, Chapters 101, 68
Ralls, Ed, Chapter 110
Ralph Community, Chapter 133
Rawlins, Henry, Chapter 64
Rawlins, Sally, Chapter 64
Reconstruction, Chapter 25, 29, 45, 64, 84, 68, 140
Red Hill, Chapter 137
Red Oak, Chapter 29
Regions Bank, Chapter 112
Reverse S-Curve, Chapter 87
Reynolds, Lily, Chapter 94
Rice, Zechariah A., Chapter 20
Rider, Randy, Chapter 131
Riley, James Whitcomb, Chapter 55
Road Crew, Chapter 31
Roads and Highways, Chapters 85, 88
Robberies, Chapter 78
Robbins, Jenny Loring, Chapter 55
Roberts-Mozley House, Chapter 82
Roberts, Melville, Chapter 82
Roberts, W.T., Chapters 38, 46, 79, 82, 138, 140
Roberts, William Harvey, Chapter 133
Robinson, Dr. Clark, Chapter 34
Rollins, Keith, Chapter 24
Rollins, Sandra, Chapter 24

Rose Avenue, Chapters 71, 88, 96, 137
Rosehaven Memorial Park, Chapter 130
Rowan, Tyler, Chapters 56, 60
Rural Electrification Administration, Chapter 102
Ruritan Club, Chapter 94
Saloons, Chapters 31, 38, 74
Salt Springs, Chapters 3, 21, 35, 37, 42, 53, 137
Sanborn Fire Insurance Maps, Chapter 34
Sandtown Place, Chapter 12
Sandtown Road, Chapter 12
Sandtown Trail, Chapter 2
Saw Tell Road, Chapter 137
School Rules, Chapter 32
Seabreeze, Chapter 69
Seales, James, Chapter 41
Seals, James, Chapters 35, 41
Seals, Robert, Chapter 41
Segal, Richard, Chapter 87
Selective Service Board, Chapter 106
Selective Services Act, Chapter 96
Selman, J.E., Chapter 63
Selman, J.L. & Son, Chapters 38, 46
Selman, J.L. (Doctor), Chapters 48, 112
Selman, Missouri Ann (Dorsett), Chapter 69
Selman, Paul, Chapter 112
Selman, T.H., Chapters 26, 62,
Selman, Willie Edna, Chapter 22
Selman Drive, Chapter 87
Seventh Day Adventist Church, Chapters 93, 125
Shadix, J.J., Chapter 14
Shadix, J.W., Chapter 106
Shadix, Phillip, Chapter 113
Shape-Note Singing, Chapter 23

SHARE House, Chapter 46
Shoe repair, Chapter 34
Shortening, Chapter 47
Silk industry, Chapter 80
Sim's Five and Dime, Chapter 34
Simmons, Nathan Bedford, Chapter 130
Sisk, James F., Chapter 35
Skinner, Chapter 14
Skint Chestnut, Chapters 24, 26, 29, 87, 127
Skint Chestnut Tree, Chapters 3, 140
Slavery, Chapter 39
Smail, Judy, Chapter 131
Small, Sam, Chapter 79
Smith, Bob, Chapters 132, 134, 136
Smith, Carrie, Chapter 89
Smith, Charles Henry, Chapter 72
Smith, J. Thad, Chapters 77, 113
Smith, Jack, Chapter 138
Smith Jared, Chapter 18
Smith, Jesse, Chapter 34
Smith, Lamar, Chapter 34
Smith, M.M., Chapter 26
Smith, Moses Mckoy, Chapter 25
Smith, Patsy, Chapter 77
Smith, R.L., Chapters 33, 90, 136
Smith Motors, Chapter 33
Smith-Dabbs Building, Chapter 77
Smith, R.M., Chapter 81
Smith, Steven Wallace, Chapters 41, 85
Smith, Tom, Chapter 78
Smith, Vander R., Chapter 89
Smith's Ferry, Chapter 9
Snowdrift Shortening, Chapters 47, 116

620

Solicitor General, Chapter 82
Souter, George M., Chapter 62
South Douglas Elementary School, Chapter 136
South Fulton, Chapter 131
South Sweetwater Road, Chapters 55, 136,
Southern Christian Leadership Conference, Chapter 129
Southern Confederacy, Chapter 51
Southern Railway, Chapter 87
Spanish American War, Chapters 75, 76, 96
Spiller, Rell, Chapter 111
Stanton, Frank L., Chapter 55
Steamboats, Chapter 5
Steed, S.A., Chapter 14
Stele, Chapter 3
Stephens, Alexander H., Chapter 43
Steverson, Rilla, Chapter 37
Steverson, Wilson, Chapter 37
Stewart Brothers General Grocery Store, Chapter 77
Stewart Middle School, Chapter 129
Stewart, Eldorado R. (Rader), Chapters 22, 77, 84
Stewart, Elizabeth Russell, Chapter 10
Stewart, Francis Marion (Doctor), Chapters 22, 77
Stewart, G.G., Chapters 31
Stewart, George W., Chapter 35
Stewart, Reece, Chapter 32
Stewart, Synthia, Chapters 10, 133
Stewart, William Washington, Chapter 10
Stewart, Willie Edna (Selman), Chapters 77, 88
Stewart's Mill, Chapters 22, 77
Stock Law, Chapter 38
Stockmar, A.H., Chapter 107
Street names, Chapter 31
Strickland Street, Chapters 24, 32, 57, 67, 68, 78, 87, 89

621

Strickland, John, Chapter 35
Strickland, W.P., Chapter 28, 44
Submarine, Chapter 109
Suggs, Johnny, Chapter 111
Suggs, Louise, Chapter 111
Summerlin, West, Chapter 38
Sunbeam Motor Company, Chapter 100
Sunday Sales, Chapter 87
Sweetwater Creek, Chapters 4, 10, 26, 42, 119, 138
Sweetwater Creek State Park, Chapters 4, 9, 133
Sweetwater, Chapters 30, 42, 46
Sweetwater Creek State Park Interpretive Center, Chapter 133
Sweetwater Park Hotel, Chapters 11, 21, 35, 40, 50, 51, 52, 55, 69, 76, 85
Sweetwater Manufacturing Site, Chapter 138
Sweetwater Road, Chapter 55
Sweetwater Shrine Club, Chapter 34
Swenson, Charles, Chapter 104
Tackett, Ella Virginia, Chapter 20
Tackett, Melissa J. (Underwood), Chapter 20
Tackett, Wylie Preston, Chapters 20, 81
Tallapoosa Judicial Circuit, Chapters 81, 82
Tallapoosa Road, Chapter 42
Tallon, Wes, Chapters 135, 136
Talmadge, T. De Witt, Chapter 54
Tariff, Chapter 53
Taste of Douglasville, Chapter 116
Taylor, T.B. (Doctor), Chapter 116
Thanksgiving, Chapter 113
The Friends of Sweetwater Creek State Park, Chapter 113
The New South, Chapters 67, 68, 82
The Oaks, Chapter 64
The Weekly Star, Chapters 16, 28, 29, 33, 38, 42, 43, 45, 46
The Wrens Nest, Chapter 55

Third Party Politics, Chapter 68
Thompson, Frances "Toots", Chapter 22
Thompson, Reuben, Chapter 5
Thornton Road, Chapter 111
Tidwell, Robert Paul, Chapter 130
Tight Squeeze, Chapter 14
Timber Ridge Stables, Chapter 103
Tovar, Dave, Chapter 14
Town & Country Upholstery, Chapter 71
Treaty of Indian Springs, Chapters 2, 5
Trout Creek, Chapter 17
Turk, R.B. (Doctor), Chapter 34
Turner, G.R., Chapter 31
Turner, Walter, Chapter 82
Typhoid Fever, Chapters 8, 75, 76
Tyree Road, Chapter 14
Union Grove Baptist Church, Chapter 110
Union Hill School, Chapter 106
United Daughters of the Confederacy, Chapter 135
United Methodist Church, Chapters 23, 27, 65
United States District Attorney Northern District, Chapter 27
Upshaw, Ada (Addie), Chapter 71
Upshaw, Charity Adeline (Stamps), Chapter 71
Upshaw, Glenn Oglesby, Chapter 71
Upshaw, Herschel McKee, Chapter 71
Upshaw, Isaac David, Chapters 71, 105
Upshaw, L.C., Chapter 79
Upshaw, Luscious C., Chapter 71
Upshaw, Sarah (Sallie) Blanche, Chapter 71
Upshaw, William D., Chapter 71, 105
Upshaw Brothers General Merchandise, Groceries & Fertilizer, Chapter 71
Vandergrift, C.P., Chapter 63

Vansant, Claude (Doctor), Chapter 126
Vansant, Lou, Chapter 93
Vansant, Lou, Chapter 93
Vansant, Rueben, Chapters 24, 26
Vansant, Young, Chapters 24, 26, 38, 93
Vaudeville, Chapter 89
Veterans Day, Chapter 96
Veterans Memorial Highway, Chapters 55, 130
Vietnam War, Chapters 122, 130
Villa Rica, Chapters 17, 30, 109, 114, 138
Villa Rica Elementary, Chapters 94, 114
Villa Rica Explosion, Chapter 114
Vulcan Drive, Chapter 118
Waldrop, Tommy, Chapter 126
Walton, J.E., Chapter 115
Ward, Henry, Chapter 48
Waterhouse, Mona, Chapter 127
Waterworks, Chapter 82
Watson, Hugh, Chapter 16, 99, 100
Watson, J. Penn, Chapter 48
Watson, J.M., Chapter 38
Watson, J.P., Chapter 63
Watson, James A., Chapters 21, 40, 42, 50, 71
Watson, Lillie J. (Vansant), Chapter 38
Watson, Mathias Bates, Chapters 38, 63, 100
Watson, Parks, Chapter 99
Watts, Little berry, Chapter 5
Wauchope, Robert (Doctor), Chapter 3
Weather Events, Chapter 132
Weddington, Alexander Green, Chapter 19
Weddington, C.W., Chapter 48
Weddington, Hannah (Polk), Chapter 19
Weddington, Mary "Polly" (McLarty), Chapter 19

Wedge Alley, Chapter 137
West Chapel Hill Road, Chapter 9
West Georgia Regional Library, Chapter 94
Western Pacific Railroad, Chapter 27
Westfall, A.H., Chapter 87
Westmoreland, J.W., Chapter 63
Wheeler, Anderson, Chapter 62
White, George, Chapter 3
Whitley, Evan J., Chapter 96
Whitley, Evan Riley, Chapters 11, 28
Whitley, J. Cowan, Chapter 107
Whitley, Thomas R., Chapters 34, 38, 43, 46, 48, 67, 68, 69, 71, 79, 81, 94, 95
Wier, Mamie, Chapter 104
Will Love School (Segregated), Chapter 38
William, J.L., Chapter 62
Williams, I.C., Chapter 110
Williams, Tom, Chapter 38
Wills, Steve, Chapter 134
Wilson, Elaine (Banks), Chapter 77
Wilson, Hannah, Chapter 14
Wilson, James Harwell, Chapter 12
Wilson, John A., Chapters 14, 25
Wilson, Lucinda, Chapter 14
Wilson, Martha (Milller), Chapter 15
Wilson, Mary Frances (Dorsett), Chapter 15
Wilson, Moses, Chapter 14
Wilson, Noah, Chapter 14
Wilson, Peter, Chapter 14
Wilson, Richard M., Chapter 15
Wilson, Richard T., Chapter 15
Wilsonville, Chapter 14
Winn, Annette, Chapter 94

Winn, F.M., Chapters 18, 34, 106
Winn, J.H., Chapter 26
Winn, Mac (Mrs.), Chapter 106
Winston, Chapters 106, 131, 137
Winston, Ezekiel Polk, Chapter 95
Winston School (Segregated), Chapter 106
Witham, W.S., Chapter 84
Witham Banking System, Chapter 84
WMU, Chapter 124
Women's Christian Temperance League, Chapter 105
Women's History, Chapters 88, 94, 107
Wood, David Beavers, Chapter 130
Wood, Henry D., Chapter 9, 64
Wood, Louie, Chapter 94
Wood, Rosa Emory, Chapters 9, 64
Woods, Carrie (Vansant), Chapter 93
Woods, Claudie Mae, Chapter 93
Woods, Curtis, Chapter 93
Woods, Edgar, Chapter 93
Woods, Fannie Lou, Chapter 93
Woods, John David, Chapter 93
Woods, Orella, Chapter 93
Woods, Ottis, Chapter 93
World War I, Chapters 88, 95, 96, 97, 99
World War II, Chapters 106, 109
Worthan, Tom, Sr., Chapter 126
Worthan, Tom, Jr., Chapter 126
Wright, J.C., Chapter 38
Wright, Michelle, Chapter 33
WSB Radio, Chapter 117
Wylie, Jule, Chapter 78
Yeager, Chapter 137
Yeager School, Chapter 106

Young, C.B.F. (Doctor), Chapter 121
Young Refining Company, Chapter 121
Zellars, Dr. W.S., Chapter 25